Clued in to Politics

3rd Edition

Clued in to Politics

A Critical Thinking Reader in American Government

Edited by

Christine Barbour
Indiana University

Matthew J. Streb
Northern Illinois University

CQ PRESS

A Division of SAGE
Washington, D.C.

CQ Press
2300 N Street, NW, Suite 800
Washington, DC 20037

Phone: 202-729-1900; toll-free, 1-866-4CQ-PRESS (1-866-427-7737)

Web: www.cqpress.com

Cover design: www.thedesignfarm.com
Composition: C&M Digitals (P) Ltd.

♾ The paper used in this publication exceeds the requirements of the American National Standard for Information Sciences—Permanence of Paper for Printed Library Materials, ANSI Z39.48-1992.

Printed and bound in the United States of America

13 12 11 10 09   1 2 3 4 5

Library of Congress Cataloging-in-Publication Data

Barbour, Christine
    Clued in to politics : a critical thinking reader in American government / edited by Christine Barbour, Matthew J. Streb. — 3rd ed.
        p. cm.
    ISBN 978-1-60426-519-4 (pbk. : alk. paper) 1. United States—Politics and government. I. Streb, Matthew J. (Matthew Justin), 1974- II. Title.
JK21.B37 2010
320.973—dc22

                                                                    2009040272

About the Editors

Christine Barbour teaches in the political science department and the Honors College at Indiana University, where she has become increasingly interested in how teachers of large classes can maximize what their students learn. At Indiana, Professor Barbour has been a Lilly Fellow, working on a project to increase student retention in large introductory courses, and a member of the Freshmen Learning Project, a university-wide effort to improve the first-year undergraduate experience. She has served on the *New York Times* College Advisory Board, working with other educators to develop ways to integrate newspaper reading into the undergraduate curriculum. She has won several teaching honors. The two awarded by her students mean the most to her: the Indiana University Student Alumni Association Award for Outstanding Faculty and the Indiana University Chapter of the Society of Professional Journalists Brown Derby Award. She is the author, with Gerald Wright, of *Keeping the Republic: Power and Citizenship in American Politics,* 4th edition (2009). When not teaching or writing textbooks, Professor Barbour enjoys playing with her dogs, traveling, and writing about food. She is the food editor for *Bloom Magazine* and is a coauthor of *Indiana Cooks!* (2005) and *Home Grown Indiana* (2009). She is currently working on a book about local politics, development, and the fishing industry in Apalachicola, Florida.

Matthew J. Streb is associate professor and director of undergraduate studies in the department of political science at Northern Illinois University. His most recent research examines the effects of the politicization of judicial elections. Streb received his PhD from Indiana University in 2000. He is the author of *The New Electoral Politics of Race* (2002) and *Rethinking American Electoral Democracy* (2008) and the editor or coeditor of several other books, including *Polls and Politics* (2004), *Academic Freedom at the Dawn of a New Century* (2006), and *Running for Judge* (2007). Streb has published articles in such journals as *Political Research Quarterly, Public Opinion Quarterly, Social Science Quarterly, Election Law Journal,* and *American Politics Research*. In 2008, Streb received the NIU Foundation Award for Faculty Excellence. He specializes and teaches in the areas of parties, elections, polling and public opinion, Congress, civil rights movements, and research methods, and regularly teaches sections of Introduction to American Government.

Contents

Chapter 8   Bureaucracy   138

Chapter 9   The Courts   159

Chapter 10   Public Opinion   195

Preface to the Instructor

Sometimes in our efforts to get students to think critically about the texts they read, we resemble nothing so much as tourists in a foreign land, convinced that if we only make our requests louder and more insistent, we will suddenly be understood by uncomprehending native shopkeepers. "NO, NO," we say loudly. "Don't just report what the author is saying. ANALYZE it." If repeating the word *ANALYZE* in stentorian tones were enough to do the trick, all of our students would have been ace critical thinkers long ago. It isn't enough.

The reason it's not enough is that many, if not most, of our students don't really understand what it means to analyze, or to evaluate, or to assess—in short, to think critically. It isn't something that comes naturally, and we have learned the hard way that if we don't model it for students, they will be stuck at a level of descriptive understanding.

In this book we present the CLUES model—a tool for prodding students out of that descriptive rut. CLUES is an acronym (fully defined in the Preface to the Student) for the five essential steps of critical thinking that students need to internalize so that they can get the hang of thinking critically in their academic and everyday lives. We use these steps to help students work through readings together in class and, eventually, at home on their own.

In this reader we teach students to think critically about important substantive areas of American politics by means of the following features:

- Engaging, contemporary articles from a variety of sources—newspapers, magazines, radio, and the Internet—that illustrate American government at all levels
- Consistent end-of-reading questions that walk students through the CLUES method of critical thinking, helping to model the process for them so that they can learn to do it automatically
- Classic readings, such as John F. Kennedy's inaugural address and *Federalist* No. 51, that close each chapter and help students understand and observe the changes or constants in key political arguments over time
- Readings that are balanced between objective and opinion-based points of view and vary in length and format to provide instructors with maximum flexibility
- Chapters that correspond with the chapters of a typical introductory American politics text for easy incorporation into course syllabi

How to Use the Book in the Classroom

There are several ways *Clued in to Politics* can be incorporated in the classroom. These suggestions work for small classes or large lecture classes with discussion sections, but most of them are applicable for large lecture classes without discussion sections as well (see below for more on how to use the reader in large lecture classes without discussion sections). Certainly, one does not have to use all these pedagogical approaches, nor is this list exhaustive.

Answering/Creating CLUES Questions

This assignment is an excellent starting point to teach students critical thinking skills. It works well in all sizes of classes because instructors have a variety of options available to them. In a smaller class, students can begin by answering the CLUES questions for the assigned article on their own as homework or in small groups in class. The work can be given a numerical grade for the assignment or a pass/fail. The class should review the answers to the CLUES questions, especially early in the semester when students are getting familiar with the method.

In large classes, individual assignments usually work best. The instructor can collect the assignments and grade them pass/fail or use the assignments as a way to take attendance. As in smaller classes, the instructor should walk the class through the answers for the first few readings.

As the students become more advanced and independent, they can choose their own articles, figuring out what argument the author is making and creating their own questions to fit each step of the model (it is helpful early on if the instructor approves the student's article to be sure there is a clear argument to analyze). They can then answer their own questions. Getting students to apply the CLUES framework to articles on their own will help them develop immensely as critical thinkers.

Class Discussion/Class Debate

This pedagogical approach is best suited for small classes and classes that hold discussion sections. The instructor can take a variety of approaches. The class can work as a whole, or in small groups, deconstructing the author's argument. This pedagogical approach works especially well in discussing the political implications (the "S" in the CLUES framework) of the author's argument.

Even in larger classes, instructors can ask students to work with the person sitting next to them to come up with answers to the CLUES questions and then share them with the class. These "pair and share exercises" need only take a few minutes, but they can break up a lecture format and get students engaged in the readings.

Minute Reaction Papers

The use of short reaction papers to the articles is an excellent way to make sure students are both completing and understanding the readings. Instructors have a few options here. Students could write a paragraph or two simply discussing their reactions to the readings, relating the article to a concept discussed in lecture, or just responding to one of the CLUES questions.

Minute reaction papers are successful because they allow the instructor to measure whether the class grasped the author's argument and how the students' critical thinking skills are progressing. This type of assignment is particularly effective in large classes because it can be used to take attendance. Minute reaction papers are typically graded pass/fail.

Rebuttal Papers

Once students have finished several CLUES assignments on their own and are beginning to use the CLUES framework automatically, we raise the degree of difficulty a notch. Perhaps we ask students to find an editorial they disagree with and ask them to write their own editorial in opposition, using the CLUES model to guide their writing (for example, cautioning them to be aware of their audience, to set out their values and argument clearly, to supply evidence). The instructor should approve each student's article so that the student does not choose one that is too difficult to analyze.

By this point, students should have a solid understanding of evaluating evidence; this assignment will help them learn to rebut arguments with which they do not agree. Again, an assignment such as this one should be done well into the semester after the students have had much practice working through several articles using the CLUES framework. This assignment works well in all types of classes (although large lecture classes without discussion sections would need graders).

Persuasive Papers

This assignment is similar to the rebuttal paper. Instead of focusing on one article, choose a topic that is discussed in the reader (for example, Title IX, Electoral College) and have the students take a side. Students should go beyond simply analyzing the author's argument. Instead, they should bring in many different points of view on the topic, make an argument, and refute the opposition.

Like the rebuttal paper, this assignment should be given later in the semester once students have had more experience analyzing arguments. This assignment works well in all types of classes (although large lecture classes without discussion sections would need to have graders).

Classic Reading Papers

Each chapter in *Clued in to Politics* contains a classic reading designed to help students understand and observe the changes or constants in key political arguments over time. As a way to integrate the classic readings in class, students could choose or be assigned a classic reading and then write a paper relating the classic to current-day government. For example, students who read *Federalist* No. 78 could examine whether Hamilton was correct. This assignment will make students contemplate history and think critically about how important arguments of the past apply or don't apply to American politics today.

Large Lectures without Discussion Sections

Many of us find ourselves teaching larger and larger classes solely based on lecture and with little opportunity for class discussion. This can make the use of a reader difficult. As stated before, students will learn a great deal from *Clued in to Politics* simply by reading on their own. That said, students will benefit even more from additional instruction and help in learning to think critically. This can seem daunting for the instructor of such a large class (and in many cases without any help from teaching assistants), but *Clued in to Politics* can still be easily incorporated into this kind of class.

Instructors should explain the CLUES concept to the class early in the semester. This will help reinforce what students have read and will clear up any areas of confusion. At the beginning of each chapter, instructors might briefly highlight some of the questions they want students to contemplate as they are reading. Instructors can also tie in some of the major concepts of the class to the readings. For example, when discussing the role of pork barrel projects in a lecture on Congress, an instructor might mention the *Washington Times* article on criticism of current members of Congress for accepting pork. This instruction will help students understand the reading and tie it in to the "big picture."

To further help students grasp the concept of critical thinking, instructors might assign each student a partner or to a small group. Students can walk through the CLUES questions together, or later in the semester they can develop their own CLUES questions and answers in response to an article they have found. The instructor can then randomly collect the assignments to make sure they are being completed.

Other assignments that work well in a large lecture setting—and that were mentioned previously—are minute reaction papers and answering CLUES questions. These assignments can be used to monitor how well the class comprehends the readings and to take attendance. The instructor may randomly read a few of the reaction papers to see whether the students are grasping the concepts behind critical thinking.

Acknowledgments

Several people have helped us with this project, and we are grateful for their assistance. In particular, we would like to thank Gerald Wright of Indiana University; Michael Genovese and Evan Gerstmann of Loyola Marymount University (LMU); Brian Frederick of Bridgewater State College; David Kessler of the Bancroft Library at the University of California, Berkeley; and Carol Briley of the Truman Presidential Museum and Library. We are also indebted to research assistants Caroline Guidi and Jennie Haubenschild for their good work on this project.

We would also like to thank David Pace and Joan Middendorf of the Freshman Learning Project (FLP) at Indiana University for reminding us that students cannot learn to think like we do unless we model it for them. The FLP experience, and particularly David's own work with modeling critical thinking for students, has been invaluable in the conception of this book.

We have benefited from feedback from a terrific panel of reviewers over the course of three editions, and their help has been invaluable as well. We would like to thank

Craig Albert, Augusta State University
Sheldon Appleton, Oakland University

Thomas J. Barth, University of North Carolina, Wilmington

Daniel Coffey, University of Akron

Renee A. Cramer, California State University, Long Beach

Debra L. Delaet, Drake University

Richard N. Engstrom, University of Wyoming

Willoughby Jarrell, Kennesaw State University

Kelechi A. Kalu, University of Northern Colorado

Rebecca Klase, Greensboro College

Edward C. Olson, Angelo State University

Tracy Osborn, Bridgewater State College

Lisa Parshall, Daemon College

Donald Robinson, Casper College

Joseph Romance, Drew University

Andrew Rudalevige, Dickinson College

Gene T. Straughan, Lewis and Clark State College

Andrew J. Taylor, North Carolina State University

Robert Weissberg, University of Illinois, Urbana-Champaign

Joseph Wert, Indiana University Southeast

Michael Wolf, Indiana University–Purdue University Fort Wayne

David E. Woodard, Concordia University, St. Paul

We are grateful to Jean Woy for her help in developing this project and to all the folks at CQ Press who helped put this edition together: Brenda Carter and Charisse Kiino for their vision, patience, and support; Christina Mueller for coordinating the work—gathering permissions and keeping us on track; Amy Marks for her gentle and able editing; and Sarah Fell for her excellent work managing production.

Preface to the Student

This is a book of readings about politics. Although politics has its tedious moments, it also has an exhilarating side. It can be exciting, challenging, and even inspiring. It touches all of our lives much more often and more deeply than we may think. The readings in this book, although they will inevitably cover some heavy ground, were chosen to showcase the dramatic, fun, quirky, personal side of politics.

This is also a book about critical thinking. There's just no point in reading about politics if we aren't going to do it with a laser-like vision that cuts through the fog and sees the light, as it were, that separates myth from reality, lies from truth, stupidity from intelligence. If we don't think critically, we risk becoming the dupes of politicians and the system. Where's the sense in that?

So this book has two goals: first, to assemble readings on American politics that capture the excitement, drama, and interest of the political world, and second, to model the kind of critical thinking about that world that will give you the tools you need to deal with it.

What Kind of Readings Are We Using?

In our search for selections for this book, we combed a variety of news sources, from mainstream newspapers and news magazines, to opinion journals, to radio shows, to the Internet. It is both our good fortune and our curse to be living in an age when so much information about politics is available to us: our good fortune because it truly is possible for us to become informed on most matters today, and our curse because there is so much more work to be done in sorting the trustworthy from the unreliable, the true from the fraudulent, the reality from the spin. Long gone are the days when the words from a single trusted news source like Walter Cronkite could sway or soothe a nation. Today we have to dig deeper, ask tougher questions, and raise a more skeptical eyebrow to understand our world.

The news items we have selected show many faces of politics: idiosyncratic and amusing, as well as serious, weighty, and consequential. They show the good that government can do as well as its darker side. Our goal is to shake the image you may have of politics as totally irrelevant, hopelessly corrupt, or just deadly dull, and give you a healthy appreciation for what it is: a vibrant and important activity that reflects all sides of human nature and that affects our lives in many ways.

Why Bother with Critical Thinking When It's So Much Easier Not To?

Critical thinking sounds like work, and it sounds like fault-finding—two potentially unpleasant activities. It may be hard work at first (what skill worth having isn't difficult to begin with?), but what we mean by critical thinking has nothing to do with fault-finding or being negative. *Critical* in this case means careful evaluation and vigilant judgment. It means being wary of the surface appearance of what we hear and read and digging deeper to look for the subtext—what a person means and intends, whether that person has evidence for his or her conclusions, and what the political implications of the conclusions really are.

Becoming adept at critical thinking has a number of benefits:

- **We become much better students.** The skills of the critical thinker are not just the skills of the good citizen; they are the skills of the scholar. When we read we figure out what is important quickly and easily, we know which questions to ask to tease out more meaning, we can decide whether what we are reading is worth our time, and we know what to take with us and what to discard.
- **We are better able to hold our own in political (or other) arguments.** We think more logically and clearly, we are more persuasive, and we impress people with our grasp of reason and fact. There is not a career in the world that is not enhanced by critical thinking skills.
- **We learn to be good democratic citizens.** Critical thinking helps us sort through the barrage of information that assails us regularly and teaches us to process this information thoughtfully. Critical awareness of what our leaders are doing and the ability to understand and evaluate what they tell us is the lifeblood of democratic government.

Although it sounds like a dull and dusty activity, critical thinking can be vital and enjoyable. When we are good at it, it empowers and liberates us. We are not at the mercy of others' conclusions and decisions; we can evaluate facts and arguments for ourselves, turning conventional wisdom upside down and exploring the world of ideas with confidence.

How Does One Learn to Think Critically?

The trick to learning how to think critically is to do it. It helps to have a model to follow, however, and in this book we provide one. The focus of critical thinking here is the understanding of political argument. *Argument* in this case doesn't refer to a confrontation or a fight, but rather to a political contention, based on a set of assumptions, supported by evidence, leading to a clear, well-developed conclusion with consequences for how we understand the world.

Critical thinking involves constantly asking questions about the arguments you read: Whose argument is it? What is the basic case and what values underlie it? What evidence is used to back it up? What conclusions are drawn? What difference does the whole thing make? On the assumption that it will be easier for you to remember the questions to ask if you have a little help, we present here a mnemonic device that creates an acronym from the five major steps of critical thinking. Eventually, asking these questions will become second nature, but in the meantime, thinking of them as CLUES to critical thinking about American politics will help you to keep them in mind as you read.

This is what CLUES stands for:

Consider the source and the audience

Lay out the argument, the values, and the assumptions

Uncover the evidence

Evaluate the conclusion

Sort out the political implications

We'll investigate each of these steps in a little more depth.

Consider the Source and the Audience

Who is writing the news item? Where did the item appear? Why was it written? What audience is it directed toward? What must the author or publisher do to attract and keep the audience? How might that affect content?

Knowing the source and the audience goes a long way in helping you understand where the author is coming from, what his or her intentions are. If the person is a mainstream journalist, he or she probably has a reputation as an objective reporter to preserve and will at least make an honest attempt to provide unbiased information. Even so, knowing the actual news source helps you nail that down. Even in a reputable national paper like the *New York Times* or the *Wall Street Journal*, if the item comes from the editorial pages, you can count on its having an ideological point of view— usually (but not exclusively) liberal in the case of the *Times*, conservative in the case of the *Journal*. Opinion magazines have even more blatant points of view. Readers go to these sources looking for a particular perspective, and that perspective may affect the reliability of the information you find.

Lay Out the Argument, the Values, and the Assumptions

What is the basic argument the author wants to make? What assumptions about the world does he or she make? What values does the author hold about what is important and what government should do? Are all the important terms clearly defined?

If these points aren't clear, the author may be unclear on them as well. A lot of substandard thinking can be found out there, and being able to identify and discard it is a valuable skill. Often we are intimidated by a smart-sounding argument, only to discover on closer examination that it is just a piece of fuzzy thinking. A more insidious case occurs when the author is trying to obscure the point in order to get you to sign on to something you might not otherwise accept. If the argument, values, and assumptions are not perfectly clear and upfront, there may be a hidden agenda you should know about. You don't want to be persuaded by someone who claims to be an advocate for democracy, only to find out that, by *democracy*, he or she means something completely different than you do.

Uncover the Evidence

Has the author done basic research to back up his or her argument with facts and evidence? Good arguments cannot be based on gut feelings, rumor, or wishful thinking. They should be based on hard evidence, either empirical, verifiable observations about the world or solid, logical reasoning. If the argument is worth being held, it should stand up to rigorous examination, and the author should be able to defend it on these grounds. If the evidence or logic is missing, the argument can usually be dismissed.

Evaluate the Conclusion

Is the argument successful? Does it convince you? Why or why not? Does it change your mind about any beliefs you held previously? Does accepting this argument require you to rethink any of your other beliefs?

Conclusions should follow logically from the assumptions and values of an argument, if solid evidence and reasoning support it. What is the conclusion here? What is the author asking you to accept as the product of his or her argument? Does it make sense to you? Do you "buy" it? If you do, does it fit with your other ideas, or do you need to refine what you thought previously? Have you learned from this argument, or have you merely had your own beliefs reinforced?

Sort Out the Political Implications

What is the political significance of this argument? What difference does this argument make to your understanding of the way the political world works? How does it affect who gets what scarce resources, and how they get them? How does it affect who wins in the political process and who loses?

Political news is valuable if it means something. If it doesn't, it may entertain you, but essentially it wastes your time if it claims to be something more than entertainment. Make the information you get prove its importance. If it doesn't, find a different news source to rely on.

So, How Does This Book Work?

Each chapter of this book focuses on one of the main topics in a typical introductory American politics course. In each chapter we provide a selection of articles, transcripts, and other forms of political information. There are endless possibilities to include in the reader, so at the beginning of each piece we discuss our thought process in including the particular selection. Although our goal is to provide new and current information, the last selection in each chapter is typically much older, presenting a classic perspective on the subject. These classics can be as vitally relevant as the current daily news, and it is crucial that we be able to bring the same critical thinking skills to bear on them.

Sometimes the best way to learn how to do something is to watch someone else doing it. While that might be easy when it comes to tying a knot or chopping an onion, it is difficult when it comes to thinking. To model the way the CLUES steps work, we conclude each article with a CLUES box that sets out several questions you should be asking yourself as you take each step. Don't just gloss over these questions. Think about them, and answer each of them carefully. As you do, your understanding of the article will deepen, you will see more clearly what its strengths and weaknesses are, and you will be able to evaluate it more thoroughly. Eventually you will figure out what questions you should be asking on your own. When you get to that point, feel free to leave the CLUES boxes behind. You will be well on your way to being a critical thinker in your own right—an effective citizen and a promising scholar.

1

Introduction to American Politics

It's a riddle fit for a sphinx:

What is both an inspiring pursuit and a mind-numbing turn-off? A noble calling to serve an interest greater than oneself, and a degrading scramble for personal advantage? A spellbinding spectacle of the human passion for excellence, and a tedious litany of scandal and corruption?

The newest reality show on TV? Hardly. It's *politics*…the oldest reality show on earth.

How can politics embody so many contradictions? Politics is a reflection of human nature, itself a strange brew of opposites and incongruities. After all, politics is the process by which we distribute scarce resources like power and influence. Everybody wants them, but not everybody can have them. The stakes are high, and the methods are often cutthroat. But politics is also the means by which we come together to do what we cannot do alone—to build governments, construct highway systems, feed the poor, work for peace, and explore the skies. The same process of politics exploits our worst nature, and embraces our best nature.

As such, politics is a distinctively human activity, and in many ways it is our saving grace. Watch the family dogs when they want the same bone—they bite and snarl and pull each other away by the throat. Never once do they stop, call a meeting, attempt to reason or compromise or share. The strongest wins by violence and intimidation—every time. Human beings sometimes resort to the same tactics, but politics offers us an alternative—a way to resolve disputes without fighting and without coercion. Politics is the process of making decisions about who should get what valued resources, through discussion and debate, compromise and cooperation, bargaining, trade-offs, even bribery and graft sometimes, but always through human interaction that offers the possibility of a peaceful resolution.

American Government: The Democratic Experiment

In the United States we are fortunate to be living in the midst of a grand democratic experiment. In democracies, the people who are governed have rights that government cannot infringe upon, and what's more, they have a voice in the way they are governed. To the extent that they make their voice heard through the political process, their rights are expanded and protected. To the extent that they keep silent, they are often ignored by the system. Their rights can shrink or be trumped by the demands and concerns of more vocal citizens.

The United States is the first case of democracy being practiced for such a long time, on such a large scale. We call it an experiment because, like all experiments, we really do not know how it will turn out, although we have hopes and expectations. It is tempting to think that it will last for all time—that human beings, in America anyway, have solved the myriad problems that have afflicted societies through the ages and discovered the key to living in freedom and peace forever. But that is not likely. The founders themselves warned that they had put together a system requiring careful maintenance. Benjamin Franklin adjured a woman outside Constitution Hall that they had created a republic, "if you can keep it."

Democracies take time and effort, and lots of it, if they are to survive. They require that those who live in them be vigilant and careful, that they know something about how the system works, that they keep an eye on their leaders, that they be jealous of their rights and conscious of their obligations—that they be, in short, good citizens. Political philosopher Benjamin Barber notes that "the price of liberty is citizenship" and that "free societies are sustained only by hard work."[1]

A Civic Crisis?

And yet, at least until recently, many observers of American politics have argued that we are in a crisis of citizenship—a civic crisis manifested by vast public ignorance about the political system and by something worse, an indifference and cynicism that leaves citizens cold, untouched, and uninterested in learning who their leaders are and how they lead. In an important book about this problem, *Why Americans Hate Politics, Washington Post* columnist E. J. Dionne warns that "[a] nation that hates politics will not long survive as a democracy."[2]

Political apathy and low levels of political knowledge are not spread equally throughout the population—there are decided generational effects. Those raised during the Depression and World War II are far more likely to see government in a positive light and are far more likely to vote for the things they want. Baby boomers raised in the fifties, sixties, and seventies may have lived through the disillusionment of Watergate, but they also had the positive political experiences of working for civil rights, protesting the Vietnam War, and supporting early environmental efforts in this country. They too vote in fairly large numbers. As they get ready to retire, they are lobbying government to protect Social Security, to build up Medicare, to look after the interests of an aging but politically active cohort.

It is the generation of young Americans who scholars and pundits have worried about being most truly lost politically. Generation X, Generation Y, Generation Next—poll after poll of people from their thirties to their teens tell us that most young people have not seen government as relevant to their lives, responsive to their concerns, or worth their time and trouble. Although this same generation volunteers in churches, neighborhoods, and schools in record numbers, its interest in community life has not extended to government life. And in a giant self-fulfilling prophecy, most politicians continued to respond to the issues of the middle-aged and elderly people who vote, and not the young people who have become ever more cynical about the process.

The Readings in This Chapter

The first two readings in this chapter suggest that the presidential elections in 2004 and, even more, in 2008 have given observers reason to hope that younger generations of Americans might be reengaging in the political system. Political scientist Robert Putnam, writing in the *Boston Globe*, suggests that they are members of a generation shaped by 9/11 and captured by the idea of national service. National Public Radio's Scott Horsley contrasts the two visions of national service offered by the 2008 candidates for the presidency. Finally, President John F. Kennedy's inaugural address, presents a classic American view of patriotism and national service. As he notes, his election represented the passing of the torch to a new political generation, much as President Barack Obama's election did. What views of national service and political engagement are likely to hold sway with the newest generation of citizens?

Notes

1. Benjamin R. Barber, "Foreword." In *Education for Citizenship*, edited by Grant Reeher and Joseph Cammarano, ix. Lanham, Md.: Rowman & Littlefield, 1997.
2. E. J. Dionne Jr., *Why Americans Hate Politics*, 355. New York: Touchstone Books, 1991.

 1.1 The Rebirth of American Civic Life

Robert D. Putnam, Boston Globe

Why We Chose This Piece

In 1995 political scientist Robert Putnam wrote a book called Bowling Alone *about declining civic life and community in America. In this 2008 article he changes his tune, talking about a "rebirth of American civic life," prompted by the effect of the national tragedy of 9/11 on young people. He is happy to see the excitement as this generation of Americans comes of political age, but he is worried that their enthusiasm for politics will wane if the rules of the game appear to be rigged. His specific concern is with some pretty arcane rules in the Democratic Party that have the potential to overrule the results of the primaries and caucuses by choosing a nominee other than the winner of the most delegates in those contests. Note that his concern here is with the Democrats because*

Selection published: March 2, 2008

(1) Obama had generated unusual levels of enthusiastic support from younger voters and (2) Republicans have different primary rules than the Democrats. John McCain, the winner of the Republican primaries and caucuses, was never in danger of not being selected by his party.

As you read the article, don't worry too much about the details of the Florida and Michigan primaries or the Democratic "superdelegates"—you will learn more about those topics as you get further into the study of American politics. For now, concentrate on what Putnam has to say about civic engagement and young people—what he calls the "new Greatest Generation"—and the importance of "the simple playground rules of fairness" to keeping people engaged in the system. If you are between eighteen and twenty-four years old, do you think he has accurately described your generation's political experience? If you were a Democratic voter, how would you have felt if party officials had chosen Clinton over Obama?

In the mushrooming procedural debate about Democratic superdelegates and the uncontested Florida and Michigan primaries, more is at stake than the identity of the presidential nominee or even the Democrats' chances of victory in November. Primaries and caucuses coast to coast in the last two months have evinced the sharpest increase in civic engagement among American youth in at least a half-century, portending a remarkable revitalization of American democracy. But that rebirth of American civic life would be aborted if the decision rendered by millions of ordinary Americans could be overturned by a backroom deal among political insiders. The issue is not public jurisprudence or obscure party regulations or the alleged "wisdom" of party elders, but simple playground notions of fairness.

Throughout the last four decades of the 20th century, young people's engagement in American civic life declined year after year with depressing regularity. In fall 1966, well before the full flowering of Vietnam War protests, a UCLA poll of college freshmen nationwide found that "keeping up with politics" was a "very important" goal in their lives for fully 60 percent.

Thirty-four years later that figure had plummeted to 28 percent. In 1972, when the vote was first extended to 18-year-olds, turnout in the presidential election among 18- to 24-year-olds was a disappointing 52 percent. But even beginning at that modest level, rates of voting in presidential elections by young people steadily fell throughout the '70s, '80s, and '90s, reaching barely 36 percent in 2000. National commissions bemoaned the seemingly inexorable increase in youthful apathy and incivism. The National Commission on Civic Renewal said, "When we assess our country's civic and moral condition, we are deeply troubled.... We are in danger of becoming a nation of spectators."

Then came the attacks of Sept. 11, 2001, a national tragedy, but also a vivid reminder that we are all in this together. Civic seismometers across the land showed a sharp spike in virtually every measure of community-mindedness. It was, I wrote at the time, not only a tragedy, but also the sort of opportunity for civic revival that comes along once or twice a century. Just as Pearl Harbor had spawned the civic-minded "Greatest Generation," so too Sept. 11 might turn out to produce a more civically engaged generation of young people.

For most Americans the half-life of the civic boomlet after the attacks was barely six months. Within a year measures of civic engagement had returned to the previous levels, from which they have barely budged since. Except among young people.

Among the cohort of Americans caught by 9/11 in their formative years, the effects of the attacks on their civic consciousness were more enduring. The annual UCLA chart of interest in politics jumped upward in 2001 for the first time in decades and has kept rising every year since.

Last month the UCLA researchers reported that "For today's freshmen, discussing politics is more prevalent now than at any point in the past 41 years." This and other evidence led us and other observers to speak hopefully of a 9/11 generation, perhaps even a "new Greatest Generation." In the 2004 and 2006 elections, turnout among young people began at last to climb after decades of decline, reaching the highest point in 20 years in 2006. As we approached the presidential season of 2008, young Americans were, in effect, coiled for civic action, not because of their stage of life, but because of the lingering effects of the unifying national crisis they had experienced in their formative years.

The exceptionally lively presidential nominating contests of this year—and, it must be said, the extraordinary candidacy of Barack Obama—have sparked into white hot flame a pile of youthful kindling that had been stacked and ready to flare for more than six years. The 18-year-olds first eligible to vote in 2008 were in sixth grade when the twin towers fell, and their older sisters and brothers who were college seniors in September 2001 are now 28 or 29. It is precisely this group, above all others in America, that has pushed participation rates in this spring's caucuses and primaries to record levels. Turnout in this spring's electoral contests so far has generally been higher than in previous presidential nominating contests, but for twentysomethings the rise has been truly phenomenal—turnout often three or four times greater than ever before measured.

The 2008 elections are thus the coming-out party of this new Greatest Generation. Their grandparents of the original Greatest Generation were the civic pillars of American democracy for more than a half-century, and at long last, just as that generation is leaving the scene, reinforcements are arriving. Americans of every political persuasion should rejoice at this epochal swing of the generational pendulum, for it portends precisely the sort of civic renaissance for which Jeremiahs have been calling for many years.

This, then, is what is at stake in the otherwise inside-baseball controversies about superdelegates and pledged delegates and the uncontested Florida and Michigan primaries—controversies now roiling Democratic party leaders. If the results of the caucuses and primaries are, despite record-breaking rates of popular participation, overturned by unelected (though officially legitimate) superdelegates or by delegates from states that all candidates had previously agreed not to contest, the lesson for the young civic stalwarts would be unmistakable—democratic politics is a sham. Politics is actually controlled by party bosses behind the scenes. Civic engagement is for suckers.

From Little League to student council races, we all learn to accept defeats we have lost fair and square. But losing in a contest in which the rules can be rigged teaches that the game is not worth the candle. Who can honestly doubt that if the Democratic presidential candidate preferred by a majority of the delegates elected in this spring's competitive contests (and by the overwhelming majority of young voters) were to be rejected solely by the power of unelected delegates (or those "elected" without any serious competition), the unmistakable civics lesson would be catastrophic for this incipient cadre of super citizens?

So as the superdelegates, the two campaigns, and Democratic Party leaders contemplate how to resolve the procedural issues before them—what to do about Michigan and Florida, and how superdelegates should vote—let's hope that they weigh the consequences not merely for their own candidates this year, and not merely for the Democratic prospects in the fall, but for the future vitality of American democracy.

*C*onsider the source and the audience.

- This article appeared in the *Boston Globe* in March 2008, just as it began to sink in that Barack Obama was going to do better than anyone had guessed in the Democratic nominating contest, but when Hillary Clinton had a lead in the unelected superdelegate count as well as "victories" in the uncontested and uncounted primaries in Florida and Michigan. Who is Putnam speaking to here—the young people excited about Obama's candidacy or the Democratic Party officials he feared would "throw" the election to Clinton?

*L*ay out the argument, the values, and the assumptions.

- What does Putnam mean by referring to the "Greatest Generation?" Why does he value civic participation? How does he define "fairness?"
- What is the link between civic engagement and fairness, in his mind?

*U*ncover the evidence.

- What evidence does Putman provide that today's young people are a "new Greatest Generation?"
- Does he have empirical evidence to back up his claim that if Democratic officials overrule the result of the Democratic primary process, then "the rebirth of American civic life would be aborted?" Does he need evidence for that claim?

*E*valuate the conclusion.

- Was Putnam right? Do you think that 18–24-year-olds have been shaped to be more politically active by growing up in the shadow of 9/11?
- What impact would it have had on young Democratic voters you know if Clinton had been made the nominee despite Obama's primary and caucus victories? How important is it in securing your own investment in a system that the rules be perceived to be "fair"?

*S*ort out the political implications.

- The Democrats eventually decided not to count the Michigan and Florida primary results at full strength, and the superdelegates ended up moving overwhelmingly to Obama. Do you think they and the Democratic officials might have been persuaded by arguments about the probability of disillusioning and alienating a generation of new voters?

1.2 McCain, Obama View Public Service Differently

Scott Horsley, All Things Considered, *National Public Radio*

Why We Chose This Piece

We argue in this chapter that democracies are not self-sustaining—that they take careful tending by their citizens in order to thrive. But what form should that tending take? In this selection by National Public Radio's Scott Horsley, we see that the two nominees for the presidency in 2008 both advocated national service, but their ideas of what that service should mean were different. While you read this story, consider those different concepts of national service. Which form of national service does a democracy need to thrive—one, the other, or both?

Illinois Sen. Barack Obama has issued a challenge for greater national service. During a speech to college students in Colorado on Wednesday, the presumptive Democratic presidential nominee said he wants to expand the military and the Peace Corps and provide other opportunities for people of all ages to serve.

"Loving your country shouldn't just mean watching fireworks on the Fourth of July," Obama said. "Loving your country must mean accepting your responsibility to do your part to change it."

Obama's Republican rival, John McCain, also talks frequently on the campaign trail about inspiring national service.

"I think after 9/11 we made a mistake," McCain said. "I think after 9/11, instead of telling Americans to take a trip or go shopping, I think we had an opportunity to call Americans to serve."

Despite the two men's agreement on the benefits of national service, the issue plays a very different role in their overall platforms. And it's no surprise that both Obama and McCain are big believers in public service. They both devoted their careers to it, and in a way, both men found themselves through their service to others.

Obama recalled on Wednesday how working as a community organizer in Chicago allowed him to finally put down roots after years adrift. "I began to realize I wasn't just helping other people," he said. "Through service, I found a community that embraced me—citizenship that was meaningful, the direction that I'd been seeking. Through service I discovered how my own improbable story fit into the larger American story."

For McCain, that realization came in Vietnam, where the fiercely independent young man learned that teaming up with others didn't have to mean losing himself. McCain writes in his memoir, "Nothing in life is more liberating than to fight for a

---

Selection aired: July 2, 2008

cause larger than yourself, something that encompasses you, but is not defined by your existence alone."

He often sounds that theme on the campaign trail, as he did in the "volunteer state" of Tennessee. "My one job and my one accomplishment will be to inspire Americans to serve a cause greater than their self-interest. I will tell Americans of the beauty and the nobility of serving a cause greater than their self-interest."

The Role of Government in Service

Where McCain and Obama diverge on the issue is the ways in which the government should act in fostering or reflecting that spirit.

McCain's domestic agenda is all about harnessing self-interest for positive ends—whether it be tax cuts aimed at boosting the economy or personal insurance policies designed to control healthcare costs.

Speaking to students at his old high school, McCain said military service is the noblest of all causes. But otherwise, he seems to view public service as something that happens more or less outside of government—much like the first President Bush, who pictured Americans volunteering for religious, business or neighborhood groups.

"Like a thousand points of light in a broad and peaceful sky," McCain said. "Does government have a place? Yes. Government is part of the nation of communities—not the whole, just a part."

Obama, on the other hand, sees government as both a catalyst and an expression of service to a larger cause. He described that central role earlier this year during a speech in Wisconsin.

"The most important thing that we can do right now is to re-engage the American people in the process of governance. To get them excited and interested again in what works and what can work in our government. To make politics cool again and important again and relevant again," he said.

For Obama, the notion that Americans are all in this together is a central driver of domestic policy on taxes, health care and the like. Democratic campaign strategist Eric Sapp says that message about a "common good" was originally aimed at religious voters, but it has broad appeal to secular voters as well.

"What's made America strong historically is this idea of coming together as Americans," Sapp says. "Not seeing the 'others' within our groups, but coming together for a common purpose around a call to something greater than ourselves."

Both Obama and McCain are tapping into that ideal—Obama as a blueprint for government policy, McCain as a civic-minded alternative.

*C*onsider the source and the audience.

- This segment appeared on National Public Radio's *All Things Considered*—a public radio program that strives for political neutrality. Is there any difference in how the story treats the Democratic and the Republican candidates for president?

*L**ay out the argument, the values, and the assumptions.*

- Horsley argues that the McCain and Obama campaigns represent two different views of national service. What are those two views, and what is the essential difference between them?
- What values underlie each perspective, and what about the men's personal history might lead them to hold each view?

*U**ncover the evidence.*

- Does Horsley provide evidence that the men hold these two views? What besides the candidates' own words might help illustrate the difference Horsley is trying to show?

*E**valuate the conclusion.*

- According to Horsley, Obama's view of national service is based on government—"to make politics cool again"—while McCain's, aside from the importance he places on military service, is largely in the private sector—"a thousand points of light," of which government is only part. Do you agree with Horsley that these views are divergent? Even if differences exist, do the two views have anything in common?

*S**ort out the political implications.*

- Is there room in American politics for both of these views of civic engagement? How might they work together?

 1.3 Inaugural Address

John F. Kennedy

Why We Chose This Piece

> *John F. Kennedy's inaugural address, now more than forty years old, calls on Americans facing a long battle to preserve their ideals and their way of life to exhibit a selfless citizenship and devotion to country. His words to a nation challenged by the Cold War are poignant today, when the same nation is struggling with war of a different but equally destructive kind. One definition of an effective leader may be that a leader holds up a mirror before a nation's citizens and helps them see themselves as a people bound by values and heritage, willing to sacrifice for worthy common goals. How does Kennedy take the opportunity presented by this speech to establish himself as a national leader?*

Selection delivered: January 20, 1961

W e observe today not a victory of party, but a celebration of freedom—symbolizing an end, as well as a beginning—signifying renewal, as well as change. For I have sworn before you and Almighty God the same solemn oath our forebears prescribed nearly a century and three-quarters ago.

The world is very different now. For man holds in his mortal hands the power to abolish all forms of human poverty and all forms of human life. And yet the same revolutionary beliefs for which our forebears fought are still at issue around the globe—the belief that the rights of man come not from the generosity of the state, but from the hand of God.

We dare not forget today that we are the heirs of that first revolution. Let the word go forth from this time and place, to friend and foe alike, that the torch has been passed to a new generation of Americans—born in this century, tempered by war, disciplined by a hard and bitter peace, proud of our ancient heritage, and unwilling to witness or permit the slow undoing of those human rights to which this nation has always been committed, and to which we are committed today at home and around the world.

Let every nation know, whether it wishes us well or ill, that we shall pay any price, bear any burden, meet any hardship, support any friend, oppose any foe, to assure the survival and the success of liberty.

This much we pledge—and more.

To those old allies whose cultural and spiritual origins we share, we pledge the loyalty of faithful friends. United there is little we cannot do in a host of cooperative ventures. Divided there is little we can do—for we dare not meet a powerful challenge at odds and split asunder.

To those new states whom we welcome to the ranks of the free, we pledge our word that one form of colonial control shall not have passed away merely to be replaced by a far more iron tyranny. We shall not always expect to find them supporting our view. But we shall always hope to find them strongly supporting their own freedom—and to remember that, in the past, those who foolishly sought power by riding the back of the tiger ended up inside.

To those people in the huts and villages of half the globe struggling to break the bonds of mass misery, we pledge our best efforts to help them help themselves, for whatever period is required—not because the Communists may be doing it, not because we seek their votes, but because it is right. If a free society cannot help the many who are poor, it cannot save the few who are rich.

To our sister republics south of our border, we offer a special pledge: to convert our good words into good deeds, in a new alliance for progress, to assist free men and free governments in casting off the chains of poverty. But this peaceful revolution of hope cannot become the prey of hostile powers. Let all our neighbors know that we shall join with them to oppose aggression or subversion anywhere in the Americas. And let every other power know that this hemisphere intends to remain the master of its own house.

To that world assembly of sovereign states, the United Nations, our last best hope in an age where the instruments of war have far outpaced the instruments of peace, we renew our pledge of support—to prevent it from becoming merely a forum for invective, to strengthen its shield of the new and the weak, and to enlarge the area in which its writ may run.

Finally, to those nations who would make themselves our adversary, we offer not a pledge but a request: that both sides begin anew the quest for peace, before the dark powers of destruction unleashed by science engulf all humanity in planned or accidental self-destruction.

We dare not tempt them with weakness. For only when our arms are sufficient beyond doubt can we be certain beyond doubt that they will never be employed.

But neither can two great and powerful groups of nations take comfort from our present course—both sides overburdened by the cost of modern weapons, both rightly alarmed by the steady spread of the deadly atom, yet both racing to alter that uncertain balance of terror that stays the hand of mankind's final war.

So let us begin anew—remembering on both sides that civility is not a sign of weakness, and sincerity is always subject to proof. Let us never negotiate out of fear, but let us never fear to negotiate.

Let both sides explore what problems unite us instead of belaboring those problems which divide us.

Let both sides, for the first time, formulate serious and precise proposals for the inspection and control of arms, and bring the absolute power to destroy other nations under the absolute control of all nations.

Let both sides seek to invoke the wonders of science instead of its terrors. Together let us explore the stars, conquer the deserts, eradicate disease, tap the ocean depths, and encourage the arts and commerce.

Let both sides unite to heed, in all corners of the earth, the command of Isaiah—to "undo the heavy burdens, and [to] let the oppressed go free."

And, if a beachhead of cooperation may push back the jungle of suspicion, let both sides join in creating a new endeavor—not a new balance of power, but a new world of law—where the strong are just, and the weak secure, and the peace preserved.

All this will not be finished in the first one hundred days. Nor will it be finished in the first one thousand days; nor in the life of this Administration; nor even perhaps in our lifetime on this planet. But let us begin.

In your hands, my fellow citizens, more than mine, will rest the final success or failure of our course. Since this country was founded, each generation of Americans has been summoned to give testimony to its national loyalty. The graves of young Americans who answered the call to service surround the globe.

Now the trumpet summons us again—not as a call to bear arms, though arms we need—not as a call to battle, though embattled we are—but a call to bear the burden of a long twilight struggle, year in and year out, "rejoicing in hope; patient in tribulation," a struggle against the common enemies of man: tyranny, poverty, disease, and war itself.

Can we forge against these enemies a grand and global alliance, North and South, East and West, that can assure a more fruitful life for all mankind? Will you join in that historic effort?

In the long history of the world, only a few generations have been granted the role of defending freedom in its hour of maximum danger. I do not shrink from this responsibility—I welcome it. I do not believe that any of us would exchange places with any other people or any other generation. The energy, the faith, the devotion which we bring to this endeavor will light our country and all who serve it. And the glow from that fire can truly light the world.

And so, my fellow Americans, ask not what your country can do for you; ask what you can do for your country.

My fellow citizens of the world, ask not what America will do for you, but what together we can do for the freedom of man.

Finally, whether you are citizens of America or citizens of the world, ask of us here the same high standards of strength and sacrifice which we ask of you. With a good conscience our only sure reward, with history the final judge of our deeds, let us go forth to lead the land we love, asking His blessing and His help, but knowing that here on earth God's work must truly be our own.

*C*onsider the source and the audience.

- Here you are reading a president's inaugural address. What are the goals of such a speech? Is it addressed only to Americans?

*L*ay out the argument, the values, and the assumptions.

- Is Kennedy making an argument in this speech? How might the claims made in an inaugural address differ from those in a more traditional argument?
- What is Kennedy's major point? Who are the new generation of Americans to which the torch is being passed? How does their political experience make them different?
- What is Kennedy's view of a good government? What is his view of how the world should be ordered? What values are worth fighting for? What is his view of national service?

*U*ncover the evidence.

- What kind of evidence is Kennedy obliged to provide in support of the claims he makes here?
- When can ideals, convictions, and historical tradition substitute for factual evidence?

*E*valuate the conclusion.

- What does Kennedy see as the fundamental tasks to be done?
- Were there other visions of America and its role in the world that he might have offered then? What values might this role have been based on?

*S*ort out the political implications.

- How effective do you imagine this speech was as a political call to arms and a call "to bear the burden?" How might it have shaped the generations to whom it was addressed?
- How might such a speech be received today?

2

Political Culture

How do we recognize "people like us"—the people we grow up with, go to school with, attend church with, hang out with? The people who live in our neighborhoods, our towns, our cities, and our states? How do we identify Americans from all the other people in the world? That odd, intangible thing that separates "us" from "them," that answers the question "who are we?" is called political culture, the set of ideas, beliefs, and values about who we are as a nation, what we believe in, what kind of government we should have, and what our relationship to that government should be.

Political culture can be a hard concept to grasp because it is abstract. We can't see it or touch it, and in fact, it is very difficult to be aware of our own political culture when we are immersed in it. Like kids looking through play glasses with tinted lenses, we see everything colored by the lens of our culture. We think we are seeing truth—the way things really are—but really we see just our version of reality, shaped by our cultural preferences and values. Other people observing us from other cultures can often see more easily what our own familiarity with our values and beliefs hides from us. Sometimes we see the differences most clearly when we are traveling in another country among people who are not "like us."

Understanding political culture is important because the way we think about ourselves politically and the values we share help to shape our political systems and the way politics takes place within them. Today our political culture is based on a commitment to individual freedom from extensive government action; on the value of equality, defined as equal opportunity rather than equality of results; and on the principle that decisions should be made through a representative democracy, heeding the voices of individuals and organized interests in the formation of public policy. All these values together go into the ideal of the "American dream"—the idea that all citizens have the opportunity to live prosperous lives, that they are entitled to "life, liberty and the pursuit of happiness." Within these values there is room for plenty of disagreement about what sorts of political, economic, and cultural choices we as a nation should make.

But while political culture can be thought of as the ideas that bring us together, that unite us as a people, we are also a nation of immigrants, whose culture is continually being added to and enhanced by the values and beliefs of the new people who come here. From the time we are schoolchildren, we are taught two competing views of ourselves as a people. One view holds that we are a melting pot, where our identities merge together into a kind of homogeneous American soup. The other holds that we are a crazy salad, with each of us keeping our unique identities, even as we share the same bowl. The question of which of these views should hold sway has itself become a defining issue in American culture. As we approach a point in the not very distant future where white Americans of European extraction will become a minority in the United States, it is worth asking how our political culture will respond to and reflect this change.

We have chosen the selections in this chapter to showcase different interpretations of the ideas that unite us as Americans and of the role of immigration in shaping us as a people. The first article, by David Brooks of the *New York Times*, compares our political culture and the individualism on which it is based with the collectivism of China— the new powerhouse on the international stage. Will the "Chinese dream" someday be as compelling an idea around the world as the American dream? The second article, from the *New York Review of Books*, is by Zadie Smith, a young British novelist of mixed race, who explores the phenomenon of having multiple voices related to her different cultural heritages and sees in U.S. president Barack Obama's experience a mirror of her own. The third piece, written by an academic in the *Christian Science Monitor*, contrasts with Smith's, which sees value in multiculturalism, by arguing that such a blend of cultures can be threatening to democratic stability. The fourth article elaborates on some of these ideas, taking on the issue of language and national identity and examines the impact of recent immigration on American culture. Finally, a selection that touches on concerns in all these pieces is Martin Luther King Jr.'s classic "I Have a Dream" speech. Here King looks at the whole culture that ties Americans together, especially its commitment to freedom and equality, and demands access to that culture for African Americans and, by implication, other excluded groups.

 ## 2.1 Harmony and the Dream

David Brooks, The New York Times

Why We Chose This Piece

> *Contemplating the opening ceremonies of the Beijing Olympics, David Brooks, a conservative columnist at the* New York Times, *nails one of the central elements of American political culture—our tendency to see the whole as no more than a collection of individual parts. In contrast with collectivist cultures like China's, we credit individuals with their*

Selection published: August 11, 2008

successes and blame them for their failures, generally without looking to see what aspects of society might have boosted the chances of some, or damaged those of others. Even American liberals, who tend to be slightly more willing to look at society in a collectivist way than conservatives, come down firmly in the individualist camp. Although as a conservative American he clearly finds individualism more attractive, Brooks sees certain advantages in China's culture.

When you read this article, you will not only get an appreciation for a part of American culture you probably share, but may never have articulated, but you will also get a comparative sense of how our approach measures up with that of another country. Such comparisons can be valuable when you are looking at as pervasive and all-encompassing a phenomenon as political culture because it gives us an external standpoint from which to consider our own cultural assumptions. Why would such an external standpoint be helpful?

The world can be divided in many ways—rich and poor, democratic and authoritarian—but one of the most striking is the divide between the societies with an individualist mentality and the ones with a collectivist mentality.

This is a divide that goes deeper than economics into the way people perceive the world. If you show an American an image of a fish tank, the American will usually describe the biggest fish in the tank and what it is doing. If you ask a Chinese person to describe a fish tank, the Chinese will usually describe the context in which the fish swim.

These sorts of experiments have been done over and over again, and the results reveal the same underlying pattern. Americans usually see individuals; Chinese and other Asians see contexts.

When the psychologist Richard Nisbett showed Americans individual pictures of a chicken, a cow and hay and asked the subjects to pick out the two that go together, the Americans would usually pick out the chicken and the cow. They're both animals. Most Asian people, on the other hand, would pick out the cow and the hay, since cows depend on hay. Americans are more likely to see categories. Asians are more likely to see relationships.

You can create a global continuum with the most individualistic societies—like the United States or Britain—on one end, and the most collectivist societies—like China or Japan—on the other.

The individualistic countries tend to put rights and privacy first. People in these societies tend to overvalue their own skills and overestimate their own importance to any group effort. People in collective societies tend to value harmony and duty. They tend to underestimate their own skills and are more self-effacing when describing their contributions to group efforts.

Researchers argue about why certain cultures have become more individualistic than others. Some say that Western cultures draw their values from ancient Greece, with its emphasis on individual heroism, while other cultures draw more on tribal philosophies. Recently, some scientists have theorized that it all goes back to microbes. Collectivist societies tend to pop up in parts of the world, especially around the equator, with plenty of disease-causing microbes. In such an environment, you'd want to shun outsiders, who might bring strange diseases, and enforce a certain conformity over eating rituals and social behavior.

Either way, individualistic societies have tended to do better economically. We in the West have a narrative that involves the development of individual reason and conscience during the Renaissance and the Enlightenment, and then the subsequent flourishing of capitalism. According to this narrative, societies get more individualistic as they develop.

But what happens if collectivist societies snap out of their economic stagnation? What happens if collectivist societies, especially those in Asia, rise economically and come to rival the West? A new sort of global conversation develops.

The opening ceremony in Beijing was a statement in that conversation. It was part of China's assertion that development doesn't come only through Western, liberal means, but also through Eastern and collective ones.

The ceremony drew from China's long history, but surely the most striking features were the images of thousands of Chinese moving as one—drumming as one, dancing as one, sprinting on precise formations without ever stumbling or colliding. We've seen displays of mass conformity before, but this was collectivism of the present—a high-tech vision of the harmonious society performed in the context of China's miraculous growth.

If Asia's success reopens the debate between individualism and collectivism (which seemed closed after the cold war), then it's unlikely that the forces of individualism will sweep the field or even gain an edge.

For one thing, there are relatively few individualistic societies on earth. For another, the essence of a lot of the latest scientific research is that the Western idea of individual choice is an illusion and the Chinese are right to put first emphasis on social contexts.

Scientists have delighted to show that so-called rational choice is shaped by a whole range of subconscious influences, like emotional contagions and priming effects (people who think of a professor before taking a test do better than people who think of a criminal). Meanwhile, human brains turn out to be extremely permeable (they naturally mimic the neural firings of people around them). Relationships are the key to happiness. People who live in the densest social networks tend to flourish, while people who live with few social bonds are much more prone to depression and suicide.

The rise of China isn't only an economic event. It's a cultural one. The ideal of a harmonious collective may turn out to be as attractive as the ideal of the American Dream.

It's certainly a useful ideology for aspiring autocrats.

*C*onsider the source and the audience.

- The *New York Times* is a mainstream print media outlet, with a slightly left-of-center orientation and an educated readership. How might that affect the way Brooks couches his argument?

Lay out the argument, the values, and the assumptions.

- What are the basic principles of the individualism Brooks describes? Of collectivism?
- What does he indicate might be the advantages of each?
- Why does he think collectivism might have an edge? What is its attraction for autocrats—that is, rulers who have unlimited power?

Uncover the evidence.

- Brooks uses a variety of kinds of evidence to support his case. Who are his experts and what kinds of evidence does he provide? Is such an eclectic collection of sources more or less persuasive than a single source?

Evaluate the conclusion.

- Brooks thinks that China's cultural identity might end up being as persuasive as the American dream. How would you describe the "Chinese dream" he is thinking of?

Sort out the political implications.

- Must collectivism go hand in hand with autocracy? Is there such a thing as democratic collectivism?
- Are individualistic cultures necessarily at a disadvantage when confronting collectivist cultures?

 ## 2.2 Speaking in Tongues

Zadie Smith, New York Review of Books

Why We Chose This Piece

> *Zadie Smith is a British novelist, the child of an English father and a Jamaican mother. Born on London's north side, she grew up speaking one voice and then, as a student at Cambridge, developed another, more cultured voice. In this speech, printed in the* New York Review of Books *and excerpted here, she explores what it means to be multilingual—in this sense, how being able to speak to multiple audiences in her world enhances her ability to communicate but also makes her doubt in some ways the authenticity of her voice.*

> *We've chosen such an unusual piece for this chapter on American political culture for several reasons. First, Smith explicitly compares her own experience to that of Barack Obama, finding in his own multilingual past an echo of her own. She argues that Obama's ability to speak authentically to multiple audiences—to white ones as well as African*

Selection published: February 26, 2009

American ones—helped him communicate his message in ways other black politicians in the United States have not been able to do. But she also raises the issue of multicultural-ism, seeing it as a good thing, a way for different cultures to find connections and become stronger. As we will see, the author of the next selection takes a very different view.

What can we learn from a foreign observer, looking in at our political culture? How can such a perspective enhance our own understanding? What are its limits?

*T*he following is based on a lecture given at the New York Public Library in Decem-ber 2008.

1.

Hello. This voice I speak with these days, this English voice with its rounded vowels and consonants in more or less the right place—this is not the voice of my childhood. I picked it up in college, along with the unabridged *Clarissa* and a taste for port. Maybe this fact is only what it seems to be—a case of bald social climbing—but at the time I genuinely thought *this* was the voice of lettered people, and that if I didn't have the voice of lettered people I would never truly be lettered. A braver person, perhaps, would have stood firm, teaching her peers a useful lesson by example: not all lettered people need be of the same class, nor speak identically. I went the other way. Partly out of cowardice and a constitutional eagerness to please, but also because I didn't quite see it as a straight swap, of this voice for that.

My own childhood had been the story of this and that combined, of the synthesis of disparate things. It never occurred to me that I was leaving the London district of Willesden for Cambridge. I thought I was *adding* Cambridge to Willesden, this new way of talking to that old way. Adding a new kind of knowledge to a different kind I already had. And for a while, that's how it was: at home, during the holidays, I spoke with my old voice, and in the old voice seemed to feel and speak things that I couldn't express in college, and vice versa. I felt a sort of wonder at the flexibility of the thing. Like being alive twice.

. . .

Whoever changes their voice takes on, in Britain, a queerly tragic dimension. They have betrayed that puzzling dictum "To thine own self be true," so often quoted approv-ingly as if it represented the wisdom of Shakespeare rather than the hot air of Polonius. "*What's to become of me? What's to become of me?*" wails Eliza Doolittle, realizing her middling dilemma. With a voice too posh for the flower girls and yet too redolent of the gutter for the ladies in Mrs. Higgins's drawing room.

But Eliza—patron saint of the tragically double-voiced—is worthy of closer inspec-tion. The first thing to note is that both Eliza and *Pygmalion* are entirely didactic, as Shaw meant them to be. "I delight," he wrote, in throwing [*Pygmalion*] at the heads of the wiseacres who repeat the parrot cry that art should never be didactic. It goes to prove my contention that art should never be anything else.

He was determined to tell the unambiguous tale of a girl who changes her voice and loses her self. And so she arrives like this:

Don't you be so saucy. You ain't heard what I come for yet. Did you tell him I come in a taxi?... Oh, we are proud! He ain't above giving lessons, not him: I heard him say so. Well, I ain't come here to ask for any compliment; and if my moneys not good enough I can go elsewhere.... Now you know, don't you? I'm come to have lessons, I am. And to pay for em too: make no mistake.... I want to be a lady in a flower shop stead of selling at the corner of Tottenham Court Road. But they wont take me unless I can talk more genteel.

And she leaves like this:

I can't. I could have done it once; but now I can't go back to it. Last night, when I was wandering about, a girl spoke to me; and I tried to get back into the old way with her; but it was no use. You told me, you know, that when a child is brought to a foreign country, it picks up the language in a few weeks, and forgets its own. Well, I am a child in your country. I have forgotten my own language, and can speak nothing but yours.

By the end of his experiment, Professor Higgins has made his Eliza an awkward, in-between thing, neither flower girl nor lady, with one voice lost and another gained, at the steep price of everything she was, and everything she knows. Almost as afterthought, he sends Eliza's father, Alfred Doolittle, to his doom, too, securing a three-thousand-a-year living for the man on the condition that Doolittle lecture for the Wannafeller Moral Reform World League up to six times a year. This burden brings the philosophical dustman into the close, unwanted embrace of what he disdainfully calls "middle class morality." By the time the curtain goes down, both Doolittles find themselves stuck in the middle, which is, to Shaw, a comi-tragic place to be, with the emphasis on the tragic. What are they fit for? What will become of them?

How persistent this horror of the middling spot is, this dread of the interim place! It extends through the specter of the tragic mulatto, to the plight of the transsexual, to our present anxiety—disguised as genteel concern—for the contemporary immigrant, tragically split, we are sure, between worlds, ideas, cultures, voices—whatever will become of them? Something's got to give—one voice must be sacrificed for the other. What is double must be made singular.

But this, the apparent didactic moral of Eliza's story, is undercut by the fact of the play itself, which is an orchestra of many voices, simultaneously and perfectly rendered, with no shade of color or tone sacrificed. Higgins's Harley Street high-handedness is the equal of Mrs. Pierce's lower-middle-class gentility, Pickering's kindhearted aristocratic imprecision every bit as convincing as Arthur Doolittle's Nietzschean Cockney-by-way-of-Wales. Shaw had a wonderful ear, able to reproduce almost as many quirks of the English language as Shakespeare's. Shaw was in possession of a gift he wouldn't, or couldn't, give Eliza: he spoke in tongues.

It gives me a strange sensation to turn from Shaw's melancholy Pygmalion story to another, infinitely more hopeful version, written by the new president of the United States of America. Of course, his ear isn't half bad either. In *Dreams from My Father*, the new president displays an enviable facility for dialogue, and puts it to good use, animating a cast every bit as various as the one James Baldwin—an obvious influence—conjured for his own many-voiced novel *Another Country*. Obama can do young Jewish male, black old lady from the South Side, white woman from Kansas, Kenyan elders, white Harvard nerds, black Columbia nerds, activist women, churchmen, security guards, bank tellers, and even a British man called Mr. Wilkerson, who on a starry night on safari says credibly British things like: "I believe that's the Milky Way." This new president doesn't just speak *for* his people. He can *speak* them. It is a disorienting talent in a president; we're so unused to it. I have to pinch myself to remember who wrote the following well-observed scene, seemingly plucked from a comic novel:

> "Man, I'm not going to any more of these bullshit Punahou parties."
>
> "Yeah, that's what you said the last time...."
>
> "I mean it this time.... These girls are A-1, USDA-certified racists. All of 'em. White girls. Asian girls—shoot, these Asians worse than the whites. Think we got a disease or something."
>
> "Maybe they're looking at that big butt of yours. Man, I thought you were in training."
>
> "Get your hands out of my fries. You ain't my bitch, nigger...buy your own damn fries. Now what was I talking about?"
>
> "Just 'cause a girl don't go out with you doesn't make her a racist."

This is the voice of Obama at seventeen, as remembered by Obama. He's still recognizably Obama; he already seeks to unpack and complicate apparently obvious things ("Just 'cause a girl don't go out with you doesn't make her a racist"); he's already gently cynical about the impassioned dogma of other people ("Yeah, that's what you said the last time"). And he has a sense of humor ("Maybe they're looking at that big butt of yours"). Only the voice is different: he has made almost as large a leap as Eliza Doolittle. The conclusions Obama draws from his own Pygmalion experience, however, are subtler than Shaw's. The tale he tells is not the old tragedy of gaining a new, false voice at the expense of a true one. The tale he tells is all about addition. His is the story of a genuinely many-voiced man. If it has a moral it is that each man must be true to his selves, plural.

For Obama, having more than one voice in your ear is not a burden, or not solely a burden—it is also a gift. And the gift is of an interesting kind, not well served by that dull publishing-house title *Dreams from My Father: A Story of Race and Inheritance* with its suggestion of a simple linear inheritance, of paternal dreams and aspirations passed down to a son, and fulfilled. *Dreams from My Father* would have been a fine title for John McCain's book *Faith of My Fathers*, which concerns exactly this kind of linear masculine inheritance, in his case from soldier to soldier. For Obama's book, though, it's wrong, lopsided. He corrects its misperception early on, in the first chapter, while discussing the failure of his parents' relationship, characterized by their only son as the end of a dream. "Even as that spell was broken," he writes, "and the worlds that they thought they'd left behind reclaimed each of them, I *occupied the place* where their dreams had been."

To *occupy* a dream, to exist in a dreamed space (conjured by both father and mother), is surely a quite different thing from simply *inheriting* a dream. It's more interesting. What did Pauline Kael call Cary Grant? "*The Man from Dream City.*" When Bristolian Archibald Leach became suave Cary Grant, the transformation happened in his voice, which he subjected to a strange, indefinable manipulation, resulting in that heavenly sui generis accent, neither west country nor posh, American nor English. It came from nowhere, *he* came from nowhere. Grant seemed the product of a collective dream, dreamed up by moviegoers in hard times, as it sometimes feels voters have dreamed up Obama in hard times. Both men have a strange reflective quality, typical of the self-created man—we see in them whatever we want to see. "*Everyone wants to be Cary Grant,*" said Cary Grant. "*Even I want to be Cary Grant.*" It's not hard to imagine Obama having that same thought, backstage at Grant Park, hearing his own name chanted by the hopeful multitude. *Everyone wants to be Barack Obama. Even I want to be Barack Obama.*

2.

But I haven't described Dream City. I'll try to. It is a place of many voices, where the unified singular self is an illusion. Naturally, Obama was born there. So was I. When your personal multiplicity is printed on your face, in an almost too obviously thematic manner, in your DNA, in your hair and in the neither this nor that beige of your skin—well, anyone can see you come from Dream City. In Dream City everything is doubled, everything is various. You have no choice but to cross borders and speak in tongues. That's how you get from your mother to your father, from talking to one set of folks who think you're not black enough to another who figure you insufficiently white. It's the kind of town where the wise man says "I" cautiously, because "I" feels like too straight and singular a phoneme to represent the true multiplicity of his experience. Instead, citizens of Dream City prefer to use the collective pronoun "we."

Throughout his campaign Obama was careful always to say we. He was noticeably wary of "I." By speaking so, he wasn't simply avoiding a singularity he didn't feel, he was also drawing us in with him. He had the audacity to suggest that, even if you can't see it stamped on their faces, most people come from Dream City, too. Most of us have complicated back stories, messy histories, multiple narratives.

It was a high-wire strategy, for Obama, this invocation of our collective human messiness. His enemies latched on to its imprecision, emphasizing the exotic, un-American nature of Dream City, this ill-defined place where you could be from Hawaii and Kenya, Kansas and Indonesia all at the same time, where you could jive talk like a street hustler and orate like a senator. What kind of a crazy place is that? But they underestimated how many people come from Dream City, how many Americans, in their daily lives, conjure contrasting voices and seek a synthesis between disparate things. Turns out, Dream City wasn't so strange to them.

Or did they never actually see it? We now know that Obama spoke of *Main Street* in Iowa and of *sweet potato pie* in Northwest Philly, and it could be argued that he succeeded because he so rarely misspoke, carefully tailoring his intonations to suit the sensibility of his listeners. Sometimes he did this within one speech, within one line: "We worship an *awesome* God in the blue states, and we don't like federal agents poking around our libraries in the red states." *Awesome God* comes to you straight from the pews of a Georgia church; *poking around* feels more at home at a kitchen table in South Bend, Indiana. The balance was perfect, cunningly counterpoised and never accidental. It's only now that it's over that we see him let his guard down a little, on *60 Minutes*, say, dropping in that culturally, casually black construction "Hey, I'm not stupid, *man*, that's why I'm president," something it's hard to imagine him doing even three weeks earlier. To a certain kind of mind, it must have looked like the mask had slipped for a moment.

Which brings us to the single-voiced Obamanation crowd. They rage on in the blogs and on the radio, waiting obsessively for the mask to slip. They have a great fear of what they see as Obama's doubling ways. "He says one thing but he means another"—this is the essence of the fear campaign. He says he's a capitalist, but he'll spread your wealth. He says he's a Christian, but really he's going to empower the Muslims. And so on and so forth. These are fears that have their roots in an anxiety about voice. *Who is he?* people kept asking. *I mean, who is this guy, really?* He says *sweet potato pie* in Philly and *Main Street* in Iowa! When he talks to us, he sure *sounds* like us—but behind our backs he says we're clinging to our religion, to our guns. And when Jesse Jackson heard that Obama had lectured a black church congregation about the epidemic of absent black fathers, he experienced this, too, as a tonal betrayal; Obama was "talking down to black people." In both cases, there was the sense of a double-dealer, of someone who tailors his speech to fit the audience, who is not *of* the people (because he is able to look at them objectively) but always above them.

The Jackson gaffe, with its Oedipal violence ("I want to cut his nuts out"), is especially poignant because it goes to the heart of a generational conflict in the black community, concerning what we will say in public and what we say in private. For it has been a point of honor, among the civil rights generation, that any criticism or negative analysis of our community, expressed, as they often are by white politicians, without context, without real empathy or understanding, should not be repeated by a black politician when the white community is listening, even if (*especially* if) the criticism happens to be true (more than half of all black American children live in single-parent households). Our business is our business. Keep it in the family; don't wash your dirty linen in public; stay unified. (Of course, with his overheard gaffe, Jackson unwittingly broke his own rule.)

Until Obama, black politicians had always adhered to these unwritten rules. In this way, they defended themselves against those two bogeymen of black political life: the Uncle Tom and the House Nigger. The black politician who played up to, or even simply echoed, white fears, desires, and hopes for the black community was in danger of earning these epithets—even Martin Luther King was not free from such suspicions. Then came Obama, and the new world he had supposedly ushered in, the postracial world, in which what mattered most was not blind racial allegiance but factual truth. It was felt that Jesse Jackson was sadly out of step with this new postracial world: even his own son felt moved to publicly repudiate his "ugly rhetoric." But Jackson's anger was not incomprehensible nor his distrust unreasonable. Jackson lived through a bitter struggle, and bitter struggles deform their participants in subtle, complicated ways. The idea that one should speak one's cultural allegiance first and the truth second (and that this is a sign of authenticity) is precisely such a deformation.

Right up to the wire, Obama made many black men and women of Jackson's generation suspicious. How can the man who passes between culturally black and white voices with such flexibility, with such ease, be an honest man? How *will* the man from Dream City keep it real? Why won't he speak with a clear and unified voice? These were genuine questions for people born in real cities at a time when those cities were implacably divided, when the black movement had to yell with a clear and unified voice, or risk not being heard at all. And then he won. Watching Jesse Jackson in tears in Grant Park, pressed up against the varicolored American public, it seemed like he, at least, had received the answer he needed: only a many-voiced man could have spoken to that many people.

. . .

And the concept of a unified black voice is a potent one. It has filtered down, these past forty years, into the black community at all levels, settling itself in that impossible injunction "keep it real," the original intention of which was unification. We were going to unify the concept of Blackness in order to strengthen it. Instead we confined and restricted it. To me, the instruction "keep it real" is a sort of prison cell, two feet by five. The fact is, it's too narrow. I just can't live comfortably in there. "*Keep it real*" replaced the blessed and solid genetic fact of Blackness with a flimsy imperative. It made Blackness a quality each individual black person was constantly in danger of losing. And almost anything could trigger the loss of one's Blackness: attending certain universities, an impressive variety of jobs, a fondness for opera, a white girlfriend, an interest in golf. And of course, any change in the voice. There was a popular school of thought that maintained the voice was at the very heart of the thing; fail to keep it real there and you'd never see your Blackness again.

How absurd that all seems now. And not because we live in a postracial world—we don't—but because the reality of race has diversified. Black reality has diversified. It's black people who talk like me, and black people who talk like L'il Wayne. It's black conservatives and black liberals, black sportsmen and black lawyers, black computer technicians and black ballet dancers and black truck drivers and black presidents. We're all black, and we all love to be black, and we all sing from our own hymn sheet. We're all surely black people, but we may be finally approaching a point of human history where you can't talk up or down to us anymore, but only *to us*. *He's talking down to white people*—how curious it sounds the other way round! In order to say such a thing one would have to think collectively of white people, as a people of one mind who speak with one voice—a thought experiment in which we have no practice. But it's worth trying. It's only when you play the record backward that you hear the secret message.

3.

. . .

It's my audacious hope that a man born and raised between opposing dogmas, between cultures, between voices, could not help but be aware of the extreme contingency of culture. I further audaciously hope that such a man will not mistake the happy accident of his own cultural sensibilities for a set of natural laws, suitable for general application. I even hope that he will find himself in agreement with George Bernard Shaw when he declared, "Patriotism is, fundamentally, a conviction that a particular country is the best in the world because you were born in it." But that may be an audacious hope too far. We'll see if Obama's lifelong vocal flexibility will enable him to say proudly with one voice "I love my country" while saying with another voice "It is a country, like other countries." I hope so. He seems just the man to demonstrate that between those two voices there exists no contradiction and no equivocation but rather a proper and decent human harmony.

Consider the source and the audience.

- Smith is a young author whose mother is Jamaican and whose father is a white Englishman. Could this article have been written by someone who is *not* biracial?
- This article is an excerpt from a talk Smith gave at the New York Public Library, reprinted in the *New York Review of Books*, a source for long, thoughtful discourses about literature, culture, and life. What kind of attitude might Smith expect her readers to bring to her work?

Lay out the argument, the values, and the assumptions.

- Smith connects "voice" with personal, racial, and cultural identity. What is the relationship? What does it mean to her to have many voices or to be multilingual? Why does she value multiculturalism?
- What does she mean by "authenticity?" What is an authentic voice? Is it the same as "keeping it real?"
- Smith makes an explicit comparison between her experience and that of the fictional Eliza Doolittle (from the play that became the movie *My Fair Lady*), and between both of those experiences and President Barack Obama's biography. How does Obama's ability to speak authentically in many voices help him avoid the pitfalls Eliza encountered? How did it help him get elected, and why did he nonetheless make some whites and some blacks suspicious?

Uncover the evidence.

- There is no reporting in this article. It is a reflection on Smith's own experience and what she has observed in President Obama, including what she has read in his books. Is this sufficient to support her argument, or does she need to cite harder evidence, say, public opinion poll data, election returns, or anthropological studies of race in America?

Evaluate the conclusion.

- Smith argues that Obama's ability to speak authentically in many voices, which he acquired by being born in what she calls the "dream space" between two different worlds, allows him to connect with the many cultures in a multicultural world, or what she calls "the collective human messiness." How much did the fact that he is biracial have to do with his election as president?

Sort out the political implications.

- What difference does it make politically whether we think our country is multicultural or homogenous?
- Is there any way Obama can ever win over the people who are still convinced that he is not authentic (that is, the white conservatives who are sure he is really a racist, a Muslim, or a socialist)? Does he need to?

2.3 The End of Multiculturalism

The US Must be a Melting Pot

Lawrence E. Harrison, Christian Science Monitor

Why We Chose This Piece

Lawrence E. Harrison, a professor at Tufts University, is interested in the role of culture in shaping human progress. We chose this version of his argument, which appeared in the Christian Science Monitor, to contrast with Zadie Smith's very different argument about multiculturalism in the preceding selection. Multiculturalism and assimilation (or the crazy salad and the melting pot) have been the two major paradigms for understanding American political culture. One view has us celebrating our diversity, and the other has us downplaying our differences in favor of our similarities.

Where Smith saw multiculturalism as a tool that allows us to include parts of the population that previously were excluded, Harrison clearly thinks multiculturalism can carry a heavy cost, especially in the United States, where we have long had a political culture that supports democracy. According to Harrison, the influx of new cultures, especially when they are not conducive to democracy, can threaten political stability.

Is his argument an all-or-nothing argument? If you buy part of it (that some cultures are more supportive of democracy than others), do you have to buy the rest (that the addition of other cultures must do damage to democracy)?

Future generations may look back on Iraq and immigration as the two great disasters of the Bush presidency. Ironically, for a conservative administration, both of these policy initiatives were rooted in a multicultural view of the world.

Since the 1960s, multiculturalism has become a dominant feature of the political and intellectual landscape of the West. But multiculturalism rests on a frail foundation: cultural relativism, the notion that no culture is better or worse than any other—it is merely different.

When it comes to democratic continuity, social justice, and prosperity, some cultures do far better than others. Research at Tufts University's Fletcher School of Law and Diplomacy, summarized in my recent book, "The Central Liberal Truth: How Politics Can Change a Culture and Save It From Itself," makes this clear.

Extensive data suggest that the champions of progress are the Nordic countries—Denmark, Finland, Iceland, Norway, and Sweden—where, for example, universal literacy was a substantial reality in the 19th century. By contrast, no Arab country today is democratic, and female illiteracy in some Arab countries exceeds 50 percent.

Selection published: February 26, 2008

Culture isn't about genes or race; it's about values, beliefs, and attitudes. Culture matters because it influences a society's receptivity to democracy, justice, entrepreneurship, and free-market institutions.

What, then, are the implications for a foreign policy based on the doctrine that "These values of freedom are right and true for every person, in every society"? The Bush administration has staked huge human, financial, diplomatic, and prestige resources on this doctrine's applicability in Iraq. It is now apparent that the doctrine is fallacious.

A key component of a successful democratic transition is trust, a particularly important cultural factor for social justice and prosperity. Trust in others reduces the cost of economic transactions, and democratic stability depends on it.

Trust is periodically measured in 80-odd countries by the World Values Survey. The Nordic countries enjoy very high levels of trust: 58 to 67 percent of respondents in four of these countries believe that most people can be trusted, compared with 11 percent of Algerians and 3 percent of Brazilians.

The high levels of identification and trust in Nordic societies reflect their homogeneity; common Lutheran antecedents, including a rigorous ethical code and heavy emphasis on education; and a consequent sense of the nation as one big family imbued with the golden rule.

Again, culture matters—race doesn't. The ethnic roots of both Haiti and Barbados lie in the Dahomey region of West Africa. The history of Haiti, independent in 1804 in the wake of a slave uprising against the French colonists, is one of corrupt, incompetent leadership; illiteracy; and poverty. Barbados, which gained its independence from the British in 1966, is today a prosperous democracy of "Afro-Saxons."

Immigration

Hispanics now form the largest US minority, approaching 15 percent—about 45 million—of a total population of about 300 million. They're projected by the Pew Research Center to swell to 127 million in 2050—29 percent of a total population of 438 million. Their experience in the United States recapitulates Latin America's culturally shaped underdevelopment. For example, the Hispanic high school dropout rate in the US is alarmingly high and persistent—about 20 percent in second and subsequent generations. It's vastly higher in Latin America.

Samuel Huntington was on the mark when he wrote in his latest book "Who Are We? The Challenges to America's National Identity": "Would America be the America it is today if it had been settled not by British Protestants but by French, Spanish, or Portuguese Catholics? The answer is no. It would not be America; it would be Quebec, Mexico, or Brazil."

In "The Americano Dream," Mexican-American Lionel Sosa argues that the value system that has retarded progress in Latin America is an impediment to upward mobility of Latino immigrants. So does former US Rep. Herman Badillo, a Puerto Rican whose book, "One Nation, One Standard," indicts Latino undervaluing of education and calls for cultural change.

The progress of Hispanic immigrants, not to mention harmony in the broader society, depends on their acculturation to mainstream US values. Efforts—for example, long-term bilingual education—to perpetuate "old country" values in a multicultural salad bowl undermine acculturation to the mainstream and are likely to result in continuing underachievement, poverty, resentment, and divisiveness. So, too, does the willy-nilly emergence of bilingualism in the US. No language in American history has ever before competed with English to the point where one daily hears, on the telephone, "If you want to speak English, press one; *Si quiere hablar en español, oprima el botón número dos.*"

Although border security and environmental concerns are also in play, the immigration debate has been framed largely in economic terms, producing some odd pro-immigration bedfellows, for example the editorial pages of The New York Times and The Wall Street Journal. Among the issues: whether the US economy needs more unskilled immigrants; whether immigrants take jobs away from US citizens; to what extent illegal immigrants drain resources away from education, healthcare, and welfare; and whether population growth, largely driven by immigration, is necessary for a healthy economy.

But immigration looks very different when viewed in cultural terms, particularly with respect to the vast legal and illegal Latino immigration, a million or more people a year, most of them with few skills and little education. To be sure, the US has absorbed large numbers of unskilled and uneducated immigrants in the past, and today the large majority of their descendants are in the cultural mainstream. But the numbers of Latino immigrants and their geographic concentration today leave real doubts about the prospects for acculturation: 70 percent of children in the Los Angeles public schools and 60 percent in the Denver schools are Latino.

In a letter to me in 1991, the late Mexican-American columnist Richard Estrada captured the essence of the problem:

"The problem in which the current immigration is suffused is, at heart, one of numbers; for when the numbers begin to favor not only the maintenance and replenishment of the immigrants' source culture, but also its overall growth, and in particular growth so large that the numbers not only impede assimilation but go beyond to pose a challenge to the traditional culture of the American nation, then there is a great deal about which to be concerned."

Some recommendations

If multiculturalism is a myth, how do we avoid the woes that inevitably attend the creation of an enduring and vast underclass alienated from the upwardly mobile cultural mainstream? Some policy implications, one for Latin America, the others for the US and Canada, are apparent.

We must calibrate the flow of immigrants into the US to the needs of the economy, mindful that immigration has adversely affected low-income American citizens, disproportionately African-American and Hispanic, as Barbara Jordan stressed as chair of the 1990s Immigration Reform Commission. But the flow must also be calibrated to the country's capacity to assure acculturation of the immigrants.

We must be a melting pot, not a salad bowl. The melting pot, the essence of which is the Anglo-Protestant cultural tradition, is our way of creating the homogeneity that has contributed so much to the trust and mutual identification—and progress—of the Nordic societies.

As with immigration flows of the late 19th and early 20th centuries, an extensive program of activities designed to facilitate acculturation, including mastery of English, should be mounted. A law declaring English to be the national language would be helpful.

The costs of multiculturalism—in terms of disunity, the clash of classes, and declining trust—are likely to be huge in the long run. All cultures are not equal when it comes to promoting progress, and very few can match Anglo-Protestantism in this respect. We should be promoting acculturation to the national mainstream, not a mythical, utopian multiculturalism. And we should take care that the Anglo-Protestant virtues that have brought us so far do not fall into disrepair, let alone disrepute.

*C*onsider the source and the audience.

- The *Christian Science Monitor* is a well-respected, independently owned newspaper, with no clear ideological slant. Is this article more compelling appearing here than it would be if it appeared in a conservative source?

*L*ay out the argument, the values, and the assumptions.

- What is the connection, according to Harrison, between culture and democracy? What is the danger threatened by multiculturalism?
- How does immigration figure in Harrison's argument? What new cultures is he particularly worried about in the United States and why?

*U*ncover the evidence.

- What kind of evidence does Harrison provide to support his claim about the connections between culture, democracy, and immigration? Is this evidence adequate?

*E*valuate the conclusion.

- Is it enough to show that those in thriving democracies hold certain values to conclude that those who hold different values are a threat to democracy?
- Are there ways to assimilate cultures in terms of their democratic values while still celebrating the languages, foods, and traditions that mark different cultures?

*S*ort out the political implications.

- If we buy Harrison's conclusions, what kind of immigration policy should we enact? Are there other policies we could put in place to offset the effects he is worried about?

2.4 Get Out, but Leave the Quesadilla

Michael Skube, Los Angeles Times

Why We Chose This Piece

As the debate about immigration rages in the United States, two visions of America are at stake. One is the image of this country as a melting pot, a smooth synthesis of many ethnicities into a single, predominantly Anglo-Protestant American culture. The other vision sees the nation as a "crazy salad," celebrating the identities and participation of multiple ethic groups.

In this opinion piece, Michael Skube is taking a stand for one of these two culinary-sociological metaphors (melting pot versus crazy salad), interestingly with a food argument of his own. He raises an interesting question: can we keep the food but reject the cooks?

It's 9 o'clock, the sun has set and I'm going to chill out. I take two soft tortillas, spread on each a layer of fat-free refried beans, follow that up with a generous sprinkling of jack cheese, pop 'em in the microwave for a minute and then give 'em a few squirts of Texas Pete.

I'd like to say I have a more sophisticated palate, and once in a while I do. But when I want to put the cares of the day behind me, I head south of the border. It's the meal of a Mexican peasant, and it's as American as pizza.

The proliferation of Mexican restaurants in the United States began decades ago, before the proliferation of illegal Mexican workers. But the two do not intersect. We've appropriated the quesadillas and the enchiladas. We can make them well enough here. The workers—well, better that they stay home. Or go home.

Such is the ambivalence—to put it mildly—of many Americans toward Mexican immigrants, especially the illegal ones. We like what they've given us to eat, but we wouldn't much like them at the table with us. We see them at Wal-Mart, bronze as pennies and so different from us. There are so many of them, enough that we feel like a minority. Like Anglos feel when they go to Dade County, Fla., and hear nothing but Spanish. Doesn't anyone speak English here? Hey, this is America, y'know.

Miami and Dade County were Cubanized. Spanish achieved dominance. The huge influx of Mexican immigrants since 1980—not just to Los Angeles and Southern California but also to the Southwest and the South—portends a broader erosion of English. A nation whose first language was once English could become bilingual, its identity part Latino and part Anglo.

This is the unstated reason that many people oppose President Bush's plan to legalize as many as 11 million undocumented workers. Conservative Republicans in the House, in opposing both Bush's plan and a Senate immigration bill close to the president's wishes, object to legalizing undocumented workers, calling it amnesty.

Selection published: May 21, 2006

Polls suggest that a majority of Americans are with them. They expect immigrants to play by the rules, as many of their forebears did.

But there is something else at work: Many Americans sense that the nation's identity, long under siege in the schools and universities by multiculturalism, is up for grabs. More than religion or race, more than ethnicity or political persuasion, language defines us as a people. Before long, many worry, an American is going to be anyone who merely lives and works here, and there's a good chance he will speak Spanish.

The cliché—colorfully emblazoned on some wall of elementary schools across the land—is that "We Are All Immigrants." True enough, wave upon wave of immigrants have come ashore, from Germany and Ireland, Italy and Poland, from Asia and Africa. None was welcomed but most, in time, assimilated, leaving one culture and one language behind and adopting a new culture and learning a new language. They became Americans. And in doing so, they enriched the nation in immeasurable ways. We all know the story, even if we forget the resentment and prejudice.

Now comes another wave, except these immigrants are mostly coming not from across an ocean but from next door. And they are coming by the millions, some legally, others slipping across the border, unseen. Because they are coming from a contiguous country, many see them as threatening the nation's ability to control who does and who does not enter—and, by extension, its sovereignty.

Here are some figures. In 1960, the census showed that immigrants to the U.S. came principally from five countries—Italy, Germany, Canada, Britain and Poland. They numbered 4.7 million in total, with Italy's 1.25 million leading all others.

According to the 2000 census, the Mexican immigrant population in the U.S. was 7.8 million—and that counts only those who came here legally. No other country was even close; China, with 1.4 million immigrants in the U.S., was second.

"Contemporary Mexican immigration is unprecedented in American history," Harvard political scientist Samuel P. Huntington wrote in his 2004 book, "Who Are We? The Challenges to America's National Identity." The United States, he argued, might be a nation of immigrants, but it was also one whose institutions and political culture were Anglo-Protestant. What's more, that foundation was laid not by immigrants who came later but by English settlers. Huntington's book provoked a firestorm of dissent. But it also touched a nerve because of his unapologetic reverence for an Anglo heritage and his analysis of recent Mexican immigration.

No one questioned Huntington's numbers, only his interpretation of what they mean. Unabated immigration from Mexico, he argued, can only alter the nation's character and identity. "No other First World country," he wrote, "has a land frontier with a Third World country, much less one of 2,000 miles. Japan, Australia, New Zealand are islands; Canada is bordered only by the United States; the closest [that] Western European countries come to Third World countries are the Strait of Gibraltar between Spain and Morocco and the Straits of Otranto between Italy and Albania."

Not only do the United States and Mexico share a long border, but one is rich and the other poor. Huntington quotes Stanford historian David Kennedy: "The income gap between the United States and Mexico is the largest between any two contiguous countries in the world."

The Southwest, by this reasoning, could become an American Quebec—or one gigantic Dade County. Only a Canadian could fathom the former. But you don't have to live in Dade County—as I did in the '70s—to know that the latter would not be a happy prospect.

To say as much is not to diminish its vitality. To the contrary, Cubans have rebuilt Miami. But they have rebuilt it as a Spanish-speaking territory within the U.S. It is a city Americans no longer recognize as fully American. A parallel transformation in Southern California and elsewhere would begin with language that heretofore has been a foreign language, like German and French, Russian and Italian, but now asks for parity with English.

It is asking more than what many are willing to give.

Consider the source and the audience.

- Skube's piece appeared in the *Los Angeles Times*. Would this issue have special significance for California readers? Why?
- Skube appears to have some very strong views about American politics, many of which are just hinted at here. He is the winner of the Pulitzer Prize for Criticism. How can you find out more about him and his views?

Lay out the argument, the values, and the assumptions.

- What notion of national identity underlies Skube's argument here—that is, to which of the two views described in the introduction to this chapter does he subscribe? What is the role of language in national identity? For that matter, what is the role of food?
- Why does Skube believe that for most Americans the case of Mexican immigration is different from that of other ethnic groups?
- Skube mentions that a majority of Americans reject Bush's immigration plan because they expect immigrants to play by the rules. How does this belief in playing by the rules factor into American political culture?

Uncover the evidence.

- Skube relies on the example of Cuban migration into Miami to illustrate his point. Does it work? How is Cuban immigration similar to or different from the Mexican example?
- Does he offer other evidence of the disintegrating effect on American culture of allowing extensive Mexican immigration into the United States?

Evaluate the conclusion.

- Skube says that giving Spanish equal status with English is asking for more than many Americans are willing to give, and on this basis he seems to believe that immigration from Mexico should be restricted. Does one conclusion follow from the other?

Sort out the political implications.

- If protection of language and culture from Mexican dominance is Skube's goal, can that goal be achieved in other ways, without restricting immigration?
- Is it practical to say we can accept the parts of Mexican culture we like (for example, food) but reject the parts we don't like?

2.5 I Have a Dream

Martin Luther King Jr.

Why We Chose This Piece:

> *Several of the pieces in this chapter have attempted to define the "American dream," and some have looked specifically at the place of race in that dream. We will deal with the civil rights movement in a later chapter, but for now we cannot separate the pervasive issue of race from fundamental questions about American political culture, particularly when we attempt to understand the central American ideal of equality.*

> *This famous speech by Martin Luther King Jr., given at a Washington, D.C., civil rights rally in August 1963, is a classic statement about the meaning of equality in the American dream. In this speech, King outlines the many ways that the United States had failed African Americans in the middle of the twentieth century, and he describes his hopes for an America in which the equality promised in the Declaration of Independence becomes a reality for all Americans, black and white. How does King define equality? How does his definition compare with others we have seen in this chapter? Has the election of President Obama realized King's dream, or moved us closer to it?*

I am happy to join with you today in what will go down in history as the greatest demonstration for freedom in the history of our nation.

Five score years ago, a great American, in whose symbolic shadow we stand today, signed the Emancipation Proclamation. This momentous decree came as a great beacon light of hope to millions of Negro slaves who had been seared in the flames of withering injustice. It came as a joyous daybreak to end the long night of their captivity.

But 100 years later, the Negro still is not free. One hundred years later, the life of the Negro is still sadly crippled by the manacles of segregation and the chains of discrimination. One hundred years later, the Negro lives on a lonely island of poverty in the midst of a vast ocean of material prosperity. One hundred years later, the Negro is still languishing in the corners of American society and finds himself an exile in his own land. And so we've come here today to dramatize a shameful condition.

In a sense we've come to our nation's capital to cash a check. When the architects of our republic wrote the magnificent words of the Constitution and the Declaration of Independence, they were signing a promissory note to which every American was to fall heir. This note was a promise that all men—yes, black men as well as white men—would be guaranteed the unalienable rights of life, liberty, and the pursuit of happiness.

Selection delivered: August 28, 1963

It is obvious today that America has defaulted on this promissory note insofar as her citizens of color are concerned. Instead of honoring this sacred obligation, America has given the Negro people a bad check, a check that has come back marked "insufficient funds."

But we refuse to believe that the bank of justice is bankrupt. We refuse to believe that there are insufficient funds in the great vaults of opportunity of this nation. And so we've come to cash this check, a check that will give us upon demand the riches of freedom and security of justice. We have also come to his hallowed spot to remind America of the fierce urgency of now. This is no time to engage in the luxury of cooling off or to take the tranquilizing drug of gradualism. Now is the time to make real the promises of democracy. Now is the time to rise from the dark and desolate valley of segregation to the sunlit path of racial justice. Now is the time to lift our nation from the quicksands of racial injustice to the solid rock of brotherhood. Now is the time to make justice a reality for all of God's children.

It would be fatal for the nation to overlook the urgency of the moment. This sweltering summer of the Negro's legitimate discontent will not pass until there is an invigorating autumn of freedom and equality. Nineteen sixty-three is not an end but a beginning. Those who hoped that the Negro needed to blow off steam and will now be content will have a rude awakening if the nation returns to business as usual. There will be neither rest nor tranquility in America until the Negro is granted his citizenship rights. The whirlwinds of revolt will continue to shake the foundations of our nation until the bright day of justice emerges.

But there is something that I must say to my people who stand on the warm threshold which leads into the palace of justice. In the process of gaining our rightful place we must not be guilty of wrongful deeds. Let us not seek to satisfy our thirst for freedom by drinking from the cup of bitterness and hatred. We must forever conduct our struggle on the high plane of dignity and discipline. We must not allow our creative protest to degenerate into physical violence. Again and again we must rise to the majestic heights of meeting physical force with soul force. The marvelous new militancy which has engulfed the Negro community must not lead us to a distrust of all white people, for many of our white brothers, as evidenced by their presence here today, have come to realize that their destiny is tied up with our destiny. And they have come to realize that their freedom is inextricably bound to our freedom. We cannot walk alone.

And as we walk, we must make the pledge that we shall always march ahead. We cannot turn back. There are those who are asking the devotees of civil rights, "When will you be satisfied?" We can never be satisfied as long as the Negro is the victim of the unspeakable horrors of police brutality. We can never be satisfied as long as our bodies, heavy with the fatigue of travel, cannot gain lodging in the motels of the highways and the hotels of the cities. We cannot be satisfied as long as the Negro's basic mobility is from a smaller ghetto to a larger one. We can never be satisfied as long as our children are stripped of their selfhood and robbed of their dignity by signs stating "for whites only." We cannot be satisfied as long as a Negro in Mississippi cannot vote and a Negro in New York believes he has nothing for which to vote. No, no we are not satisfied and we will not be satisfied until justice rolls down like waters and righteousness like a mighty stream.

I am not unmindful that some of you have come here out of great trials and tribulations. Some of you have come fresh from narrow jail cells. Some of you have come from areas where your quest for freedom left you battered by storms of persecution and staggered by the winds of police brutality. You have been the veterans of creative suffering. Continue to work with the faith that unearned suffering is redemptive.

Go back to Mississippi, go back to Alabama, go back to South Carolina, go back to Georgia, go back to Louisiana, go back to the slums and ghettos of our northern cities, knowing that somehow this situation can and will be changed.

Let us not wallow in the valley of despair. I say to you today my friends—so even though we face the difficulties of today and tomorrow, I still have a dream. It is a dream deeply rooted in the American dream.

I have a dream that one day this nation will rise up and live out the true meaning of its creed: "We hold these truths to be self-evident, that all men are created equal."

I have a dream that one day on the red hills of Georgia the sons of former slaves and the sons of former slave owners will be able to sit down together at the table of brotherhood.

I have a dream that one day even the state of Mississippi, a state sweltering with the heat of injustice, sweltering with the heat of oppression, will be transformed into an oasis of freedom and justice.

I have a dream that my four little children will one day live in a nation where they will not be judged by the color of their skin but by the content of their character.

I have a dream today.

I have a dream that one day down in Alabama, with its vicious racists, with its governor having his lips dripping with the words of interposition and nullification—one day right there in Alabama little black boys and black girls will be able to join hands with little white boys and white girls as sisters and brothers.

I have a dream today.

I have a dream that one day every valley shall be exalted, and every hill and mountain shall be made low, the rough places will be made plain, and the crooked places will be made straight, and the glory of the Lord shall be revealed and all flesh shall see it together.

This is our hope. This is the faith that I go back to the South with. With this faith we will be able to hew out of the mountain of despair a stone of hope. With this faith we will be able to transform the jangling discords of our nation into a beautiful symphony of brotherhood. With this faith we will be able to work together, to pray together, to struggle together, to go to jail together, to stand up for freedom together, knowing that we will be free one day.

This will be the day, this will be the day when all of God's children will be able to sing with new meaning "My country 'tis of thee, sweet land of liberty, of thee I sing. Land where my father's died, land of the Pilgrim's pride, from every mountainside, let freedom ring!"

And if America is to be a great nation, this must become true. And so let freedom ring from the prodigious hilltops of New Hampshire. Let freedom ring from the mighty mountains of New York. Let freedom ring from the heightening Alleghenies of Pennsylvania.

Let freedom ring from the snow-capped Rockies of Colorado. Let freedom ring from the curvaceous slopes of California.

But not only that; let freedom ring from Stone Mountain of Georgia.

Let freedom ring from Lookout Mountain of Tennessee.

Let freedom ring from every hill and molehill of Mississippi—from every mountainside.

Let freedom ring. And when this happens, and when we allow freedom to ring— when we let it ring from every village and every hamlet, from every state and every city, we will be able to speed up that day when all of God's children— black men and white men, Jews and Gentiles, Protestants and Catholics—will be able to join hands and sing in the words of the old Negro spiritual: "Free at last! Free at last! Thank God Almighty, we are free at last!"

*C*onsider the source and the audience.

- King is gaining access to a real national audience for the first time in this speech. How does he use symbols, language, and history to appeal to that audience?

*L*ay out the argument, the values, and the assumptions.

- How would King define the basic values of equality and freedom he talks about? What is his dream?
- What political tactics does he think will make his dream reality?

*U*ncover the evidence.

- Does King offer evidence to make his case? What kind?
- What rhetorical tactics does he use to support his case? What is the purpose of laying claim to important symbols like the Declaration of Independence, the American dream, and "My Country 'Tis of Thee"?

*E*valuate the conclusion.

- Is King successful in claiming for black Americans the fundamental American rights and dreams that white people take for granted?
- What kind of case would his opponents have to make to argue against him?

*S*ort out the political implications.

- What strategies does King use to make his declaration and his intentions nonthreatening to whites? How did his strategy advance the civil rights movement in the 1960s?
- What might King have said if he could have witnessed the presidential election of 2008?
- What groups today might want to give their own "I Have a Dream" speech?

3

Federalism and the Constitution

By most estimations, the U.S. Constitution is a marvel. It provides a stable yet flexible political structure that guarantees us unprecedented individual freedom, although most of the time we are barely aware it is there. In normal times we take it for granted, but when times turn tough—when a president is impeached, an election is contested, the nation is attacked, or the country launches a war—we are sharply aware of the value of what the founders wrought. Since September 11, 2001, Americans have had more cause than usual to appreciate the brilliance of Madison and his colleagues, as events that might have blown another nation off its course have ultimately been no more than choppy seas for the American ship of state.

In this chapter we explore three of the central principles that make our Constitution work: federalism, separation of powers, and checks and balances. Sometimes American government texts cover these subjects in one chapter; sometimes they are divided between a chapter on federalism and one on the founding. Because we make this chapter do the work of two, there are more readings here than in most of our other chapters.

Federalism is the concept of dividing power between the national government and its regional governments (in our case, the states). With the Articles of Confederation the founders had tried a system in which the power was grounded in the states, but most of them rejected it because the absence of a strong center led to political and economic instability. The alternative, a unitary system in which all the power was centralized, was unacceptable to men who feared a strong government on the English model. A federal system, in which states possessed some constitutional power but the national government was supreme, was a compromise that has proved flexible enough to weather many constitutional storms. Indeed, the balance of power has shifted back and forth between nation and states throughout our history, driven by historical events and judicial interpretation.

The principles of separation of powers and checks and balances hold that liberty is best preserved and power limited when it is divided between three branches of government that are mostly separate but with each given a little power over the others to keep an eye on them. The founders believed that by dividing power between the two federal levels, and then among three branches at each level, they were providing the best security for the new republic.

The readings in this chapter give you a variety of perspectives on the Constitution and the principles on which it is based. The opening piece, by Keith Olbermann of MSNBC, uses humor to mock the notion that Texas should secede from the United States. The second piece, by a *Chicago Tribune* editorial and opinion writer, looks at the issue of gay marriage through the lens of federalism. In a *Washington Post* column, Sanford Levinson writes that the Constitution is rife with outmoded mechanisms that don't work, and he proposes a new constitutional convention to get it fixed. Charlie Savage of the *Boston Globe* examines the Bush administration's practice of issuing signing statements, which altered the balance of power between the executive and the legislature. These pieces raise arguments made in that classic on checks and balances, Madison's *Federalist* No. 51, our final selection.

 ### 3.1 "Countdown with Keith Olbermann" for Friday, May 15, 2009

Keith Olbermann, MSNBC

Why We Chose This Piece

You might be surprised to run in to Keith Olbermann in these pages, but even liberal figures like MSNBC's Olbermann (or Bill O'Reilly, his conservative nemesis on Fox News) can raise interesting issues—the trick is to recognize their ideology and be careful to process what they have to say accordingly.

In this transcript, Olbermann is on a rant about the issue of Texas secession, a possibility Texas governor Rick Perry had raised earlier. While Olbermann's goal is to be funny (a goal you might think he has met if you are a liberal, or failed dismally at if you are conservative), he makes a point often overlooked in the debate that followed Perry's pronouncement.

Perry had hinted that secession might be on the agenda because President Barack Obama's stimulus package was forcing states to adopt spending programs, possibly in violation of the Tenth Amendment, which says that all powers not given to the national government by the Constitution are reserved to the states. What Olbermann focuses on is not the

Selection aired: May 15, 2009

federal programs that Texas would be forced to adopt by the stimulus plan, but the ones Texas would be forced to give up if it seceded. By Olbermann's reckoning, secession would be very costly to Texas, indeed.

As you read this piece, remember that Olbermann is (1) pretty liberal and (2) an entertainer. (He made the leap to political commentary from sports commentary and sometimes treats the two activities like halves of the same whole.) So strip out the drama and rhetoric and just look at the contrast Olbermann draws between Texas as part of the United States and Texas as its own country. What are the political and economic advantages of belonging to a greater union? What would Texas give up if it decided to go it alone? What does this tell us about the strengths and weaknesses of federalism from a states' rights point of view?

OLBERMANN: Finally, as promised, tonight's number one story, our new regular feature, the WTF moment. An elected governor of an American state continues to flirt with treason. Rick Perry of Texas, who probably would advocate stoning the heathen in Valverde if it would win him 37 extra votes, has once again refused the opportunity to step back from the stupidity that is secession.

(BEGIN VIDEO CLIP)

GOV. RICK PERRY, TEXAS: We live in a great country. America is -

Texas is a very unique state inside that great country. And there's no reason for us to be even talking at seceding.

But if Washington continues to force these programs on the states, if Washington continues to disregard the Tenth Amendment, you know, who knows what happens. There may be people standing up all the country in tea parties saying, enough. All right.

(END VIDEO CLIP)

OLBERMANN: How about them standing up in Texas and saying enough, all right, governor ass hat. Recent polling suggests more than a third of all Texans believe the place would be better off independent of the United States. It is a split among Republicans. But when you reduce it to just the bully's threat to take his ball and go home, 51 percent of all Texas Republicans approve of the suggestion that Texas may need to leave the United States.

You know what the South Carolina politician James Lewis Pettigrew said of his state, just before the Civil War, too small for a republic and too big for an insane asylum.

Governor, have you or your separatist friends considered what would happen if you actually seceded? Assuming the rest of the country did not decide it was a rebellion, and didn't send in federal troops, and didn't try to capture you and hang you, and, in a bitter irony, did not suspend habeas corpus in the rebellious territory, so that former President George W. Bush could be detained without charge and without access to attorneys?

I'm talking about what would happen if we all just sat back and said, bye, have fun storming the castle.

Let's start internally. Your taxes would shoot through the roof. Just FEMA has sent $3,449,000,000 to Texas since 2001. Other agencies sent you another billion just for Hurricane Ike last year.

When NASA pulls out of Houston, that's 26,000 jobs, another 2.5 billion you just lost from your economy. We'd obviously move everybody out of Ft. Hood, Texas, whose financial impact on your new kingdom is another six billion.

Your own country? Get your own damn forts, and you're own damn Air Force, Army, Navy. What is that, 10 billion a year, 100, a trillion? You'll need some form of welfare, Social Security. You'll have to get your own FDA, CDC, FDC, FEC, FBI, CIA, NSA, Post Office. You'll need a lot of new investments after the Americans—I'm sorry, the Gringos pull out. You've got four nuclear power plants there. Good for you. Where were you going to put all the nuclear waste? The Alamo?

Remember, these are all the startup costs. I lost track at about 500 billion and we haven't even gotten to annual maintenance or expansion or improvements. Pell Grants, I forgot Pell Grants. The U.S. gave Texas students a billion dollars in Pell Grants for the academic year 2006–2007. Good luck with that.

What are you going do about your sports franchises? The Cowboys just spent a billion on that new stadium. "America's team." That's funny, the Cowboys, "North Texas' team."

Now, no American network is going to want to televise their games, because the ratings in Texas will no longer count in America. You'll be Canada with something of a twang. Do you think it's a coincidence that half the Canadian baseball teams went out of business because of TV revenues and other reasons, and half of the Canadian basketball teams?

So take your choice, Astros or Rangers. One of them is going to move to Charlotte. Who exactly do you think your University of Texas football team is going to play now? USC? Oklahoma? Try Sul Ross or San Jacinto JC or the new big rivalry with Tom Delay Exterminator University.

Now, security. You'll need your own Gitmo. Starting wars is optional, of course. See your Mr. Bush about that. And since you'll be surrounded by the United States and Mexico, presumably the U.S. will continue this knuckle headed border fence you guys started, only it won't be on your southern border anymore. Now it will be on your northern one, because the rest of us here, we can't risk the economic impact of hordes of illegal aliens fleeing the chaos of the United State of Texas, or the Texican nation, or Texaco, or whatever you're going to call yourselves.

So you'll have to put up your own fence at your own expense.

We'll talk politics for a second too. Let's look at what your departure will mean back here in the northern 49. Congratulations to the Democrats and their filibuster proof 60 seats in the 98 seat, Texas-free Senate. And thanks from the Dems in California, New York, Florida, Illinois and Michigan, which will take the lion's portions of those Texas electoral college seats, 13. Eleven more would go to other blue states. The other red states would, of course, get the leftovers, ten.

Per Nate Silver's calculation, if Texas had left last year, Obama would have won the electoral college by 242 votes, not by 192. And also speaking of politics, remember sovereign republic of Texas, you've got your big political nightmare coming up 11 years from now. The big political nightmare, the big political nightmare, you know, when the Mexican Texans get the ballot initiative passed on whether or not Texas should become part of Mexico.

Right now, Texas is 48 percent Anglo, 36 percent Hispanic. With no major change in population, just progressing things outward, by 2020, every projection has Anglos being outnumbered by Hispanics in Texas. That's in 2020. By 2040, the Anglos will comprise barely a fourth of the population of Texas.

I'm sorry, of Tejas. Texas state in Mexico. Hasta la vista, baby.

Don't let Oklahoma hit you on the backside on the way out.

Secession; what the—

That's COUNTDOWN for this the 2,206th day since the previous president declared mission accomplished in Iraq. I'm Keith Olbermann, good night and good luck.

*C*onsider the source and the audience.

- "Countdown with Keith Olbermann" is an unabashedly liberal source, and Olbermann is clearly mocking the Republican governor of Texas in this piece. Does his bias render everything he says suspect? How can you sort the worthwhile from the purely ideological?
- There is no doubt that Olbermann is "preaching to the choir" on his show—that is, he is speaking to people who already agree with him. Would this piece be likely to sway any stray conservative watchers who happened to tune in? Why or why not?

*L*ay out the argument, the values, and the assumptions.

- What is Olbermann's point about federalism? Is there much to be gained by states in the relationship? If so, why would a state threaten to withdraw from the union?

*U*ncover the evidence.

- What kinds of evidence does Olbermann use to make the case that states benefit from federalism and big states like Texas benefit greatly?
- Besides data on the monetary value of the programs that Texas receives, Olbermann raises cultural issues such as sports, language, and identity. Does that strengthen or weaken his case?

*E*valuate the conclusion.

- Olbermann clearly thinks that Governor Perry is foolish for talking about secession, given what his state gains by being part of the Union. How effectively does he make that point in this segment?
- Olbermann uses humor as a tool to drive home his point. Does humor make a serious conclusion easier or harder to absorb?

S*ort out the political implications.*

- What political motivation might Perry have had for talking about secession? Who would be attracted by such talk, and who repelled?
- How important is the federal relationship to our identities as citizens of states and of the United States?

3.2 Stacking the Deck on Gay Marriage

Steve Chapman, Chicago Tribune

Why We Chose This Piece

You might think of gay marriage as a civil rights issue, but as this opinion piece by Chicago Tribune *columnist Steve Chapman shows, the way it has been handled in the United States opens up intriguing issues of federalism and states' rights as well.*

As Chapman explains, generally speaking, marriage laws are up to states to determine. (There are limits to a state's autonomy. When some states forbade people of different races to marry, for instance, the Supreme Court stepped in—eventually—to prohibit such laws.) Despite the difference in how states treat marriage, Article IV, Section 1, of the U.S. Constitution says that each state has to respect the "public acts, records, and judicial proceedings" of the others, giving them "full faith and credit." Even if you run away to get married in Las Vegas, you are considered to be married in all fifty states.

Unless, that is, you happen to be gay. Fearing that the courts in the state of Hawaii might legalize gay marriage, and that other states might be forced to follow suit, legislators rushed to write what they called the Defense of Marriage Act (DOMA), which specifically defined marriage as taking place between one man and one woman. It said that a gay marriage did not need to be recognized outside the state where it had taken place and such marriage did not confer any of the federal benefits of marriage. Both houses of Congress passed DOMA handily, and in September 1996, President Bill Clinton signed it into law.

Hawaii did not legalize gay marriage, but in May 2004 the Supreme Judicial Court of the state of Massachusetts decided that gay marriage would be legal there. A few other states have since followed suit. As of this writing, gay marriage is also legal in Vermont, Maine, Connecticut, and Iowa. However, couples married in those states (and those who were married in California before the passage of Proposition 8 put an end to gay marriage there) still are not married in the eyes of the federal government. In the article you are about to read, Chapman argues that DOMA violates the principle of federalism by foreclosing the option of gay marriage at the federal level. Can a state marriage be genuine if it lacks the federal underpinnings?

Selection published: April 26, 2009

The country used to be unanimous in rejecting gay marriage. But that consensus, like the polar ice sheets, is showing some cracks. Vermont recently became the fourth state to allow gays to wed, and New York may be next. Elsewhere, marriage remains as Miss California prefers—solely between a man and a woman.

It's at moments like this that the framers of the Constitution begin to look even wiser than usual. Somehow they anticipated that people in Massachusetts would not want to live under exactly the same laws as people in Mississippi. So they set up a system known as federalism, which allows different states to choose different policies. Thus we simultaneously uphold majority rule and minority rights.

This, at least, is how federalism is supposed to operate—letting subsets of the national population get their way in their own locales. There's only one hitch: In this case, it doesn't quite work that way.

Why not? Because of a huge imbalance created by that longtime nemesis of state sovereignty—the federal government. Under the 1996 Defense of Marriage Act, Virginia has complete authority to deny the privileges and responsibilities of marriage to same-sex partners. But Iowa doesn't have the complete authority to grant them.

Oh, Iowa can provide recognition to gay marriages under all its laws and policies. But that's a surprisingly small part of what marriage encompasses. Under federal law, there are more than 1,100 rights and privileges that go with being a husband or wife. And none of them is available to married same-sex couples.

Under federal law, a person may transfer property to a spouse tax-free. Married couples may file their income taxes jointly. Someone whose spouse dies is assured Social Security survivor's benefits. A married person has the authority to make medical decisions for an incapacitated partner.

Or say you're an American citizen living in this country who marries a foreigner. Normally, you would be entitled to bring your beloved to this country to live permanently and become a citizen.

But if you're both of the same sex, you can forget all of the above. Even though Iowa might like to put heterosexual and homosexual married couples on the same footing, it can't, because the federal statute blocks the way.

"In determining the meaning of any act of Congress, or of any ruling, regulation or interpretation of the various administrative bureaus and agencies of the United States," says DOMA, "the word 'marriage' means only a legal union between one man and one woman as husband and wife."

That decree may sound reasonable: Since most Americans and most states reject same-sex marriage, federal policy should as well. But it conflicts with how the nation has handled marriage up till now, which is to leave it up to individual states to decide who may wed—and then honor those diverse choices.

Some states, for instance, allow marriages between first cousins; others forbid it. Some states allow 15-year-olds to marry with parental consent, while most set the minimum age higher.

And the feds? They have consistently observed a policy of staying the hell out. Washington doesn't tell Colorado and New York which marriages it will acknowledge. Colorado and New York tell it.

Not so with same-sex unions. Under DOMA, the federal government insists that some marriages are not marriages.

That's particularly hard to justify because the other major provision of the law bends over backward to protect state authority over matters marital. It says no state is obligated to recognize a same-sex marriage that took place somewhere else. Gays married in Vermont magically become single when they venture into New Hampshire.

This part of the law goes beyond the norm to accommodate different preferences. Usually, states are obligated to enforce contracts made in other states. Back in the segregationist years, Southern states often honored interracial marriages transacted beyond their borders even though they regarded them as "so unnatural that God and nature seem to forbid them."

Given the strong feelings about gay marriage, the local option is the best option. States that abhor the idea should be free to implement policies reflecting that sentiment. But the other side should have exactly the same prerogative: giving both heterosexual and homosexual couples access to marriage in full.

Our system, unlike Mao's China, is supposed to let a hundred flowers bloom. But for the best growth, the federal sun has to shine on all of them.

*C*onsider the source and the audience.

- The *Chicago Tribune* is a major urban newspaper in the Midwest. Chapman is an opinion writer and a member of the *Trib*'s editorial board. He's married, with kids and a house in the Chicago suburbs. Does this piece have a different impact coming from such a mainstream source than if it appeared, say, in a gay outlet like the *Advocate?*

*L*ay out the argument, the values, and the assumptions.

- Is Chapman in favor of gay marriage, or against it? Does it matter to his argument?
- What rights does he think marriage entails? What is the relationship of state to federal marriage rights?
- On what grounds does Chapman object to DOMA?

*U*ncover the evidence.

- What kind of evidence does an argument like Chapman's require? Does he need data, or is it sufficient to rest it on the Constitution and on principles of logic?

*E*valuate the conclusion.

- Is Chapman right that DOMA violates the principle of federalism?
- What kind of solution to gay marriage does Chapman favor? Does he argue that gay marriage should be legal in all fifty states?

*S*ort out the political implications.

- Why was DOMA written the way it was? What do you think was its authors' primary motivation?
- As more states allow gay marriage as an equal right, what might happen to DOMA if it ends up challenged in the Supreme Court?

3.3 I Dissent! The Constitution Got Us Into This Mess

Sanford Levinson, Washington Post

Why We Chose This Piece

Even though this piece is somewhat dated (University of Texas law professor Sanford Levinson wrote it in the immediate wake of the 2000 presidential election), it is worth reading now. Levinson pulls no punches. In this opinion piece in the Washington Post, *he clearly feels that some elements of the U.S. Constitution need correction. He is the coeditor of a book called* Constitutional Stupidities, Constitutional Tragedies, *and he doesn't confine himself to critiquing the way we handle presidential elections through the Electoral College. Indeed, he also takes on the House of Representatives' role in contested elections, lifetime tenure for Supreme Court justices, and the amendment process—all constitutional "stupidities" that he thinks should be addressed.*

Are you a fan of the U.S. Constitution? Before you get offended by Professor Levinson's critique, read his argument very carefully. If the constitutional provisions he isolates don't qualify as "stupidities," they are certainly oddities, and we should understand exactly how they work and what they mean for American politics. What are the implications of the idea that we should adapt the Constitution today to contemporary needs and events and not be limited to the document as the founders wrote it in 1787?

We have crossed the constitutional bridge into the 21st century and discovered that it is rickety, maybe even falling down. An electoral system that might have made sense when devised in the late 18th and early 19th centuries has turned out to be shockingly problematic in this new millennium.

This should come as no surprise. So often, we almost literally idolize the United States Constitution, treating it with the reverence due a sacred text. But the Constitution is a most-human product, and therefore an imperfect document, with flaws and weaknesses that can threaten our stability at any time. The kind of tottering we've witnessed over the past few weeks was thoroughly predictable. But warnings that we were heading for a wreck have generally been either dismissed with a round of constitutional cheerleading, or met with denial. "It happened before, but it can't happen again," we say, when reminded of earlier crises. (Remember early 1998, when no one believed we'd see another impeachment?) Or we take refuge in the delusory belief that God has the United States in his special care.

Both responses are equally foolish, as we have seen in the post-election crisis. Our task now is to figure out how much repair is necessary to prevent a future systemic collapse. In just this past month, several of the Constitution's "stupidities" have been revealed. Chief among these is the electoral college. Not only does this feature make it

---

Selection published: December 17, 2000

possible to deny the presidency to the candidate who wins the popular vote, it also gives a significant advantage to small states, each of which is guaranteed at least three electoral votes. This means that a candidate gets significantly more benefit from carrying, say, Wyoming and the two Dakotas, with a total of nine electoral votes, than New Mexico, which has roughly the same total population as the three states combined but only five electoral votes.

The electoral college, and the disproportionate power it gives to small states, has rightly been put under the microscope. But a number of other flawed constitutional features also deserve closer scrutiny and discussion:

How the House would pick a president

This is my choice for the most dubious feature of the Constitution. It provides that deadlocks over the choice of president in the electoral college be broken by the U.S. House of Representatives on a one-state, one-vote basis. Although this hasn't happened since 1824, when the House picked John Quincy Adams as president over Andrew Jackson, it loomed as a possibility in 1948 and 1968, when third-party presidential candidates in those years each won more than 20 votes. Even if you believe that the electoral college is a good idea, and that the advantage held there by small states is defensible, there is no defense, in 2000, for allowing Vermont's single representative to offset the entire 30-member congressional delegation of my home state of Texas in the instance of a House vote for president.

If the House ever has to select the president—provided we retain the electoral college and accept its risk of deadlocks—then it should do so on a one-member, one-vote basis, the theory of representation that the Supreme Court has endorsed now for almost 40 years. As it happens, if this year's election had come down to the House's choosing, it probably would not have mattered which rule we had, since the Republicans both hold a majority of individual seats and control 29 of the state delegations. Consider the situation, though, if only half a dozen congressional districts had gone Democrat instead of Republican, giving the Democrats control of the House. In that case, if the election had come to the House, Gore—the choice of the people as well [as] of a majority of the people's representatives—could have been deprived of the presidency due to the happenstance that the Republicans control most state delegations.

Life tenure on the Supreme Court

The Supreme Court's role in the just-ended campaign highlighted the questionable wisdom of lifetime appointments for Supreme Court justices. One unfortunate consequence of lifetime tenure is revealed in a recent article in the *Wall Street Journal*, which suggested that Chief Justice William Rehnquist and Associate Justice Sandra Day O'Connor have put off resigning from the court so that their replacements could be named by a Republican president. There is every reason to believe that former justice Byron White waited, for the same purpose, until a Democratic president took office before retiring in 1993. If the United States followed the practice of many other countries—and many of the states—in imposing term limits on the justices, then the opportunity for such partisan behavior would be limited. Moreover, as Emory University professor David Garrow writes in an article in the current *University of Chicago Law*

Review, over the years, several justices, including some in the recent past, have remained on the bench far too long, even after mental debilities made it impossible for them to serve the nation well. There is no reason to believe this is true of any current members of the court, but we should not continue to rely on the judges to have the self-discipline to set their own retirement dates.

Article V

The clause for enacting amendments is one of the Constitution's most dubious features, because, as a practical matter, it makes formal constitutional change exceedingly difficult. The problems posed by Article V are a primary reason why obvious defects in the constitutional structure, like those discussed above, have not been addressed, and why more train wrecks like this year's are possible in the future. Article V provides that two-thirds of each house of Congress must first agree to propose an amendment, which then must be ratified by three-fourths of the states. Winning the "amendment game" and changing the status quo thus requires triumphing first in both Houses of Congress and then in at least 75 state legislative chambers (for example, bicameral legislatures in 37 states plus the unicameral legislature in Nebraska). Winning the game on defense—that is, preventing formal change—requires only one-third plus one of the votes in either the House of Representatives (146 votes) or the U.S. Senate (34 votes), or prevailing in at least one house of 13 state legislatures.

Having been forewarned by last month's events, responsible political leaders have a duty to promote a serious analysis of the quality of our political infrastructure and to suggest necessary changes that will either prevent, or at least lower the cost of, future problems.

There is an alternative to constitutional amendments. It is drawn from Article V itself: Two-thirds of the states can petition Congress to call a constitutional convention, a gathering of elected state delegates to reflect on the adequacy of our present institutional structure. The current problems posed by the way we elect our presidents would certainly justify extended discussion by a cross-section of American leaders empowered to propose constitutional amendments for consideration by state conventions (as allowed by Article V) elected by the people of the states.

It would be foolish to deny that an Article V convention would raise many problems of its own. Like much of the Constitution, Article V is poorly drafted, and it provides no clue as to how, precisely, a convention would be organized. For example, would votes be cast on a one-member, one-vote basis, as in the House, or on the basis of equal votes for each state, as in the Senate? (Obviously, I favor the former.) Other problems will occur to readers. But a constitutional convention is, for better or worse, the best procedure given us, by the Constitution itself, to respond to what are the decided imperfections of the document we were handed in 1787.

To reject even thinking about the possibility of changing aspects of our governmental structure is to say, in effect, that we really shouldn't worry, that the last month has been perfectly all right and that it speaks only to the strengths, and not at all to the weaknesses, of our constitutional order. One might be touched by such displays of faith, but this is no time for constitutional cheerleading. Even the Framers recognized the possibilities of imperfections, the frailties of humans, and the importance of learning from experience.

*C*onsider the source and the audience.

- The *Washington Post* is a major national newspaper, and one that is particularly popular with Washington insiders. Moreover, Levinson is a professor at the flagship law school of the state of Texas, critiquing the constitutional arrangements that gave the presidency to Texas governor George W. Bush. Why would the *Post* print such a provocative piece?

*L*ay out the argument, the values, and the assumptions.

- This is clearly an abbreviated version of an argument that appears in Levinson's book. What are the argument's essential elements?
- Is the argument driven by Levinson's scholarly views or his political values? Can we tell? Does it matter?
- If Levinson doesn't place his faith in the U.S. Constitution, who is he counting on to get it right? Is that confidence warranted?

*U*ncover the evidence.

- What evidence does Levinson provide to support his argument that the Constitution is flawed?
- What other kinds of evidence might be convincing here?

*E*valuate the conclusion.

- Can the "totteriness" of the Constitution and Levinson's critique support any conclusions other than the one that Levinson arrives at? What might they be?

*S*ort out the political implications.

- What results might follow if we had another constitutional convention? What forces would argue for what provisions?
- Would a new convention produce a Constitution better than the one we have? Why or why not?

 ### 3.4 Bush Challenges Hundreds of Laws

President Cites Powers of His Office

Charlie Savage, Boston Globe

Why We Chose This Piece

Unlike some of the constitutional procedures that Levinson talks about in the previous article, one that makes a good deal of sense is checks and balances, a constitutional principle that not just liberals but many conservatives and libertarians felt was under siege

---

Selection published: April 30, 2006

during the Bush administration. The Globe *reporter here focuses on one particular threat to checks and balances, the attachment of presidential signing statements to bills passed by Congress and signed by the president that indicate how he believes the law should or should not be enforced. This article was one of the first in the mainstream media to analyze the Bush administration's signing statements and the impact they might have on the constitutional balance in this country. President Obama has said he does not intend to use signing statements the way Bush used them but will restrict them to clarifying his constitutional position as earlier presidents have done. How would the founders have felt about these signing statements as issued by the Bush administration?*

President Bush has quietly claimed the authority to disobey more than 750 laws enacted since he took office, asserting that he has the power to set aside any statute passed by Congress when it conflicts with his interpretation of the Constitution.

Among the laws Bush said he can ignore are military rules and regulations, affirmative-action provisions, requirements that Congress be told about immigration services problems, "whistle-blower" protections for nuclear regulatory officials, and safeguards against political interference in federally funded research.

Legal scholars say the scope and aggression of Bush's assertions that he can bypass laws represent a concerted effort to expand his power at the expense of Congress, upsetting the balance between the branches of government. The Constitution is clear in assigning to Congress the power to write the laws and to the president a duty "to take care that the laws be faithfully executed." Bush, however, has repeatedly declared that he does not need to "execute" a law he believes is unconstitutional.

Former administration officials contend that just because Bush reserves the right to disobey a law does not mean he is not enforcing it: In many cases, he is simply asserting his belief that a certain requirement encroaches on presidential power.

But with the disclosure of Bush's domestic spying program, in which he ignored a law requiring warrants to tap the phones of Americans, many legal specialists say Bush is hardly reluctant to bypass laws he believes he has the constitutional authority to override.

Far more than any predecessor, Bush has been aggressive about declaring his right to ignore vast swaths of laws, many of which he says infringe on power he believes the Constitution assigns to him alone as the head of the executive branch or the commander in chief of the military.

Many legal scholars say they believe that Bush's theory about his own powers goes too far and that he is seizing for himself some of the law-making role of Congress and the Constitution-interpreting role of the courts.

Phillip Cooper, a Portland State University law professor who has studied the executive power claims Bush made during his first term, said Bush and his legal team have spent the past five years quietly working to concentrate ever more governmental power into the White House.

"There is no question that this administration has been involved in a very carefully thought-out, systematic process of expanding presidential power at the expense of the other branches of government," Cooper said. "This is really big, very expansive, and very significant."

For the first five years of Bush's presidency, his legal claims attracted little attention in Congress or the media. Then, twice in recent months, Bush drew scrutiny after challenging new laws: a torture ban and a requirement that he give detailed reports to Congress about how he is using the Patriot Act.

Bush administration spokesmen declined to make White House or Justice Department attorneys available to discuss any of Bush's challenges to the laws he has signed.

Instead, they referred a *Globe* reporter to their response to questions about Bush's position that he could ignore provisions of the Patriot Act. They said at the time that Bush was following a practice that has "been used for several administrations" and that "the president will faithfully execute the law in a manner that is consistent with the Constitution."

But the words "in a manner that is consistent with the Constitution" are the catch, legal scholars say, because Bush is according himself the ultimate interpretation of the Constitution. And he is quietly exercising that authority to a degree that is unprecedented in U.S. history.

Bush is the first president in modern history who has never vetoed a bill, giving Congress no chance to override his judgments. Instead, he has signed every bill that reached his desk, often inviting the legislation's sponsors to signing ceremonies at which he lavishes praise upon their work.

Then, after the media and the lawmakers have left the White House, Bush quietly files "signing statements," official documents in which a president lays out his legal interpretation of a bill for the federal bureaucracy to follow when implementing the new law. The statements are recorded in the *Federal Register*.

In his signing statements, Bush has repeatedly asserted that the Constitution gives him the right to ignore numerous sections of the bills—sometimes including provisions that were the subject of negotiations with Congress—in order to get lawmakers to pass the bill. He has appended such statements to more than one of every 10 bills he has signed.

"He agrees to a compromise with members of Congress, and all of them are there for a public bill-signing ceremony, but then he takes back those compromises and more often than not, without the Congress or the press or the public knowing what has happened," said Christopher Kelley, a Miami University of Ohio political science professor who studies executive power.

Military link

Many of the laws Bush said he can bypass including the torture ban involve the military.

The Constitution grants Congress the power to create armies, to declare war, to make rules for captured enemies, and "to make rules for the government and regulation of the land and naval forces." But, citing his role as commander in chief, Bush says he can ignore any act of Congress that seeks to regulate the military.

On at least four occasions while Bush has been president, Congress has passed laws forbidding U.S. troops from engaging in combat in Colombia, where the U.S. military is advising the government in its struggle against narcotics-funded Marxist rebels.

After signing each bill, Bush declared in his signing statement that he did not have to obey any of the Colombia restrictions because he is commander in chief.

Bush has also said he can bypass laws requiring him to tell Congress before diverting money from an authorized program in order to start a secret operation, such as the "black sites" where suspected terrorists are secretly imprisoned.

Congress has also twice passed laws forbidding the military from using intelligence that was not "lawfully collected," including any information on Americans that was gathered in violation of the Fourth Amendment's protections against unreasonable searches.

Congress first passed this provision in August 2004, when Bush's warrantless domestic spying program was still a secret, and passed it again after the program's existence was disclosed in December 2005.

On both occasions, Bush declared in signing statements that only he, as commander in chief, could decide whether such intelligence can be used by the military.

In October 2004, five months after the Abu Ghraib torture scandal in Iraq came to light, Congress passed a series of new rules and regulations for military prisons. Bush signed the provisions into law, then said he could ignore them all. One provision made clear that military lawyers can give their commanders independent advice on such issues as what would constitute torture. But Bush declared that military lawyers could not contradict his administration's lawyers.

Other provisions required the Pentagon to retrain military prison guards on the requirements for humane treatment of detainees under the Geneva Conventions, to perform background checks on civilian contractors in Iraq, and to ban such contractors from performing "security, intelligence, law enforcement, and criminal justice functions." Bush reserved the right to ignore any of the requirements.

The new law also created the position of inspector general for Iraq. But Bush wrote in his signing statement that the inspector "shall refrain" from investigating any intelligence or national security matter, or any crime the Pentagon says it prefers to investigate for itself.

Bush had placed similar limits on an inspector general position created by Congress in November 2003 for the initial stage of the U.S. occupation of Iraq. The earlier law also empowered the inspector to notify Congress if a U.S. official refused to cooperate. Bush said the inspector could not give any information to Congress without permission from the administration.

Oversight questioned

Many laws Bush has asserted he can bypass involve requirements to give information about government activity to congressional oversight committees.

In December 2004, Congress passed an intelligence bill requiring the Justice Department to tell them how often, and in what situations, the FBI was using special national security wiretaps on U.S. soil. The law also required the Justice Department to give oversight committees copies of administration memos outlining any new interpretations of domestic-spying laws. And it contained 11 other requirements for reports about such issues as civil liberties, security clearances, border security, and counternarcotics efforts.

After signing the bill, Bush issued a signing statement saying he could withhold all the information sought by Congress.

Likewise, when Congress passed the law creating the Department of Homeland Security in 2002, it said oversight committees must be given information about vulnerabilities at chemical plants and the screening of checked bags at airports.

It also said Congress must be shown unaltered reports about problems with visa services prepared by a new immigration ombudsman. Bush asserted the right to withhold the information and alter the reports.

On several other occasions, Bush contended he could nullify laws creating "whistle-blower" job protections for federal employees that would stop any attempt to fire them as punishment for telling a member of Congress about possible government wrongdoing.

When Congress passed a massive energy package in August, for example, it strengthened whistle-blower protections for employees at the Department of Energy and the Nuclear Regulatory Commission.

The provision was included because lawmakers feared that Bush appointees were intimidating nuclear specialists so they would not testify about safety issues related to a planned nuclear-waste repository at Yucca Mountain in Nevada, a facility the administration supported, but both Republicans and Democrats from Nevada opposed.

When Bush signed the energy bill, he issued a signing statement declaring that the executive branch could ignore the whistle-blower protections.

Bush's statement did more than send a threatening message to federal energy specialists inclined to raise concerns with Congress; it also raised the possibility that Bush would not feel bound to obey similar whistle-blower laws that were on the books before he became president. His domestic spying program, for example, violated a surveillance law enacted 23 years before he took office.

David Golove, a New York University law professor who specializes in executive-power issues, said Bush has cast a cloud over "the whole idea that there is a rule of law," because no one can be certain of which laws Bush thinks are valid and which he thinks he can ignore.

"Where you have a president who is willing to declare vast quantities of the legislation that is passed during his term unconstitutional, it implies that he also thinks a very significant amount of the other laws that were already on the books before he became president are also unconstitutional," Golove said.

Defying Supreme Court

Bush has also challenged statutes in which Congress gave certain executive branch officials the power to act independently of the president. The Supreme Court has repeatedly endorsed the power of Congress to make such arrangements. For example, the court has upheld laws creating special prosecutors free of Justice Department oversight and insulating the board of the Federal Trade Commission from political interference.

Nonetheless, Bush has said in his signing statements that the Constitution lets him control any executive official, no matter what a statute passed by Congress might say.

In November 2002, for example, Congress, seeking to generate independent statistics about student performance, passed a law setting up an educational research institute to conduct studies and publish reports "without the approval" of the Secretary of Education. Bush, however, decreed that the institute's director would be "subject to the supervision and direction of the secretary of education."

Similarly, the Supreme Court has repeatedly upheld affirmative-action programs, as long as they do not include quotas. Most recently, in 2003, the court upheld a race-conscious university admissions program over the strong objections of Bush, who argued that such programs should be struck down as unconstitutional.

Yet despite the court's rulings, Bush has taken exception at least nine times to provisions that seek to ensure that minorities are represented among recipients of government jobs, contracts, and grants. Each time, he singled out the provisions, declaring that he would construe them "in a manner consistent with" the Constitution's guarantee of "equal protection" to all, which some legal scholars say amounts to an argument that the affirmative-action provisions represent reverse discrimination against whites.

Golove said that to the extent Bush is interpreting the Constitution in defiance of the Supreme Court's precedents, he threatens to "overturn the existing structures of constitutional law."

A president who ignores the court, backed by a Congress that is unwilling to challenge him, Golove said, can make the Constitution simply "disappear."

Common practice in '80s

Though Bush has gone further than any previous president, his actions are not unprecedented.

Since the early 19th century, American presidents have occasionally signed a large bill while declaring that they would not enforce a specific provision they believed was unconstitutional. On rare occasions, historians say, presidents also issued signing statements interpreting a law and explaining any concerns about it.

But it was not until the mid-1980s, midway through the tenure of President Reagan, that it became common for the president to issue signing statements. The change came about after then–Attorney General Edwin Meese decided that signing statements could be used to increase the power of the president.

When interpreting an ambiguous law, courts often look at the statute's legislative history, debate and testimony, to see what Congress intended it to mean. Meese realized that recording what the president thought the law meant in a signing statement might increase a president's influence over future court rulings.

Under Meese's direction in 1986, a young Justice Department lawyer named Samuel A. Alito Jr. wrote a strategy memo about signing statements. It came to light in late 2005, after Bush named Alito to the Supreme Court.

In the memo, Alito predicted that Congress would resent the president's attempt to grab some of its power by seizing "the last word on questions of interpretation." He suggested that Reagan's legal team should "concentrate on points of true ambiguity, rather than issuing interpretations that may seem to conflict with those of Congress."

Reagan's successors continued this practice. George H. W. Bush challenged 232 statutes over four years in office, and Bill Clinton objected to 140 laws over his eight years, according to Kelley, the Miami University of Ohio professor.

Many of the challenges involved longstanding legal ambiguities and points of conflict between the president and Congress.

Throughout the past two decades, for example, each president including the current one has objected to provisions requiring him to get permission from a congressional committee before taking action. The Supreme Court made clear in 1983 that only the full Congress can direct the executive branch to do things, but lawmakers have continued writing laws giving congressional committees such a role.

Still, Reagan, George H. W. Bush, and Clinton used the presidential veto instead of the signing statement if they had a serious problem with a bill, giving Congress a chance to override their decisions.

But the current President Bush has abandoned the veto entirely, as well as any semblance of the political caution that Alito counseled back in 1986. In just five years, Bush has challenged more than 750 new laws, by far a record for any president, while becoming the first president since Thomas Jefferson to stay so long in office without issuing a veto.

"What we haven't seen until this administration is the sheer number of objections that are being raised on every bill passed through the White House," said Kelley, who has studied presidential signing statements through history. "That is what is staggering. The numbers are well out of the norm from any previous administration."

Exaggerated fears?

Some administration defenders say that concerns about Bush's signing statements are overblown. Bush's signing statements, they say, should be seen as little more than political chest-thumping by administration lawyers who are dedicated to protecting presidential prerogatives.

Defenders say the fact that Bush is reserving the right to disobey the laws does not necessarily mean he has gone on to disobey them.

Indeed, in some cases, the administration has ended up following laws that Bush said he could bypass. For example, citing his power to "withhold information" in September 2002, Bush declared that he could ignore a law requiring the State Department to list the number of overseas deaths of U.S. citizens in foreign countries. Nevertheless, the department has still put the list on its website.

Jack Goldsmith, a Harvard Law School professor who until last year oversaw the Justice Department's Office of Legal Counsel for the administration, said the statements do not change the law; they just let people know how the president is interpreting it.

"Nobody reads them," said Goldsmith. "They have no significance. Nothing in the world changes by the publication of a signing statement. The statements merely serve as public notice about how the administration is interpreting the law. Criticism of this practice is surprising, since the usual complaint is that the administration is too secretive in its legal interpretations."

But Cooper, the Portland State University professor who has studied Bush's first-term signing statements, said the documents are being read closely by one key group of people: the bureaucrats who are charged with implementing new laws.

Lower-level officials will follow the president's instructions even when his understanding of a law conflicts with the clear intent of Congress, crafting policies that may endure long after Bush leaves office, Cooper said.

"Years down the road, people will not understand why the policy doesn't look like the legislation," he said.

And in many cases, critics contend, there is no way to know whether the administration is violating laws or merely preserving the right to do so.

Many of the laws Bush has challenged involve national security, where it is almost impossible to verify what the government is doing. And since the disclosure of Bush's domestic spying program, many people have expressed alarm about his sweeping claims of the authority to violate laws.

In January, after the *Globe* first wrote about Bush's contention that he could disobey the torture ban, three Republicans who were the bill's principal sponsors in the Senate—John McCain of Arizona, John W. Warner of Virginia, and Lindsey O. Graham of South Carolina—all publicly rebuked the president.

"We believe the president understands Congress's intent in passing, by very large majorities, legislation governing the treatment of detainees," McCain and Warner said in a joint statement. "The Congress declined when asked by administration officials to include a presidential waiver of the restrictions included in our legislation."

Added Graham: "I do not believe that any political figure in the country has the ability to set aside any . . . law of armed conflict that we have adopted or treaties that we have ratified."

And in March, when the *Globe* first wrote about Bush's contention that he could ignore the oversight provisions of the Patriot Act, several Democrats lodged complaints.

Senator Patrick J. Leahy of Vermont, the ranking Democrat on the Senate Judiciary Committee, accused Bush of trying to "cherry-pick the laws he decides he wants to follow."

And Representatives Jane Harman of California and John Conyers Jr. of Michigan—the ranking Democrats on the House Intelligence and Judiciary committees, respectively—sent a letter to Attorney General Alberto R. Gonzales demanding that Bush rescind his claim and abide by the law.

"Many members who supported the final law did so based upon the guarantee of additional reporting and oversight," they wrote. "The administration cannot, after the fact, unilaterally repeal provisions of the law implementing such oversight. . . . Once the president signs a bill, he and all of us are bound by it."

Lack of court review

Such political fallout from Congress is likely to be the only check on Bush's claims, legal specialists said.

The courts have little chance of reviewing Bush's assertions, especially in the secret realm of national security matters.

"There can't be judicial review if nobody knows about it," said Neil Kinkopf, a Georgia State law professor who was a Justice Department official in the Clinton administration. "And if they avoid judicial review, they avoid having their constitutional theories rebuked."

Without court involvement, only Congress can check a president who goes too far. But Bush's fellow Republicans control both chambers, and they have shown limited interest in launching the kind of oversight that could damage their party.

"The president is daring Congress to act against his positions, and they're not taking action because they don't want to appear to be too critical of the president, given that their own fortunes are tied to his because they are all Republicans," said

Jack Beermann, a Boston University law professor. "Oversight gets much reduced in a situation where the president and Congress are controlled by the same party."

Said Golove, the New York University law professor: "Bush has essentially said that 'We're the executive branch and we're going to carry this law out as we please, and if Congress wants to impeach us, go ahead and try it.'"

Bruce Fein, a deputy attorney general in the Reagan administration, said the American system of government relies upon the leaders of each branch "to exercise some self-restraint." But Bush has declared himself the sole judge of his own powers, he said, and then ruled for himself every time.

"This is an attempt by the president to have the final word on his own constitutional powers, which eliminates the checks and balances that keep the country a democracy," Fein said. "There is no way for an independent judiciary to check his assertions of power, and Congress isn't doing it, either. So this is moving us toward an unlimited executive power."

*C*onsider the source and the audience.

- The *Boston Globe* is owned by the *New York Times*, whose editorial pages tend to be liberal, and Boston is a liberal northeastern city. Would this article have appeared in a more conservative outlet? (Think about the previous selection as you answer.)

*L*ay out the argument, the values, and the assumptions.

- Though this is a news article, it is also an analytic piece and it is making an argument. What is Savage's opinion about signing statements? How can you tell?
- What does he suggest that signing statements threaten? Why would he probably prefer to see Bush veto more bills instead?
- What does Savage focus on as the most damaging things done by signing statements?

*U*ncover the evidence.

- Savage suggests that signing statements are injurious to the constitutional order in the United States. How does he use authorities and experts to help him make the case? How does he use empirical evidence?
- Does he give equal hearing to experts and evidence on the other side? What might such contrary evidence look like?

*E*valuate the conclusion.

- Savage's conclusion, in the words of his "experts," is that signing statements move us toward an unlimited executive. Do the examples of signing statements that he provides back this up?

*S*ort out the political implications.

- How much power should the president have, anyway?
- Even if you like the signing statements Bush has issued, what are the inherent dangers in institutionalizing such a practice?

3.5 *Federalist* No. 51

James Madison, The Federalist Papers

Why We Chose This Piece

Here speaks the main author of the U.S. Constitution, many of whose provisions have been debated, critiqued, and revered in this chapter's previous selections. Federalist No. 51 is James Madison's famous justification of the principles of federalism, separation of powers, and checks and balances. It is based on his notion that if people are too ambitious and self-interested to produce good government, then government will have to be adapted to the realities of human nature. A mechanism must be created by which the product of government will be good, even if the nature of the human beings participating in it cannot be counted on to be so. The solution, according to Madison, is to create a government that prevents one person or one group from obtaining too much power. How does he make human nature, warts and all, work for the public interest in the Constitution? [We present Madison's Federalist No. 51, slightly abridged in order to throw into sharper relief his argument about the constitutional protections of liberty.]

I n order to lay a due foundation for that separate and distinct exercise of the different powers of government, which to a certain extent is admitted on all hands to be essential to the preservation of liberty, it is evident that each department should have a will of its own; and consequently should be so constituted, that the members of each should have as little agency as possible in the appointment of the members of the others. Were this principle rigorously adhered to, it would require that all the appointments for the supreme executive, legislative, and judiciary magistracies should be drawn from the same fountain of authority, the people, through channels having no communication whatever with one another. Perhaps such a plan of constructing the several departments would be less difficult in practice than it may in contemplation appear. Some difficulties, however, and some additional expense would attend the execution of it. Some deviations, therefore, from the principle must be admitted. In the constitution of the judiciary department in particular, it might be inexpedient to insist rigorously on the principle; first, because peculiar qualifications being essential in the members, the primary consideration ought to be to select that mode of choice which best secures these qualifications; secondly, because the permanent tenure by which the appointments are held in that department, must soon destroy all sense of dependence on the authority conferring them.

It is equally evident that the members of each department should be as little dependent as possible on those of the others, for the emoluments annexed to their offices. Were the executive magistrate, or the judges, not independent of the legislature in this particular, their independence in every other would be merely nominal.

Selection published: February 6, 1788

But the great security against a gradual concentration of the several powers in the same department, consists in giving to those who administer each department the necessary constitutional means and personal motives to resist encroachments of the others. The provision for defense must in this, as in all other cases, be made commensurate to the danger of attack. Ambition must be made to counteract ambition. The interest of the man must be connected with the constitutional right of the place. It may be a reflection on human nature, that such devices should be necessary to control the abuses of government. But what is government itself, but the greatest of all reflections on human nature? If men were angels, no government would be necessary. If angels were to govern men, neither external nor internal controls on government would be necessary. In framing a government which is to be administered by men over men, the great difficulty lies in this: You must first enable the government to control the governed; and in the next place, oblige it to control itself. A dependence on the people is, no doubt, the primary control on the government; but experience has taught mankind the necessity of auxiliary precautions.

This policy of supplying, by opposite and rival interests, the defect of better motives, might be traced through the whole system of human affairs, private as well as public. We see it particularly displayed in all the subordinate distributions of power, where the constant aim is to divide and arrange the several offices in such a manner as that each may be a check on the other that the private interest of every individual, may be a sentinel over the public rights. These inventions of prudence cannot be less requisite in the distribution of the supreme powers of the state.

But it is not possible to give each department an equal power of self defense. In republican government, the legislative authority necessarily predominates. The remedy for this inconvenience is to divide the legislative into different branches; and to render them, by different modes of election and different principles of action, as little connected with each other as the nature of their common functions and their common dependence on the society will admit. It may even be necessary to guard against dangerous encroachments by still further precautions. As the weight of the legislative authority requires that it should be thus divided, the weakness of the executive may require, on the other hand, that it should be fortified. An absolute negative on the legislature appears, at first view, to be the natural defense with which the executive magistrate should be armed. But perhaps it would be neither altogether safe nor alone sufficient. On ordinary occasions it might not be exerted with the requisite firmness, and on extraordinary occasions it might be perfidiously abused. May not this defect of an absolute negative be supplied by some qualified connection between this weaker department and the weaker branch of the stronger department, by which the latter may be led to support the constitutional rights of the former, without being too much detached from the rights of its own department?

If the principles on which these observations are founded be just, as I persuade myself they are, and they be applied as a criterion to the several State constitutions, and to the federal Constitution, it will be found that if the latter does not perfectly correspond with them, the former are infinitely less able to bear such a test.

There are, moreover, two considerations particularly applicable to the federal system of America, which place the system in a very interesting point of view.

First. In a single republic, all the power surrendered by the people is submitted to the administration of a single government; and usurpations are guarded against by a division of the government into distinct and separate departments. In the compound republic of America, the power surrendered by the people is first divided between distinct governments, and then the portion allotted to each subdivided among distinct and separate departments. Hence a double security arises to the rights of the people. The different governments will control each other; at the same time that each will be controlled by itself.

Second. It is of great importance in a republic not only to guard the society against the oppression of its rulers, but to guard one part of the society against the injustice of the other part. Different interests necessarily exist in different classes of citizens. If a majority be united by a common interest, the rights of the minority will be insecure. There are but two methods of providing against this evil: The one by creating a will in the community independent of the majority that is, of the society itself; the other, by comprehending in the society so many separate descriptions of citizens as will render an unjust combination of a majority of the whole very improbable, if not impracticable. The first method prevails in all governments possessing an hereditary or self-appointed authority. This, at best, is but a precarious security; because a power independent of the society may as well espouse the unjust views of the major, as the rightful interests of the minor party, and may possibly be turned against both parties. The second method will be exemplified in the federal republic of the United States. While all authority in it will be derived from and dependent on the society, the society itself will be broken into so many parts, interests, and classes of citizens, that the rights of individuals, or of the minority, will be in little danger from interested combinations of the majority. . . . In the extended republic of the United States, and among the great variety of interests, parties, and sects which it embraces, a coalition of a majority of the whole society could seldom take place on any other principles than those of justice and the general good; whilst there being thus less danger to a minor from the will of the major party, there must be less pretext, also, to provide for the security of the former, by introducing into the government a will not dependent on the latter, or, in other words, a will independent of the society itself. It is no less certain than it is important, notwithstanding the contrary opinions which have been entertained, that the larger the society, provided it lie within a practicable sphere, the more duly capable it will be of self-government. And happily for the *republican cause*, the practicable sphere may be carried to a very great extent, by a judicious modification and mixture of the *federal principle*.

*C*onsider the source and the audience.

- This piece was originally published in a New York newspaper in 1788, at a time when New Yorkers were debating whether to ratify the new Constitution. What was its political purpose? Who was Madison arguing against?

*L*ay out the argument, the values, and the assumptions.

- What two ways did Madison think the Constitution would undertake to preserve liberty?
- What assumptions did he make about the purpose of government?

*U*ncover the evidence.

- What sort of evidence did Madison rely on to make his case? Was any other evidence available to him at that time?

*E*valuate the conclusion.

- Was Madison right about the best way to preserve liberty in a republic? How would the other authors we've read in this chapter answer this question?

*S*ort out the political implications.

- What will the political process be like in a political system that is divided between national and state levels, and at each level among executive, legislative, and judicial branches? Will policymaking be quick and efficient, gradual and judicious, or slow and sluggish? Why?
- How much power do everyday citizens end up having in such a system? Why didn't Madison give us more power?

4 ★

Civil Liberties

It's awfully easy to take our freedoms for granted when no one is trying to take them away. For many Americans, as the twenty-first century dawned, our civil liberties—things like freedom of speech, freedom of religion, due process of law—almost seemed like part of the landscape. Certain rights for certain people may have seemed controversial, and there were perennial, irresolvable debates such as where the line between church and state should be drawn, or whether women had a right to an abortion, but as far as the fundamentals went, Americans knew they lived in the freest country in history.

They still do, but since September 11, 2001, the premises and the stakes have changed, and with them some of the unalterable freedoms we have been accustomed to. Indeed, it was our very openness and freedom that made us vulnerable to terrorist attack, and many observers argued that to become less vulnerable we had to be a little less open, a little less free. Individual freedoms often conflict with the common good, and an inevitable tension exists between freedom and security—we could be completely secure if we gave up all of our liberty to a caretaker state, but very few of us are willing to make that deal.

Our civil liberties are the individual freedoms we possess that government cannot take away. Although they exist to empower us, they also exist to limit government. Because they deal with power, both individual and governmental, civil liberties will always be controversial. Since everyone wants power, since there is not enough to go around, and since some people's power gain will always be other people's loss, our civil liberties can be controversial, to say the least.

In fact, one of the great debates at our Constitution's founding concerned civil liberties—whether that document established a government that was powerful enough to need limiting through the addition of the first ten amendments, or whether it was so weak as it stood that it would not try to infringe on our lives. Those making the first of those arguments won, of course, and the Bill of Rights is an established part of our constitutional law. But we continue to debate the centrality of civil liberties in this country—many argue that the election of Barack Obama as president in 2008 was a reassertion of the idea that the United States is a nation of laws, and in the protection of our freedoms we can also find security.

In the United States we rarely have to resort to violence to solve our conflicts over rights and freedom (although people do occasionally try to take the law into their own hands). Generally, however, there is a consensus that we should look to politics to resolve clashes of rights—specifically to the Supreme Court, with some assistance from the Congress and the presidency and even the American public, organized into interest groups like the American Civil Liberties Union or the National Rifle Association.

In this chapter we look at readings that examine several contemporary civil liberties issues. The first, a *Washington Post* article, is about a man who is fighting the military's willingness to allow senior officers to proselytize their subordinates—what he sees as a violation of the First Amendment separation between church and state. The second, from the *Christian Science Monitor*, looks at religious freedom from a different angle, examining the way that some people's freedom to believe can come into conflict with the demand by gays for equal treatment by the state when it comes to marriage law. The third, from *Time*, looks at some of the civil liberties issues and ethical dilemmas raised by the treatment of foreign prisoners held during wartime. This reading is followed by another piece that raises war-related concerns—an *Economist* article that asks whether torture is ever justified. Finally, we look at an excerpt from Alexander Hamilton's *Federalist* No. 84, in which he objects to the addition of the Bill of Rights to our Constitution.

 ## 4.1 Marching as to War

Alan Cooperman, Washington Post

Why We Chose This Piece

The subject of this article, Mikey Weinstein, believes that there is a common practice in today's military of senior officers proselytizing subordinates, hoping to convert them to evangelical Christianity, and that it violates the First Amendment clause protecting against establishment of religion. Christians in the military don't dispute what is going on but insist it is their right. They say their behavior is protected by the other half of the First Amendment's religious guarantees—the free exercise clause. Are these two parts of the First Amendment—the establishment clause and the free exercise clause—necessarily incompatible? When they conflict, which should prevail?

Porcelain figurines are perched on the mantelpiece behind Mikey Weinstein. Guests are seated on chintz couches in front of him. It's a nice crowd at a polite fundraising party.

Selection published: July 16, 2006

But Mikey—his friends, his enemies, even complete strangers call him "Mikey"—has had it with nice.

He's done with polite.

"We've created this foundation to be a weapon. We're going to lay down a withering field of fire and leave sucking chest wounds," he says, glaring through the floor-to-ceiling windows of an Arlington high-rise at a panoramic view of Washington.

Weinstein, 51, was once a White House lawyer who defended the Reagan administration during the Iran-contra investigation. Three generations of his family—his father, himself, both of his sons and a daughter-in-law—have gone to U.S. military academies.

Now he's declaring war against what, for him, is an improbable enemy: the defense establishment. He is suing the Air Force in federal court, demanding a permanent injunction against alleged religious favoritism and proselytizing in the service. He has also formed a nonprofit organization, the Military Religious Freedom Foundation, to combat what he sees as a concerted effort by evangelical Christian organizations to treat the armed forces as a mission field, ripe for conversions.

Weinstein's head is big and bald, like a cannonball mounted on his short, powerful frame. He keeps a powerful stereo in the garage of his home in Albuquerque and listens to heavy metal at full volume. The incongruity of his sheepish first name is exceeded only by the incongruity of a middle-aged corporate lawyer quoting Meat Loaf, Mudvayne and Marilyn Manson.

Yet one of his favorite lines these days—right up there with "sucking chest wounds"—comes from the Officers' Christian Fellowship, a private organization with 14,000 active-duty members on more than 200 U.S. military bases around the world. In its mission statement, the OCF says its goal is "a spiritually transformed military, with ambassadors for Christ in uniform, empowered by the Holy Spirit."

Ambassadors for Christ in uniform. According to the OCF's executive director, retired Air Force Lt. Gen. Bruce Fister, it means that "the people around a military leader ought to see the characteristics of Christ in that leader." It is a national tradition reflected in "hundreds of writings and proclamations issued down through the ages by American leaders who claim divine protection for our nation, place our nation's trust in God and claim God as our source of strength."

Ambassadors for Christ in uniform. To Weinstein, who is both a Jew and a member of a military family, it is an abomination. It "evokes the Crusades." He says he can't believe that generals talk like this when the United States is fighting a global war on terror and trying to win hearts and minds in Muslim countries.

He starts to get riled up—waving his arms, quoting the Constitution, saying "the Christian right wants people to think that separation of church and state is a myth, like Bigfoot." And then he pauses, something he does not do often.

"Let me make it clear. I would shed my last drop of blood to defend their right to hold that biblical worldview. They are absolutely entitled to believe that Anne Frank is burning in hell along with Dr. Seuss, Gandhi and Einstein," he says. "But I will not accept my government telling me who are the children of the greater God and who are the children of the lesser God. That's the difference. I will not defend—I will fight them tooth and nail, and lay down a withering field of fire and leave sucking chest wounds—if they engage the machinery of the state, which is what they're doing."

The last straw

To Weinstein, it's also personal, and has been from the start: July 29, 2004.

He visited the Air Force Academy in Colorado Springs that day as a proud parent. His son Curtis, who was entering his second year at the academy, had just finished three weeks of combat survival training. Weinstein spotted him across a room and knew instantly that something was wrong. They drove off campus, in stormy silence, and pulled into a McDonald's.

"All right, Curtis...I can't take any more of this. What the hell have you done?" Weinstein remembers asking.

"It's not what I've done, Dad. It's what I'm going to do," Curtis answered, according to his father. "I'm going to beat the [...] out of the next person that calls me a [...] Jew or accuses me or our people of killing Jesus Christ."

At that moment, Weinstein says, "everything kind of telescoped. I could hear my heart in my ears. For a guy who talks a lot...I was speechless."

Weinstein says Curtis recounted eight or nine separate incidents in which cadets and officers had made anti-Semitic remarks. One came in the heat of athletic competition, when an upperclassman taunted: "How does it make you feel to know that you killed Jesus Christ?"

"What hurt me the most was...you know, he's a tough kid, he was the city wrestling champ of Albuquerque as a sophomore in high school...[but] he said, 'Dad, I don't really know what to do when they say that,'" Weinstein recalls.

Since that day, Weinstein says, he has talked with hundreds of present and former cadets and staff at the academy, and has become convinced that the conflict is not between Christians and Jews, but between aggressively evangelical Christians and everybody else.

Weinstein's passion already has shaken the Pentagon. His complaints about the Air Force Academy led last year to congressional hearings, an internal Air Force investigation and new Air Force guidelines on religious tolerance.

The internal inquiry substantiated virtually all of his specific allegations. It found, for example, that Brig. Gen. Johnny Weida, the commandant of cadets, taught the entire incoming class a "J for Jesus" hand signal; that football coach Fisher DeBerry hung a "Team Jesus" banner in the locker room; and that more than 250 faculty members and senior officers signed a campus newspaper advertisement saying: "We believe that Jesus Christ is the only real hope for the world."

But the Air Force's report concluded that there was "no overt religious discrimination," merely a "lack of awareness over where the line is drawn between permissible and impermissible expression of beliefs." In its motion to dismiss Weinstein's lawsuit, the Air Force maintains that it has already addressed and remedied the religious climate at the Academy, and that Weinstein's complaint cites no specific incidents in the Air Force at large.

The pushback from evangelicals has been intense. Focus on the Family and like-minded groups, many of which are headquartered near the academy, succeeded early this year in persuading the Air Force to soften its guidelines, so that the latest rules explicitly allow commanders to share their faith with subordinates.

More than 70 members of Congress have urged President Bush to issue an executive order guaranteeing the right of military chaplains to pray "in the name of Jesus" at mandatory ceremonies attended by service members of all faiths.

The National Association of Evangelicals and the Alliance Defense Fund, a conservative legal group, also have filed motions to intervene in the suit on behalf of Christian chaplains and service members. They argue that the injunction Weinstein is seeking would infringe on their rights to free speech and free exercise of religion.

"I consider my constitutional right to discuss my faith without censorship or fear of retribution as valuable to the military and the future of our nation as the aircraft, bombs and bullets I am trained to employ," Air Force Capt. Karl Palmberg, one of the would-be interveners, said in an affidavit.

Judge James Parker, who is hearing the case, has not yet ruled on the preliminary motions. As a result, the Air Force has not yet had to respond to the substance of Weinstein's allegation that it has a pervasive, unconstitutional bias in favor of evangelical Christianity.

Weinstein has amended his lawsuit, filed last October in U.S. District Court in New Mexico, to add several active-duty officers (including his older son, First Lt. Casey Weinstein) as co-plaintiffs. He is girding for a long legal battle, which is why he has formed a foundation with 501(c)(3) tax-exempt status and traveled from Albuquerque to Arlington on a recent weekend to raise money.

When the Air Force allows superior officers to evangelize their subordinates, Weinstein contends, it is doing something that no private company would allow. "Imagine if your boss were constantly coming by your desk to talk about his faith and invite you to his church," he says. "When it's your superior officer, it's much worse."

"I don't care what the admirals and generals say anymore," he says in an interview a few hours before the fundraiser, which took in about $20,000. "I'm done with the politicians. What I say to the Pentagon, and to George Bush, and to the people on Capitol Hill, and to all these mega-evangelical church folks, is just five simple words: Tell it to the judge. Because we're in federal court now."

The field general

Fellow members of the Air Force Academy's Class of 1977 say Weinstein was always like this. His nicknames at the academy, where he graduated in the top 15 percent of his class, were "Motor Mouth" and "Ticktock," for his loquacity and his hurry. He is perpetually on the move, talking fast, driving fast. He just traded in his yellow Dodge Viper, an $85,000 roadster, for an even more exotic Lotus.

"There's this line where Meat Loaf in 'Bat Out of Hell II' says: 'We were born out of time.' That's my attitude exactly," Weinstein says. "In archaeological time, we're already dead. We're only here a nanosecond. You got to make it count."

If half of Weinstein's persona is Clint Eastwood, however, the other half is Rodney Dangerfield. The combination, more surprising and appealing than either of its parts, is his real charm, his unique *shtick*.

When his wife, Bonnie, takes one of his favorite See's chocolates, he reminds her of the label given him by a mega-church in the southeastern United States.

"I'm the Field General of the Godless Armies of Satan!" he says. "You can't just steal my candy like that."

The Weinsteins were married 29 years ago in the Air Force Academy's modernist chapel, its 17 gleaming spires lined up like fighter jets shooting into the sky. It was a Jewish ceremony, but the clergyman under the *huppah* was a Protestant chaplain.

Back then, Weinstein says, military chaplains "were like Father Mulcahy in 'M*A*S*H,' type O universal blood donor chaplains" who gave equally to all, who tried to serve the troops, not convert them.

Weinstein writes, travels and exercises as frenetically as he speaks. He corresponds by e-mail with U.S. soldiers, sailors and airmen around the world who report incidents of proselytizing and religious pressure. He lectures at synagogues and Rotary Clubs.

He is writing a book, tentatively titled "With God on Our Side," for publication by St. Martin's Press in the fall. He may soon make his film debut, too: He was followed through Arlington by documentary maker Oren Jacoby, who is adapting James Carroll's best-selling history of the church and the Jews, "Constantine's Sword."

Last year, Weinstein exchanged vitriolic e-mails with the Rev. Ted Haggard, pastor of the 14,000-member New Life Church in Colorado Springs and president of the National Association of Evangelicals. The private messages became public when one of Haggard's associate pastors gave them to a blogger, hoping to embarrass Weinstein by publishing his torrent of incomplete sentences punctuated with !!! and ??? together with Haggard's calm, composed replies.

Since then, Weinstein, who boxed in his academy days, has repeatedly offered to go three rounds in the ring with Haggard, a former football player. "We'll do it for charity. That can include the Christian Children's Fund and also, I think, the United Way and the United Jewish Appeal," Weinstein says. And though he is smiling, he is not kidding.

On the morning of the Arlington fundraiser, he spends 61 minutes on an elliptical trainer. By his reckoning, it is Day 2,572 in a row without missing a cardiovascular workout.

The allies

In spite of his pugnacity—or maybe because of it—Weinstein has enlisted a growing number of big-name allies.

The guest of honor at the party in Arlington is Joe Wilson, a career diplomat whose criticism of the Bush administration's rationale for war in Iraq led to the unmasking of his wife, Valerie Plame, as a CIA officer and, ultimately, to perjury charges against I. Lewis "Scooter" Libby, Vice President Cheney's former chief of staff.

He and Weinstein are natural allies, Wilson explains, "because I'm fighting the neo-cons, and he's fighting the theo-cons."

The party, held in the posh apartment of a Weinstein cousin, is the first event organized for the new foundation by David Rosen, once the campaign finance director for Sen. Hillary Clinton (D-N.Y.) and now Weinstein's chief fundraiser. After deliberating for just five hours, a jury acquitted Rosen last year of underreporting the cost of an August 2000 Hollywood gala in honor of Hillary and Bill Clinton.

Among the guests in Arlington are several members of Weinstein's advisory board, which he has stocked with retired senior officers and decorated combat veterans that he says the Pentagon cannot simply dismiss as "Chardonnay-sipping liberals." Its luminaries include retired Air Force Gen. Robert T. Herres, who was the first vice chairman of the Joint Chiefs of Staff; retired Vice Adm. Bernard Kauderer, former commander of the Pacific submarine fleet; and retired Air Force Col. Richard Klass, who won a Silver Star as a pilot in Vietnam.

Some of them think Weinstein is over the top. And they like it.

"It's sort of like Howard Dean and the 2004 campaign," Klass says. "It took someone like him to get out in front and bring the issue to people's attention. If this is going to be a long, hard slog—which I'm afraid it is—maybe some years down the line we'll need someone who's more politic than Mikey. But at this stage I think it absolutely requires hell-raising.... You can't have a man in a gray flannel suit as the point man on this issue right now."

The military has been a path of upward mobility for Weinstein's family, as for so many others. His father grew up poor, enlisted in the Navy as a teenager and got into the Naval Academy through its prep school; one of his close buddies in the class of 1953 at Annapolis was H. Ross Perot.

Weinstein himself was born on an Air Force base. The military gave him his entire education, including at the University of the Pacific McGeorge School of Law. After 10 years in the JAG corps and three years in the Reagan White House, he went to work for his father's old friend, becoming general counsel of Perot Systems Corp. in 1988. During the 1990s, Weinstein launched a series of his own ventures. Last year, he rejoined Perot as a director of business development.

Judging by his taste in cars, Weinstein appears to have plenty of disposable income, but he declines to discuss his finances: "I'm wealthy in the love I have for my family, that's all I'll say."

He is more forthcoming about the battle's emotional toll. His sons have stopped giving interviews to the media. Bonnie, who has multiple sclerosis, has been diagnosed with a painful, stress-induced jaw disorder. Since anonymous callers began leaving threats on their home telephone, they now live with two attack-trained German shepherds. But Mikey is not about to duck a fight.

"When somebody threatens me," he says, "I usually tell them to pack a picnic lunch and stand in line."

*C*onsider the source and the audience.

- The *Washington Post* is read by a mainstream national audience and by Washington insiders. Does the author sound sympathetic to Mikey Weinstein's cause?
- How might Weinstein be portrayed differently in a more conservative or rural outlet?

*L*ay out the argument, the values, and the assumptions.

- Weinstein's argument begins with the First Amendment. What does he think is the most important part of Americans' religious freedoms?
- What does he think is wrong with evangelical Christians being allowed to recruit in the military?
- Weinstein has a military background and has worked for a Republican administration. Is any part of his argument inconsistent with traditional conservative ideology?

*U*ncover the evidence.

- What evidence does Weinstein accumulate to persuade the court that religious pressure is brought to bear in the military?
- Did the Air Force's internal inquiry dispute that evidence?

*E*valuate the conclusion.

- Weinstein believes that the dominance and active recruitment of evangelical Christians in the military amounts to religious discrimination against non-Christians and that the civil liberties of military personnel are being infringed. He is also concerned that the war on terror begins to look like the Crusades when it is waged against Muslims by a self-proclaimed Christian army. His opponents believe they are within their rights. How can a court decide which conclusion is right?

*S*ort out the political implications.

- Why did the founders put the establishment clause in the Bill of Rights? What would a nation look like in which everyone could practice religious freedom without restraint?

4.2 Gay Marriage Looms as "Battle of Our Times"

Jane Lampman, Christian Science Monitor

Why We Chose This Piece

The establishment clause of the First Amendment that we discussed in reading the previous selection means that the state cannot enshrine religious views in public policy, and if a group wants to promote a view that denies Americans fundamental rights, the group runs the risk of losing federal support, lest the state subsidize that particular religious belief.

Conflicts other than those faced by Mikey Weinstein can result. In 1983 Bob Jones University, a fundamentalist Christian school that did not allow interracial dating, lost its tax-exempt status. As this article makes clear, the growing acceptance of gay rights is raising similar issues. As civil laws in America become more accepting of gay rights, conservative Christian groups whose members believe that homosexuality is a sin are claiming that being forced to observe those laws threatens their religious freedom. What is really at stake in the dispute between fundamentalist Christians and the supporters of gay rights?

The battle over same-sex marriage is shaping into something more than deep societal tradition vs. civil rights. It is becoming a conflict of equality vs. religious liberty.

As gays make gains, some religious institutions are coming under pressure. For instance:

- A Christian high school in Wildomar, Calif., is being sued for expelling two students on suspicion of being lesbian. The parents' suit claims that the school is a business under state civil rights law, which prohibits discrimination based on sexual orientation.

Selection published: June 1, 2006

- Catholic Charities in Boston, where same-sex marriage is legal, recently shuttered its adoption agency rather than serve gay and lesbian couples in conflict with church teaching. The church's request for a religious waiver from state antidiscrimination rules has made no headway.
- Christian clubs at several universities are fighting to maintain school recognition while restricting their leadership to those who conform to their beliefs on homosexuality.

Meanwhile, the Christian Legal Society and similar groups are mounting a national effort to challenge antidiscrimination policies in court, claiming they end up discriminating against conservative Christians.

"The fight over same-sex marriage—and two very different conceptions of the ordering of society—will be a knock-down, drag-out battle," predicts Marc Stern, a religious liberty attorney at the American Jewish Congress.

Both sides are pursuing their agendas in state legislatures, courts, and public schools. Both sides tend to view the struggle as a zero-sum, society-defining conflict. For supporters of gay marriage, it represents the last stage in America's long road to equality, from racial to gender to sexual equality. For opponents, traditional marriage stands as the God-ordained bedrock of society, essential to the well-being of children and the healthy functioning of the community.

While no one expects the courts to force unwilling clergy to perform weddings for same-sex couples, some see a possibility that religious groups (other than houses of worship) could lose their tax-exempt status for not conforming to public policy, as did fundamentalist Bob Jones University, over racial issues in 1983.

Legal experts of various views met last December, hosted by the Becket Fund, a nonpartisan institute promoting religious free expression, to consider the implications of same-sex marriage for religious liberty.

Writing about the conference in *The Weekly Standard*, Maggie Gallagher quoted participants as seeing the coming litigation as "a train wreck," "a collision course," and "the battle of our times."

To ameliorate such conflict, some insist that, given the nation's commitment to both equal rights and religious liberty, accommodations must be found.

"This set of issues tests us in new ways, and I don't think either side is going to win the day," says Charles Haynes, of the First Amendment Center in Washington, in an interview. "For the foreseeable future, we are going to be living with two important claims, and we have to find ways to protect the rights of people on all sides."

Douglas Laycock, of the University of Texas Law School, suggests a modification to the current joint administration of marriage by the state and religious groups.

"We can never resolve the debate over same-sex marriage until we separate legal marriage from religious marriage," he says in a conference paper. "The state should administer legal marriage, and its rules...should be made through the political process. Religious organizations should administer religious marriages," making their own rules. The legal relationship "could be called 'civil union' for gays and straights alike."

Ms. Gallagher, head of the Institute for Marriage and Public Policy, worries about any delegalizing of marriage. "That would be a good solution if there weren't a great public purpose to marriage that needs legal support to sustain.... If you chop it into pieces, that's a powerful statement by the law that there's no important purpose to marriage as a public institution."

The most immediate skirmish in the battle takes place next week, when the U.S. Senate will debate and possibly vote on a federal constitutional amendment defining marriage as only between a man and a woman. While the amendment may not gain the needed two-thirds majority, the debate positions the issue as a hot-button topic for the coming political campaign.

Religious leaders on both sides of the Marriage Protection Amendment have formed coalitions, demonstrating that religious perceptions vary considerably.

Some 50 leaders from Roman Catholic, Mormon, Southern Baptist, Orthodox, Evangelical, and Orthodox Jewish traditions formed the Religious Coalition for Marriage, focused on strengthening its traditional role in society. They see the amendment as essential to protect "marriage from...activist courts determined to reinterpret this fundamental institution...against the will of the American people," says Richard Land, a leader of the Southern Baptist Convention.

(A recent Gallup poll found 58 percent of Americans opposing same-sex marriage and 39 percent favoring it. The country is split on a constitutional amendment: 50 percent in favor, 47 percent opposed.)

On the other side, Clergy for Fairness—including leaders from mainline Protestant and Reform Jewish denominations—says that people of faith disagree on same-sex marriage and that religious denominations, not the federal government, should decide whether they'll sanctify marriages. The group also says it opposes the amendment because it would mark the first time the Constitution would be used "to restrict the rights of an entire group of Americans."

Chai Feldblum, a Georgetown University law professor active on gay rights issues, argues that the government should view both heterosexuality and homosexuality as morally neutral—"though how you 'deploy' your sexual activity can be very morally laden," she says.

"It's an incredible stain on the government that it is denying governmental structures for loving relationships and families," she adds. Yet she acknowledges the genuine difficulty that same-sex marriage presents for some religious people.

"I'd like gay people to understand that when religious people have to do something against their belief," Professor Feldblum says, "that impinges on their deep sense of self, just as I would like religious people to understand that when gay people are told they...can't marry their loved one, that impinges on that person's deep sense of self."

She's wary of granting religious waivers on these issues, however.

In Gallagher's view, "We are in a situation where courts are declaring our great historic, cross-cultural understanding of marriage to be a form of bigotry. That's a very destructive message," when research shows that children do much better in households with a mother and a father.

Others worry about the harm litigation battles could do. "People on both sides see this as good vs. evil," says the First Amendment Center's Dr. Haynes, "and those positions are going to tear us apart, deeply hurt the nation and our commitment to civil rights and religious freedom."

Haynes has just worked with groups on both sides to develop sexual-orientation guidelines for public schools.

"I've been involved in brokering nine different guidelines on issues like the Bible and religious holidays, and this has been the hardest," Haynes says. After eight months, Christian educators and a gay group involved in school issues did agree on a process for local districts to use that each side thought was fair. Whether local districts pick up on the guidelines remains to be seen.

Clamor over textbooks, for example, has erupted in Massachusetts and in Canada, where kindergartners are being introduced to stories about families with same-sex parents. Although schools must reflect the legal status of such relationships in the curriculum, some parents are demanding notice and protections.

"Some will ask why those parents should be given consideration," Haynes says. "The answer is that this is America, and we try to do the best we can to protect the religious liberty of even the smallest minority.... This takes more work than simply saying 'winner takes all.'"

Yet who is going to broker common ground is the question as advocates on both sides seek complete victory. Legal experts expect a patchwork of legislation and court decisions to emerge.

"Then we will have to worry about how to deal with the fact we have different rules in different states," Mr. Stern says. "If two or three big states move to same-sex marriage, however, it's not going to work to have different definitions across the U.S."

*C*onsider the source and the audience.

- The source of this article is the *Christian Science Monitor*, one of the most respected newspapers in the country and winner of seven Pulitzer Prizes. It has no overt religious purpose, though its founding mission was "to injure no man, but to bless all mankind." Would you expect the fact that the paper is owned by the First Church of Christ, Scientist, to affect the content of this article? How?
- How might the article look different if it appeared elsewhere?

*L*ay out the argument, the values, and the assumptions.

- What is at stake in the clash between those demanding equal rights and those demanding religious freedom? Why does one source say it goes to people's "deep sense of self?"
- How can both sides see it as a fight between good and evil?

*U*ncover the evidence.

- Does either side offer evidence that its side is right? What kind of evidence is relevant here?
- Can one side be "proven to be right?"

*E*valuate the conclusion.

- Why do sources say that this is not a "winner-take-all" conflict? Are they right?
- What kind of solution do the sources in the story point to? Is accommodation possible? If fundamental identity is at stake, can each side afford to give in at all?

*S*ort out the political implications.

- If some kind of common ground is to be found, who is to find it, especially when one side rejects the decisions of what they call "activist courts?"

4.3 At Guantanamo, Dying Is Not Permitted

Adam Zagorin, Time *magazine Web exclusive*

Why We Chose This Piece

Wartime raises special issues with regard to civil liberties. How many freedoms do we give up to keep ourselves safe? And what about prisoners of war—are they entitled to the same protections we give our own citizens? Generally we answer yes, because we want our own warriors to be protected by our enemies, but since the start of the war on terror, waged since September 11, 2001, the United States has played by different rules.

The treatment of prisoners held in Guantanamo Bay, Cuba, is a case in point. The Supreme Court has stepped in to guarantee some protections, but as this Time *article makes clear, many civil liberties issues remained, even after President Obama decided to close down the prisons there. The controversy over force feeding prisoners, and prisoners who have not actually been charged, is a particularly interesting one. Do these prisoners have any of the basic rights of criminal defendants or even those convicted of crimes, like a protection against cruel and inhuman punishment? Do they have fundamental rights to privacy? To life? To death?*

The prisoners at Guantanamo Bay, Cuba, won a major victory this week when the Supreme Court struck down the Bush administration's planned military tribunals. But for many prisoners at the detention facility, the protests haven't stopped. Hunger strikes persist, in what Guantanamo commander Rear Adm. Harry Harris, Jr. has called "asymmetric warfare"—a means to attract attention to their increasingly controversial detention. As a result, the camp's administrators have sought to keep prisoners alive at all cost—because a prisoner's death (as the U.S. found out three weeks ago, when three Gitmo inmates committed suicide) can be a major embarrassment for the U.S. and add fuel to widespread demands for the facility to be shut down.

Civil-liberties advocates point out that Guantanamo's 460 inmates have few other means to make their voices heard, given that most have been detained for more than four years without even being charged with a crime. Indeed, though the U.S. has condemned the hunger strikers at Gitmo, just last year the White House hailed a hunger-striking Iranian dissident for showing "that he is willing to die for his right to express his opinion."

At Gitmo, however, dead prisoners are something the U.S. military wishes devoutly to avoid. So force-feeding has been standard policy at the camp ever since hunger strikes began in early 2002. The facility's top physicians have also told *TIME* that prisoners who resist are subjected to especially harsh methods. In one case, according to medical records obtained by *TIME*, a 20-year-old named Yusuf al-Shehri, jailed since

Selection published: June 30, 2006

he was 16, was regularly strapped into a specially designed feeding chair that immobilizes the body at the legs, arms, shoulders and head. Then a plastic tube that is 50% larger, and more painful to insert, than the commonly used variety was inserted up through his nose and down his throat, carrying a nutritional formula into his stomach.

Thousands of people, of course, endure some form of voluntary intra-nasal feeding every day in hospital settings. But when force-feeding is involuntary and the recipient is in a state of high anxiety, the muscles tense up and the procedure can trigger nausea, bleeding, diarrhea and vomiting. "We are humane and compassionate," Guantanamo commander Harris told *TIME*, "but if we tell a detainee to do something, we expect the detainee to do it." As a note scrawled in al-Shehri's medical records put it: "[The prisoner] was informed that dying is not permitted."

Before this year, the feeding chair—marketed as a "padded cell on wheels" by its Iowa manufacturer—was evidently used sparingly. In comments several months ago, SOUTHCOM commander Gen. Bantz Craddock, who oversees Gitmo, joked that at least hunger strikers got to choose the color of their feeding tube (yellow was a favorite), and the flavor of the lozenges used to soothe throats irritated by the feeding tubes. "Look, they get choices," Craddock said at the time. And that's part of the problem. At the peak of a protest last fall, 131 protesters, or more than 25%, were on hunger strikes.

But in January, say lawyers for the prisoners and other critics of conditions there, camp overseers finally got fed up with protesters undermining camp discipline and overtaxing the medical staff, who often had to spend 15 hours a day feeding obstreperous inmates. Dr. Ronald Sollock, the camp's chief physician, told *TIME* bluntly that gentler force-feeding techniques of the past were a "failure." He says that without being strapped down, some inmates would try to pull out their nasal tubes, and even strike medical personnel. Worse, some continued to lose weight, by forcing themselves to vomit after being force-fed. "We had to take steps to prevent that, but we only do what is medically necessary in a humane and compassionate manner," says Sollock.

The tougher stance on feeding did have an effect on prisoners' willingness to go on hunger strikes. "A lot of detainees said, 'I don't want to put up with this. This is too much of a hassle,'" says Craddock. Asked whether the new methods represented an "effective deterrent" to hunger striking, he answered, "Yeah."

Officially, force-feeding at Gitmo is done with a tube 3 mm. (or about .1 in.) across, the same size used in American hospitals. In a sworn statement last year, Gitmo's top physician at the time, Dr. John Edmondson, noted that "smaller tubes which remained in the patient for longer periods were more comfortable [and] easier to manage for medical personnel."

Al-Shehri's medical records, however, document the use of the larger tubes, which experts say have no medical purpose in this context. Al-Shehri's lawyer has also filed court documents citing lesions and bleeding caused when guards held him by the chin and hair, strapped down, as a medical staffer "forcefully inserted the tube in his nose and down his throat." The lawyer also charges that al-Shehri was subject to verbal and religious abuse during force-feeding, asserting that the tubes "were viewed by the detainees as objects of torture." The records also show that instead of leaving the tube in place to avoid the possible trauma of repeated insertions, al-Shehri had his introduced and withdrawn at each of his two daily feedings.

And this leads to another problem. According to al-Shehri's records and Gitmo doctors, a typical feeding lasts about two hours, with the inmate left in the restraint chair for roughly 45 minutes afterward. During the feeding period, the prisoner will receive as much as 1.5 liters of formula, which, in the case of hunger strikers, can be more than their stomachs can comfortably hold. This can produce what is euphemistically called "dumping syndrome," an uncomfortable, even painful bout of nausea, vomiting, bloating, diarrhea, and shortness of breath. And those are precisely the symptoms that al-Shehri and many other force-fed prisoners have reported to their lawyers.

In March, as a result of these allegations, more than 250 medical professionals signed an open letter to the British medical journal *The Lancet*, demanding an end to force-feeding. They cited the code of ethics of the American Medical Association and the World Medical Association, both of which condemn the force-feeding of prisoners as an assault on human dignity—so long as they're capable of making an informed decision not to eat. But that's the conundrum: How do you know what is an informed decision at Gitmo? Are detainees there, who are imprisoned in an isolated environment far from their families for an indefinite period, capable of making a rational and autonomous choice to starve themselves?

The code of ethics has been put to the test several times in the past, most notably during the 1980s, when several Irish Republican Army prisoners staged hunger strikes in British prisons. A handful died, and the episode was seen as evidence of Margaret Thatcher's toughness. At Gitmo, however, the death of a prisoner could ignite riots in the Muslim world. In that context, the Pentagon believes that keeping detainees alive at all costs is very much in the nation's security interest.

It's equally in the prisoners' interests to have someone die. According to Col. Mike Bumgarner, who oversees the detention camps on a day-to-day basis, several prisoners have told him of a "vision, or a dream—implicitly a message from God—that if three detainees die it will attract enough attention so that they will all get out of Guantanamo." It needn't be by starvation: according to newly declassified documents, two prisoners, one of whom was al-Shehri, tried to commit suicide on May 18 by swallowing hoarded anti-anxiety medication. Those attempts triggered a search, which in turn led to the most serious rioting in the history of Camp Delta. And on May 29, yet another round of hunger strikes began. It started with 75 prisoners, rose to 89 a few days later, and then suddenly began to fade away. Recent communications by Gitmo inmates with their lawyers, and obtained by *TIME*, indicate that harsh force-feeding methods were used to end the hunger strikes. The military has offered no explanation for the drop-off in hunger strikers.

Bumgarner has said the prisoners' objective is to push the number of strikers above 100, as they did last fall. But additional medical personnel are ready to be shipped in to force-feed them if they do. "We used to over-react, and the detainees saw that we got worried if they were not eating," he says. "Now we have a system. I tell them, 'Have at it. If you want to have 460 hunger strikers, we'll get 460 doctors in here to take care of you.' They will not succeed."

Yet hunger strikers have already won a measure of success. In part because of their protests, and the attention focused on Guantanamo, the U.S. is facing growing criticism—from both allies and enemies—for the rules of detention at the camp. Now the Supreme Court's Hamdan decision effectively grants prisoners at least some of their longstanding demands, including more rights at trial. All the same, most of them are unlikely to be released soon. Indeed, authorities are currently constructing a new, state-of-the-art, $30 million prison at Guantanamo, where they plan to consolidate many of the camp's maximum-security inmates. Harris argues the camp will be needed for the foreseeable future, and that refusing to eat is not a cry for help, but a ploy drawn from the al-Qaeda playbook calculated to attract media attention and force the U.S. government to back down. "The will to resist of these detainees is high," says Harris. "They are waging their war, their jihad against America, and we just have to stop them."

*C*onsider the source and the audience.

- In writing for *Time*, Zagorin can expect to reach a broad national American audience that will presumably be concerned, but hardened by the events of September 11, 2001. How might this article have been received in, say, 2000?
- How might this article be read differently if it were published in another country?

*L*ay out the argument, the values, and the assumptions.

- Why do prisoners at Guantanamo Bay want to kill themselves?
- Why do U.S. officials want to prevent the suicide of prisoners? What measures do they take to ensure suicides do not take place? Are there any limits to how far they would go?
- What are the ethical issues that underlie the question of suicide, forced feeding, and humane treatment? How do these ethical issues fare when confronted with wartime reality? Does war trump ethics?

*U*ncover the evidence.

- How does Zagorin know what is going on at Guantanamo? Why would those sources be talking to him?
- Are Zagorin's sources balanced? Do we get a fair idea of both sides of the story?

*E*valuate the conclusion.

- U.S. officials suggest that prisoner suicide is an act of war, justifying warlike behavior on the part of the United States. Are they right? Do the benefits of denying these prisoners their rights outweigh the costs?
- Does the fact that these prisoners are captive and have not been charged change the calculation of what rights, if any, they are due?

*S*ort out the political implications.

- What kind of precedent is being set in Guantanamo? What do our actions there mean for future wars?
- What kind of protections of our soldiers can we expect in future wars?

4.4 Is Torture Ever Justified?

Terrorism and Civil Liberties

The Economist

Why We Chose This Piece

In the early months of 2009, a continuing debate about the place of torture in democratic societies took place between President Obama and the officials of his new administration on the one hand, and the defenders of George W. Bush's administration, in particular former vice president Dick Cheney, on the other. Obama insisted that protection of civil liberties is central to who we are, that only when we respect the rights of all can we be truly secure, as our bad treatment of prisoners helps strengthen recruitment of enemy combatants against us, and that in any case, torture has never been proved an effective way to get reliable information. Cheney argued just the opposite and said that we face a direct choice—that what he called "enhanced interrogation techniques" were necessary to keep us safe and by refusing to engage in them and by bringing some transparency to our previous use of them, Obama was risking the security of the nation.

Although this Economist *article was written in 2007, when Bush still had a year and a half to serve, it captures the issues at stake nicely. Can a debate such as this one ever be settled conclusively? How?*

In every war, information is a weapon. In a "war against terrorism," where the adversary wears no uniform and hides among the civilian population, information can matter even more. But does that mean that torture can sometimes be justified to extract information?

The answer in international law is categorical: no. As laid down in treaties such as the Geneva Conventions, the UN Convention against Torture and the International Covenant on Civil and Political Rights, the ban on torture or any cruel, inhuman or degrading treatment is absolute, even in times of war. Along with genocide, torture is the only crime that every state must punish, no matter who commits it or where. Defenders of this blanket prohibition offer arguments that range from the moral (torture degrades and corrupts the society that allows it) to the practical (people will say anything under torture so the information they provide is unreliable anyway).

The September 11th attacks have not driven any rich democracy to reverse itself and make torture legal. But they have encouraged the bending of definitions and the turning of blind eyes. There is a greater readiness among governments that would never practise torture themselves to use information which less squeamish states have obtained—through torture.

Selection published: September 22, 2007

Start with definitions. Most civilised people squirm at the thought of putting sus-pected terrorists on the rack or pulling off toenails. What if that prisoner knew the whereabouts of a ticking bomb—maybe a biological, chemical or even nuclear one? Wouldn't a little sleep deprivation, sexual humiliation or even water-dunking be justi-fied to save hundreds and perhaps thousands of lives? Whatever the law says, a lot of people seem to think so.

In a BBC survey of 27,000 people in 25 countries last October, more than one out of three people in nine of those countries, including America, considered a degree of torture acceptable if it saved lives. Opposition was highest in most European and English-speaking countries. . . . Another poll in 2005 by the Pew Research Centre found that nearly half of all Americans thought the torture of suspected terrorists was sometimes justified.

Two Republican presidential hopefuls, Rudy Giuliani and Mitt Romney, support the "enhanced" interrogation of suspects in the event of an imminent attack. Dick Cheney, America's vice-president, recently suggested that "dunking" a terrorist in water to save lives was a "no-brainer." The ensuing uproar led him to backtrack, claiming that he was not, of course, referring to "water-boarding," or simulated drowning, a technique regarded as tantamount to torture and banned in the American army's own interrogation manual.

One objection to allowing moderate physical pressure is the difficulty of knowing where to draw the line. If stress positions and sleep deprivation do not work, do you progress to branding with red-hot irons and beating to a pulp? And can you rely on interrogators to heed such distinctions? It is the danger of a slippery slope that makes opponents of torture insist on a total ban.

Israel is the only country in modern times to have openly allowed "moderate physi-cal pressure" as a "last resort." Since interrogators used such methods anyway, it was argued, passing an explicit law would at least make it possible to set out some limits. But in 1999, citing the slippery-slope argument, Israel's Supreme Court ruled that tor-ture could never be justified, even in the case of a ticking bomb. It went on to outlaw techniques such as sleep deprivation, exposure to extremes of hot and cold, prolonged stress positions, hooding and violent shaking.

In the 1970s Britain used similar techniques against suspected terrorists in North-ern Ireland. These were banned in 1978 following a case brought by the Republic of Ireland to the European Court of Human Rights. Although not torture, such methods did amount to inhumane treatment, the court ruled. In 2002 the International Crimi-nal Court for ex-Yugoslavia in The Hague decided that prolonged solitary confinement constituted torture. Such rulings did not prevent America from resorting to such harsh techniques when interrogating suspects in Afghanistan, Iraq and Guantánamo Bay, however. Former detainees in those places have spoken of severe beatings, water-boarding, excruciating stress positions, mock executions, sleep deprivation and much else besides.

Administration lawyers argued that since al-Qaeda and its Taliban allies were not a state party to the Geneva Conventions they were not covered by its ban on torture and other maltreatment. True, America had ratified (in 1988) the Convention against Tor-ture, but that applied only to acts carried out on American soil, they said. And though America's own 1994 federal statute against torture did cover acts by Americans abroad, this applied only to full-blown torture, not lesser abuses.

In the notorious "torture memos" drawn up by the Department of Justice and the Pentagon in 2002 and 2003, the same lawyers sought to restrict the normal definition of torture—"severe pain or suffering"—to extreme acts equivalent to "serious physical injury, organ failure, or even death." Furthermore, as a wartime commander in chief whose main duty was to protect the American people, the president had the power to override both domestic and international law, they argued. After being leaked in 2004 most of these memos were "withdrawn," though not the one on the president's wartime powers.

Mr Bush and his colleagues have always said that America neither authorises nor condones torture. "We don't do torture," the president famously said. But Mr Bush has been vaguer about the grey area between torture and more moderate pressure. Soon after suspected terrorists were first sent to Guantánamo in January 2002 he said that America's armed forces would treat the detainees "humanely" in a manner "consistent with the Geneva Conventions"—but only "to the extent appropriate and consistent with military necessity."

Not until the Supreme Court's ruling in Hamdan in 2006 did the administration accept that all detainees, wherever held, were protected by Common Article 3 of the Geneva Conventions, which bans all forms of cruel, inhuman or degrading treatment as well as torture. The 2005 Detainee Treatment Act, incorporating an amendment by Senator John McCain, already prohibited such treatment by American soldiers any-where in the world. But it did not apply to the CIA.

Yet it is the CIA that has been responsible for the "extraordinary rendition" of sus-pects to clandestine prisons in third countries for "enhanced" interrogation (whether by that country's agents or the CIA itself) amounting at times, many suspect, to torture. The programme's existence was not officially confirmed until Mr Bush announced last year the transfer to Guantánamo of the last 14 "high-value" detainees then being held in so-called "black sites" around the world. Of some 100 suspected terrorists believed to have been "rendered" over the past six years, 39 remain unaccounted for, Human Rights Watch, a New York-based lobby, says.

In July this year Mr Bush set out new broad guidelines for interrogations under a resumed CIA programme. He says the newly authorised techniques now comply fully with the Geneva Conventions' ban on "outrages upon personal dignity, in particular humiliating and degrading treatment" as well as torture. Even if true (which is hard to know because the details have not been disclosed), the programme itself with its enforced disappearances and black sites, which even the International Red Cross is not allowed to visit, violates basic tenets of international law.

Even if a country bans torture, how should it treat information that others have extracted this way? In 2004 Britain's Court of Appeal ruled that information acquired through torture was admissible as evidence in court. David Blunkett, then Britain's home secretary, welcomed the ruling. Although the government "unreservedly" con-demned torture, he said, it would be "irresponsible not to take appropriate account of any information which could help protect national security and public safety." But the ruling was later overturned by the House of Lords.

A separate question is whether governments should use information extracted under torture by others for counter-terrorist purposes, even if it is not admissible as evidence. Most probably agree with Mr Blunkett that it would be irresponsible not to. But a case can be made that this is, in effect, condoning the use of torture by allies.

Britain has also run into trouble when trying to deport suspected foreign terrorists against whom it has not got enough evidence to secure a conviction in court. Under international law, a country must make sure that the person it wishes to expel is not in danger of being tortured or subjected to other abuse in the receiving country. In 2005 the UN's special rapporteur on torture criticised Britain for relying on "diplomatic assurances" that deportees would not be tortured. Charles Clarke, who had succeeded Mr Blunkett as home secretary, retorted that the rights of the victims of the London Tube bombings that year mattered more than those of the perpetrators. The UN should "look at human rights in the round," he said, "rather than simply focusing all the time on the terrorist." Fine—except that no British court had convicted these suspects as terrorists.

To date, 144 countries have ratified the Convention against Torture. (The hold-outs include such usual suspects as Sudan, North Korea, Myanmar and Zimbabwe, but also India.) And yet, the UN's special rapporteur told the Security Council in June, torture remains widespread. Amnesty International noted cases of state-sponsored torture or other inhumane treatment in 102 of the 153 countries included in its 2007 report. The worst offenders were China, Egypt (both of which are parties to the convention), Myanmar and North Korea, along with several African countries. America's transgressions are trivial by comparison. The worry, argues Kenneth Roth, director of Human Rights Watch, is that when America breaks the rules it encourages others to do the same.

Why does torture endure? Part of the reason, argues Michael Ignatieff, a Canadian writer, may be that it is at times motivated not so much by a desire to extract vital information but by something baser, such as an urge to inflict pain, exact revenge, or even just for fun. That seems to have been part of the motivation of the Americans who abused prisoners in Abu Ghraib, for example. But torture may also endure because it sometimes works.

Many critics of torture claim that it is ineffective as well as repugnant. Since people will say anything just to stop the pain, the information gleaned may not be reliable. On the other hand, if people do say anything under torture, you might expect some of what they say to be true and therefore—if those being tortured really are terrorists— useful to the authorities. Torture certainly helped induce Guy Fawkes to betray his co-conspirators after they had tried to blow up King James I and the British Parliament on November 5th 1605.

Asked recently about the CIA's use of enhanced interrogation in secret prisons, George Tenet, the CIA's director until 2004, replied that the agency's widely condemned rendition programme had saved lives, disrupted plots and provided "invaluable" information in the war against terrorism. Indeed, while denying the use of full-blown torture, he said that the programme on its own was "worth more than the FBI, the CIA and the National Security Agency put together have been able to tell us."

Mr Ignatieff, for his own part, sees no trumping argument on behalf of terrorists that makes their claims to human rights and dignity prevail over the security interests— and right to life—of the majority. Yet he continues to advocate a total ban. "We cannot torture, in other words, because of who we are," he says. He knows that many will disagree.

*C*onsider the source and the audience.

- *The Economist* is an international newsmagazine, with a clear free-market, free-trade bent that usually manifests itself as a more conservative-libertarian point of view. How might that affect an article that, though about a general issue, is clearly focused on the behavior of the United States?

*L*ay out the argument, the values, and the assumptions.

- This article doesn't make its own argument about torture, but it tries to illuminate the strands of several arguments that are already out there. What is the argument made by those who blur the definition of torture? What value do those people put a priority on?
- What argument is made by people who say that we cannot torture because of "who we are?" What value do they prioritize?
- Is there any middle ground here, or are there any shades of gray? What are they?

*U*ncover the evidence.

- What sorts of evidence does *The Economist* provide? What kind of evidence would you need to show that torture "works?"
- Does the "who we are" argument require any evidence?

*E*valuate the conclusion.

- *The Economist* carefully refrains from drawing a conclusion in this piece. What conclusions do you draw based on what you have read? Is torture ever justified? Can we torture and remain true to ourselves?

*S*ort out the political implications.

- The United States has clearly engaged in activities that its critics define as torture and that even its friends say enters a gray area. How has that changed how we are viewed in the world? Does it make us stronger or weaker in the war on terror?

 ## 4.5 *Federalist* No. 84

Alexander Hamilton, **The Federalist Papers**

Why We Chose This Piece

> *The original text of the Constitution contained no Bill of Rights, and that would almost be its undoing. Fearful of a strong central government, the Anti-Federalists insisted that they would not vote to ratify the Constitution unless it contained some built-in limitations to its*

Selection published: May 28, 1788

own power. In Federalist No. 84, the second-to-last of The Federalist Papers, Alexander Hamilton was busy tying up loose ends that had not been dealt with in previous essays. It was here that he chose to rebut the Anti-Federalist claim that a Bill of Rights was needed. It was not necessary, he argued, because many of the state constitutions admired by the Anti-Federalists did not have bills of rights, and in any case the text of the Constitution had many rights built in, among them the protection against the suspension of habeas corpus, the prohibition against bills of attainder and ex post facto laws, and the entitlement to trial by jury.

Hamilton went further than arguing that a Bill of Rights was unnecessary, however. In the excerpt reprinted here, he claimed that it was actually dangerous to liberty. Are we freer or less free than we were at the time of the founding?

It has been several times truly remarked that bills of rights are, in their origin, stipulations between kings and their subjects, abridgements of prerogative in favor of privilege, reservations of rights not surrendered to the prince. Such was MAGNA CHARTA, obtained by the barons, sword in hand, from King John. Such were the subsequent confirmations of that charter by succeeding princes. Such was the PETITION OF RIGHT assented to by Charles I, in the beginning of his reign. Such, also, was the Declaration of Right presented by the Lords and Commons to the Prince of Orange in 1688, and afterwards thrown into the form of an act of parliament called the Bill of Rights. It is evident, therefore, that, according to their primitive signification, they have no application to constitutions professedly founded upon the power of the people, and executed by their immediate representatives and servants. Here, in strictness, the people surrender nothing; and as they retain every thing they have no need of particular reservations. "WE, THE PEOPLE of the United States, to secure the blessings of liberty to ourselves and our posterity, do ORDAIN and ESTABLISH this Constitution for the United States of America." Here is a better recognition of popular rights, than volumes of those aphorisms which make the principal figure in several of our State bills of rights, and which would sound much better in a treatise of ethics than in a constitution of government.

But a minute detail of particular rights is certainly far less applicable to a Constitution like that under consideration, which is merely intended to regulate the general political interests of the nation, than to a constitution which has the regulation of every species of personal and private concerns. If, therefore, the loud clamors against the plan of the convention, on this score, are well founded, no epithets of reprobation will be too strong for the constitution of this State. But the truth is, that both of them contain all which, in relation to their objects, is reasonably to be desired.

I go further, and affirm that bills of rights, in the sense and to the extent in which they are contended for, are not only unnecessary in the proposed Constitution, but would even be dangerous. They would contain various exceptions to powers not granted; and, on this very account, would afford a colorable pretext to claim more than were granted. For why declare that things shall not be done which there is no power to do? Why, for instance, should it be said that the liberty of the press shall not be restrained, when no power is given by which restrictions may be imposed? I will not contend that such a provision would confer a regulating power; but it is evident that it would furnish, to men disposed to usurp, a plausible pretense for claiming that power. They might urge with a semblance of reason, that the Constitution ought not to be charged with the absurdity of providing against the abuse of an authority which was not given, and that the provision against restraining the liberty of the press afforded a clear implication, that a power to prescribe proper regulations concerning it was intended to be vested in the national government. This may serve as a specimen of the numerous handles which would be given to the doctrine of constructive powers, by the indulgence of an injudicious zeal for bills of rights.

On the subject of the liberty of the press, as much as has been said, I cannot forbear adding a remark or two: in the first place, I observe, that there is not a syllable concerning it in the constitution of this State; in the next, I contend, that whatever has been said about it in that of any other State, amounts to nothing. What signifies a declaration, that "the liberty of the press shall be inviolably preserved?" What is the liberty of the press? Who can give it any definition which would not leave the utmost latitude for evasion? I hold it to be impracticable; and from this I infer, that its security, whatever fine declarations may be inserted in any constitution respecting it, must altogether depend on public opinion, and on the general spirit of the people and of the government. And here, after all, as is intimated upon another occasion, must we seek for the only solid basis of all our rights.

There remains but one other view of this matter to conclude the point. The truth is, after all the declamations we have heard, that the Constitution is itself, in every rational sense, and to every useful purpose, A BILL OF RIGHTS. The several bills of rights in Great Britain form its Constitution, and conversely the constitution of each State is its bill of rights. And the proposed Constitution, if adopted, will be the bill of rights of the Union. Is it one object of a bill of rights to declare and specify the political privileges of the citizens in the structure and administration of the government? This is done in the most ample and precise manner in the plan of the convention; comprehending various precautions for the public security, which are not to be found in any of the State constitutions. Is another object of a bill of rights to define certain immunities and modes of proceeding, which are relative to personal and private concerns? This we have seen has also been attended to, in a variety of cases, in the same plan. Adverting therefore to the substantial meaning of a bill of rights, it is absurd to allege that it is not to be found in the work of the convention. It may be said that it does not go far enough, though it will not be easy to make this appear; but it can with no propriety be contended that there is no such thing. It certainly must be immaterial what mode is observed as to the order of declaring the rights of the citizens, if they are to be found in any part of the instrument which establishes the government. And hence it must be apparent, that much of what has been said on this subject rests merely on verbal and nominal distinctions, entirely foreign from the substance of the thing.

*C*onsider the source and the audience.

- Hamilton was directing this essay to staunch opponents of the Constitution, and on this point, at least, they were winning. He was also speaking to citizens of New York who admired their own state constitution. How did these considerations shape the way he framed his argument?

Lay out the argument, the values, and the assumptions.

- How powerful a government did Hamilton believe was established by the Constitution?
- Why did he think a Bill of Rights would be unnecessary?
- Why did he think it would be dangerous? What mischief would be done if the government were told it was not allowed to do things it didn't have the power to do anyway?

Uncover the evidence.

- Hamilton used historical evidence to discuss why bills of rights had existed in the past. Did that evidence have anything to do with the case he was discussing?
- How did he use logic to make the case that a Bill of Rights was dangerous?

Evaluate the conclusion.

- Did Hamilton persuade you that a Bill of Rights would empower government officials to argue that government had all the powers not specifically listed in a written Bill of Rights? Would the burden be on us to prove that we had any rights other than those listed?

Sort out the political implications.

- Today many Americans argue that we have a right to privacy. People who interpret the Constitution strictly, as did many members of the Bush administration, believe that we have only the rights that are written down in the Constitution. How does this debate relate to Hamilton's argument here?

★ *★* 5 *★* ★

Civil Rights

For all the lip service we pay to the principle that "all men are created equal," American history has been a story of exclusion from the very beginning. The early colonies excluded people from political power who were not members of the right church, or who did not have the right amount of land or the right sum of money in their pockets. At various times we have excluded people from the rights of American citizenship because of the color of their skin, their gender, the country in which they were born, or the language they spoke. Today groups like the disabled, gays and lesbians, and noncitizens still find themselves excluded from access to some of the basic rights that others in America enjoy. The search for equality in the United States has been a perennial theme of those who stand outside the charmed circle of the privileged and the free, fighting hard to get their share of the American dream.

We call the battle for equality in this country a battle for civil rights—citizenship rights guaranteed by the Constitution or, when the Constitution has not been specific enough to protect some groups, its provisions in the Thirteenth, Fourteenth, Fifteenth, Nineteenth, and Twenty-sixth Amendments. The struggle for civil rights that produced those amendments and the laws that enforce them has been harrowing and long because so much is at stake. Rights are more than words on paper—they are political power. To deny people the right to do something is to have power over them and make them conform to your will. If they gain rights despite your efforts, they have acquired power to stop you from doing what you want. People fight furiously to restrict and to gain rights because they care so deeply about who shall have the power to decide what kind of society we live in—whose will counts and whose does not.

Groups that fight for civil rights—for recognition of their will and inclusion in the system—are handicapped from the start by the fact that, by definition, they are outside the system in significant ways. The initial challenge these groups face is finding an arena in which they can begin their fight. Consider the plight of African Americans after the Civil War, which officially ended slavery. The southern states had shut blacks out of political power; the justices on the Supreme Court had previously refused to consider them as potential citizens and within several decades would declare that segregation was legal; Congress refused to pass legislation enforcing the newly passed Thirteenth, Fourteenth, and Fifteenth Amendments; and the president, himself a southerner, had no interest in protecting their newfound rights. It took nearly a hundred years—until the composition of the Supreme Court changed sufficiently to be receptive to a brilliant legal strategy mapped out by the National Association for the Advancement of Colored People—for African Americans to get a toehold in the courts, and into the political arena where the fight for enforcement of their civil rights could eventually be won. Civil rights struggles are very much about politics, about using the rules of the system to change public opinion, to change the laws, and to change the way the laws are enforced.

In this chapter we look at the civil rights battles still being fought by various groups in the political, legal, and cultural arenas. The first selection, from the *New York Times*, looks at the continued segregation of some high school proms in the South. It raises the difficult question of how private discrimination should be handled. The second piece, from the conservative *National Review Online*, looks at gender equality in the schools and argues that the efforts to make things more equal for girls ignores a growing inequality for boys. The third article, also directed to a conservative audience, argues that gay political groups exploit the issue of race when they call for equal rights to marry, and that that language should be reserved for blacks only. Finally, for our classic statement about civil rights, we look at the speech given by then-candidate Barack Obama during his race for the Democratic nomination. He argues that we need to break our stalemate when it comes to discussing race. Have we done that? What does Obama's election as president say about race in America today?

 ## 5.1 A Prom Divided

Sara Corbett, New York Times

Why We Chose This Piece

In the 1950s the Supreme Court declared that the doctrine of separate but equal was unconstitutional. When it came to education, the court ruled in Brown v. Board of Education *that the very act of separation created inequality, so that separate was unequal by definition. Black students, forced to go to separate schools, felt inferior, and consequently the education they received was inferior.*

A half-century later, most of us think that the issue of legal segregation of public facilities is dead. As this article from the New York Times *reveals, however, some unsettled gray areas remain that look like a throwback to a more racist past. At some southern high schools, separate junior-senior proms are held for white students and black students,*

Selection published: May 21, 2009

despite black student requests to merge them. In the case described here, the white students say it's their parents' choice, not their own, to hold a whites-only prom. Since both proms are held outside of school, they are private, not subject to civil rights laws. What do you think should be the school district's response to these separate proms?

About now, high-school seniors everywhere slip into a glorious sort of limbo. Waiting out the final weeks of the school year, they begin rightfully to revel in the shared thrill of moving on. It is no different in south-central Georgia's Montgomery County, made up of a few small towns set between fields of wire grass and sweet onion. The music is turned up. Homework languishes. The future looms large. But for the 54 students in the class of 2009 at Montgomery County High School, so, too, does the past. On May 1—a balmy Friday evening—the white students held their senior prom. And the following night—a balmy Saturday—the black students had theirs.

Racially segregated proms have been held in Montgomery County—where about two-thirds of the population is white—almost every year since its schools were integrated in 1971. Such proms are, by many accounts, longstanding traditions in towns across the rural South, though in recent years a number of communities have successfully pushed for change. When the actor Morgan Freeman offered to pay for last year's first-of-its-kind integrated prom at Charleston High School in Mississippi, his home state, the idea was quickly embraced by students—and rejected by a group of white parents, who held a competing "private" prom. (The effort is the subject of a documentary, "Prom Night in Mississippi," which will be shown on HBO in July.) The senior proms held by Montgomery County High School students—referred to by many students as "the black-folks prom" and "the white-folks prom"—are organized outside school through student committees with the help of parents. All students are welcome at the black prom, though generally few if any white students show up. The white prom, students say, remains governed by a largely unspoken set of rules about who may come. Black members of the student council say they have asked school administrators about holding a single school-sponsored prom, but that, along with efforts to collaborate with white prom planners, has failed. According to Timothy Wiggs, the outgoing student council president and one of 21 black students graduating this year, "We just never get anywhere with it." Principal Luke Smith says the school has no plans to sponsor a prom, noting that when it did so in 1995, attendance was poor.

Students of both races say that interracial friendships are common at Montgomery County High School. Black and white students also date one another, though often out of sight of judgmental parents. "Most of the students do want to have a prom together," says Terra Fountain, a white 18-year-old who graduated from Montgomery County High School last year and is now living with her black boyfriend. "But it's the white parents who say no.... They're like, if you're going with the black people, I'm not going to pay for it."

"It's awkward," acknowledges JonPaul Edge, a senior who is white. "I have as many black friends as I do white friends. We do everything else together. We hang out. We play sports together. We go to class together. I don't think anybody at our school is racist." Trying to explain the continued existence of segregated proms, Edge falls back on the same reasoning offered by a number of white students and their parents. "It's how it's always been," he says. "It's just a tradition."

Earlier this month, on the Friday night of the white prom, Kera Nobles, a senior who is black, and six of her black classmates drove over to the local community center where it was being held. Standing amid a crowd of about 80 parents, siblings and grandparents, they snapped pictures and whooped appreciatively as their white friends—blow-dried, boutonniered and glittering in a way that only high-school seniors can—did their "senior walk," parading in elegant pairs into the prom. "We got stared at a little, being there," said one black student, "but it wasn't too bad."

After the last couple were announced, after they watched the white people's father-daughter dance and then, along with the other bystanders, were ushered by chaperones out the door, Kera and her friends piled into a nearby KFC to eat. Whatever elation they felt for their dressed-up classmates was quickly wearing off.

"My best friend is white," said one senior girl, a little glumly. "She's in there. She's real cool, but I don't understand. If they can be in there, why can't everybody else?"

The seven teenagers—a mix of girls and boys—slowly worked their way through two buckets of fried chicken. They cracked jokes about the white people's prom ("I feel bad for them! Their prom is lame!"). They puzzled merrily over white girls' devotion both to tanning beds ("You don't like black people, but you're working your hardest to get as brown as I am!") and also to the very boys who were excluded from the dance ("Half of those girls, when they get home, they're gonna text a black boy"). They mused about whether white parents really believed that by keeping black people out of the prom, it would keep them out of their children's lives ("You think there aren't going to be black boys at college?"). And finally, more somberly, they questioned their white friends' professed helplessness in the face of their parents' prejudice ("You're 18 years old! You're old enough to smoke, drive, do whatever else you want to. Why aren't you able to step up and say, 'I want to have my senior prom with the people I'm graduating with?'").

It was getting late now. KFC was closing. Another black teenager was mopping the floor nearby. A couple of the boys mentioned they had to wash their cars in the morning. Kera had an early hair appointment. The next night, they would dress up and dance raucously for four hours before tumbling back outside, one step closer to graduating. In the meantime, a girl named Angel checked her cellphone to see if any of the white kids had texted from inside their prom. They hadn't. Angel shrugged. "I really don't understand," she said. "Because I'm thinking that these people love me and I love them, but I don't know. Tonight's a different story."

Consider the source and the audience.

- The *New York Times* is a northern paper, writing for a national audience, albeit probably a more liberal one. How might the article be written differently in a southern newspaper? Or would it be written at all?

Lay out the argument, the values, and the assumptions.

- In her article, Corbett doesn't make an argument in her own voice, though she clearly makes a tacit, or implied, argument. In whose voice is this argument made?
- Whose "side" would you say Corbett is on? What does she think of separate proms, and why? How can you tell? Can you guess what values underlie her thinking?

*U*ncover the evidence.

- Corbett interviews both white and black students for this article, but she spends time only with the black students during the white prom, not the other way around. How does the conversation she reports support her tacit argument?
- Who else might she have interviewed? Why do no parents appear in this story?

*E*valuate the conclusion.

- Corbett shows that the black students would like to join the white prom and that they question the nature of their friendships with those white students who let their parents dictate the two-prom system. The implication is that this practice is a racist one, a throwback to a racist past. Is that the correct conclusion?
- If the parents are still acting in a racist fashion, are their children doing the same if they fail to repudiate their parents' values?

*S*ort out the political implications.

- Government's role ends when public segregation is outlawed. What strategies are available for combating private segregation?
- In a time when the United States has elected its first African American president, does continued discrimination in private life matter? Why or why not?

 ## 5.2 Nine Nonsense

Carrie Lukas, National Review Online

Why We Chose This Piece

In 1972 Congress passed Title IX of the Educational Amendments, which said that no one can be excluded from participating in sports at an institution supported by federal funds for reasons of gender. Title IX revolutionized the world of girls' athletics. In a relatively short period of time, sports for girls became common in public schools and scholars began to note a variety of side benefits, including higher self-esteem among female students who participate in sports.

Title IX has also been the target of heavy criticism, however, from those who believe that the insistence on gender equity has resulted in discrimination against men, many of whose athletic programs had to be phased out to fund women's. Lukas is a particularly scathing critic, taking on here the quota system that resulted from Title IX's requirement that athletic funding be in proportion to gender enrollment. Lukas addresses those who propose that Title IX might be a mechanism for getting more female participation in disciplines

Selection published: April 6, 2006

where women are typically underrepresented, like the hard sciences, by imagining what might happen if this idea were taken to what she imagines might be its logical extremes. Does Title IX have any utility beyond school athletics? Should schools try to equalize gender representation across academic disciplines?

Consistency isn't a concept particularly valued by feminists. Feminists deny there are natural differences between men and women—except that women are more empathetic, more verbally adept, and less violent than men. Differences can exist, but only if they are in the female's favor.

According to the *National Journal*, some officials at the National Science Foundation and Education Department share the feminists' immunity to cognitive dissonance. They are exploring Title IX's applications to specific areas of study, but only in disciplines where Title IX's application will benefit women.

It's well-known that fewer women study the hard sciences than men. As the *National Journal* details, men earned about 80 percent of engineering degrees in 2001 and 75 percent of degrees in computer science. Universities, non-profits, and the government pour money into programs to address this discrepancy by encouraging more women to pursue these fields.

Academics frequently meet to ponder the particular problem. Larry Summers was at such a conference when he speculated that innate differences in ability might play a role. Dr. Summers should have realized that, for the gender warriors that populate academia, there is only one acceptable explanation—discrimination—for women's under-representation in the upper echelons of science and math. His mistake contributed to the loss of his job as Harvard's president.

The specter of discrimination fuels current efforts to apply Title IX to science departments. The *National Journal* reports that Education Department officials are investigating specific campuses with departments suspected of treating women "differently." The officials declined to name specific universities under investigation, leaving university administrators to feel as though they are all potential targets.

But why limit the investigation to science and engineering departments? If the Department of Education is interested in the numbers game, then they should be just as concerned about areas in which women dominate men. Women earn nearly eight in ten degrees in education and psychology, and six in ten degrees in accounting and biology. Overall, women earn 58 percent of bachelor's degrees. The ratio among African Americans is even more skewed, with women earning nearly two-thirds of all bachelor's degrees.

The increasingly poor performance of young men is the most significant, troubling trend in American education. Imagine if this trend were reversed and men's academic achievement were soaring relative to women's. Women's groups would howl and the media would be awash in stories covering the crisis.

For years, the only way that a university could inoculate itself from Title IX litigation was to have athletic participation mirror enrollment. In other words, if 58 percent of students were women, then 58 percent of athletes had to be women. Universities trying to meet this criterion struggled to attract female athletes. But, all too often, they resorted to the surefire method of balancing the equation: eliminating men's teams. More than 90 universities cut men's track and field, and more than 20 cancelled wrestling.

If similar standards were applied to academic departments, university biology and accounting programs would be forced to try desperately to attract young men to the major. But if they fell short, they could opt to expel women to make the numbers balance. Engineering programs would face the inverse problem: attracting women and cutting men.

Gender warriors may be willing to take this deal. Feminists hardly celebrate that women gravitate toward majors like education that lead to lower-paying jobs after graduation. They may embrace a policy that pushes women toward more prestigious careers. But if academic departments are fair game, then why shouldn't similar standards be applied to enrollment?

If Title IX were applied to enrollment, schools would face the uncomfortable proposition of trying to attract more men or artificially reduce women's enrollment to reach the magic proportional balance. To achieve enrollment parity today, more than one million women would have to be expelled from colleges and universities around the country.

It's ridiculous to imagine a quota system taken to this extreme. And, of course, men would gain little from the enforcement of such a quota system. They wouldn't receive a better education or be better prepared to participate in the modern economy if women were denied educational opportunities. Policymakers concerned about the lack of men in higher education need to focus on root causes, such as the government-run public-school monopoly that often fails to educate children.

Expanding Title IX is not the answer, and the Bush administration knows this. The administration has courageously taken on Title IX fanatics by providing much-needed clarity about how schools can comply with Title IX in the athletic arena through the use of surveys, instead of relying solely on proportionality. It's unlikely they'll let this effort move forward. But the news that some agency bureaucrats are seeking to selectively apply Title IX to academic disciplines is a reminder of how the gender warriors' bias infects government policy.

Feminists are consistent about one thing—they consistently ignore problems facing American men.

*C*onsider the source and the audience.

- Writing for the conservative *National Review Online*, Lukas can be fairly sure that her audience will agree with her about feminism and Title IX. Would she have been forced to temper her argument at all in a more mainstream journal?
- Lukas is identified as vice president for policy and economics at the Independent Women's Forum. How could you find out more about that organization, what it stands for, and what impact it might have on the argument she is making?

*L*ay out the argument, the values, and the assumptions.

- What does Lukas think is wrong with feminism? What is the chief gender equity problem in higher education that concerns her?
- What is her strategy in answering critics who say women are underrepresented in some disciplines? How does she change the focus of the argument?
- What does she think the government's role should be in achieving equal rights? What does she think is the root problem of gender inequity in higher education?

*U*ncover the evidence.

- Lukas describes feminism as an inconsistent, foolish, and self-serving ideology. When people create a caricature of their opponent that is easily knocked down, we say they are setting up a straw man (or straw woman, in this case). Is that what Lukas is doing here? What evidence might convince you that there is more to her characterization?
- Lukas tries to demonstrate the absurdity of the values she claims feminists hold by showing what would happen if they were taken to the extreme. Does she have any evidence that feminists would want to do what she claims or that the consequences she predicts would result? Does raising a hypothetical scenario exempt her from having to back up her argument?

*E*valuate the conclusion.

- Lukas implies that the real gender problem in schools today is that men are underrepresented in higher education. If that is true, does it mean that feminists' concerns are unwarranted?
- Lukas claims that the root problem of male underrepresentation is the public school system. Does she tell you enough about this conclusion to allow you to decide if it is correct?

*S*ort out the political implications.

- How can we know which gender differences are due to innate ability and which to discrimination?
- What should be government's role in creating gender equity in higher education?

 ## 5.3 Same-Sex Marriage: Hijacking the Civil Rights Legacy

Eugene F. Rivers, Weekly Standard

Why We Chose This Piece

> *Because so much emotion and meaning are attached to the issue of race in the United States, it can be strategically useful for a group (or individual) to harness its particular cause to that larger one, a practice that has come to be known, disreputably, as "playing the race card." If we accuse someone of playing the race card we imply that he or she is exploiting the issue of race for some self-serving purpose.*

> *In this article, Rivers accuses gay rights groups of using race to legitimate their demand for rights when, the author claims, they are really seeking only to enshrine their preferences in law. The risk one runs when accusing someone of using race for political purposes is that one instantly becomes vulnerable to the same criticism. How does Rivers use race here to support his preference for a traditional vision of marriage?*

Selection published: June 1, 2006

The movement to redefine marriage to include same-sex unions has packaged its demands in the rhetoric and images of the civil rights movement. This strategy, though cynical, has enormous strategic utility. For what reasonable, fair-minded American could object to a movement that conjures up images of Martin Luther King Jr. and his fellows campaigners for racial justice facing down dogs and fire hoses? Who is prepared to risk being labeled a bigot for opposing same-sex marriage?

As an exercise in marketing and merchandising, this strategy is the most brilliant playing of the race card in recent memory. Not since the "poverty pimps" of 35 years ago, who leveraged the guilt and sense of fair play of the American public to hustle affirmative action set-asides, have we witnessed so brazen a misuse of African-American history for partisan purposes.

But the partisans of homosexual marriage have a problem. There is no evidence in the history and literature of the civil rights movement, or in its genesis in the struggle against slavery, to support the claim that the "gay rights" movement is in the tradition of the African-American struggle for civil rights. As the eminent historian Eugene D. Genovese observed more than 30 years ago, the black American experience as a function of slavery is unique and without analogue in the history of the United States. While other ethnic and social groups have experienced discrimination and hardship, none of their experiences compare with the physical and cultural brutality of slavery. It was in the crucible of the unique experience of slavery that the civil rights movement was born.

The extraordinary history of the United States as a slaveholding republic included the kidnapping and brutal transport of blacks from African shores, and the stripping of their language, identity, and culture in order to subjugate and exploit them. It also included the constitutional enshrining of these evils in the form of a Supreme Court decision—Dred Scott v. Sandford—denying to blacks any rights that whites must respect, and the establishment of Jim Crow and *de jure* racial discrimination after *Dred Scott* was overturned by a civil war and three historic constitutional amendments.

It is these basic facts that embarrass efforts to exploit the rhetoric of civil rights to advance the goals of generally privileged groups, however much they wish to depict themselves as victims. Whatever wrongs individuals have suffered because some Americans fail in the basic moral obligation to love the sinner, even while hating the sin, there has never been an effort to create a subordinate class subject to exploitation based on "sexual orientation." It is precisely the indiscriminate promotion of various social groups' *desires and preferences* as "rights" that has drained the moral authority from the civil rights industry. Let us consider the question of rights. What makes a gay activist's aspiration to overturn thousands of years of universally recognized morality and practice a "right"? Why should an institution designed for the reproduction of civil society and the rearing of children in a moral environment in which their interests are given pride of place be refashioned to accommodate relationships integrated around intrinsically non-marital sexual conduct?

One must, in the current discussion, address directly the assertion of discrimination. The claim that the definition of marriage as the union of one man and one woman constitutes discrimination is based on a false analogy with statutory prohibitions on interracial marriages in many states through much of the 20th century. This alleged analogy collapses when one considers that skin pigmentation is utterly irrelevant to the procreative and unitive functions of marriage. Racial differences do not interfere with the ability of sexually complementary spouses to become "one-flesh," as the Book of Genesis puts it, by sexual intercourse that fulfills the behavioral conditions of procreation. As the law of marital consummation makes clear, and always has made clear, it is this bodily union that serves as the foundation of the profound sharing of life at every level—biological, emotional, dispositional, rational, and spiritual—that marriage is. This explains not only why marriage can only be between a man and a woman, but also why marriages cannot be between more than two people—despite the desire of "polyamorists" to have their sexual preferences and practices legally recognized and blessed.

Moreover, the analogy of same-sex marriage to interracial marriage disregards the whole point of those prohibitions, which was to maintain and advance a system of racial subordination and exploitation. It was to maintain a caste system in which one race was relegated to conditions of social and economic inferiority. The definition of marriage as the union of a man and a woman does not establish a sexual caste system or relegate one sex to conditions of social and economic inferiority. It does, to be sure, deny the recognition as lawful "marriages" to some forms of sexual combining—including polygyny, polyandry, polyamory, and same-sex relationships. But there is nothing invidious or discriminatory about laws that decline to treat all sexual wants or proclivities as equal.

People are equal in worth and dignity, but *sexual choices* and lifestyles are not. That is why the law's refusal to license polygamous, polyamorous, and homosexual unions is entirely right and proper. In recognizing, favoring, and promoting traditional, monogamous marriage, the law does not violate the "rights" of people whose "lifestyle preferences" are denied the stamp of legal approval. Rather, it furthers and fosters the common good of civil society, and makes proper provision for the physical and moral protection and nurturing of children.

Well-intentioned liberals shudder upon hearing the word "discrimination." Its simple enunciation instills guilt and dulls their critical faculties. But once malcontented members of any group—however privileged—can simply invoke the term and launch their own personalized civil rights industry, the word has been emptied of its normative and historical content.

Defending the civil rights legacy should prove cold comfort to its historic advocates, because the loss of its distinctive nature is our own fault. It was our failure, philosophically and politically, to develop a compelling historiography of the movement that contributed to its decline and decay. From the teaching in schools, to the use of the phrase in political discourse, the notion of civil rights has been diluted, ahistoricized, and nearly emptied of content in relation to the lived historical experience of black Americans.

It is especially sad and disturbing that many self-proclaimed civil rights leaders have failed to resist corruption and co-optation by the homosexual movement. People who should be vitally concerned with promoting marriage and rebuilding the institution of marriage in African-American communities are either silent or complicit in a campaign which, if successful, will trivialize marriage.

In light of the prospect of judicially mandated homosexual marriage, we believe that black leaders—and especially black clergy—need to speak forcefully in favor of President George W. Bush's proposal for a Federal Marriage Amendment. If their support for true marriage alienates them from their white liberal friends, so be it. No community has suffered more than has ours from the weakening of the institution of marriage at the hands of purveyors of the doctrines of the sexual revolution. It is our sons and our daughters who have paid the costs imposed by a cultural elite that seeks to overthrow cultural and Biblical principles of sexual restraint and responsibility. Leaders of our community should therefore be in the vanguard of the movement to prevent further moral erosion and begin reversing historical declines.

Consider the source and the audience.

- Writing for the *Weekly Standard*, a conservative journal, Rivers is directing his argument to a sympathetic, conservative audience. But, as the last paragraph makes clear, he has a broader audience in mind. What does he gain by persuading black clergy to support his views?

Lay out the argument, the values, and the assumptions.

- Is the main goal of this article to stake out the unique claim of blacks to the rhetoric of civil rights or to promote a particular, traditional view of marriage?
- What exactly does that view of marriage entail? Why the emphasis on procreation?
- Why is it useful for the author to group gays with polygamists, polyamorists, and the like? Why does the author call homosexuality a choice, a preference, or a lifestyle?

Uncover the evidence.

- What evidence does Rivers use to convince readers that marriage ought to be between one man and one woman? Is an appeal to history convincing?
- What evidence does he summon to support the claim that procreation is the central purpose of marriage? Can appeals to religious doctrine be proved or disproved?
- What evidence does the author offer that homosexuality is a choice or a preference? Does he need to refute the scientific evidence that it is biologically determined?

Evaluate the conclusion.

- Rivers concludes that gays play the race card when they compare their quest for equal legal rights to marry with the historical ban on interracial marriage in the United States. Is he right that gays can make no claim to being denied their civil rights?
- When he appeals to black clergy to support him in his denial of marriage rights to gays, is Rivers immune from criticism that he too is playing the race card?

Sort out the political implications.

- Is it possible to refer to race in a political context without exploiting it?
- What groups can legitimately use the rhetoric of civil rights to make claims on society?

5.4 A More Perfect Union

Barack Obama

Why We Chose This Piece

In March 2008, then-senator Barack Obama's promising campaign for the Democratic nomination for the presidency appeared to be hitting turbulent waters. Cable stations were playing video of his former pastor, the Reverend Jeremiah Wright, shouting spiteful words about white America from his pulpit, and even some Obama supporters were wondering if their candidate had spent his Sunday mornings listening to the rantings of a disillusioned and angry man. Many African Americans, more familiar with the proceedings of traditionally black churches than their white compatriots, found Wright's shouting to be normal and his words to be understandable, even if they did not agree with the message. Wright, a former marine who had lived through segregation, could not help but note where the promise of America fell short for black America. A glass that many Americans wanted to view as half full still looked half empty to blacks from Wright's generation.

Obama, born of a white mother and an African father, and self-educated in the culture of black America, had hoped to keep race off the front burner in his campaign, but the old Wright videos made that impossible. He saw himself as facing not only a critical moment in his campaign but also a "teachable moment." He could hunker down and hope the scandal faded, or he could tackle it with a speech on race. He chose to do the latter, a response viewed as risky at the time, though in hindsight it may have been the very thing to set his campaign back on track. He says he wants his speech to open a new conversation about race in this country. Does it do that? How?

"We the people, in order to form a more perfect union..."—221 years ago, in a hall that still stands across the street, a group of men gathered and, with these simple words, launched America's improbable experiment in democracy. Farmers and scholars, statesmen and patriots who had traveled across an ocean to escape tyranny and persecution finally made real their declaration of independence at a Philadelphia convention that lasted through the spring of 1787.

The document they produced was eventually signed but ultimately unfinished. It was stained by this nation's original sin of slavery, a question that divided the colonies and brought the convention to a stalemate until the founders chose to allow the slave trade to continue for at least 20 more years, and to leave any final resolution to future generations.

Of course, the answer to the slavery question was already embedded within our Constitution—a Constitution that had at its very core the ideal of equal citizenship

---

Selection delivered: March 18, 2008

under the law; a Constitution that promised its people liberty and justice and a union that could be and should be perfected over time.

And yet words on a parchment would not be enough to deliver slaves from bondage, or provide men and women of every color and creed their full rights and obligations as citizens of the United States. What would be needed were Americans in successive generations who were willing to do their part—through protests and struggles, on the streets and in the courts, through a civil war and civil disobedience, and always at great risk—to narrow that gap between the promise of our ideals and the reality of their time.

This was one of the tasks we set forth at the beginning of this presidential campaign—to continue the long march of those who came before us, a march for a more just, more equal, more free, more caring and more prosperous America. I chose to run for president at this moment in history because I believe deeply that we cannot solve the challenges of our time unless we solve them together, unless we perfect our union by understanding that we may have different stories, but we hold common hopes; that we may not look the same and we may not have come from the same place, but we all want to move in the same direction—toward a better future for our children and our grandchildren.

This belief comes from my unyielding faith in the decency and generosity of the American people. But it also comes from my own story.

I am the son of a black man from Kenya and a white woman from Kansas. I was raised with the help of a white grandfather who survived a Depression to serve in Patton's Army during World War II and a white grandmother who worked on a bomber assembly line at Fort Leavenworth while he was overseas. I've gone to some of the best schools in America and lived in one of the world's poorest nations. I am married to a black American who carries within her the blood of slaves and slaveowners—an inheritance we pass on to our two precious daughters. I have brothers, sisters, nieces, nephews, uncles and cousins of every race and every hue, scattered across three continents, and for as long as I live, I will never forget that in no other country on Earth is my story even possible.

It's a story that hasn't made me the most conventional of candidates. But it is a story that has seared into my genetic makeup the idea that this nation is more than the sum of its parts—that out of many, we are truly one.

Throughout the first year of this campaign, against all predictions to the contrary, we saw how hungry the American people were for this message of unity. Despite the temptation to view my candidacy through a purely racial lens, we won commanding victories in states with some of the whitest populations in the country. In South Carolina, where the Confederate flag still flies, we built a powerful coalition of African-Americans and white Americans.

This is not to say that race has not been an issue in this campaign. At various stages in the campaign, some commentators have deemed me either "too black" or "not black enough." We saw racial tensions bubble to the surface during the week before the South Carolina primary. The press has scoured every single exit poll for the latest evidence of racial polarization, not just in terms of white and black, but black and brown as well.

And yet, it has only been in the last couple of weeks that the discussion of race in this campaign has taken a particularly divisive turn.

On one end of the spectrum, we've heard the implication that my candidacy is somehow an exercise in affirmative action; that it's based solely on the desire of wide-eyed liberals to purchase racial reconciliation on the cheap. On the other end, we've heard my former pastor, Jeremiah Wright, use incendiary language to express views that have the potential not only to widen the racial divide, but views that denigrate both the greatness and the goodness of our nation, and that rightly offend white and black alike.

I have already condemned, in unequivocal terms, the statements of Reverend Wright that have caused such controversy and, in some cases, pain. For some, nagging questions remain. Did I know him to be an occasionally fierce critic of American domestic and foreign policy? Of course. Did I ever hear him make remarks that could be considered controversial while I sat in the church? Yes. Did I strongly disagree with many of his political views? Absolutely—just as I'm sure many of you have heard remarks from your pastors, priests, or rabbis with which you strongly disagreed.

But the remarks that have caused this recent firestorm weren't simply controversial. They weren't simply a religious leader's efforts to speak out against perceived injustice. Instead, they expressed a profoundly distorted view of this country—a view that sees white racism as endemic, and that elevates what is wrong with America above all that we know is right with America; a view that sees the conflicts in the Middle East as rooted primarily in the actions of stalwart allies like Israel, instead of emanating from the perverse and hateful ideologies of radical Islam.

As such, Reverend Wright's comments were not only wrong but divisive, divisive at a time when we need unity; racially charged at a time when we need to come together to solve a set of monumental problems—two wars, a terrorist threat, a falling economy, a chronic health care crisis and potentially devastating climate change—problems that are neither black or white or Latino or Asian, but rather problems that confront us all.

Given my background, my politics, and my professed values and ideals, there will no doubt be those for whom my statements of condemnation are not enough. Why associate myself with Reverend Wright in the first place, they may ask? Why not join another church? And I confess that if all that I knew of Reverend Wright were the snippets of those sermons that have run in an endless loop on the television sets and YouTube, or if Trinity United Church of Christ conformed to the caricatures being peddled by some commentators, there is no doubt that I would react in much the same way.

But the truth is, that isn't all that I know of the man. The man I met more than 20 years ago is a man who helped introduce me to my Christian faith, a man who spoke to me about our obligations to love one another, to care for the sick and lift up the poor. He is a man who served his country as a United States Marine; who has studied and lectured at some of the finest universities and seminaries in the country, and who for over 30 years has led a church that serves the community by doing God's work here on Earth—by housing the homeless, ministering to the needy, providing day care services and scholarships and prison ministries, and reaching out to those suffering from HIV/AIDS.

In my first book, *Dreams From My Father*, I describe the experience of my first service at Trinity:

"People began to shout, to rise from their seats and clap and cry out, a forceful wind carrying the reverend's voice up into the rafters. And in that single note—hope!—I heard something else: At the foot of that cross, inside the thousands of churches across the city, I imagined the stories of ordinary black people merging with the stories of David and Goliath, Moses and Pharaoh, the Christians in the lion's den, Ezekiel's field of dry bones. Those stories—of survival and freedom and hope—became our stories, my story. The blood that spilled was our blood, the tears our tears, until this black church, on this bright day, seemed once more a vessel carrying the story of a people into future generations and into a larger world. Our trials and triumphs became at once unique and universal, black and more than black. In chronicling our journey, the stories and songs gave us a meaning to reclaim memories that we didn't need to feel shame about—memories that all people might study and cherish, and with which we could start to rebuild."

That has been my experience at Trinity. Like other predominantly black churches across the country, Trinity embodies the black community in its entirety—the doctor and the welfare mom, the model student and the former gang-banger. Like other black churches, Trinity's services are full of raucous laughter and sometimes bawdy humor. They are full of dancing and clapping and screaming and shouting that may seem jarring to the untrained ear. The church contains in full the kindness and cruelty, the fierce intelligence and the shocking ignorance, the struggles and successes, the love and, yes, the bitterness and biases that make up the black experience in America.

And this helps explain, perhaps, my relationship with Reverend Wright. As imperfect as he may be, he has been like family to me. He strengthened my faith, officiated my wedding, and baptized my children. Not once in my conversations with him have I heard him talk about any ethnic group in derogatory terms, or treat whites with whom he interacted with anything but courtesy and respect. He contains within him the contradictions—the good and the bad—of the community that he has served diligently for so many years.

I can no more disown him than I can disown the black community. I can no more disown him than I can disown my white grandmother—a woman who helped raise me, a woman who sacrificed again and again for me, a woman who loves me as much as she loves anything in this world, but a woman who once confessed her fear of black men who passed her by on the street, and who on more than one occasion has uttered racial or ethnic stereotypes that made me cringe.

These people are a part of me. And they are part of America, this country that I love.

Some will see this as an attempt to justify or excuse comments that are simply inexcusable. I can assure you it is not. I suppose the politically safe thing to do would be to move on from this episode and just hope that it fades into the woodwork. We can dismiss Reverend Wright as a crank or a demagogue, just as some have dismissed Geraldine Ferraro, in the aftermath of her recent statements, as harboring some deep-seated bias.

But race is an issue that I believe this nation cannot afford to ignore right now. We would be making the same mistake that Reverend Wright made in his offending sermons about America—to simplify and stereotype and amplify the negative to the point that it distorts reality.

The fact is that the comments that have been made and the issues that have surfaced over the last few weeks reflect the complexities of race in this country that we've never really worked through—a part of our union that we have not yet made perfect. And if we walk away now, if we simply retreat into our respective corners, we will never be able to come together and solve challenges like health care or education or the need to find good jobs for every American.

Understanding this reality requires a reminder of how we arrived at this point. As William Faulkner once wrote, "The past isn't dead and buried. In fact, it isn't even past." We do not need to recite here the history of racial injustice in this country. But we do need to remind ourselves that so many of the disparities that exist between the African-American community and the larger American community today can be traced directly to inequalities passed on from an earlier generation that suffered under the brutal legacy of slavery and Jim Crow.

Segregated schools were and are inferior schools; we still haven't fixed them, 50 years after Brown v. Board of Education. And the inferior education they provided, then and now, helps explain the pervasive achievement gap between today's black and white students.

Legalized discrimination—where blacks were prevented, often through violence, from owning property, or loans were not granted to African-American business owners, or black homeowners could not access FHA mortgages, or blacks were excluded from unions or the police force or the fire department—meant that black families could not amass any meaningful wealth to bequeath to future generations. That history helps explain the wealth and income gap between blacks and whites, and the concentrated pockets of poverty that persist in so many of today's urban and rural communities.

A lack of economic opportunity among black men, and the shame and frustration that came from not being able to provide for one's family contributed to the erosion of black families—a problem that welfare policies for many years may have worsened. And the lack of basic services in so many urban black neighborhoods—parks for kids to play in, police walking the beat, regular garbage pickup, building code enforcement—all helped create a cycle of violence, blight and neglect that continues to haunt us.

This is the reality in which Reverend Wright and other African-Americans of his generation grew up. They came of age in the late '50s and early '60s, a time when segregation was still the law of the land and opportunity was systematically constricted. What's remarkable is not how many failed in the face of discrimination, but how many men and women overcame the odds; how many were able to make a way out of no way, for those like me who would come after them.

For all those who scratched and clawed their way to get a piece of the American Dream, there were many who didn't make it—those who were ultimately defeated, in one way or another, by discrimination. That legacy of defeat was passed on to future generations—those young men and, increasingly, young women who we see standing on street corners or languishing in our prisons, without hope or prospects for the future. Even for those blacks who did make it, questions of race and racism continue to define their worldview in fundamental ways. For the men and women of Reverend Wright's generation, the memories of humiliation and doubt and fear have not gone away; nor has the anger and the bitterness of those years. That anger may not get expressed in public, in front of white co-workers or white friends. But it does find voice in the bar-bershop or the beauty shop or around the kitchen table. At times, that anger is exploited by politicians, to gin up votes along racial lines, or to make up for a politician's own failings.

And occasionally it finds voice in the church on Sunday morning, in the pulpit and in the pews. The fact that so many people are surprised to hear that anger in some of Reverend Wright's sermons simply reminds us of the old truism that the most segre-gated hour of American life occurs on Sunday morning. That anger is not always pro-ductive; indeed, all too often it distracts attention from solving real problems; it keeps us from squarely facing our own complicity within the African-American community in our condition, and prevents the African-American community from forging the alli-ances it needs to bring about real change. But the anger is real; it is powerful. And to simply wish it away, to condemn it without understanding its roots, only serves to widen the chasm of misunderstanding that exists between the races.

In fact, a similar anger exists within segments of the white community. Most work-ing- and middle-class white Americans don't feel that they have been particularly priv-ileged by their race. Their experience is the immigrant experience—as far as they're concerned, no one handed them anything. They built it from scratch. They've worked hard all their lives, many times only to see their jobs shipped overseas or their pen-sions dumped after a lifetime of labor. They are anxious about their futures, and they feel their dreams slipping away. And in an era of stagnant wages and global competi-tion, opportunity comes to be seen as a zero sum game, in which your dreams come at my expense. So when they are told to bus their children to a school across town; when they hear an African-American is getting an advantage in landing a good job or a spot in a good college because of an injustice that they themselves never committed; when they're told that their fears about crime in urban neighborhoods are somehow preju-diced, resentment builds over time.

Like the anger within the black community, these resentments aren't always expressed in polite company. But they have helped shape the political landscape for at least a generation. Anger over welfare and affirmative action helped forge the Rea-gan Coalition. Politicians routinely exploited fears of crime for their own electoral ends. Talk show hosts and conservative commentators built entire careers unmasking bogus claims of racism while dismissing legitimate discussions of racial injustice and inequality as mere political correctness or reverse racism.

Just as black anger often proved counterproductive, so have these white resent-ments distracted attention from the real culprits of the middle class squeeze—a corpo-rate culture rife with inside dealing, questionable accounting practices and short-term greed; a Washington dominated by lobbyists and special interests; economic policies that favor the few over the many. And yet, to wish away the resentments of white Americans, to label them as misguided or even racist, without recognizing they are grounded in legitimate concerns—this too widens the racial divide and blocks the path to understanding.

This is where we are right now. It's a racial stalemate we've been stuck in for years. Contrary to the claims of some of my critics, black and white, I have never been so naïve as to believe that we can get beyond our racial divisions in a single election cycle, or with a single candidacy—particularly a candidacy as imperfect as my own.

But I have asserted a firm conviction—a conviction rooted in my faith in God and my faith in the American people—that, working together, we can move beyond some of our old racial wounds, and that in fact we have no choice if we are to continue on the path of a more perfect union.

For the African-American community, that path means embracing the burdens of our past without becoming victims of our past. It means continuing to insist on a full measure of justice in every aspect of American life. But it also means binding our particular grievances—for better health care and better schools and better jobs—to the larger aspirations of all Americans: the white woman struggling to break the glass ceiling, the white man who has been laid off, the immigrant trying to feed his family. And it means taking full responsibility for our own lives—by demanding more from our fathers, and spending more time with our children, and reading to them, and teaching them that while they may face challenges and discrimination in their own lives, they must never succumb to despair or cynicism; they must always believe that they can write their own destiny.

Ironically, this quintessentially American—and yes, conservative—notion of self-help found frequent expression in Reverend Wright's sermons. But what my former pastor too often failed to understand is that embarking on a program of self-help also requires a belief that society can change.

The profound mistake of Reverend Wright's sermons is not that he spoke about racism in our society. It's that he spoke as if our society was static; as if no progress had been made; as if this country—a country that has made it possible for one of his own members to run for the highest office in the land and build a coalition of white and black, Latino and Asian, rich and poor, young and old—is still irrevocably bound to a tragic past. But what we know—what we have seen—is that America can change. That is the true genius of this nation. What we have already achieved gives us hope—the audacity to hope—for what we can and must achieve tomorrow.

In the white community, the path to a more perfect union means acknowledging that what ails the African-American community does not just exist in the minds of black people; that the legacy of discrimination—and current incidents of discrimination, while less overt than in the past—are real and must be addressed, not just with words, but with deeds, by investing in our schools and our communities; by enforcing our civil rights laws and ensuring fairness in our criminal justice system; by providing this generation with ladders of opportunity that were unavailable for previous generations. It requires all Americans to realize that your dreams do not have to come at the expense of my dreams; that investing in the health, welfare and education of black and brown and white children will ultimately help all of America prosper.

In the end, then, what is called for is nothing more and nothing less than what all the world's great religions demand—that we do unto others as we would have them do unto us. Let us be our brother's keeper, scripture tells us. Let us be our sister's keeper. Let us find that common stake we all have in one another, and let our politics reflect that spirit as well.

For we have a choice in this country. We can accept a politics that breeds division and conflict and cynicism. We can tackle race only as spectacle—as we did in the O.J. trial—or in the wake of tragedy—as we did in the aftermath of Katrina—or as fodder for the nightly news. We can play Reverend Wright's sermons on every channel, every day and talk about them from now until the election, and make the only question in this campaign whether or not the American people think that I somehow believe or sympathize with his most offensive words. We can pounce on some gaffe by a Hillary supporter as evidence that she's playing the race card, or we can speculate on whether white men will all flock to John McCain in the general election regardless of his policies.

We can do that.

But if we do, I can tell you that in the next election, we'll be talking about some other distraction. And then another one. And then another one. And nothing will change.

That is one option. Or, at this moment, in this election, we can come together and say, "Not this time." This time, we want to talk about the crumbling schools that are stealing the future of black children and white children and Asian children and Hispanic children and Native American children. This time, we want to reject the cynicism that tells us that these kids can't learn; that those kids who don't look like us are somebody else's problem. The children of America are not those kids, they are our kids, and we will not let them fall behind in a 21st century economy. Not this time.

This time we want to talk about how the lines in the emergency room are filled with whites and blacks and Hispanics who do not have health care, who don't have the power on their own to overcome the special interests in Washington, but who can take them on if we do it together.

This time, we want to talk about the shuttered mills that once provided a decent life for men and women of every race, and the homes for sale that once belonged to Americans from every religion, every region, every walk of life. This time, we want to talk about the fact that the real problem is not that someone who doesn't look like you might take your job; it's that the corporation you work for will ship it overseas for nothing more than a profit.

This time, we want to talk about the men and women of every color and creed who serve together and fight together and bleed together under the same proud flag. We want to talk about how to bring them home from a war that should have never been authorized and should have never been waged. And we want to talk about how we'll show our patriotism by caring for them and their families, and giving them the benefits that they have earned.

I would not be running for President if I didn't believe with all my heart that this is what the vast majority of Americans want for this country. This union may never be perfect, but generation after generation has shown that it can always be perfected. And today, whenever I find myself feeling doubtful or cynical about this possibility, what gives me the most hope is the next generation—the young people whose attitudes and beliefs and openness to change have already made history in this election.

There is one story in particularly that I'd like to leave you with today—a story I told when I had the great honor of speaking on Dr. King's birthday at his home church, Ebenezer Baptist, in Atlanta.

There is a young, 23-year-old white woman named Ashley Baia who organized for our campaign in Florence, S.C. She had been working to organize a mostly

African-American community since the beginning of this campaign, and one day she was at a roundtable discussion where everyone went around telling their story and why they were there.

And Ashley said that when she was 9 years old, her mother got cancer. And because she had to miss days of work, she was let go and lost her health care. They had to file for bankruptcy, and that's when Ashley decided that she had to do something to help her mom.

She knew that food was one of their most expensive costs, and so Ashley convinced her mother that what she really liked and really wanted to eat more than anything else was mustard and relish sandwiches—because that was the cheapest way to eat. That's the mind of a 9-year-old.

She did this for a year until her mom got better. So she told everyone at the round-table that the reason she joined our campaign was so that she could help the millions of other children in the country who want and need to help their parents, too.

Now, Ashley might have made a different choice. Perhaps somebody told her along the way that the source of her mother's problems were blacks who were on welfare and too lazy to work, or Hispanics who were coming into the country illegally. But she didn't. She sought out allies in her fight against injustice.

Anyway, Ashley finishes her story and then goes around the room and asks every-one else why they're supporting the campaign. They all have different stories and dif-ferent reasons. Many bring up a specific issue. And finally they come to this elderly black man who's been sitting there quietly the entire time. And Ashley asks him why he's there. And he does not bring up a specific issue. He does not say health care or the economy. He does not say education or the war. He does not say that he was there because of Barack Obama. He simply says to everyone in the room, "I am here because of Ashley."

"I'm here because of Ashley." By itself, that single moment of recognition between that young white girl and that old black man is not enough. It is not enough to give health care to the sick, or jobs to the jobless, or education to our children.

But it is where we start. It is where our union grows stronger. And as so many gen-erations have come to realize over the course of the 221 years since a band of patriots signed that document right here in Philadelphia, that is where the perfection begins.

*C*onsider the source and the audience.

- Obama is speaking at once to white Americans who might have been offended by Reverend Wright's words and to black Americans who believe that many of Wright's words were justi-fied. How does he navigate these two different audiences?
- How does his background enable him to straddle the two cultures to which he is speaking?

*L*ay out the argument, the values, and the assumptions.

- Why does Obama call his speech "A More Perfect Union?" Why does he see our Constitu-tion as "unfinished?" What are the values he sees underlying it that might be the means to finishing it?

- How does he explain Reverend Wright's words? What does Obama believe is wrong with those words? What is right about them?
- What makes race so difficult for Americans to talk about? What is the racial stalemate we have been stuck in for years, what has kept us stuck, and how might we get out of it?

*U*ncover the evidence.

- Is any evidence required for Obama's argument? When a speaker or writer relies on historical evidence, how can he or she respond to others who believe that the historical record says something different?
- Besides history, what does Obama use to back up his case?

*E*valuate the conclusion.

- Obama essentially argues that we are at a crossroads with respect to race and if we don't move out of the stalemate we are in we will stay stuck. Is this conclusion reasonable? What is required of us to move beyond this racial stalemate?

*S*ort out the political implications.

- Obviously, this speech did the trick in terms of keeping Obama's campaign alive. Did it also meet his goal of starting a new conversation about race? How would we know?

6

Congress

The founders' passion for checks and balances reached a high point in their design of the U.S. Congress. Not only is that institution checked by the executive and judicial branches of government, but it is checked and balanced internally as well, by the requirement that both chambers, the large, unwieldy House of Representatives and the smaller, more disciplined Senate, agree on all bills that become national law. Though we citizens may fuss and fume over what seems like endless gridlock or legislative logjams, slow, painstaking lawmaking is just what our cautious founders wanted.

In some ways though, the Congress of today does not look like the founders' ideal. Their hope was that the House of Representatives would be responsive to public opinion and that it would be balanced by the more mature Senate, which would be focused on longer-term issues of the public interest. In truth, members of both institutions are subject to a legislative dilemma. They are torn between two roles—representing the particular interests of their constituencies (either a legislative district or a state) or engaging in lawmaking that serves the national interest but might not serve their constituency's interests nearly as well. Since the former course is far more likely to lead to their reelection, and reelection is the primary concern of almost every member of Congress, they have every incentive to ignore critical national problems, particularly in the House, where members come up for reelection every two years.

The readings in this chapter touch on some, but by no means all, of the many critical issues concerning legislative politics. The first article, written by a history professor, discusses Speaker of the House Nancy Pelosi's possible place in history. Obviously as the first female Speaker, Pelosi will be more than a footnote in history books. But the author of this article believes that Pelosi has the potential to become one of the most successful Speakers in history, an argument that no doubt would be rejected by most Republicans and possibly even some Democrats. The second piece, an op-ed article from the *New York Times*, examines the struggles of another Democratic leader, Senate majority leader Harry Reid. Even with a strong majority in the Senate, the author argues that Reid faces many difficulties in leading his party. Third, an article from the *Washington Times* reports on the criticisms that some members of Congress are receiving for bringing home pork-barrel projects—special projects that members of

Congress vote to fund in their districts that may not be particularly worthy, at least not to the national taxpayers who foot the bill. In the fourth piece, a political science professor and a statistician analyze the reasons behind remarkably uncompetitive congressional elections. The final selection is a 1950 speech made by Sen. Margaret Chase Smith, decrying the incivility and damage to personal liberty that came with the attempt by her colleague Sen. Joseph McCarthy to root out what he saw as a communist threat in American government.

 ## 6.1 The Pelosi Factor

Julian E. Zelizer, Politico.com

Why We Chose This Piece

Speakers of the House of the Representatives, particularly in recent years, have been lightening rods for criticism. This has been especially true of the current Speaker, Nancy Pelosi. Polls indicate that the public has been no more satisfied with a Democratic-controlled House than it was before 2006, when Republicans and Speaker Dennis Hastert were in charge. Here, Julian E. Zelizer, a professor of history and public affairs, argues that although the public appears to say otherwise, Pelosi has the potential to leave a positive legacy.

The article, however, is about much more than the strengths and weaknesses of Pelosi. It illustrates nicely the complexities of being Speaker, a position that any student of Congress must understand. As you read, ask yourself what powers—both formal and informal—the Speaker has to accomplish her goals. What limitations are there on those powers?

In November 2004, the day after President George W. Bush's reelection and the padding of Republican congressional majorities, Richard Viguerie, a pioneer of the modern conservative movement, said, "Now comes the revolution.... If you don't implement a conservative agenda now, when do you?"

Four years later, the situation looks very different. Democrats control the White House and Congress. Pundits are talking about the crisis in the Republican Party, and Democrats are pushing forward a bold domestic agenda—including health care and the environment—that has the potential to rival the Great Society.

House Speaker Nancy Pelosi (D-Calif.) has been instrumental to the reversal of Democratic fortunes even though most of the attention has been focused on President Barack Obama.

With new reports that Pelosi was briefed about the CIA's use of torture in 2003, there are likely to be some Democrats who raise questions about her future as a party leader.

But before they do, they should closely consider what they would lose. Since taking over as speaker 2½ years ago, Pelosi has proved to be a formidable leader who might

Selection published: May 13, 2009

very well amass the kind of legendary record that House Speaker Sam Rayburn (D-Texas) achieved in the 1940s and '50s. It is still too early to tell, but she is off to a good start. Pelosi's speakership has relied on ideas and muscle. She comes from the progressive Democratic tradition and has not been shy about taking on Republicans or centrist Democrats. Even though Republicans immediately tried to put her on the defensive after their losses in 2006 by warning voters of the "San Francisco values" that she would bring into the House, Pelosi has not shied away from defending progressive policies. Pelosi and House Democrats directly challenged Bush's policies in Iraq and called for an immediate withdrawal.

Pelosi has also been a driving force at pushing for progressive domestic policies, including with the current administration. In her first session, House Democrats obtained an increase in the minimum wage, higher benefits for veterans and improved gas standards. Since January 2009, House Democrats have shaped much of the economic stimulus package to include funding for progressive programs such as schooling, Medicaid, infrastructure and state assistance that had been neglected in the conservative era.

Nonetheless, Pelosi is also adept at using the carrot and the stick. She took power in an age of strong speakers and lives by these rules. She has proved to be skilled at fundraising, and members of the House realize that there is a high cost to be incurred to their campaigns if they break from the party line. When a fight broke out between Reps. Henry Waxman (D-Calif.) and John Dingell (D-Mich.) over who would chair the House Energy and Commerce Committee, the leadership stood behind the environmentally friendly Waxman.

At the same time, behind the scenes, she made sure that more progressive voices in the Democratic Party did not defect when Senate Democrats failed to obtain an immediate withdrawal from Iraq and when they were forced to agree to spending reductions in the economic stimulus bill.

The challenges for Pelosi will increase over the coming year. In some ways, the economic stimulus bill and the financial bailout were the easy part for House Democrats. Now come the two issues that have the potential to divide the party: health care reform and environmental regulation. Though there is general consensus that bold legislation is needed in both areas, the devil is in the details. House Ways and Means Committee Chairman Charles Rangel recently issued a warning to the leadership and the White House that he would oppose a tax on employer-provided benefits.

There has also been a notable drop in poll numbers about how Americans perceive Pelosi even at a time when favorable ratings for Democrats in Congress have risen. Now the torture briefing stories will cause more problems.

But if she can emerge from these struggles with her reputation and the party relatively intact, Pelosi might very well be on her way to joining the list of some of the legendary speakers of the House. She is certainly already one of the crucial forces behind the reconstruction of the Democratic Party.

---

*C*onsider the source and the audience.

- Zelizer is a well-known professor of American political history, especially regarding Congress. How might that influence his ability to evaluate the potential legacy of a sitting Speaker?

*L*ay out the argument, the values, and the assumptions.

- Why does Zelizer believe that Pelosi has been an effective Speaker? Why does he believe that she has the potential to be "legendary?"

*U*ncover the evidence.

- Zelizer writes that Pelosi "has been instrumental to the reversal of Democratic fortunes even though most of the attention has been focused on President Barack Obama." Has he shown this to be the case? How does he know that it is true?

*E*valuate the conclusion.

- Zelizer is making an argument about Pelosi's legacy. Do we have to wait for history to play itself out before we know if what he argues is true, or can we evaluate his claims without knowing the future?
- Does Zelizer give appropriate attention to Pelosi's possible negatives?

*S*ort out the political implications.

- How might Pelosi's success or failure as Speaker influence the kinds of policies that Congress passes?
- How might Pelosi's role as Speaker change with Barack Obama as president, as opposed to George W. Bush?

6.2 Guns, Geysers, and Mr. Reid

Gail Collins, New York Times

Why We Chose This Piece

In the previous article, Julian E. Zelizer examined the speakership of Nancy Pelosi. Here, Gail Collins discusses the problems facing another Democratic congressional leader, Senate majority leader Harry Reid. Like the Zelizer article, this piece is about much more than the subject of the article. It raises all kinds of interesting issues with which students of Congress must grapple. The article illustrates the unique nature of the federal legislative process (How does a bill about credit cards get a provision that allows people to carry firearms in national parks?), the limitations on majority-party power in the Senate because of the filibuster, and the difficulties congressional leaders have controlling party members with competing points of view.

Whenever life feels dark and difficult, it's always helpful to think about people who have it worse. Be thankful, for instance, that you're not one of those co-pilots for regional airlines who make $16,000 a year and have to

Selection published: May 16, 2009

commute from Seattle to Newark. Or a person currently riding in a plane with a $16,000 co-pilot in the cockpit. Be thankful you aren't a Chrysler dealer. Or Senate Majority Leader Harry Reid.

Nothing is simple if you're Harry Reid. This week the Senate was working on a consumer rights bill for credit card holders when Tom Coburn, an Oklahoma Republican, suddenly proposed an amendment to allow people to carry loaded guns in national parks.

This would seem relevant only if consumers are worried that they will not be able to use their American Express at a souvenir stand in Yellowstone, and will need to hold up the cashier in order to bring home a much-anticipated geyser refrigerator magnet.

Coburn said it was not a "gotcha" aimed at forcing the opposition into a corner on a hot-button issue, although when you say you're offering an amendment "to protect innocent Americans from violent crime in national parks and refuges" I think you are kind of stacking the deck.

But one way or another, the Democrats clearly did feel trapped into placating the gun lobby. Twenty-seven of them wound up voting yes on an amendment that would arm the tourists and make final passage of the credit card bill more complicated. Including Reid. Then Reid tried to get the Senate to confirm David Hayes, Obama's nominee to be deputy secretary of the interior. This proved to be impossible even though Hayes was both uncontroversial and a man whose qualifications for the job include having already been deputy secretary of the interior. But no, the Republicans threatened a filibuster because Senator Robert Bennett of Utah was ticked off at the Department of the Interior for canceling the sale of oil and gas leases on public lands in his state.

Secretary of the Interior Ken Salazar told Bennett that he'd review the leases and could probably reinstate some of the sales, but that it would be a lot easier to do all that if he had, um, a deputy. No deal.

This is exactly the sort of procedural roadblock that you need 60 votes to overcome, and people are beginning to ask why the majority leader can't handle these things since Arlen Specter's defection gave the Democrats 60 votes. Do not say this to Harry Reid! For one thing, Al Franken is still in court in Minnesota, and when you ask the Republicans how long they're going to litigate the results of an election that took place last November, they murmur vaguely about how Rome wasn't built in a day.

Anyhow, Ted Kennedy is sick and Robert Byrd is 91 and it's a miracle some of the other ones can find their way to the Capitol. Even if you eventually get all 60 Democratic votes in the same room, how do you get them to do the same thing? You will remember that when Specter came over, Democrat Ben Nelson of Nebraska instantly said: "They might have a 60-member majority. That doesn't mean they have 60 votes." Reid must have found the point Nelson was making less chilling than the fact that the senator kept referring to his own party as "they."

Next week, some supporters of Dawn Johnsen are hoping that Reid will take up Johnsen's nomination to run the Office of Legal Counsel, the place where the president goes for advice on whether whatever he wants to do is legal. This causes the majority leader's office to hold its collective head and moan.

Johnsen actually is controversial. She was once a lawyer for the National Abortion Rights Action League. Twenty years ago, she put a footnote in a legal brief saying that forcing a woman to give birth to a child against her will was "disturbingly suggestive of involuntary servitude." This has been creatively translated into the charge that Johnsen, the mother of two, believes pregnancy is akin to slavery.

Also, she has spoken out so forcefully against the Bush administration's politicizing the Office of Legal Counsel that Republicans are claiming she'd ... politicize the office.

The inevitable filibuster threats have been made. Since the Office of Legal Counsel doesn't actually have anything to do with abortion, it might be reasonable for Reid to expect that anti-choice Democratic senators could throw him a vote on the procedural issues and then oppose the actual nomination, when Johnsen would only need 51 votes and Reid would not require their help.

That, however, would presume a degree of consistency that is hard to get in a place that holds one important aspect of credit card reform is giving people the ability to pack a handgun at the Grand Canyon.

*C*onsider the source and the audience.

- Who does Collins, a frequent op-ed contributor to the *New York Times*, appear to be writing for here? Liberals? Conservatives? A general audience?

*L*ay out the argument, the values, and the assumptions.

- Why does Collins think you should be thankful that you are not Harry Reid? Why, according to her, is nothing simple for him?

*U*ncover the evidence.

- Collins provides several examples to illustrate the challenges in front of Reid. What are they? Are they persuasive?

*E*valuate the conclusion.

- Are the problems Reid faces unique to the current political situation, or are these likely to be issues for any Senate majority leader?
- Collins uses humor to make her case. Does this make her conclusion more or less persuasive, or is her tone irrelevant?

*S*ort out the political implications.

- What might be some positives regarding the limits on congressional leaders' power? Negatives?
- One of Reid's biggest hurdles is that to get a bill that his party supports out of the Senate, he needs sixty votes to break a filibuster. Some observers argue that the filibuster promotes debate and is needed to protect the rights of numerical minorities. Others believe the filibuster is nothing more than a stall tactic that prevents the will of the majority from being enacted into law. Which side is correct? Can a legitimate case be made for the filibuster, or does it undermine the legislative process?

6.3 Lawmakers Fried for Bringing Home Bacon

Hypocrisy Charges Hit GOP

S.A. Miller, Washington Times

Why We Chose This Piece

Public opinion polls show consistently that the American public generally likes its individual members of Congress but is not too fond of the institution as a whole. An explanation that some political scientists have offered for this finding is that we like when our individual members of Congress provide perks for our districts—for example, money to build a new park or improve roads, securing a government contract for a business in the district—but we view Congress as a whole as engaging in nothing but wasteful and inefficient spending.

At the center of this controversy are earmarks, also known as pork. Pork is congressional spending on projects in a particular congressperson's district. It may benefit the district, but it generally has no real benefit for the public at large, whose tax dollars pay for the project. Pork is frequently slipped into bills on other issues and gets passed without the rigorous debate, hearings, and scrutiny to which other spending bills are subjected. Both Barack Obama and John McCain called for earmark reform when running for president, and members of Congress often make similar pleas. Yet meaningful earmark reform has been remarkably difficult to achieve. After reading this article, ask yourself why this might be the case.

Capitol Hill lawmakers still brag about the federal dollars and projects they bring home. But in an age of taxpayer-financed bailouts and massive budget deficits, members are increasingly on the defensive about pork-barrel spending.

Pet projects are targets for charges of government waste during tough economic times, and earmarks stuffed into appropriations bills smack of Washington backroom dealing.

Republicans, laboring to re-establish the party's reputation for fiscal restraint, are bearing the brunt of the criticism and being hit from all sides.

Rep. Mary Fallin, a Republican contender in the 2010 Oklahoma governor's race, was criticized last week by her primary rival for not "practicing what she preaches" when it comes to pork spending.

"She is just as guilty on the runaway federal spending that she rails against," said state Sen. Randy Brogdon, who pointed out that Mrs. Fallin requested more than $243 million in pet projects for the upcoming fiscal year.

Lawmakers rarely acquire all the federal funding they request for the projects, but all of the requests are posted on their office Web pages under new earmark disclosure rules.

Selection published: April 20, 2009

Mrs. Fallin secured 13 projects worth $4.8 million in the 2009 appropriations bills, according to an earmark tally by Citizens Against Government Waste.

The nonprofit watchdog group's annual "Pig Book," published last week, spawned scores of news reports about pet projects sponsored by members of both parties and supplied fodder for campaign attacks.

Mrs. Fallin, who voted against every Democratic spending bill this year, said her earmark requests, including for defense projects and law enforcement programs, were legitimate. She said the earmark system needs reform but she will keep requesting projects until Congress adopts a better process.

"I want to make sure the taxpayer dollars we send to Washington come back to Oklahoma," Mrs. Fallin said. "There will be people who will try to score political points until we get that system developed."

Reps. Jerry Moran and Todd Tiahrt also are trading shots about pork spending as they face off in the Republican primary race in Kansas for the seat being vacated by retiring Sen. Sam Brownback, a Republican.

"The congressman has heard from across the state that people want real earmark reform," Moran campaign spokesman Travis Murphy said. "We expect the issue of reform that prevents situations like what we have seen with PMA and other firms to be among the many issues debated in this campaign."

The PMA Group is a lobbying firm that closed this year after the FBI raided its office in a corruption probe of campaign contributions and spending earmarks. According to the watchdog group Center for Responsive Politics, PMA donated about $27,000 to Mr. Tiahrt and $1,500 to Mr. Moran.

Mr. Moran has given the money to charity, but Mr. Tiahrt has not.

Tiahrt campaign manager Robert Noland said the candidate supports an "across-the-board" overhaul of the earmark system but also backs projects that benefit Kansas, including job-creation programs and the construction of flood-control levees.

"It is unfortunate that Congressman Moran plays politics by criticizing earmarks one moment but then gets caught by having one of his own earmarks highlighted in the ... 2009 'Pig Book,'" Mr. Noland said.

The book listed a $2.1 million project for trade centers in six states sponsored by a bipartisan group of 10 lawmakers that included Mr. Moran.

Democrats are seizing on the same arguments to counter Republicans who say President Obama and the Democrat-led Congress are on a spending spree that threatens to bankrupt the country.

"We've been hitting [Republicans] for their hypocrisy on projects—specifically, either saying they won't request them and then they did or voting against the economic recovery bill and then heralding the projects at home," said Jennifer Crider, a spokeswoman for the Democratic Congressional Campaign Committee.

Republicans are highlighting Democrats' pork spending to reinforce their message.

The National Republican Congressional Committee announced an offensive Friday targeting 43 vulnerable House Democrats with robocalls and TV and radio ads that highlight the $1.2 trillion in new spending authorized so far this year.

"Democrats have failed to be honest about their willingness to support a pork-filled stimulus package and a budget that taxes, spends and borrows in excess at the expense of their constituents," NRCC spokesman Ken Spain said.

*C*onsider the source and the audience.

- The *Washington Times* is considered to be the more conservative of the two major daily Washington newspapers. Why might it publish an article such as this one? How might its readers react to the article?

*L*ay out the argument, the values, and the assumptions.

- According to the article, why are earmarks considered to be problematic, especially during a tough economic climate?
- Why are Republican candidates, in particular, being charged with hypocrisy?

*U*ncover the evidence.

- The article gives some examples of earmarks that members of Congress have requested. Do these examples illustrate the issues often associated with pork-barrel spending? Are more systematic data needed?

*E*valuate the conclusion.

- Representative Fallin said that her earmark requests were "legitimate." What is the difference between legitimate and illegitimate earmark requests? Are all earmarks bad?

*S*ort out the political implications.

- If Congress severely limited earmarks, what effect might that have on how constituents view their members of Congress? On how they view the institution of Congress as a whole?
- How might curtailing federal earmarks affect state and local governments?

 ## 6.4 No Country for Close Calls

Nate Silver and Andrew Gelman, New York Times

Why We Chose This Piece

> *Most political scientists agree that competitive elections—or at least the potential for competitive elections—are at the heart of a healthy democracy. With few exceptions, however, the results of the overwhelming majority of congressional elections are foregone conclusions, and the lack of competitiveness has only increased over time. Although most political scientists champion the notion of competitive elections and agree that congressional elections have become less competitive over time, there is disagreement over what exactly has led to the lack of competitive elections. Here, a statistician—the same one you are introduced to in Chapter 13—and a political scientist provide what they see as the reasons behind the lack of competitive elections.*

Selection published: April 19, 2009

We like this reading because it exposes you to the "science" of politics. Moreover, it contributes to an interesting debate. What is responsible for the lack of competitive congressional elections and, perhaps more important, what can be done to fix the problem?

E lection junkies like us can't help but savor the excitement of races where the advantage shifts with nearly every click-refresh of the Board of Elections' Web site.

Right now, there's plenty to savor: the courts are still hammering out the Senate race in Minnesota, where Al Franken leads by 312 votes out of nearly three million cast. The special election in the 20th Congressional District in upstate New York, where at one point the candidates were tied at 77,225 votes each, may be headed along the same trajectory. Contests as close as these—not to mention Florida's electoral adventures in 2000—have led to an impression that the margin between Democrats and Republicans is pretty narrow. That is why when Barack Obama defeated John McCain by 7.3 points last November, historically a fairly average margin, the victory was widely hailed as a landslide.

In truth, these nail-biters have become, at least in elections to the House of Representatives, exceedingly rare.

Consider that, in the past decade, there were 2,175 elections to the United States House of Representatives held on Election Days 2000, 2002, 2004, 2006 and 2008. Among these, there were 41 instances—about 1.9 percent—in which the Democratic and Republican candidates each received 49 percent to 51 percent of the vote (our calculations exclude votes cast for minor parties). In the 1990s, by contrast, there were 65 such close elections. And their number increases the further one goes back in time: 88 examples in the 1950s, 108 in the 1930s, 129 in the 1910s.

Although "wave" elections like 1994 and 2006, in which a relatively high number of incumbents are unseated, can deliver momentarily higher numbers of close contests, the trend has generally been toward less competition. Indeed, it may be precisely because close Congressional races are so atypical that the exceptions get so much attention.

Why is it that there are fewer close elections than there once were? We can think of three reasons:

POWERFUL INCUMBENTS The incumbency advantage has generally been increasing over time. A 2002 paper by Stephen Ansolabehere and James M. Snyder Jr. of M.I.T. examined the incumbency advantage in elections since World War II, and found that it had increased from about a two-point head start in the 1940s to eight points in the 1990s.

Since there are no term limits for Congress, and since most senators and representatives today are career politicians who won't retire until age or scandal forces them to, this means that elections in the vast majority of states and Congressional districts are never competitive.

There are many theories as to why this is the case—in the television and Internet era, name recognition may be a more powerful advantage. Increasingly, gerrymandered districts may also be helping to protect incumbents, although academic research disagrees on whether gerrymandering is itself a direct cause of declining competition.

SELF-SORTING VOTERS While America as a whole is becoming more diverse, individual localities are becoming less so, according to "The Big Sort," written by Bill Bishop of The Austin American-Statesman and Robert Cushing of the University of Texas.

In the 1976 election between Jimmy Carter and Gerald Ford, only about a quarter of Americans lived in counties that were decided by 20 or more points. But by the 2004 election between George W. Bush and John Kerry, that number had nearly doubled. Mr. Bishop and Mr. Cushing's thesis is that, as the economy has become more virtual, individuals can now choose where to live on an ideological rather than an occupational basis: a liberal computer programmer in Texas can settle in blue Austin, and a conservative one in the ruby-red suburbs of Houston.

These effects can be especially acute in Congressional districts, which contain, on average, about 700,000 citizens each, and which can be as small as 10 square miles.

INFLEXIBLE PARTIES In theory, the major party candidates in each Congressional district should be able to adapt themselves to their constituents: a Republican Congressional candidate in San Francisco should be very liberal, just not quite as liberal as her Democratic counterpart, whereas a Democrat in the Oklahoma panhandle should be quite conservative, if slightly to the left of his opponent.

This sometimes still holds in elections at the state and local levels, where candidates can better divorce themselves from the priorities of national parties—Wyoming, for instance, has a very moderate Democratic governor, while Vermont has a moderate Republican one. But candidates for national office have become increasingly constrained as Congress has become more partisan.

Candidates who don't follow the party line may have trouble eliciting support from activists and national campaign committees. Voters, moreover, may have difficulty reconciling the positions the candidate is advancing with their impressions of what it means to be a Democrat or Republican on Capitol Hill.

And so Rockefeller Republicans are all but extinct in New England, whereas conservative Democrats have been all but banished from their former stronghold in the South. Gone with them are competitive elections in those districts.

The good news for fans of competitive elections is that some of these factors could conceivably be changed through acts of Congress. Congressional districts could be drawn along strictly geographic lines, for instance, or campaign finance laws could be reformed to give incumbents less of an advantage. The bad news is that the first instinct of our senators and representatives is self-preservation, and reforms that would threaten the safety of their seats are likely to encounter stiff resistance.

In an age when the country remains pretty evenly divided politically, presidential elections will likely continue to be close. But the geographical separation of Democratic and Republican voters, the rigidity of our political parties, and the ability of incumbents to win re-election in all but the most unusual circumstances have made close elections for Congress increasingly rare. Elections like those in New York's 20th district or in Minnesota, as contentious as they are, actually hark back to a less divisive era in American politics.

*C*onsider the source and the audience.

- Nate Silver and Andrew Gelman are both statisticians (Gelman is also a political scientist). Why might their backgrounds give them credibility on this issue? Does one have to understand statistics to make a persuasive case for the reasons behind the lack of competitive elections?

*L*ay out the argument, the values, and the assumptions.

- Silver and Gelman provide three reasons for the lack of competitive congressional elections. What are they?
- What do the authors believe can be done to promote competitive elections?

*U*ncover the evidence.

- Silver and Gelman raise a complex question that is difficult to address fully in a short op-ed piece. What kinds of evidence do they provide to support their argument? Is this enough, or is more detailed analysis needed?
- Do Silver and Gelman provide any evidence that their ideas to promote competitive elections will actually do so?

*E*valuate the conclusion.

- Are you convinced that the three explanations provided by Silver and Gelman are responsible for the lack of competitive elections? Is one more persuasive than the others?
- Can you think any other explanations for the decline in competitive congressional elections?

*S*ort out the political implications.

- If elections are not competitive, how might that affect the quality of representation constituents receive from their member of Congress?
- If elections were more competitive, what problems might emerge as a result?

 ## 6.5 Declaration of Conscience

Margaret Chase Smith, Speech on the Senate Floor

Why We Chose This Piece

> *Many commentators and scholars have noted an increasingly polarized atmosphere in Congress, whose members are more extreme in their views than the majority of the population. Democrats accuse Republicans of being racists and elitist warmongers; Republicans accuse Democrats of being big spenders and un-American peaceniks. In a closely divided, already partisan Congress, the post–September 11 pressures of fear, war, and antiterrorist zeal have sharpened ideological differences and heightened existing animosities.*

Selection delivered: June 1, 1950

It's hard to imagine, however, a time as rancorous in U.S. legislative history as the 1950s, also a time of national fear and unease, when Republican senator Joe McCarthy used the Senate as a platform for rooting out anyone he thought had Communist sympathies. As a result of his frequently unsubstantiated accusations and innuendo, many people lost reputations, jobs, and security. Democrats and Republicans accused each other of being too soft on communism or too restrictive of civil liberties.

Congressional politics may seem partisan and nasty in the early years of the twenty-first century, but clearly it is not a new phenomenon. On the flip side, but also not new, is the kind of integrity and concern for the national good that led Republican senator Margaret Chase Smith (the first woman to have been elected to both the House and the Senate) to break with her party and make this speech on the Senate floor, condemning the politics of personal destruction. Following Smith's speech, others gathered to condemn McCarthy, including journalists such as Edward R. Murrow, and McCarthy was officially censured by the Senate in 1954. How could one go about building such a bridge between acrimonious partisans in Congress today?

I would like to speak briefly and simply about a serious national condition. It is a national feeling of fear and frustration that could result in national suicide and the end of everything that we Americans hold dear. It is a condition that comes from the lack of effective leadership in either the Legislative Branch or the Executive Branch of our Government.

That leadership is so lacking that serious and responsible proposals are being made that national advisory commissions be appointed to provide such critically needed leadership.

I speak as briefly as possible because too much harm has already been done with irresponsible words of bitterness and selfish political opportunism. I speak as simply as possible because the issue is too great to be obscured by eloquence. I speak simply and briefly in the hope that my words will be taken to heart.

I speak as a Republican. I speak as a woman. I speak as a United States Senator. I speak as an American.

The United States Senate has long enjoyed worldwide respect as the greatest deliberative body in the world. But recently that deliberative character has too often been debased to the level of a forum of hate and character assassination sheltered by the shield of congressional immunity.

It is ironical that we Senators can in debate in the Senate directly or indirectly, by any form of words, impute to any American who is not a Senator any conduct or motive unworthy or unbecoming an American—and without that non-Senator American having any legal redress against us—yet if we say the same thing in the Senate about our colleagues we can be stopped on the grounds of being out of order.

It is strange that we can verbally attack anyone else without restraint and with full protection and yet we hold ourselves above the same type of criticism here on the Senate Floor. Surely the United States Senate is big enough to take self-criticism and self-appraisal. Surely we should be able to take the same kind of character attacks that we "dish out" to outsiders.

I think that it is high time for the United States Senate and its members to do some soul-searching—for us to weigh our consciences—on the manner in which we are performing our duty to the people of America—on the manner in which we are using or abusing our individual powers and privileges.

I think that it is high time that we remembered that we have sworn to uphold and defend the Constitution. I think that it is high time that we remembered that the Constitution, as amended, speaks not only of the freedom of speech but also of trial by jury instead of trial by accusation.

Whether it be a criminal prosecution in court or a character prosecution in the Senate, there is little practical distinction when the life of a person has been ruined.

Those of us who shout the loudest about Americanism in making character assassinations are all too frequently those who, by our own words and acts, ignore some of the basic principles of Americanism:

The right to criticize;
The right to hold unpopular beliefs;
The right to protest;
The right of independent thought.

The exercise of these rights should not cost one single American citizen his reputation or his right to a livelihood nor should he be in danger of losing his reputation or livelihood merely because he happens to know someone who holds unpopular beliefs. Who of us doesn't? Otherwise none of us could call our souls our own. Otherwise thought control would have set in.

The American people are sick and tired of being afraid to speak their minds lest they be politically smeared as "Communists" or "Fascists" by their opponents. Freedom of speech is not what it used to be in America. It has been so abused by some that it is not exercised by others.

The American people are sick and tired of seeing innocent people smeared and guilty people whitewashed. But there have been enough proved cases such as the Amerasia case, the Hiss case, the Coplon case, the Gold case, to cause nationwide distrust and suspicion that there may be something to the unproved, sensational accusations.

As a Republican, I say to my colleagues on this side of the aisle that the Republican Party faces a challenge today that is not unlike the challenge that it faced back in Lincoln's day. The Republican Party so successfully met that challenge that it emerged from the Civil War as the champion of a united nation—in addition to being a Party that unrelentingly fought loose spending and loose programs.

Today our country is being psychologically divided by the confusion and the suspicions that are bred in the United States Senate to spread like cancerous tentacles of "know nothing, suspect everything" attitudes. Today we have a Democratic Administration that has developed a mania for loose spending and loose programs. History is repeating itself—and the Republican Party again has the opportunity to emerge as the champion of unity and prudence.

The record of the present Democratic Administration has provided us with sufficient campaign issues without the necessity to resorting to political smears. America is rapidly losing its position as leader of the world simply because the Democratic Administration has pitifully failed to provide effective leadership.

The Democratic Administration has completely confused the American people by its daily contradictory grave warnings and optimistic assurances—that show the people that our Democratic Administration has no idea of where it is going.

The Democratic Administration has greatly lost the confidence of the American people by its complacency to the threat of communism here at home and the leak of vital secrets to Russia through key officials of the Democratic Administration. There are enough proved cases to make this point without diluting our criticism with unproved charges.

Surely these are sufficient reasons to make it clear to the American people that it is time for a change and that a Republican victory is necessary to the security of this country. Surely it is clear that this nation will continue to suffer as long as it is governed by the present ineffective Democratic Administration.

Yet to displace it with a Republican regime embracing a philosophy that lacks political integrity or intellectual honesty would prove equally disastrous to this nation. The nation sorely needs a Republican victory. But I don't want to see the Republican Party ride to political victory on the Four Horsemen of Calumny—Fear, Ignorance, Bigotry, and Smear.

I doubt if the Republican Party could—simply because I don't believe the American people will uphold any political party that puts political exploitation above national interest. Surely we Republicans aren't that desperate for victory.

I don't want to see the Republican Party win that way. While it might be a fleeting victory for the Republican Party, it would be a more lasting defeat for the American people. Surely it would ultimately be suicide for the Republican Party, and the two-party system that has protected our American liberties from the dictatorship of a one-party system.

As members of the Minority Party, we do not have the primary authority to formulate the policy of our Government. But we do have the responsibility of rendering constructive criticism, of clarifying issues, of allaying fears by acting as responsible citizens.

As a woman, I wonder how the mothers, wives, sisters, and daughters feel about the way in which members of their families have been politically mangled in Senate debate—and I use the word "debate" advisedly.

As a United States Senator, I am not proud of the way in which the Senate has been made a publicity platform for irresponsible sensationalism. I am not proud of the reckless abandon in which unproved charges have been hurled from this side of the aisle. I am not proud of the obviously staged, undignified countercharges that have been attempted in retaliation from the other side of the aisle.

I don't like the way the Senate has been made a rendezvous for vilification, for selfish political gain at the sacrifice of individual reputations and national unity. I am not proud of the way we smear outsiders from the Floor of the Senate and hide behind the cloak of congressional immunity and still place ourselves beyond criticism on the Floor of the Senate.

As an American, I am shocked at the way Republicans and Democrats alike are playing directly into the Communist design of "confuse, divide, and conquer." As an

American, I don't want a Democratic Administration "whitewash" or "coverup" any more than I want a Republican smear or witch hunt.

As an American, I condemn a Republican "Fascist" just as much as I condemn a Democrat "Communist." I condemn a Democrat "Fascist" just as much as I condemn a Republican "Communist." They are equally dangerous to you and me and to our country. As an American, I want to see our nation recapture the strength and unity it once had when we fought the enemy instead of ourselves.

It is with these thoughts that I have drafted what I call a "Declaration of Conscience." I am gratified that Senator Tobey, Senator Aiken, Senator Morse, Senator Ives, Senator Thye, and Senator Hendrickson have concurred in that declaration and have authorized me to announce their concurrence.

Consider the source and the audience.

- This is a speech on the Senate floor made by a female junior senator (the only woman in the Senate at the time), criticizing a colleague from her own party (whom she never mentions by name). How might these circumstances have affected her credibility with her other colleagues and the way the speech was perceived?

Lay out the argument, the values, and the assumptions.

- Why does Smith call this speech a "Declaration of Conscience?" What does she reveal explicitly about her basic values here—for instance, in terms of what it means to be an American, what is her view of the public interest and what values are more important than winning? What does she reveal about her values by her willingness to take McCarthy on when her other colleagues remained silent?
- How does Smith think the Senate should conduct itself? Why?
- What does Smith think are proper grounds for criticizing the Democrats, and how does she think that criticism is undermined by the Senate's behavior?

Uncover the evidence.

- What kinds of evidence does Smith use to support her claims? Why were her claims about what Americans want persuasive even in the days before there was extensive polling evidence to back her up?
- How does she use historical evidence to support her views?

Evaluate the conclusion.

- What does Smith imply are the proper limits of partisanship? Should the effort to advance one's own party's fortunes stop? How can partisanship be balanced against the public interest?

Sort out the political implications.

- What would this speech sound like coming from a Democrat or a Republican today? What vision of the public interest could be offered to offset partisan views?

7 ★

The Presidency

Since the New Deal in the 1930s, we have developed increasingly huge expectations of our presidents—to solve our problems and ensure us the good life—while giving them limited constitutional power to do the things we demand. In addition, we expect them to be both head of government—sort of the politician in chief, passing legislation and leading their party—at the same time that we require them to take the more lofty role of head of state, guiding the government through difficult times and symbolizing all that is good and unifying in America.

Different presidents respond to these conflicting demands in different ways, but all of them are forced to confront a tough truth. If they do not have sufficient popularity with the public to convince Congress not to cross them, they will not have the leverage needed to get their laws passed and their appointments approved. In many ways, the chief resource of the American president, on which he depends to shape the country and its institutions in the direction he desires, is his power to persuade, and to control the way the media portray him (which in turn affects his standing with the public).

Many commentators believed that the presidency of George W. Bush, which began so ignominiously with the contested election of 2000, would last only one term—that his tentative electoral victory had denied him the mandate that would persuade the public to endorse his policies and enable him to govern effectively. Almost from the start, however, Bush confounded his critics.

The events of 2001, particularly the terror attacks on September 11, convinced the public that President Bush did have what it would take to lead during difficult times. With the support of his soaring approval ratings, Bush began to craft a presidency along lines stronger than those seen since the days of Richard Nixon. Arguing that, since Watergate, the power of the office had been nibbled away by Congress (and its stature diminished by White House occupants of whom they did not approve), the Bush administration set out to create an executive branch arguably more powerful than any we had seen before. Barack Obama ran for the presidency, in part, on a platform of restoring checks and balances. Himself a constitutional law professor, Obama argues that the executive is a co-equal branch of government with the legislature and the judiciary.

In this chapter we look at several dimensions of the executive office. We begin with an editorial that is strong in its condemnation of what its authors see as an unconstitutional accrual of executive power on the part of the Bush administration. Second is an analysis of Bush's leadership style, looking to see how well he fulfilled his promise to be "a uniter, not a divider" in Washington and asking what strategies the president is justified in using in the name of getting his policies passed. Third, we take a look at a blog post by *Atlantic* writer Andrew Sullivan, comparing the leadership styles of Bush and Obama. Our fourth article, from *CQ Weekly*, looks to see whether in its early days the Obama administration was rolling back the scope of executive power, as the new president had promised to do. Finally, we turn to Abraham Lincoln, who also makes an "ends justify the means" argument about presidential power. In this speech excerpt he explains to Congress why he defied a ruling from a Supreme Court justice that his suspension of habeas corpus during wartime was unconstitutional.

 ## 7.1 The Real Agenda

Editorial, **New York Times**

Why We Chose This Piece

> *Written two years before the end of President George W. Bush's second term, this piece is concerned with the expanding reach of executive power under Bush's administration. Reading 3.4 examined the effect of presidential signing statements on the principle of checks and balances. This editorial looks at two other instances of growing executive power: the administration's claims of authority over the detention camps at Guantánamo Bay and over the practice of domestic spying by the National Security Agency. How do these critiques of the growth of executive power compare with the founders' concerns about a limited executive?*

It is only now, nearly five years after Sept. 11, that the full picture of the Bush administration's response to the terror attacks is becoming clear. Much of it, we can see now, had far less to do with fighting Osama bin Laden than with expanding presidential power.

Over and over again, the same pattern emerges: Given a choice between following the rules or carving out some unprecedented executive power, the White House always shrugged off the legal constraints. Even when the only challenge was to get required approval from an ever-cooperative Congress, the president and his staff preferred to go it alone. While no one questions the determination of the White House to fight terrorism, the methods this administration has used to do it have been shaped by another, perverse determination: never to consult, never to ask and always to fight against any constraint on the executive branch.

One result has been a frayed democratic fabric in a country founded on a constitutional system of checks and balances. Another has been a less effective war on terror.

Selection published: July 16, 2006

The Guantánamo Bay Prison

This whole sorry story has been on vivid display since the Supreme Court ruled that the Geneva Conventions and United States law both applied to the Guantánamo Bay detention camp. For one brief, shining moment, it appeared that the administration realized it had met a check that it could not simply ignore. The White House sent out signals that the president was ready to work with Congress in creating a proper procedure for trying the hundreds of men who have spent years now locked up as suspected terrorists without any hope of due process.

But by week's end it was clear that the president's idea of cooperation was purely cosmetic. At hearings last week, the administration made it clear that it merely wanted Congress to legalize President Bush's illegal actions—to amend the law to negate the court's ruling instead of creating a system of justice within the law. As for the Geneva Conventions, administration witnesses and some of their more ideologically blinkered supporters in Congress want to scrap the international consensus that no prisoner may be robbed of basic human dignity.

The hearings were a bizarre spectacle in which the top military lawyers—who had been elbowed aside when the procedures at Guantánamo were established—endorsed the idea that the prisoners were covered by the Geneva Convention protections. Meanwhile, administration officials and obedient Republican lawmakers offered a lot of silly talk about not coddling the masterminds of terror.

The divide made it clear how little this all has to do with fighting terrorism. Undoing the Geneva Conventions would further endanger the life of every member of the American military who might ever be taken captive in the future. And if the prisoners scooped up in Afghanistan and sent to Guantánamo had been properly processed first—as military lawyers wanted to do—many would never have been kept in custody, a continuing reproach to the country that is holding them. Others would actually have been able to be tried under a fair system that would give the world a less perverse vision of American justice. The recent disbanding of the C.I.A. unit charged with finding Osama bin Laden is a reminder that the American people may never see anyone brought to trial for the terrible crimes of 9/11.

The hearings were supposed to produce a hopeful vision of a newly humbled and cooperative administration working with Congress to undo the mess it had created in stashing away hundreds of people, many with limited connections to terrorism at the most, without any plan for what to do with them over the long run. Instead, we saw an administration whose political core was still intent on hunkering down. The most embarrassing moment came when Bush loyalists argued that the United States could not follow the Geneva Conventions because Common Article Three, which has governed the treatment of wartime prisoners for more than half a century, was too vague. Which part of "civilized peoples," "judicial guarantees" or "humiliating and degrading treatment" do they find confusing?

Eavesdropping on Americans

The administration's intent to use the war on terror to buttress presidential power was never clearer than in the case of its wiretapping program. The president had legal means of listening in on the phone calls of suspected terrorists and checking their e-mail messages. A special court was established through a 1978 law to give the executive branch warrants for just this purpose, efficiently and in secrecy. And Republicans in Congress were all but begging for a chance to change the process in any way the president requested. Instead, of course, the administration did what it wanted without asking anyone. When the program became public, the administration ignored calls for it to comply with the rules. As usual, the president's most loyal supporters simply urged that Congress pass a law allowing him to go on doing whatever he wanted to do.

Senator Arlen Specter, chairman of the Senate Judiciary Committee, announced on Thursday that he had obtained a concession from Mr. Bush on how to handle this problem. Once again, the early perception that the president was going to bend to the rules turned out to be premature.

The bill the president has agreed to accept would allow him to go on ignoring the eavesdropping law. It does not require the president to obtain warrants for the one domestic spying program we know about—or for any other program—from the special intelligence surveillance court. It makes that an option and sets the precedent of giving blanket approval to programs, rather than insisting on the individual warrants required by the Constitution. Once again, the president has refused to acknowledge that there are rules he is required to follow.

And while the bill would establish new rules that Mr. Bush could voluntarily follow, it strips the federal courts of the right to hear legal challenges to the president's wiretapping authority. The Supreme Court made it clear in the Guantánamo Bay case that this sort of meddling is unconstitutional.

If Congress accepts this deal, Mr. Specter said, the president will promise to ask the surveillance court to assess the constitutionality of the domestic spying program he has acknowledged. Even if Mr. Bush had a record of keeping such bargains, that is not the right court to make the determination. In addition, Mr. Bush could appeal if the court ruled against him, but the measure provides no avenue of appeal if the surveillance court decides the spying program is constitutional.

The Cost of Executive Arrogance

The president's constant efforts to assert his power to act without consent or consultation has warped the war on terror. The unity and sense of national purpose that followed 9/11 is gone, replaced by suspicion and divisiveness that never needed to emerge. The president had no need to go it alone—everyone wanted to go with him. Both parties in Congress were eager to show they were tough on terrorism. But the obsession with presidential prerogatives created fights where no fights needed to occur and made huge messes out of programs that could have functioned more efficiently within the rules.

Jane Mayer provided a close look at this effort to undermine the constitutional separation of powers in a chilling article in the July 3 issue of *The New Yorker*. She showed how it grew out of Vice President Dick Cheney's long and deeply held conviction that the real lesson of Watergate and the later Iran-contra debacle was that the president needed more power and that Congress and the courts should get out of the way.

To a disturbing degree, the horror of 9/11 became an excuse to take up this cause behind the shield of Americans' deep insecurity. The results have been devastating.

Americans' civil liberties have been trampled. The nation's image as a champion of human rights has been gravely harmed. Prisoners have been abused, tortured and even killed at the prisons we know about, while other prisons operate in secret. American agents "disappear" people, some entirely innocent, and send them off to torture chambers in distant lands. Hundreds of innocent men have been jailed at Guantánamo Bay without charges or rudimentary rights. And Congress has shirked its duty to correct this out of fear of being painted as pro-terrorist at election time.

We still hope Congress will respond to the Supreme Court's powerful and unequivocal ruling on Guantánamo Bay and also hold Mr. Bush to account for ignoring the law on wiretapping. Certainly, the president has made it clear that he is not giving an inch of ground.

*C*onsider the source and the audience.

- Here we have an editorial from a liberal-leaning city paper, but one that echoes concerns from across the spectrum about increased executive power. Why does this issue unite liberals and conservatives? Where might conservatives break with the *Times* on this issue?

*L*ay out the argument, the values, and the assumptions.

- Is the *Times* editorial board out to criticize only the Bush administration in particular, or does it have general concerns about the precedents that are set with expanded executive power? What are the board's concerns?
- What does the editorial board see as the results of Bush's preoccupation with "going it alone" and accruing power to the executive?

*U*ncover the evidence.

- The *Times* editorial board claims the Bush administration has taken certain actions. What evidence is offered in support of these claims?
- What evidence does the *Times* present that the consequences it dislikes follow from those actions? Could these consequences have resulted from anything else?

*E*valuate the conclusion.

- The editorial ends with a list of the "costs" of the Bush administration's actions (trampled civil liberties, damaged national image, prisoner abuse, and the like). Is the *Times* right that these things have come to pass?
- Did the Bush administration weaken checks and balances and wage a less effective war on terror as a result of acting without the support of Congress and the courts?

*S*ort out the political implications.

- Could the Bush administration have exercised its power in a way that would have protected Americans without the negative consequences the *Times* feared had come to pass? Is a stronger executive necessary to win the war against terrorists?

7.2 Bush Moves by Refusing to Budge

Ronald Brownstein, Los Angeles Times

Why We Chose This Piece

George W. Bush ran for president on the promise of being a "uniter, not a divider." More than halfway through his first term, however, the country had solidified along the Red America versus Blue America split we saw on electoral maps on election night 2000. This article, by Los Angeles Times *veteran political reporter Ronald Brownstein, analyzed Bush's leadership style and looked at why the expectations that Bush would be a consensus builder had fallen so far short of the mark. Does the responsibility to build consensus belong to a president or to members of the opposite party? What has been President Obama's approach to bipartisanship?*

From his law office in the small Texas town of Henderson, former Democratic state Rep. Paul Sadler barely recognizes George W. Bush anymore.

When Bush served as Texas governor, Sadler probably negotiated with him more extensively than any other Democrat in the Legislature, forging agreements on difficult issues from education reform to taxes. Through that partnership, Sadler came to see Bush as a conciliator committed to building consensus across party lines.

Now, as he watches Bush operate in Washington, Sadler sees "a harder edge."

"Almost all of us who had dealt with Bush, who were chairmen of committees or worked with him in Texas, have noticed the difference," Sadler says. "There has not been that collaborative spirit. I don't know if he's changed since Texas or the Democrats are different in Washington, or maybe it's both. But he is not the centrist as president that he was as governor."

At home and abroad, Bush has surprised friends and critics with the ambition of his presidential agenda—and the forceful, often confrontational, manner in which he has pursued it.

From a deal-maker in Texas, he has morphed into a back-breaker in Washington. With Congress and allies abroad, he has displayed a pugnacious style of leadership, advancing boldly ideological ideas that test the boundaries of consensus. He often has accepted compromise only when it appeared that he had no other choice.

"I remember describing Bush as an incrementalist when he was down here, and he was," said Bruce Buchanan, a professor of government at the University of Texas. "He was not throwing the long pass. He was not a policy ideologue by any stretch of the imagination. Now all of a sudden he's this guy who is deeply and passionately committed to a heavily substantive ideological agenda."

This approach has brought Bush many successes, from a major 2001 tax cut to the United Nations resolution that returned arms inspectors to Iraq. But it also has

---

Selection published: March 2, 2003

produced a more polarizing presidency than his record in Texas, or his rhetoric in the 2000 campaign, might have predicted.

Bush advisors believe that by showing his commitment to bold change, he reinforces an image as a strong leader that could become his greatest asset for reelection. But Democrats believe Bush is unnecessarily dividing Congress and the country in ways that could threaten his legislative agenda and his prospects for a second term.

In 2000, Bush pledged to govern as a "uniter, not a divider" who would "change the tone in Washington." On one level, he has succeeded—personal animosity between the parties isn't as intense as it was between congressional Republicans and President Clinton. But the policy differences between the two sides may be even wider than in the Clinton years.

Party-line voting in Congress has reached a new peak. According to *Congressional Quarterly*, Republicans went with their party on nearly 90% of the votes during Bush's first two years, while Democrats voted with their party nearly 86% of the time.

And despite the public's impulse to rally around the commander in chief in an unsettling age of global terrorism, opinion about Bush's performance and priorities is at least as polarized as it was about Clinton's. In the most recent poll conducted for *The Times*, 95% of Republicans said they approved of Bush's performance, while just 28% of Democrats agreed.

These centrifugal tendencies predate Bush's presidency. Party-line voting has increased steadily in Congress over the last 30 years. So has the gap between the president's approval rating among voters from his own party and those from the opposition, said Matthew Dowd, director of polling at the Republican National Committee.

Yet Bush's decisions have, in most respects, accelerated these trends.

The administration worked closely with Democrats on Bush's education reform bill and the legislative response to the Sept. 11 terrorist attacks. And on issues such as campaign finance reform, corporate accounting reform and the federalization of airport security workers, he eventually acquiesced when bipartisan congressional majorities insisted on a course he had resisted.

But mostly, Bush has pursued as hard a line in pushing his goals with Congress as he has with the world over Iraq. His intent was clear even before he took office.

Shortly after the 2000 election, Nick Calio, the first White House director of legislative affairs, went to see Bush in Texas. When Calio started to walk through concessions he might have to make to pass the tax cut bill, Bush cut him off. "Nicky," he said, "we will not negotiate with ourselves, ever."

It's a promise Bush has kept with a vengeance.

From his initial tax cut through a huge second round of tax reductions he has proposed this year, to his energy plan, his staunchly conservative judicial nominations and his new plans to restructure Medicare and Medicaid, Bush has consistently offered proposals that excite conservatives while holding little appeal even to centrist Democrats. Several moderate Republicans also have recoiled at elements of his new tax cut plan, and he's been forced to back off his initial Medicare plan after objections from both parties.

"What you get now from Bush is a sense that this is a White House determined to squeeze every last bit of political advantage out of every situation," says Will Marshall, president of the Progressive Policy Institute, a centrist Democratic think tank.

Indeed, centrist Democrats open to accommodation with Bush have complained that the White House has shown too little interest in working with them.

Moderate Sen. John B. Breaux (D-La.), who often has tried to operate as a bridge between the parties, has expressed frustration about being shut out on Medicare reform efforts, an issue where he has offered ideas similar to Bush's.

"There's been less negotiation on the policies that they are trying to push forward domestically—health care and taxes—than there has been in the past," Breaux says.

Many Bush advisors acknowledge pursuing a hardball approach, but argue they are applying lessons from President Reagan on how to move the policy debate in their direction.

"Reagan's approach was you push hard; Democrats come out against you; it seemed to be polarizing," said one senior White House aide. "But Reagan held firm, aggressively pushed his position, and at the last minute cut a deal if he had to. Many times Democrats, at least some Democrats, came with him—and Reagan got the legislation he wanted."

Key to this vision has been maximizing Republican unity. Bush's core legislative strategy has been to pass bills that track his preferences through the GOP-controlled House.

Then the White House tries to get whatever it can through the Senate, hoping to tilt the final product further in its direction in House-Senate negotiations.

That model worked in mid-2001 when the final bill produced a $1.35-trillion tax cut, about $200 billion more than the Senate had passed.

But after Democrats seized Senate control when Vermont's James F. Jeffords quit the GOP to become an independent, Bush's approach proved a recipe for stalemate on a series of issues.

Although the House passed measures Bush backed to reform health maintenance organizations, provide prescription drugs for seniors, increase government cooperation with religious charities and set a new energy policy, no bill ever reached him on those issues—either because the House and Senate could not agree or because the Senate deadlocked along party lines.

In all four cases, Democrats complained that the White House made little effort to resolve the disagreements.

In talks over HMO reform, for instance, Senate advocates of the bill say administration officials did little more than recite insurance industry objections to the measure.

"What the hell do we care what the insurance industry thinks?" Sen. John Edwards (D-N.C.), one of the bill's key sponsors, grumbled to Sen. John McCain (R-Ariz.) in one session.

Bush's hands-off attitude marked a stark contrast with his earlier pattern. In Texas, Bush was renowned for bringing together legislators from both parties and asking what it would take to reach a deal. "That was constantly our conversation," Sadler said.

But Senate Minority Leader Tom Daschle (D-S.D.) has told friends he has only rarely had such pragmatic conversations with Bush. In turn, White House aides said that even when the administration moved toward Daschle's position, the Democrat demanded more.

Most Bush advisors say it's not possible to re-create the consensual approach he used in Texas because the environment in Washington is much more partisan.

Somewhat wistfully, Bush on several occasions told Calio, "In Texas, everybody was a lot friendlier and a lot more interested in the result than the process."

And some Senate Republicans, such as Finance Committee Chairman Charles E. Grassley of Iowa, note that the administration, even if not typically working with Democrats, has not objected when they have done so.

On the morning after the Senate approved the final version of the 2001 tax bill with 12 Democratic votes, Bush called Grassley at 8:15 A.M. "I knew you were good," Grassley said Bush told him, "but I didn't know you were that good."

Yet it is also clear that given the choice between making concessions that create a broader bipartisan majority and narrowly passing a bill that more closely tracks his preferences, Bush will choose the latter, White House aides agree.

The aides believe his hard-line approach energizes the GOP base—his approval rating among Republicans exceeds even Reagan's—and reinforces his image as a strong, decisive leader. In effect, many of Bush's key advisors see polarization as an acceptable cost for the demonstration of resolve and vision.

Buchanan, the Texas professor, sees these assumptions as a key to Bush's different approach at the national level.

While the limited powers of the Texas governorship encourage a mediator's role, he says, the White House appears to have concluded that Bush's greatest form of leverage is his ability to change the parameters of debate with bold initiatives.

Some friends and foes also see in Bush a growing confidence after the Sept. 11 attacks in his own beliefs, which leads him to view domestic issues in the same black-and-white terms he has used to frame the war against terrorism.

The political risk is that this approach portrays Bush to swing voters as too rigid or too ideological. In polls, his presidency is dividing not only Democrats from Republicans, but drawing a bright line down the electorate's center. In the recent poll by *The Times*, 62% of independents who consider themselves conservative said they were inclined to support Bush in 2004; but just 24% of liberal-to-moderate independents agreed.

As political storms gather at home, Bush seems as unaffected as he does by the international turmoil over Iraq.

"In general, he is more a goal-oriented person than a process-oriented person," the senior White House aide said. "We are pursuing policies we believe are in the best interest of the country, which in the end will redound to his benefit. If that makes the process more contentious and polarized than we'd like, I think it is an acceptable price to pay."

*C*onsider the source and the audience.

- Brownstein is a well-known political reporter for a reputable national paper. What kind of sources is he likely to be able to tap into for a story like this?
- Would a liberal or conservative journal present this issue any differently?

*L*ay out the argument, the values, and the assumptions.

- What is Brownstein's basic argument about Bush's leadership style in Texas as opposed to the White House?

- What did Bush's advisors see as the benefits of his style? What did Democrats see as its drawback?
- What reasons for Bush's changed role were offered by the people Brownstein talks to?

*U*ncover the evidence.

- Brownstein offers data to support his claim that America is divided along partisan lines. Do these data show that the divide is due to Bush? What additional data might help support the claim?
- Brownstein talks to a number of people about Bush's leadership style and its effects on national politics. Is his selection of sources balanced? Who else might you like to hear from?

*E*valuate the conclusion.

- Did any of the people Brownstein talks to, even among Bush's supporters, contest the claim that Bush's leadership style was more contentious and polarizing than they expected?
- Were the Democrats right in saying that ultimately Bush's failure to reach out to them would damage the country?
- Were Bush's supporters right in saying that the gains in achieving Bush's goals justified the increased political polarization?

*S*ort out the political implications.

- What are the political implications of the "ends justify the means" argument made by Bush's supporters in this context? What is the national interest here—in substantive policy goals geared to one party's base or in policy driven by national political consensus?
- Is President Obama following his predecessor's model on working with Congress, or is he taking another approach?

 ## 7.3 The Presider

Andrew Sullivan, The Daily Dish *blog*

Why We Chose This Piece

Andrew Sullivan is a writer, British by birth but an American resident, whose Daily Dish *blog appears regularly at andrewsullivan.theatlantic.com and who writes for the* Atlantic *and the* London Times. *Although he considers himself a libertarian conservative and initially supported the Iraq war, he grew disillusioned with President Bush and was an early Obama supporter from 2007 on, though he became more skeptical about Obama after he took office. In this blog post, Sullivan compares Bush's and Obama's leadership styles (though in January 2009 Obama was in just the early days of his administration). His analysis takes off from Bush's frequently stated belief that he was "the Decider." How does Sullivan think those leadership styles follow from the two men's views of the executive office?*

Selection published: January 28, 2009

One impression from Obama's interactions with the Republicans and Democrats in Congress: Obama clearly sees the presidency as a different institution than his immediate predecessor. This is a good thing, it seems to me. Bush had imbibed a monarchical sense of the office from his father and his godfather (Cheney). The monarch *decided*. If you were lucky, you'd get an explanation later, usually dolled up in propaganda. But the president had one accountability moment—the election of 2004—and the rest of the time he saw the presidency as a form of power that should be used with total boldness and declarative clarity.

At times, Bush's indifference to the system around him bordered on a kind of political autism. And so one of the oddest aspects of Bush's presidency was his tendency to declare things as if merely saying them as president could make them so. The model was clear and dramatically intensified by wartime: the president pronounced; Congress anemically responded; the base rallied. At the start, it felt like magic, but as reality slipped through the fast-eroding firewall of reckless spending and military misadventure, Bush's authority disappeared all the more quickly—because his so-certain predictions were so obviously wrong. The Decider had no response to this. He just had to keep deciding and asserting, to less and less effect, that he was right all along. Hence the excruciating final months. Within a democratic system, we had replicated all the comedy and tragedy of cocooned authoritarianism.

Now look at Obama. What the critics misread in his Inaugural was its classical structure. He was not running any more. He was presiding. His job was not to rally vast crowds, but to set the scene for the broader constitutional tableau to come to life. Hence the obvious shock of some Republican Congressman at debating with a president who seemed interested in actual conversation, as opposed to pure politics. Last Tuesday, there were none of the bold declarative predictions of the Second Bush Inaugural—and none of the slightly creepy Decider idolatry. Yes, Obama set some very clear directional goals, but the key difference is what came next: a window of invitation. The invitation is to the other co-equal branches of government to play their part; and for the citizenry to play its. This is an understanding of the president as one node in a constitutional order—not a near-dictator outside and superior to other branches of government. It is a return to traditional constitutional order. And it is rooted in a traditional, small-c conservative understanding of the presidency.

If Bush was about the presidency as power, Obama is about the presidency as *authority*. It's fascinating to watch this deep difference in understanding slowly but unmistakably realize itself in public actions. Somewhere the Founders are smiling. The system is correcting itself after one of the most unbalanced periods in American history. But it took the self-restraint of one man to do it.

---

*C*onsider the source and the audience.

- This is a blog post by a writer who admittedly does not like President Bush. Can we trust anything he says about Bush, or is such analysis inevitably flawed by Sullivan's biases?
- Is a blog post a more or less reliable source than the mainstream media? To what standards should we hold it?

*L*ay out the argument, the values, and the assumptions.

- For Sullivan, what is the difference between being a Decider and a Presider? How does this difference relate to the difference between power and authority?
- Sullivan clearly believes that one of these roles is more appropriate than the other in American politics. Which role, and why? What is his constitutional claim?

*U*ncover the evidence.

- Does Sullivan offer any kind of evidence here? What kind? Would you like to see other kinds of evidence?
- Would he have had to document his evidence differently if this argument were appearing in a more mainstream outlet than his own blog? Does the absence of sources and footnotes negate the value of his argument?

*E*valuate the conclusion.

- Sullivan obviously prefers Obama's leadership style to Bush's on constitutional grounds. After one week in office, had Obama given Sullivan enough grounds to come to that conclusion? What would you say now that more time has passed?

*S*ort out the political implications.

- What do you think the founders would have made of Sullivan's argument if they were magically brought back today? Was the Constitution written with a Decider or a Presider in mind?
- If Sullivan is right about the difference between the two men, how will the Obama administration look different from the Bush administration?

 ## 7.4 Taking Giant Steps to Define Executive Powers

David Nather, CQ Weekly

Why We Chose This Piece

> *As the previous readings have indicated, the question of how much power the president should have is by no means settled in American politics. President Bush sought to expand the power of the executive, and, at least early in his administration, President Obama made good on his promise to bring it back into balance with Congress and the courts. In this article, CQ Weekly staffer David Nather looks at the evidence, one month into the new administration. Has Obama's behavior changed in this regard in the ensuing months?*

O n the campaign trail, Barack Obama swore he wouldn't be another president who grabs power for himself and resists oversight from Congress and the courts. He taught constitutional law for more than a decade, he liked to remind

Selection published: February 22, 2009

his audiences, and he promised to pull back on some of the most sweeping claims of executive power made by George W. Bush.

"The biggest problems that we're facing right now have to do with George Bush trying to bring more and more power into the executive branch and not go through Congress at all," he said in March at a town hall gathering in Lancaster, Pa. "And that's what I intend to reverse when I'm president."

Such pledges met with wide skepticism, since Washington's conventional wisdom holds that new presidents rarely find themselves in the reversing-of-their-own-power business for very long. While some of the new powers that Bush and Vice President Dick Cheney claimed for the executive branch—such as the bid for nearly unilateral control over people detained as suspected terrorists—might be readily reversed, others, such as the dramatically expanded spending authority granted to the Treasury under the law enacted last fall creating the Troubled Asset Relief Program (TARP), clearly won't be up for review in Obama's White House.

Even so, the early track record of the young administration has surprised scholars and advocates who are eager to see new restraints placed on the exercise of executive power. Some of the first steps Obama has taken as president, along with several of his early appointments, suggest that he actually is rejecting some of Bush's most expansive executive power claims, experts say, particularly on national security and secrecy.

But that's not to say that executive power watchdogs can rest easy for the next four years. There are just enough gray areas and caveats, observers caution, to suggest that Obama isn't entirely opposed to strong presidential powers in other forms. He's embraced an active approach on the economic crisis that limits the involvement of Congress. And even on national security policy, he's left a few important policies vague enough that watchdog groups say his administration still deserves close scrutiny.

Two days after his inauguration, Obama ordered the closing of the detention camp at Guantanamo Bay, Cuba, within a year; created a task force to do a top-to-bottom review of U.S. policies for detaining suspected terrorists; required that interrogations be done in compliance with the Geneva Conventions and limited to techniques authorized by the Army field manual; and told interrogators not to rely on any other legal opinions issued by the Bush administration after Sept. 11, 2001.

That's important because the authorization of "enhanced interrogation techniques"— as well as other justifications of broad executive powers, such as surveillance and military commissions—came from legal opinions written by the Justice Department's Office of Legal Counsel. Obama has also instructed agencies to adopt "a presumption in favor of disclosure" when the public asks for records and made it harder for ex-presidents to claim executive privilege to fight the release of their records.

Such moves add up to a clear signal that Obama wants to make a clean break from the most controversial aspects of the Bush record on presidential powers. "The signs are pretty strong that he is dialing back some of the more aggressive claims of executive power" that Bush made during his presidency, said Peter M. Shane, a law professor at Ohio State University who specializes in separation of powers.

Stealth Power Plays?

Still, other critics note that this collaborative outlook doesn't always extend to the most urgent issue of Obama's young presidency: helping to resuscitate the economy.

In pushing for the economic stimulus bill and follow-up disbursement of TARP funds, the White House is already embracing a powerful executive branch role in battling the economic crisis.

Treasury Secretary Timothy F. Geithner's plan for stabilizing the banking system envisions an investment of up to $2 trillion in public and private funds with little involvement from Congress, and lawmakers of both parties say it's sorely lacking in specifics. As part of that plan, Obama plans to use $350 billion in TARP funds without showing much concern for the broad spending latitude Congress wrote into the bailout law—so broad the Bush administration didn't even have to spend the first $350 billion on troubled assets.

Gene Healy, a vice president at the libertarian Cato Institute, called Obama "a bundle of contradictions" on executive power. "He's uncomfortable, and rightly so, with the Bush administration's claims of executive power in foreign affairs," said Healy, but he "seems really comfortable, through programs like TARP, with the idea that the president can remake the economy through executive fiat."

Watchdog groups, meanwhile, are paying close attention to how the administration will settle issues that are unresolved in his executive orders. Sharon Bradford Franklin, senior counsel at the Constitution Project, said the Guantanamo executive order leaves open the possibility that some suspects could be tried in some kind of national security court—rather than under the traditional criminal justice system—while the detention order refers to "other disposition" of suspected terrorists, suggesting that some of them may still be held indefinitely.

Obama already has demonstrated that he's aware of the importance of guarding presidential prerogatives. With former Bush adviser Karl Rove citing executive privilege in refusing to testify in the House Judiciary Committee's probe of the firing of several U.S. attorneys, Obama has tried to avoid taking sides. White House counsel Gregory B. Craig says Obama is "very sympathetic to those who want to find out what happened" but wants to be careful "not to do anything that would undermine or weaken the institution of the presidency."

In addition, Obama's decision to take a year to close Guantanamo hasn't won raves from critics of the Bush policies. But Mickey Edwards, a former Republican House member who specializes in constitutional issues, says Obama's caution shows that he—unlike Bush—is aware he's not the only stakeholder in these kinds of decisions.

"What's really important here is that Obama acknowledges that even though he knows what he wants to do, it's not necessarily just his call as to whether we do it," said Edwards, now a lecturer at Princeton's Woodrow Wilson School of Public and International Affairs. "He's showing some good judgment in not just rushing into these decisions."

The Bureaucrats' View

Executive power watchdogs also are keeping tabs on Obama's early appointments, especially since many of them have long track records as skeptics of Bush's broad executive-power claims.

Attorney General Eric H. Holder Jr., who once called for "a reckoning" for the Bush administration's treatment of detainees and warrantless wiretapping program, promised during his confirmation hearing to do his job "with the humility to recognize that congressional oversight and judicial review are necessary." In written answers to questions from the committee, he hinted that he might release some of the Office of Legal Counsel's still-secret memos from that period.

In addition, Dawn Johnsen, whom Obama has nominated to head the Office of Legal Counsel, was an outspoken critic of that office's justification of aggressive interrogation practices, writing in Slate.com that "we must regain our ability to feel outrage whenever our government acts lawlessly and devises bogus constitutional arguments for outlandishly expansive presidential power."

And Leon E. Panetta, the new director of the Central Intelligence Agency, made it clear at his confirmation hearings that he rejects the kinds of aggressive interrogation tactics the Bush administration used. "I understand the powers the president has under Article II, and they are broad powers," he told Republican Sen. Richard M. Burr of North Carolina. "But nobody is above the law."

Still, even Obama's appointees leave room for flexibility in what the president can do. They just set narrower boundaries than the Bush administration did. In answers to written questions from Republican Sen. Arlen Specter of Pennsylvania, Holder wrote, "A statute cannot impermissibly infringe the president's constitutional powers." But, defending his criticism of Bush's warrantless eavesdropping program, he also wrote, "There is a critical difference between the president's authority to take certain actions in the absence of a statute and his authority to take the same action in violation of a statute."

Other Obama appointees acknowledge the idea that the president should be able to control the executive branch bureaucracy, but they generally say it applies only when Congress hasn't specifically spoken on an issue. For example, Elena Kagan, the nominee for solicitor general, wrote in the Harvard Law Review in 2001 that "presidential administration"—her term for President Bill Clinton's heavy use of directives to agencies—"advances political accountability" because the president responds directly to public opinion.

In the long run, skeptics of presidential power say that without more active restraint by Congress and the courts, it can easily rebound if another terrorist attack puts pressure on the president to respond with strong measures. Obama is "a president who has decided, for the time being, to hold himself in check," said Healy. "That's rare enough in itself, and he should be commended for that. But it's not by any means a perfect solution."

*C*onsider the source and the audience.

- *CQ Weekly* is a respected source on American politics, held to be balanced and fair. Is this report therefore more persuasive than, say, what Andrew Sullivan wrote in the previous selection?
- Do you read this piece differently because of the source? Should you?

*L*ay out the argument, the values, and the assumptions.

- Nather is not so much making an argument himself, as he is letting other people make it. He cites both supporters of Obama's view of the presidency, and its critics. What are the different dimensions of presidential power they discuss?

- What is the difference between executive power wielded to make foreign policy and that power wielded in the domestic sphere? What distinction do some observers make between the president's acting where there is no law and the president's acting in conflict with the law?
- What does the Constitution say about all of this? Why are even critics of Obama seemingly inclined to give him some benefit of the doubt?
- What does this article imply is the ultimate check on Obama's executive authority?

*U*ncover the evidence.

- Does Nather use data and figures here to support the various cases people make, or does he take them at their word? Does their expertise mean that independent evidence of their claims is unnecessary?
- What other sides might be represented here? Does anyone who Nather talks to think the presidency should be more powerful than it already is? Do any of them support Bush's view of the executive? Why might that be?

*E*valuate the conclusion.

- Most of the sources Nather cites appear to believe that, one month into the job, Obama is staying pretty true to his word on a constitutional level, even if he is calling for a more muscular government to handle our economic problems. Is that still the case?

*S*ort out the political implications.

- Do emergencies (like 9/11 or the economic crash of 2008) call for strong executive power to solve them, or can they be responded to with the more measured response of a checked and balanced government?
- Can executives bulk up and acquire new powers when they need them to solve an emergency, and then give them up when normal times return? Are they likely to do so, if they could?

 ## 7.5 Excerpt from Speech to Congress

Abraham Lincoln

Why We Chose This Piece

> *In a list of restrictions on the powers of Congress, Article I, Section 9 of the U.S. Constitution says, "The Privilege of the Writ of Habeas Corpus shall not be suspended, unless when in Cases of Rebellion or Invasion the public Safety may require it." Habeas corpus, meaning literally "to have the body," is a way of protecting someone from being arrested and held for political reasons. A judge can issue a writ of habeas corpus and have the prisoner delivered before him, to inquire into the legality of the charge. For some people this writ is so essential to our notion of due process of law that they call it the "writ of liberty."*

Selection delivered: September 15, 1863

As the Civil War began, President Abraham Lincoln struggled to suppress the rebellion in the Southern states and the activities of its Northern sympathizers in the Democratic Party. In April 1861 he was fearful that the state of Maryland, leaning toward secession, would act to prevent the federal army from passing through the state. To control what he believed to be the subversive speech and actions of Maryland politicians, he suspended the writ of habeas corpus.

John Merryman was arrested in May of the same year. U.S. Supreme Court Justice Roger B. Taney issued a writ of habeas corpus to the military to show cause for Merryman's arrest. Under Lincoln's orders, the military refused. Taney issued a judgment saying that under the Constitution only Congress had the power to suspend the writ, and that by taking that power on himself, Lincoln was taking not only the legislative power, but also the judicial power, to arrest and imprison without due process of law. Taney granted that he could not enforce his judgment against the power of the military but said that if the military were allowed to take judicial power in that way, then the people of the United States had ceased to live under the rule of law.

On July 4, Lincoln appeared before Congress and, among other things, attempted to defend his assumption of the power to suspend habeas corpus and his defiance of the Supreme Court's ordering him to stop. The following is an excerpt from his speech.

Obviously we have survived what Taney saw as an overzealous power grab. Although Lincoln expanded the suspension of habeas corpus in 1862, Congress finally acted to approve it in 1863, and it remained suspended until a Supreme Court ruling in 1866 (Ex Parte Milligan) officially restored it. What did Lincoln risk in defying the Supreme Court? Was it worth it?

Soon after the first call for militia it was considered a duty to authorize the commanding general in proper cases according to his discretion, to suspend the privilege of the writ of habeas corpus, or in other words to arrest and detain, without resort to the ordinary processes and forms of law, such individuals as he might deem dangerous to the public safety. This authority has purposely been exercised but very sparingly. Nevertheless the legality and propriety of what has been done under it are questioned and the attention of the country has been called to the proposition that one who is sworn to "take care that the laws be faithfully executed" should not himself violate them. Of course some consideration was given to the questions of power and propriety before this matter was acted upon. The whole of the laws which were required to be faithfully executed were being resisted and failing of execution in nearly one-third of the States. Must they be allowed to finally fail of execution, even had it been perfectly clear that by the use of the means necessary to their execution some single law, made in such extreme tenderness of the citizen's liberty that practically it relieves more of the guilty than of the innocent, should to a very limited extent be violated? To state the question more directly, are all the laws but one to go unexecuted and the Government itself go to pieces lest that one be violated? Even in such a case would not the official oath be broken if the Government should be overthrown, when it was believed that disregarding the single law would tend to preserve it? But it was not believed that this question was presented. It was not believed that any law was violated. The provision of the Constitution that "the privilege of the writ of habeas corpus shall not be suspended unless when in cases of rebellion or invasion the public safety may require it," is equivalent to a provision—is a provision—that such privilege may be suspended when in cases of rebellion or invasion the public safety does require it. It was decided that we have a case of rebellion, and that the public safety does require the qualified suspension of the privilege of the writ which was authorized to be made. Now, it is insisted that Congress and not the Executive is vested with this power. But the Constitution itself is silent as to which, or who, is to exercise the power; and as the provision was plainly made for a dangerous emergency, it cannot be believed the framers of the instrument intended that in every case the danger should run its course until Congress could be called together, the very assembling of which might be prevented, as was intended in this case, by the rebellion.

*C*onsider the source and the audience.

- Lincoln is speaking to Congress under a state of emergency. How does that fact affect the terms in which he casts his argument? When does urgency become panic? How far should it be resisted?

*L*ay out the argument, the values, and the assumptions.

- What is Lincoln's essential purpose here, which he believes justifies some reduction in due process? What does he see as the trade-off facing him as executor of the laws?
- Why doesn't he mention the name of the person who has challenged his actions?
- How does he reason that the founders must not have intended members of Congress to be the ones to decide whether habeas corpus should be suspended?

*U*ncover the evidence.

- What does a reading of the Constitution tell us about this matter? Is the Constitution indeed silent?

*E*valuate the conclusion.

- How persuasive is the "ends justify the means" argument in this context? What are its limits? What means might not be justified by a worthy end?

*S*ort out the political implications.

- Is Lincoln's argument relevant to the Bush administration's acquisition of additional power after 9/11? What are the similarities between the two situations? What are the differences?

8

Bureaucracy

Bureaucracy. We may love to hate it—but we can't live without it. No other part of American government is so often mocked and maligned yet touches our lives more frequently or more directly. The job of American government in the twenty-first century is vast, and the people who do that job—who deliver our mail, approve our student loan checks, examine our tax returns, register us to vote, issue our driver's licenses, direct airport security, buy fighter jets, determine what intersections should have stoplights, even the people who decide how much arsenic can safely be in our drinking water—are all federal, state, or local government employees, also known as bureaucrats.

A bureaucracy is really no more than a hierarchical organization (meaning that power flows from the top down), governed by explicit rules, where workers specialize in particular tasks and advance by merit. It is decision making by experts and specialists, where those with less power defer to those with more, and everyone defers to the rules. What it especially is *not* is democratic. Democratic decisions are made when we want to take account of as many views as possible, or to serve the broadest possible interests. Democracy is often slow and cumbersome, and certainly not very efficient. We would never want to decide democratically about whether to approve a new cancer drug, for instance, because most of us don't know enough to make a very good job of it, and by the time we all finished making our views heard, several people would no doubt have died waiting for the drug's approval.

Although it's difficult for Americans to accept, democracy is not always an appropriate decision-making technique. Bureaucracy sometimes does a much better job. But the things that make bureaucracy good at what it does—the expert decisions made behind closed doors, the lack of accountability to the public, the huge number of rules and massive amounts of paperwork (known as red tape) that help to ensure that bureaucrats treat all people the same—also make it ripe for criticism by an impatient and suspicious public. And that, perhaps, is the best check of all on a bureaucracy that, although subject to executive approval and legislative oversight, still wields a great deal of power without having to answer directly to the American voters.

In this chapter we present four selections that raise different issues facing bureaucracies. The first article reports on an artist who, frustrated with the system of highways in

Los Angeles that repeatedly confused him and sent him the wrong way, decided to ignore regular bureaucratic channels and take matters into his own hands. Second, we turn to an article from the *New York Times* that discusses a recent decision by a county government to ban trans fat, a move that has become increasingly common in cities across the country. Although the decision to eliminate trans fat was not made by a bureaucrat, the issues regarding regulation that emerge from the article definitely apply to the bureaucracy—the institution typically in charge of enacting regulations at the federal level. The third article, by Jeffrey Rosen in the *New Republic*, examines whether the Department of Homeland Security, one of the most complex components of the federal bureaucracy, has kept Americans safe. Finally, we close with a speech by President Harry Truman in 1945 calling for the creation of a Department of Defense.

8.1 In Artist's Freeway Prank, Form Followed Function

Unauthorized Addition to Sign Went Unnoticed for Months. No Charges Planned.

Hugo Martin, Los Angeles Times

Why We Chose This Piece

We all like to kvetch about rules and regulations—usually the most visible sign of government bureaucracy in our lives—but few of us decide to do something about it the way Richard Ankrom did in the article below. We like this article because it embodies that American willingness to "fight City Hall," but we also like to imagine the consequences if we all took on the system the way Ankrom did. As you read this article, ask yourself what the opportunities and costs of this kind of civil disobedience are.

What more could an artist want? An unusual medium. A chance to take a jab at the establishment. An almost endless audience, speeding to see the work. Richard Ankrom created that enviable milieu above an unlikely canvas—the Harbor Freeway in downtown Los Angeles.

For two years, the rail-thin artist planned and prepared for his most ambitious project, a piece that would be seen by more than 150,000 motorists per day on the freeway, near 3rd Street.

With friends documenting his every move on camera, Ankrom clandestinely installed the finished product on a gray August morning. For nine months, no one noticed. It even failed to catch the eye of California Department of Transportation officials.

And that is exactly what Ankrom hoped for.

The 46-year-old Los Angeles artist designed, built and installed an addition to an overhead freeway sign—to exact state specifications—to help guide motorists on the

---

Selection published: May 9, 2002

sometimes confusing transition to the northbound Golden State Freeway a couple miles farther north.

He installed his handiwork in broad daylight, dressed in a hard hat and orange reflective vest to avoid raising suspicion. He even chopped off his shoulder-length blond hair to fit the role of a blue-collar freeway worker.

The point of the project, said Ankrom, was to show that art has a place in modern society—even on a busy, impersonal freeway. He also wanted to prove that one highly disciplined individual can make a difference.

Embarrassed Caltrans officials, who learned of the bogus sign from a local newspaper column, concede that the sign could be a help. They will leave it in place, for now. The transportation agency doesn't plan to press charges, for trespassing or tampering with state property.

Why didn't the counterfeit sign get noticed?

"The experts are saying that Mr. Ankrom did a fantastic job," conceded Caltrans spokeswoman Jeanne Bonfilio. "They thought it was an internal job."

Ankrom's work has also won praise from some in the art world.

Mat Gleason, publisher of the Los Angeles art magazine *Coagula*, learned about the project a few months ago. He calls it "terrific" because it shows that art can "benefit people and at the same time the bureaucracy a little."

The idea for the sign came to Ankrom back in 1999, when he found himself repeatedly getting lost trying to find the ramp to the north Golden State after the Harbor becomes the Pasadena Freeway. (The sharp left-lane exit sneaks up on drivers at the end of a series of four tunnels.)

He thought about complaining to Caltrans. But he figured his suggestion would get lost in the huge state bureaucracy. Instead, Ankrom decided to take matters into his own hands by adding a simple "North 5" to an existing sign.

"It needed to be done," he said from his downtown loft. "It's not like it was something that was intentionally wrong."

It didn't hurt that his work is displayed before 150,000 people daily. On an average day, even the Louvre gets only one-tenth that many visitors. He also didn't mind that his "guerrilla public service" made Caltrans look a bit foolish. "They are left with egg on their faces," he said.

Ankrom had planned to wait until August—a year after the installation—to reveal his forgery via video at an art show. But a photographer friend leaked the story.

From his tiny Brewery Art Complex loft, Ankrom said he tries to use his work to comment on current trends. The Seattle native fabricates hatchets embedded with roses and produces neon-illuminated laser guns. To pay the bills, he is also a freelance sign maker.

The expertise he gained in both fields helped him pull off the perfect counterfeit job.

He closely studied existing freeway signs, matching color swatches and downloading specifications from the Federal Highway Administration's Web site.

His biggest challenge was finding reflective buttons resembling those on Interstate signs—a dilemma finally resolved when he discovered a replica sold by a company in Tacoma, Wash.

The video he made of the entire process shows Ankrom snapping digital photos of existing Golden State Freeway signs and projecting the images onto paper, before tracing them onto a sheet of aluminum. He cut and painted the aluminum sign and even "aged" it with a layer of gray.

Ankrom affixed a contractor-style logo on the side of his pickup truck to add authenticity during the project. But closer examination might have raised suspicions. It read: Aesthetic De Construction. He even printed up a bogus work order, just in case he was stopped by police. "I tried to make this airtight, because I didn't want anything to go wrong," he said.

In early August, Ankrom launched the final phase of his project. After friends were in place with video and still cameras, one gave the all-clear signal via walkie-talkie: "Move in rubber ducky."

He made short work of the final installation—climbing up the sign and hanging over speeding traffic to install his addition. The main challenge was avoiding the razor wire on the way up.

Ankrom said he's not surprised that Caltrans isn't pressing charges, adding, "It wasn't straight-out vandalism."

For now, department officials say they will merely inspect the elements of Ankrom's sign to make sure they are securely fastened. They may be replaced in a few months as part of a program to retrofit all freeway signs with new, highly reflective models.

Caltrans officials had discussed adding more directional signs, but the agency spokeswoman said she is not sure why the department never followed through.

Ankrom said he would like Caltrans to return the work. "If they want to keep it up there, that is fine too," he said. "Hopefully it will help people out, which was the whole point."

*C*onsider the source and the audience.

- What does it mean that the source is a major-circulation, western-city newspaper?

*L*ay out the argument, the values, and the assumptions.

- What did Ankrom think he was doing? What were his political goals, and why did he think he was justified in pursuing them? (For our present purposes, we can set aside his artistic goals.)
- Can you put Ankrom's argument into general terms, so that it would apply to other people in other situations?
- What can you tell about Ankrom's worldview and the values that underlie his thinking about this issue?

*U*ncover the evidence.

- Does Ankrom offer any evidence to support his claim that his actions are justified?

*E*valuate the conclusion.

- Are Ankrom's actions justified? Can you imagine coming to the opposite conclusion? Which is more persuasive? Why?

*S*ort out the political implications.

- Did Ankrom's actions cause any harm? Could they have? What if everyone behaved this way?

8.2 Does That Trans-Fat Ban Grease a Slippery Slope?

Kate Stone Lombardi, New York Times

Why We Chose This Piece

Have you ever walked into a restaurant that is entirely nonsmoking and were upset that you couldn't enjoy a smoke over dinner? Maybe you've wondered why you are required to wear a seat belt or have complained that laws mandating that you wear a helmet while riding a motorcycle infringe on your personal freedoms. These examples involve regulations usually created and enforced by the bureaucracy to protect citizens. Critics complain that they limit personal freedom and create too much "red tape."

The following article highlights the debate over government regulations for public safety versus a person's individual freedom. It examines a decision by a county in the New York metropolitan area to ban trans fat, a substance that is bad for your health but gives foods, such as bakery products, a desired texture and taste. Although in this case it was a legislative body, not a bureaucratic agency, that enacted the ban, the issues the article raises can be applied to bureaucratic decision making as well. How do we decide where to draw the line between protecting the public good and allowing citizens to enjoy the personal freedom for which democracy is famous?

Westchester County government works hard to protect us, issuing warnings for every season of our lives. If it's not how to use space heaters safely in the winter, it's about potentially dangerous birdbaths in the summer. (The stagnant water may attract mosquitoes, which might breed West Nile disease.)

It's easy to make fun of these dispatches, but then again, neither electrical fires (frayed or cracked cords) nor debilitating illnesses (those bugs) are laughing matters. The question is, how much is too much? At what point is the county reasonably promoting our health and safety, and when does it turn into a "nanny state," treating adults like children and interfering with our rights to live our lives as stupidly as we choose?

The latest salvo in the battle is the county's recent ban on the use of cooking oils containing trans fat. On Jan. 15, Health Department inspectors began checking food service establishments for the now-illegal oils. After a 90-day grace period, restaurants—as well as cafeterias, nursing homes, even food carts, if they are licensed by the county—will be subject to fines if they break the new law.

No one can rationally argue that trans fats are desirable. This is the stuff created by partial hydrogenation, which turns liquid oil into a solid fat. Trans fats are used as a substitute for saturated fats in baked goods, because they can add creaminess and shelf life to commercial products. They are also used in fried foods, salad dressing, margarine and other foods.

Selection published: January 27, 2008

Trans fats are directly linked to heart disease; they raise levels of a particularly unhealthy form of cholesterol. The county health commissioner, Dr. Joshua Lipsman, likens what trans fat does to the body to what bacon grease does to a kitchen sink. The stiffer and harder the fats become, the more they clog the arteries. Dr. Lipsman estimates that once the ban is in effect, there will be 50 to 100 fewer deaths in Westchester each year.

Local chefs are not standing up to defend this artery-clogging fat. But what some of them are worried about, they say, is the slippery slope of government regulation of their business. The county Board of Legislators is considering a bill that would require chain restaurants to post the calorie content of menu items prominently. Both the trans-fat ban and the proposed calorie count law are based on New York City regulations.

"We saw it happen in New York City, and we knew it was just a matter of time before it was going to come here," said Jonathan Pratt, the owner of Peter Pratt's Inn in Yorktown Heights. He has a worried eye on California, where the health department awards restaurants a letter grade, which they require to be prominently posted. "Imagine—your restaurant has a big 'C' in front of it," Mr. Pratt said. "That will sure bring people in."

Rich Stytzer, president of the Westchester/Rockland Chapter of the New York State Restaurant Association, said his group had been working with the Health Department on a voluntary switch to non-trans-fat oils. He said about 750 of the county's roughly 3,000 food service establishments had voluntarily made the switch. But Mr. Stytzer, who runs Antun's of Westchester, a catering hall in Elmsford, would have preferred to keep the program voluntary.

"When do you stop with the legislation?" he asked. "It's hard enough to stay in business in Westchester County now. Every mandate and every penny is a hardship on a restaurant. The restaurants change to their customers' needs and wants, and we don't need the government coming in and telling us what to do."

Jay Lippin, the chef at Mighty Joe Young's, in Hartsdale, made the switch to trans-fat-free oil before he was required to do so. Of course, that doesn't mean customers should feel virtuous if they order Mr. Lippin's 28-ounce T-bone steak served with garlic mashed potatoes or 12-ounce filet mignon served with fried calamari. The chef notes that he also has fish and salads on the menu, and that "like everything, it's all about moderation."

Mr. Lippin now uses an oil called Elitra, which he said costs twice as much as the oil he had been using, but because it is more stable, it lasts longer, so it is not as expensive as it seems. Mr. Pratt said the price of non-trans-fat oils had risen sharply. In the last six months, the price of a 35-pound cube of fryer oil rose from $13 to $22.

Dr. Lipsman, who also supports the calorie-posting proposal, scoffed at the "slippery slope" concept and denied that the health department would ultimately go after cheeseburgers, fries or foie gras.

"When chefs say, 'Oh, what's next?' they are missing the concept of reasonableness," he said. "We are enforcing laws that protect public health, and this doesn't take away from people's choices. Trans fat is like lead in gasoline or lead in paint. It's something that doesn't need to be there and no one will miss."

*C*onsider the source and the audience.

- Unlike many of the readings in this book, the author is not making the argument here. Instead, this is a straight piece of news reporting in which she relies on others to argue for and against the ban. Is it clear where the author stands on the issue? Does it matter?
- The article is from the *New York Times* regarding a decision made by a county in the New York metropolitan area. Why might the audience for this article be much larger than just those who live in the county?

*L*ay out the argument, the values, and the assumptions.

- Why did the county decide to ban trans fat?
- Why do some business owners oppose such a move? Is it just the ban on trans fat that concerns them, or is it something more?

*U*ncover the evidence.

- The author writes "No one can rationally argue that trans fats are desirable." What evidence does she provide to support such a strong claim?
- What evidence do those who oppose the ban provide to back their position?

*E*valuate the conclusion.

- Do we need more evidence to reach a conclusion on the issue, or is the evidence given sufficient?
- From what you have read, on which side of the debate do you fall? Why?

*S*ort out the political implications.

- Actions like smoking have externalities that affect others. Does eating trans fats have social costs?

8.3 Man-Made Disaster

Six Years On, the Department of Homeland Security Is Still a Catastrophe

Jeffrey Rosen, New Republic

Why We Chose This Piece

> As noted in Reading 8.1, a regular criticism of bureaucracy is that it can become inefficient and unwieldy. This article portrays the Department of Homeland Security (DHS),

---

Selection published: December 24, 2008

by comparison to other bureaucratic departments a new creation, as being the poster child for government waste and inefficiency. With the creation of the DHS shortly after September 11, a bipartisan Congress and President George W. Bush intended to stream-line bureaucracy and thereby make Americans safer at home. Many observers argue that the DHS has indeed accomplished this goal. Others aren't so sure. Bureaucratic reorgani-zation does not guarantee success since battles over jurisdiction often emerge and agen-cies resist changing bureaucratic culture—the accepted values and procedures of an organization—that existed before the merge.

Jeffrey Rosen argues that the DHS has fallen victim to exactly those problems. We include this article for a few reasons. First, it is an in-depth look at one of the most talked about gov-ernment agencies today. Second, Rosen's argument is thought provoking, yet highly contro-versial. Even if you ultimately disagree with his analysis, the article provides fascinating insight into the DHS and the problems that new bureaucratic organizations often face. As you read the article, ask yourself how employees of the DHS might react to Rosen's claims.

Michael Chertoff needs an office. When I interviewed the secretary of Homeland Security this summer, we met in a pair of temporary locations between which he shuttles—first in the decaying Nebraska Avenue Complex of the naval sta-tion at Ward Circle (a center for signal analysis during World War II) and later in an unmarked and unfurnished office in the nondescript headquarters of U.S. Customs and Border Protection in the Ronald Reagan building, near the White House. Chertoff hasn't settled into an office partly because the six-year-old Department of Homeland Security (DHS) still has no permanent, consolidated headquarters. Instead, the unwieldy amal-gam of 22 separate federal agencies operates out of 70 buildings at 40 different locations in the Washington area. And the lack of a real home is just the beginning of the depart-ment's bureaucratic problems. The most recent survey by the U.S. Office of Personnel Management on the job satisfaction of federal employees in 36 agencies ranked Home-land Security last or near last in every category. Meanwhile, officials from the Pentagon who have tried to do business with DHS complained to me of organizational chaos at the department. Homeland Security employees, they said, are often unaware of overlap-ping initiatives championed by their colleagues, and even by Chertoff himself.

This can't have been what Democrats and Republicans had in mind when they celebrated the creation of the department in November 2002—arguably the last moment of bipartisan cooperation that Washington would see for six years. Although hastily thrown together, DHS was hailed by most of official Washington as a necessary response to the extreme vulnerabilities exposed by the September 11 attacks. Today, that bipartisan consensus remains largely intact. In fact, as Barack Obama prepares to take office, some Democrats want to increase the department's budget, which is now over $40 billion per year. "I do think more money has to be spent, order of magnitude twenty to twenty-five percent more," I was told in July by James Steinberg, who empha-sized that he was not speaking for the Obama campaign. (He is now expected to become deputy secretary of state.) "I don't think Secretary Chertoff has fought hard enough within the administration for his share of resources," P.J. Crowley, a homeland security expert at the Center for American Progress, told me in June. "If we continue to suggest we are at war, I wonder if DHS really is on a war-time footing." More recently, the nomination of the charismatic Janet Napolitano to head the department suggests that Obama himself is committed to a strong DHS. In announcing her nomination, Obama said, "She understands the need for a Department of Homeland Security that has the capacity to help prevent terrorist attacks and respond to catastrophe be it man-made or natural." It may still be years away from having a permanent headquarters, but the Department of Homeland Security, apparently, is here to stay.

Should that be cause for celebration or concern? This summer, I talked to security experts on both sides of the political spectrum, and had several conversations with Chertoff, in an effort to answer the following question: Is DHS achieving its mission of making us safer? My reluctant conclusion is that, although Chertoff has performed impressively in an impossible job, the department is hard to justify with any rational analysis of costs and benefits. On the contrary, it's arguably one of the most expensive marketing ventures in political history—an enterprise that seeks to make us feel safer instead of actually making us safer. The best argument for DHS is that the illusion of safety may itself provide tangible psychological and economic benefits: If people feel less afraid, they may be more likely to fly on planes. But even if conceived on these terms—as a more-than-$40-billion-dollar-a-year pacifier—the department is hard to defend, since there's no good evidence that it has, in fact, calmed Americans down rather than making us more nervous.

The only way of calming people down is political leadership that puts the terrorist threat in perspective. But, despite efforts by Chertoff to avoid the color-coded hysteria that defined the department in its early days, DHS officials inevitably feel pressure to exaggerate the terrorist threat—scaremongering that creates further public demand for promises of security that can't be fulfilled. And so the very existence of DHS creates a chain reaction of self-justifying insecurity. For this reason, Republicans (who used to be the stiff-upper-lip party of limited government) and Democrats (who don't trust the government to run the war in Iraq and are generally cautious about spending too much on defense) are willing to sink billions into an institutional money pit that has more to do with symbols than substance. Both parties seem incapable of acknowledging an uncomfortable but increasingly obvious truth: that the Department of Homeland Security was a bureaucratic and philosophical mistake.

To understand how DHS was hobbled from the beginning, it may be helpful to recall the partisan gymnastics surrounding its creation. After September 11, President Bush appointed Pennsylvania governor Tom Ridge to head a new Office of Homeland Security in the White House. When Joe Lieberman first proposed setting up a cabinet-level homeland security department in October 2001, White House conservatives balked at the prospect of a vast new federal bureaucracy. But, as Lieberman's bill began to gain momentum, the White House decided it couldn't let the GOP be out-flanked by Democrats in appearing tough on terror. In April 2002, after months of Republican senators fighting against Lieberman's bill, White House Chief of Staff Andy Card convened a secret working group to decide which federal agencies to merge into a homeland security department that would be created on Bush's terms. The mid-level White House staffers who were responsible for designing the new department met regularly with Card, Condoleezza Rice, and Cheney's chief of staff, Scooter Libby. Those staffers later told *The Washington Post* about the rushed and almost random character of much of their deliberation: The Immigration and Naturalization Service and Federal Emergency Management Agency were in, but, because of internal politics, the FBI was out. The Lawrence Livermore National Laboratory was in because a White House security expert, Richard Falkenrath, called a friend and asked which of the Department of Energy's three research labs to include.

The White House announced the plan on June 6, 2002, the same day Coleen Rowley—a whistle-blower who had accused FBI leadership of ignoring warnings before September 11 about potential terrorists taking flying lessons—testified on the Hill. The Rowley story suggested the Bush administration had all the information it needed to prevent the attacks but had failed to connect the dots. According to Representative Jane Harman, the former ranking member on the House intelligence committee, the announcement may have been timed to move the Rowley story "below the fold" and out of the headlines. "I think they rushed this," Harman told me. "I don't ever think Bush was excited about this department" but he decided it was "politically expedient."

In addition to facing the bureaucratic challenge of merging 22 federal agencies into a single organization, the department was hampered by Congress's refusal to reorganize its oversight process: As a result, DHS at one point had to report to no fewer than 88 congressional oversight committees, a byzantine challenge that wasted the time of the department's leadership.

Tom Ridge, the first secretary of Homeland Security, took over on January 24, 2003. From the beginning, he was criticized for ineffectiveness, and, on his retirement, a terrorism expert told *The New York Times* that Ridge "seemed more interested in grabbing headlines" than executing an effective terrorism-prevention strategy. (Ridge did not respond to an interview request.) He administered the widely ridiculed color-coded alerts, which were raised to "orange" six times on his watch, and he was assailed by the DHS inspector general, Clark Ervin, for showy but ineffective transportation security measures. "I was issuing one critical report after another until I lost White House support," Ervin, now director of the homeland security program at the Aspen Institute, told me. Ridge resigned after Bush's reelection. In January 2005, Bush nominated Michael Chertoff to replace him.

From the start, Chertoff—a balding man with the razor-thin build of a dedicated runner (he has been quoted in *Runner's World*)—seemed to understand that his department's ambitious mission had to be defined more precisely. DHS's official charge is to "prevent and deter terrorist attacks and protect against and respond to threats and hazards to the Nation." But trying to prevent the next attack by guessing where it might occur is usually an exercise in futility. If one target is protected, an agile terrorist can always switch to another one; and there are, at least in theory, an infinite number of targets to protect. Moreover, even if this game of haphazard prevention sometimes succeeds, there is bound to be a lot of guesswork involved and therefore a lot of wasted effort. This makes preventing terrorist attacks an extremely expensive proposition— and one that can be difficult to justify on a cost-benefit basis.

Chertoff grasps all of this. (That is one of the reasons he has won bipartisan respect. "He has a quiet intelligence, a very calm demeanor, he's nonpartisan and non-polarizing … and his instinct is to solve problems, not to score points," says Harman, whose relationship with Chertoff is so amicable that they've gone jogging together.) As Chertoff told me, "You can't eliminate the risk, so you manage the risk." And so he tried to handle public expectations about security with a thoughtfully moderate approach that he called "somewhere between complacency and hysteria." He sought to focus federal efforts on preventing attacks (such as nuclear terrorism) that would strike a significant blow against our economic system, while insisting that smaller events (such as lone bombers on buses) couldn't be prevented and weren't primarily a federal concern.

And yet, even as Chertoff conceded that there was only so much government could do in the realm of prevention, the department continued to spend lavishly on questionable prevention measures. More than one-third of homeland security spending in 2006 was devoted to protecting what DHS calls "critical infrastructure and key assets." That year, DHS asked Congress for more than $2 billion to finance state and local homeland security grants, some of which were devoted to installing surveillance cameras. The cameras were sold to the public as a way of preventing crime. But a comprehensive survey of studies published by the Home Office in Britain—which has more security cameras than any other European nation—found that cameras have "no effect" on violent crime in the United States or the United Kingdom. When I asked Chertoff about the cameras, he conceded something few other officials have been willing to admit: that they don't deter terrorist attacks. "The cameras don't prevent," he told me. "But they allow you to respond and capture. And that's maybe not the best thing, but it's maybe the second-best thing." Even as a tool of investigation, however, it's not clear cameras are worth the cost. The London subway bombers, for example, were caught after they showed up on camera, but they probably would have been caught even if they hadn't been videoed: Intelligence work, rather than the cameras, led to their capture. "The question isn't whether the cameras are useful; the question is whether they're essential— or would it be better to spend that money on the policeman on the beat?" says security expert Bruce Schneier.

Schneier argues that few of the high-profile items DHS has funded can survive a cost-benefit analysis. Sky marshals cost hundreds of millions of dollars per year but have added little to the sensible security measure of reinforcing cockpit doors; instead, sky marshals killed a mentally ill, unarmed passenger at a Florida airport in 2005. The Real ID Act—which Chertoff championed and which requires state driver's licenses and ID cards to conform to a common standard defined by DHS—might allow terrorists without a criminal background to obtain a trusted credential while encouraging security officers to let down their guard. And screening cargo at ports for radioactivity hasn't detected a single nuclear bomb, but it has generated 500 false alarms per day at the Long Beach and Los Angeles ports. John Mueller—a political scientist and author of *Overblown: How Politicians and the Terrorism Industry Inflate National Security Threats, and Why We Believe Them*—has compared federal homeland security expenditures since September 11 with the expected lives saved as a result of the increased spending and concluded that the annual cost ranged from $64 million to $600 million per life saved. By contrast, the federal government's standard regulatory goal for cost-effective prevention measures is $1 to $10 million per life saved.

Chertoff insists that at least some of the department's focus on prevention of high-impact terrorism has paid off. When I asked him whether DHS deserved credit for the fact that we haven't been attacked since September 11, he reeled off a list of half a dozen or so plots that have been blocked during that time, most notably the plot in August 2006 to use liquid explosives to blow up planes flying from London to the United States.

The 2006 airline-bombing plot, however, doesn't seem like a convincing testament to the success of the department. Last September, after a five-month trial, a British jury refused to find any of the eight bombing suspects guilty of conspiring to target transatlantic planes. (Three defendants were found guilty on conspiracy to murder charges.) One reason the charges failed to persuade a jury, according to press reports, is that British and American officials disagreed about when to arrest the suspects, with the British arguing unsuccessfully that an attack wasn't imminent. Moreover, even if the episode is considered a success for the U.S. government, it's not clear that the Department of Homeland Security deserves most of the credit: It was surveillance by British and American intelligence and law enforcement officials—not the increased security at airports overseen by DHS—that led to the arrests and halted the plot.

The department is hardly the only arm of the federal government to succumb to a prevention-at-all-costs mentality. In fact, Chertoff and DHS deserve credit for trying at times to resist that mindset. In 2007, for example, Congress mandated that, by 2012, all containers bound for the United States must first be scanned for radiation in foreign ports. Chertoff convincingly criticized this requirement as an example of the tendency to "govern by anecdote"—to allow compelling narratives to drive decision-making, as opposed to choosing policies that achieve the greatest good for the greatest number. "My belief is that the genesis of this went back to the 2004 campaign for president, when someone must have told John Kerry that only four percent of containers were being inspected, and four percent sounds like a low number, so that became an easy target," Chertoff told me. We now scan 100 percent of the cargo coming into the country in U.S. ports, but Chertoff argues that it makes little sense to insist on radiation scanning in foreign ports like England, where terrorists are unlikely to build nuclear bombs to be shipped to the United States. This year, Chertoff implemented an initiative to expand overseas scanning on the trade routes with the highest security threats; but, despite his more targeted alternative, the cumbersome congressional mandate remains in place.

If prevention measures like cameras and 100 percent port screening are largely a waste, why is there so much pressure to sink money into them? The answer, as Chertoff understands, is human psychology. When I asked him whether any books or scholars had influenced his thinking about how to measure success in the war on terrorism, he cited *Failing to Win: Perceptions of Victory and Defeat in International Politics*, by the political scientists Dominic D.P. Johnson and Dominic Tierney, published in 2006. Johnson and Tierney note that the Tet offensive, considered by historians an objective victory for U.S. troops, is widely perceived to be a loss because expectations for the United States were so much greater than for North Vietnam. For Chertoff, examples like this suggest that government officials should lower expectations about how much security the public can reasonably expect.

Nevertheless, I was surprised that Chertoff cited *Failing to Win*, since one implication of the book is that the Department of Homeland Security should never have been created. Johnson and Tierney argue that people wildly overestimate the risk of being threatened by terrorism. One reason British citizens perceived the evacuation of 340,000 troops at Dunkirk as a victory rather than what it was—a crushing defeat—was because of memorable images of a flotilla of plucky civilian volunteers sailing small vessels from England to rescue the troops. (In fact, many of them were evacuated on warships.) The same elements of psychology lead people to exaggerate the likelihood of terrorist attacks: Images of terrifying but highly unusual catastrophes on television—such as the World Trade Center collapsing—are far more memorable than images of more mundane and more prevalent threats, like dying in car crashes. Psychologists call this the "availability heuristic," in which people estimate the probability of something occurring based on how easy it is to bring examples of the event to mind.

As a result of this psychological bias, large numbers of Americans have overestimated the probability of future terrorist strikes: In a poll conducted a few weeks after September 11, respondents saw a 20 percent chance that they would be personally harmed in a terrorist attack within the next year and nearly a 50 percent chance that the average American would be harmed. Those alarmist predictions, thankfully, proved to be wrong; in fact, since September 11, international terrorism has killed only a few hundred people per year around the globe, as John Mueller points out in *Overblown*. At the current rates, Mueller argues, the lifetime probability of any resident of the globe being killed by terrorism is just one in 80,000.

This public anxiety is the central reason for both the creation of DHS and its subsequent emphasis on showy prevention measures, which Schneier calls a form of "security theater." But that raises a question: Even if DHS doesn't actually make us safer, could its existence still be justified if reducing the public's fears leads to tangible economic benefits? "If the public's response is based on irrational, emotional fears, it may be reasonable for the government to do things that make us feel better, even if those don't make us safer in a rational sense, because if they feel better, people will fly on planes and behave in a way that's good for the economy," Tierney told me. But the psychological impact of DHS still has to be subject to cost-benefit analysis: On balance, is the government actually calming people rather than making them more nervous? Tierney argues convincingly that the same public fears that encourage government officials to spend money on flashy preventive measures also encourage them to exaggerate the terrorist threat. "It's very difficult for a government official to come out and say anything like, 'Let's put this threat in perspective,'" he told me. "If they were to do so, and there isn't a terrorist attack, they get no credit; and, if there is, that's the end of their career." Of course, no government official feels this pressure more acutely than the head of homeland security. And so, even as DHS seeks to tamp down public fears with expensive and often wasteful preventive measures, it may also be encouraging those fears—which, in turn, creates ever more public demand for spending on prevention.

Michael Chertoff's public comments about terrorism embody this dilemma: Despite his laudable efforts to speak soberly and responsibly about terrorism— and to argue that there are many kinds of attacks we simply can't prevent—the incentives associated with his job have led him at times to increase, rather than diminish, public anxiety. Last March he declared that, "if we don't recognize the struggle we are in as a significant existential struggle, then it is going to be very hard to maintain the focus." If nuclear attacks aren't likely and smaller events aren't existential threats, I asked, why did he say the war on terrorism is a "significant existential struggle"? "To me, existential is a threat that shakes the core of a society's confidence and causes a significant and long-lasting line of damage to the country," he replied. But it would take a series of weekly Virginia Tech-style shootings or London-style subway bombings to shake the core of American confidence; and Al Qaeda hasn't come close to mustering that frequency of low-level attacks in any Western democracy since September 11. "Terrorism kills a certain number of people, and so do forest fires," Mueller told me. "If terrorism is merely killing certain numbers of people, then it's not an existential threat, and money is better spent on smoke alarms or forcing people to wear seat belts instead of chasing terrorists."

The threat of terrorism is deadly serious, of course, and the federal government has an important role to play in addressing it. But the focus on security theater at DHS may be distracting the federal government from the two categories of things it can do well: intelligence—that is, investigation of specific threats before strikes occur—and responding to disasters and attacks after they have happened. "The place where we can get the most leverage for our terrorism dollars is at the beginning, working with overseas police to roll up terrorist financing through effective intelligence, and at the end, with emergency response and disaster relief," says Schneier. "The stuff in the middle that requires us to guess the plot correctly really is a waste of money."

According to policing scholar Dennis Kenney of John Jay College of Criminal Justice, the prevention technologies DHS likes to fund have never been effective in revealing plots before they are hatched and tend to lead to information overload. Instead, Kenney says, "the best police department doesn't have the best technologies; it has good community relations with citizens who want to tell them what's going on." Kenney notes that the New York police uncovered a post-September 11 subway bombing plot because of a tip and arrested the suspects when they arrived at the station. During the Clinton administration, the Justice Department prevented abortion clinic bombings by winning the trust of pro-lifers, who then turned over their members at the radical fringe. And Kenney notes that the Colombian police, in one of the most striking terrorism successes of the past few years, have learned the same lesson: "Fifteen years ago, the military had no way of knowing where to strike; now they have information coming to the Colombian police from the community about where the farc terrorists and narco-terrorists are, because the police have built community trust." In other words, it's rigorous police work—not unwieldy prevention measures designed to detect every possible attack—that probably represents our best hope for stopping terrorists before they strike.

In the other realm where the federal government can play a constructive role—reacting effectively after a disaster has taken place—DHS failed its biggest test so far. Hurricane Katrina struck New Orleans six-and-a-half months after Chertoff took office, and the ineptitude of the department's response had a severe human cost. The little noticed bipartisan report on Katrina by the Senate Committee on Homeland Security and Governmental Affairs found that "Chertoff himself should have been more engaged in preparations over the weekend before landfall" and "his performance in the nation's worst domestic disaster fell short of reasonable expectations." A day after landfall, "DHS officials were still struggling to determine the 'ground truth' about the extent of the flooding despite the many reports it had received about the catastrophe," while "DHS leaders did not become fully engaged in recovery efforts" until three days after the hurricane struck. The report details failure to heed repeated warnings, poor advance planning, broken lines of communication between DHS and the military as well as between state and federal officials, pointless turf wars between DHS and the Justice Department, and incompetence at every level. But the overwhelming conclusion of the document is that the response represented a failure of political leadership. When I asked Chertoff about this, he conceded that, before Katrina, he underestimated the public leadership aspects of his job.

The failures surrounding Katrina suggest that reacting effectively to disaster involves more than coordinating emergency response; it means preparing society to cope, practically and psychologically, with the disasters that are an inevitable part of life. On the practical side, Stephen Flynn of the Council on Foreign Relations believes we need to do a better job of supporting first-responders. Republicans, he argues, have allowed a rigid states' rights ideology to create an artificial distinction between federal and state responses to natural disasters and small-scale acts of terrorism—denying local cops and firefighters the resources and support they need. As for the psychological side: Instead of a security mindset, which assumes we're either safe or not, Flynn's buzzword is resilience—the idea that you can't prevent all hazards but can organize communities to recover quickly once inevitable hazards occur. "The more resilient we become as a society, the less consequential acts of terrorism become, and that requires acting in ways DHS hasn't been acting," Flynn told me. "One is being far more open with the American people about vulnerabilities, and another is empowering us about how we address the vulnerabilities so we don't have an unbounded sense of fear."

In that sense, perhaps Janet Napolitano's best qualification for the problematic job she will soon inherit is her background as an effective and popular governor. After all, the only way to make the public more resilient is through political leadership. Before World War II, people understood that life was fraught with risk, and presidents like Lincoln and Roosevelt could challenge the public to be brave in the face of uncertainty and danger. Today, by contrast, we have come to believe that life is risk-free and that, if something bad happens, there must be a government official to blame. The Department of Homeland Security—with its doomed quest to give Americans the illusion of total security—is the ultimate monument to our anxious age. The biggest contribution Barack Obama could make in the realm of homeland security has nothing to do with port screening or security cameras or federal budgets. Perhaps our new president instead can lead us to rediscover the sense of self-reliance that we long ago forgot how to find within ourselves.

*C*onsider the source and the audience.

- Jeffrey Rosen is the legal affairs editor for the *New Republic* and a law professor. How might his background help him write a piece that seems outside his primary area of expertise?

*L*ay out the argument, the values, and the assumptions.

- The title makes it clear that Rosen believes the Department of Homeland Security was a "bureaucratic and philosophical mistake," but why?
- What does he mean when he says the creation of the Department of Homeland Security is "one of the most expensive marketing ventures in political history"?
- Why doesn't he believe that the Department of Homeland Security has improved Americans' psyche?

*U*ncover the evidence.

- Rosen uses a cost-benefit-type analysis to support his argument. What are the costs he sees regarding the Department of Homeland Security? Are there any benefits? How does he know that the costs outweigh the benefits?

*E*valuate the conclusion.

- Is it possible to know how effective the Department of Homeland Security has been in preventing terrorist attacks?
- If the Department of Homeland Security has been as ineffective as Rosen argues, then why do you think it receives strong support from politicians?

*S*ort out the political implications.

- How might the Department of Homeland Security change under the Obama administration? Do you think a new administration will allay any of Rosen's problems with the department?

8.4 Special Message to the Congress Recommending the Establishment of a Department of National Defense

Harry S. Truman

Why We Chose This Piece

The previous reading highlights the difficulties with establishing a new bureaucratic department and reorganizing government. This speech shows you that presidents have long struggled with these issues. More than sixty years ago, President Harry Truman faced some of the same challenges that President George W. Bush faced when the latter pushed for the creation of a Department of Homeland Security. Here, Truman is calling for the different branches of the military, previously managed by the War Department and the Department of the Navy, to be combined under a single command in the form of a new Department of Defense. As with the Department of Homeland Security, this move involved restructuring existing government departments, with all the associated turf battles and disputes. In this speech, Truman lays out the case for why such a move was necessary. (We reprint only the first part of his long speech here.) What similarities might exist between Truman's proposal for a Department of Defense and Bush's proposal for a Department of Homeland Security? Are any differences apparent to you?

To the Congress of the United States: In my message of September 6, 1945, I stated that I would communicate with the Congress from time to time during the current session with respect to a comprehensive and continuous program of national security. I pointed out the necessity of making timely preparation for the

---

Selection delivered: December 19, 1945

Nation's long-range security now—while we are still mindful of what it has cost us in this war to have been unprepared.

On October 23, 1945, as part of that program, there was for your consideration a proposal for universal military training. It was based upon the necessities of maintaining a well-trained citizenry which could be quickly mobilized in time of need in support of a small professional military establishment. Long and extensive hearings have now been held by the Congress on this recommendation. I think that the proposal, in principle, has met with the overwhelming approval of the people of the United States.

We are discharging our armed forces now at the rate of 1,500,000 a month. We can with fairness no longer look to the veterans of this war for any future military service. It is essential therefore that universal training be instituted at the earliest possible moment to provide a reserve upon which we can draw if, unhappily, it should become necessary. A grave responsibility will rest upon the Congress if it continues to delay this most important and urgent measure.

Today, again in the interest of national security and world peace, I make this further recommendation to you. I recommend that the Congress adopt legislation combining the War and Navy Departments into one single Department of National Defense. Such unification is another essential step—along with universal training—in the development of a comprehensive and continuous program for our future safety and for the peace and security of the world.

One of the lessons which have most clearly come from the costly and dangerous experience of this war is that there must be unified direction of land, sea and air forces at home as well as in all other parts of the world where our Armed Forces are serving.

We did not have that kind of direction when we were attacked four years ago—and we certainly paid a high price for not having it.

In 1941, we had two completely independent organizations with no well-established habits of collaboration and cooperation between them. If disputes arose, if there was failure to agree on a question of planning or a question of action, only the President of the United States could make a decision effective on both. Besides, in 1941, the air power of the United States was not organized on a par with the ground and sea forces.

Our expedient for meeting these defects was the creation of the Joint Chiefs of Staff. On this Committee sat the President's Chief of Staff and the chiefs of the land forces, the naval forces, and the air forces. Under the Joint Chiefs were organized a number of committees bringing together personnel of the three services for joint strategic planning and for coordination of operations. This kind of coordination was better than no coordination at all, but it was in no sense a unified command.

In the theaters of operation, meanwhile, we went further in the direction of unity by establishing unified commands. We came to the conclusion—soon confirmed by experience—that any extended military effort required overall coordinated control in order to get the most out of the three armed forces. Had we not early in the war adopted this principle of a unified command for operations, our efforts, no matter how heroic, might have failed.

But we never had comparable unified direction or command in Washington. And even in the field, our unity of operations was greatly impaired by the differences in training, in doctrine, in communication systems, and in supply and distribution systems, that stemmed from the division of leadership in Washington.

It is true, we were able to win in spite of these handicaps. But it is now time to take stock, to discard obsolete organizational forms and to provide for the future the soundest, the most effective and the most economical kind of structure for our armed forces of which this most powerful Nation is capable.

I urge this as the best means of keeping the peace.

No nation now doubts the good will of the United States for maintenance of a lasting peace in the world. Our purpose is shown by our efforts to establish an effective United Nations Organization. But all nations—and particularly those unfortunate nations which have felt the heel of the Nazis, the Fascists or the Japs—know that desire for peace is futile unless there is also enough strength ready and willing to enforce that desire in any emergency. Among the things that have encouraged aggression and the spread of war in the past have been the unwillingness of the United States realistically to face this fact, and her refusal to fortify her aims of peace before the forces of aggression could gather in strength.

Now that our enemies have surrendered it has again become all too apparent that a portion of the American people are anxious to forget all about the war, and particularly to forget all the unpleasant factors which are required to prevent future wars.

Whether we like it or not, we must all recognize that the victory which we have won has placed upon the American people the continuing burden of responsibility for world leadership. The future peace of the world will depend in large part upon whether or not the United States shows that it is really determined to continue in its role as a leader among nations. It will depend upon whether or not the United States is willing to maintain the physical strength necessary to act as a safeguard against any future aggressor. Together with the other United Nations, we must be willing to make the sacrifices necessary to protect the world from future aggressive warfare. In short, we must be prepared to maintain in constant and immediate readiness sufficient military strength to convince any future potential aggressor that this Nation, in its determination for a lasting peace, means business.

We would be taking a grave risk with the national security if we did not move now to overcome permanently the present imperfections in our defense organization. However great was the need for coordination and unified command in World War II, it is sure to be greater if there is any future aggression against world peace. Technological developments have made the Armed Services much more dependent upon each other than ever before. The boundaries that once separated the Army's battlefield from the Navy's battlefield have been virtually erased. If there is ever going to be another global conflict, it is sure to take place simultaneously on land and sea and in the air, with weapons of ever greater speed and range. Our combat forces must work together in one team as they have never been required to work together in the past.

We must assume, further, that another war would strike much more suddenly than the last, and that it would strike directly at the United States. We cannot expect to be given the opportunity again to experiment in organization and in ways of teamwork while the fighting proceeds. True preparedness now means preparedness not alone in armaments and numbers of men, but preparedness in organization also. It means establishing in peacetime the kind of military organization which will be able to meet the test of sudden attack quickly and without having to improvise radical readjustment in structure and habits.

The basic question is what organization will provide the most effective employment of our military resources in time of war and the most effective means for maintaining peace. The manner in which we make this transition in the size, composition, and organization of the armed forces will determine the efficiency and cost of our national defense for many years to come.

Improvements have been made since 1941 by the President in the organization of the War and Navy Departments, under the War Powers Act. Unless the Congress acts before these powers lapse, these Departments will revert to their prewar organizational status. This would be a grievous mistake.

The Joint Chiefs of Staff are not a unified command. It is a committee which must depend for its success upon the voluntary cooperation of its member agencies. During the war period of extreme national danger, there was, of course, a high degree of cooperation. In peacetime the situation will be different. It must not be taken for granted that the Joint Chiefs of Staff as now constituted will be as effective in the apportionment of peacetime resources as they have been in the determination of war plans and in their execution. As national defense appropriations grow tighter, and as conflicting interests make themselves felt in major issues of policy and strategy, unanimous agreements, will become more difficult to reach.

It was obviously impossible in the midst of conflict to reorganize the armed forces of the United States along the lines here suggested. Now that our enemies have surrendered, I urge the Congress to proceed to bring about a reorganization of the management of the Armed Forces. . . .

I recommend that the reorganization of the armed services be along the following broad lines:

(1) There should be a single Department of National Defense. This Department should be charged with the full responsibility for armed national security. It should consist of the armed and civilian forces that are now included within the War and Navy Departments.

(2) The head of this Department should be a civilian, a member of the President's cabinet, to be designated as the Secretary of National Defense. Under him there should be a civilian Under Secretary and several civilian Assistant Secretaries.

(3) There should be three coordinated branches of the Department of National Defense: one for the land forces, one for the naval forces, and one for the air forces, each under an Assistant Secretary. The Navy should, of course, retain its own carrier, ship, and water-based aviation, which has proved so necessary for efficient fleet operation. And, of course, the Marine Corps should be continued as an integral part of the Navy.

(4) The Under Secretary and the remaining Assistant Secretaries should be available for assignment to whatever duties the President and the Secretary may determine from time to time.

(5) The President and the Secretary should be provided with ample authority to establish central coordinating and service organizations, both military and civilian, where these are found to be necessary. Some of these might be placed under

Assistant Secretaries, some might be organized as central service organizations, and some might be organized in a top military staff to integrate the military leadership of the department. I do not believe that we can specify at this time the exact nature of these organizations. They must be developed over a period of time by the President and the Secretary as a normal part of their executive responsibilities. Sufficient strength in these department-wide elements of the department, as opposed to the separate Service elements, will insure that real unification is ultimately obtained. The President and the Secretary should not be limited in their authority to establish department-wide coordinating and service organizations.

(6) There should be a Chief of Staff of the Department of National Defense. There should also be a commander for each of the three component branches—Army, Navy, and Air.

(7) The Chief of Staff and the commanders of the three coordinate branches of the Department should together constitute an advisory body to the Secretary of National Defense and to the President. There should be nothing to prevent the President, the Secretary, and other civilian authorities from communicating with the commanders of any of the components of the Department on such vital matters as basic military strategy and policy and the division of the budget. Furthermore, the key staff positions in the Department should be filled with officers drawn from all the services, so that the thinking of the Department would not be dominated by any one or two of the services.

As an additional precaution, it would be wise if the post of Chief of Staff were rotated among the several services, whenever practicable and advisable, at least during the period of evolution of the new unified Department. The tenure of the individual officer designated to serve as Chief of Staff should be relatively short—two or three years—and should not, except in time of a war emergency declared by the Congress, be extended beyond that period.

Unification of the services must be looked upon as a long-term job. We all recognize that there will be many complications and difficulties. Legislation of the character outlined will provide us with the objective, and with the initial means whereby forward-looking leadership in the Department, both military and civilian, can bring real unification into being. Unification is much more than a matter of organization. It will require new viewpoints, new doctrine, and new habits of thinking throughout the departmental structure. But in the comparative leisure of peacetime, and utilizing the skill and experience of our staff and field commanders who brought us victory, we should start at once to achieve the most efficient instrument of national safety.

Once a unified department has been established, other steps necessary to the formulation of a comprehensive national security program can be taken with greater ease. Much more than a beginning has already been made in achieving consistent political and military policy through the establishment of the State-War-Navy Coordinating Committee. With respect to military research, I have in a previous message to the Congress proposed the establishment of a federal research agency, among whose responsibilities should be the promotion and coordination of fundamental research pertaining to the defense and security of the Nation. The development of a coordinated, government-wide intelligence system is in process. As the advisability of additional action to insure a broad and coordinated program of national security becomes clear, I shall make appropriate recommendations or take the necessary action to that end.

The American people have all been enlightened and gratified by the free discussion which has taken place within the Services and before the committees of the Senate and the House of Representatives. The Congress, the people, and the President have benefited from a clarification of the issues that could have been provided in no other way. But however strong the opposition that has been expressed by some of our outstanding senior officers and civilians, I can assure the Congress that once unification has been determined upon as the policy of this nation, there is no officer or civilian in any Service who will not contribute his utmost to make the unification a success.

I make these recommendations in the full realization that we are undertaking a task of greatest difficulty. But I am certain that when the task is accomplished, we shall have a military establishment far better adapted to carrying out its share of our national program for achieving peace and security.

*C*onsider the source and the audience.

- Truman is speaking to Congress and also, indirectly, to the American public. How does that affect the way he frames the issue and the stakes he emphasizes?

*L*ay out the argument, the values, and the assumptions.

- How does Truman view America's role in the world and the kind of threats that are likely to be levied against it?
- Why does he feel that the United States could not count on another victory of the sort it won in World War II? What were the flaws in the existing military command structure?
- What would increase America's ability to provide security for its own citizens and its chances of continuing its leadership role in the world? Why?

*U*ncover the evidence.

- Does Truman offer real examples of problems under the existing military structure to support his case?
- How does he use logic, examples of changes in the military, and the threat of possible future defeat as support for the kind of change he wants to bring about?

*E*valuate the conclusion.

- Was Truman right in saying that combining the two departments was sufficient to offset the kinds of problems he foresaw? Has our military history since World War II borne that out?

*S*ort out the political implications.

- What would be the situation today if we were trying to conduct the war on terror with two unlinked Departments of War and Navy?

9

The Courts

Trying to persuade New Yorkers that they had nothing to fear from the proposed Constitution, founder Alexander Hamilton wrote in *The Federalist Papers* that the judicial branch was not a threat to liberty since it possessed the power of neither the purse nor the sword. Unable to raise money or troops, insulated from political pressure and public opinion by lifetime tenure, it would be the "least dangerous branch" of the new government.

While the original Supreme Court was an institution of so little prestige that President George Washington had trouble finding qualified people who were willing to sit on it, today's Court is a monument of political power that has made decisions as central as whether someone has the right to die, to speak freely, to have an abortion, or to go to the public school of one's choice. In 2000 it took on the ultimate political role of kingmaker, when a 5–4 conservative majority decided the closely contested presidential election in favor of George W. Bush.

In this chapter we deal with complicated and abstract issues that focus on the political power of the courts. The overarching theme in all these issues is that, contrary to Hamilton's expectations, the courts are powerful and political institutions. They are deeply involved in divvying up scare resources, choosing who gets to have their way about the kind of society we live in, ruling on the most fundamental issues: who lives, who dies, and who gets to decide.

The articles in this chapter were selected to help you see how these abstract concepts play out in the political world. The first selection, an article from the online journal *Slate*, looks at possible explanations for why some justices change their minds about fundamental issues once they are on the Court. The second examines the increasingly contentious process of Senate confirmation of presidential nominations for the federal bench. The third, from the *New Yorker*, takes a close look at the views of the current chief justice, John Roberts. The fourth, from the *Washington Post's* Eugene Robinson, looks at the impact of identity politics on the composition of the Court—do one's ethnic, racial, and gender identities bias how one sees critical issues? Finally, we turn to *The Federalist Papers* themselves, for Hamilton's original explanation of why the judiciary is the least dangerous branch of government. Would he be surprised by judicial politics today?

9.1 The Souter Factor

Dahlia Lithwick, Slate

Why We Chose This Piece

> *These days the battles over Supreme Court nominees can be bitterly partisan, which*
> *makes it all the more ironic that, as many scholars have noted, some Supreme Court jus-*
> *tices have a tendency to become more liberal the longer their tenure on the Court. Dahlia*
> *Lithwick, the legal analyst for the online journal* Slate, *looks at possible explanations for*
> *this phenomenon. If justices really do change their ideological stripes once they are on the*
> *Court, is all the partisan wrangling just a waste of time?*

The much-whispered hope of liberals and much-shouted anxiety of conservatives is that John Roberts, once robed, will be sucked up into the mystical, nameless force that pulls Supreme Court justices leftward. The tendency of justices to "defect," or "evolve" (circle the word you prefer) to the left during their careers on the high court is legendary. Political guru Larry Sabato estimates that as many as a "quarter of confirmed nominees in the last half-century, end up evolving from conservative to moderate or liberal." The burning question about Roberts then is not, "What does he really believe?" so much as, "How long will he really believe it?"

Clarence Thomas is said to have bragged: "I am not evolving" following his confirmation, and he's proved true to his word. But tales of other rock-ribbed Republicans listing leftward abound. Consider the twin disappointments of President Eisenhower's administration: William Brennan—who went on to become the moral and intellectual leader of the court's liberal faction, and Chief Justice Earl Warren—an appointment Eisenhower later characterized as "the biggest damn fool mistake I ever made." Consider Harry Blackmun—the Nixon appointee who went on to author *Roe v. Wade*, and Lewis Powell, savior of affirmative action, whom Nixon also appointed. Consider John Paul Stevens (a Ford appointee), Sandra Day O'Connor (a Reagan appointee), Anthony Kennedy (ditto), and David Souter (Bush I). All presented as predictable conservatives until they hit the bench. Yes, there are a few defections in the opposite direction: FDR appointee Felix Frankfurter and Kennedy appointee Byron "Whizzer" White became more conservative on the court. But no one really disputes that the trend is largely from the right to the left. The question is, why?

Half-baked theories about the drift to the left abound. Here they are, for Roberts' watchers to consider:

1. **The Greenhouse Effect** "The Greenhouse Effect" is the name of a phenomenon popularized by D.C. Appeals Court Judge Laurence Silberman referring to federal judges whose rulings are guided solely by their need for adulation from legal

Selection published: August 3, 2005

reporters such as Linda Greenhouse of the *New York Times*. The idea is that once confirmed, justices become desperate to be invited to the right cocktail parties and conform their views to those of the liberal intelligentsia. Robert Bork recently told the *New York Times*, "It's hard to pick the right people in the sense of those who won't change, because there aren't that many of them. . . . So you tend to get people who are wishy-washy, or who are unknown, and those people tend to drift to the left in response to elite opinion." Similarly, Max Boot argues that Anthony Kennedy "is no Warren or Brennan, to be sure, but whenever he has a chance to show the cognoscenti that he's a sensitive guy—not like that meany Scalia—Justice Kennedy will grab at it."

The problem with this theory is that it accepts a great conservative fiction: that there is vast, hegemonic liberal control over the media and academia. This may have been somewhat true once, but it's patently untrue today. Jurists desperate for sweet media love can hop into bed with the Limbaugh/Coulter/FOX News crowd. Clarence Thomas has made a career of it. There is a significant and powerful conservative presence in the media, inside the Beltway, and in academia. And my own guess is that Federalist cocktail parties in D.C. are vastly more fun than their no-smoking/vegan/no-topless-dancing counterparts on the left.

A correlate of the "Greenhouse Effect" is that justices tend to grow obstinate in response to partisan criticism. As Greenhouse herself points out in her recent biography, *Becoming Justice Blackmun*, the justice reacted so strongly to the tsunamis of hate mail and media vilification following *Roe* that he became more liberal in other areas as a result. Perhaps Anthony Kennedy now takes some of his more lefty positions precisely because of the conservative calls for his impeachment following his votes in key abortion and gay rights cases.

To be sure, no judge likes to look stupid in the papers, and every justice keeps at least one eye on the history books. But it's too simple-minded to assert that judges reinvent themselves each morning to please the *New York Times* or the cafeteria at Harvard Law School.

2. **Mean ol' Nino** This theory holds generally that justices tweak their philosophies and ideologies in response to each other; and specifically, that Antonin Scalia and (to a lesser degree) Clarence Thomas have managed to drive once stalwart conservatives into the arms of the court's lefties. Mark Tushnet, a law professor at Georgetown University, argues that the failure of the Rehnquist Court to achieve the expected rollback of the social revolution spawned by the Warren Court has a good deal to do with Antonin Scalia's failure to lead the court's moderate conservatives. Tushnet suggests in a recent law-review article that Scalia's "acerbic comments on his colleagues' work," and his general tendency to run with constitutional scissors, ultimately drove both O'Connor and Kennedy to form alliances with the court's liberals, particularly David Souter and Stephen Breyer.

3. **"Seeing the Light"** This theory, a favorite of liberals, hinges on the claim that jurists eventually drift leftward because they become increasingly compassionate/sensitive/wise with age, and that each of these values is a fundamentally liberal one. In last week's *Chicago Tribune*, Geoffrey R. Stone, a professor of law at the University of Chicago, editorialized that "[j]ustices are continually exposed to the injustices that

exist in American society and to the effects of those injustices on real people. As they come more fully to understand these realities, and as they come to an ever-deeper appreciation of the unique role of the Supreme Court in our constitutional system, they become better, more compassionate justices."

The problem with this notion—that judges begin to appreciate the intrinsic rightness of tolerance, pluralism, and acceptance—is that it flies in the face of a basic human truth: We almost all become more conservative with age. This theory also fails to explain why some jurists—notably Scalia and Thomas and, to a great extent, Rehnquist—fail to budge from their ideological positions over the years. While it may feel good for liberals to assert that the drift to the left is simply a sign of wisdom, it strikes me as too simple and self-serving to be accurate.

4. **The Boys in the Bubble** This is the theory used to explain David Souter's dramatic defection from solid conservative preconfirmation to reliable liberal justice. The argument is that he had so little "real-life" experience prior to his confirmation that he only developed his jurisprudential views after donning the black robe. Souter himself has said that when he was confirmed he knew next to nothing about important federal constitutional issues—having had experience as a state attorney general and then as a state supreme court justice. At his confirmation hearings he answered truthfully but saw his views change radically once he began to truly study the issues. Because judges often hail from Ivy League institutions or from the lower courts, they may be less likely to have fully formed political ideologies. Certainly there is some truth to the proposition that justices who either rose through the executive branch (like a Clarence Thomas) or had tremendous advocacy experience (like a Ruth Bader Ginsburg) are less likely to change their views once confirmed.

5. **The Law Is a Moderate Mistress** This theory holds that there is something inherently moderating about the law itself; that the traditions and pace of the legal system tend to foster centrism and moderation. The "drifters" of the Supreme Court world—the Kennedys and O'Connors—are not so much evolving toward the left, therefore, as they are evolving toward the center.

This theory explains why Stephen Breyer has similarly moved rightward, proving to be the swing vote in this term's blockbuster case allowing displays of the Ten Commandments on state grounds, and joining the court's conservatives in matters as vital as the presidential power to detain enemies in wartime. We don't hear much from the media about Breyer's occasional defections to the conservative team, and certainly liberal pundits don't call for his impeachment the way Phyllis Schlafly does each time Justice Kennedy strays from the reservation. But it remains true that strong centripetal forces on the court tend to pull everyone slightly toward the middle.

What does all this say about the likelihood of a John Roberts "evolution" to the left? Rank speculation suggests that he may drift somewhat, but not a whole lot. Roberts' intellectual confidence points to a man unlikely to be swayed by the siren song of the opinion pages, and his ability to get along with everyone suggests that he may not only withstand Scalia's barbs but could assume the role of leader of the conservative wing—attracting moderates like Kennedy and Breyer back to the fold. Roberts' extensive experience in the executive branch and his role as successful advocate for conservative positions means he likely has a well-thought-out judicial philosophy on hot-button issues like abortion and gay marriage, and that, unlike Souter or O'Connor, he won't be crafting his views as he goes. Roberts is also a deeply religious man, which may keep him from sliding toward the center the way Scalia and Thomas have resisted the pull.

But, unlike Scalia and Thomas, Roberts seems to recognize the fundamental role and value of moderation in the law. He respects its glacial pace and tends to understand that his job is to guide, not shape, the law. In short, Roberts may shift toward the middle over time, but he is highly unlikely to become the court's staunchest liberal. However, 30 years is a long time. And Linda Greenhouse is most charming.

*C*onsider the source and the audience.

- *Slate* is a free daily online magazine, owned by but separate from the *Washington Post*. The opinion writers at the journal tend to take a more liberal point of view; it is definitely a Blue America media outlet. How might that affect the approach Lithwick takes? The way she defines her question?

*L*ay out the argument, the values, and the assumptions.

- Lithwick begins with the assumption that there is a leftward drift on the Court, although she grants that there is some movement rightward as well. Is such movement a good or bad thing? What would it say about human nature if there was no movement in a justice's views once he or she was appointed?
- Lithwick explores five possible explanations for the leftward drift she perceives. What are the values that underlie each explanation? What kinds of people would be most likely to endorse each one?

*U*ncover the evidence.

- What kinds of evidence does Lithwick use to document the leftward shift she is talking about? What further evidence would you like to see?
- Lithwick purports to evaluate each of the explanations for the change in judicial ideology. What kinds of evidence does she use to do that? Does she deal satisfactorily with each?

*E*valuate the conclusion.

- Lithwick's conclusions are not about the general leftward shift but about the potential for such a shift in Chief Justice John Roberts. Where does she think Roberts is likely to end up? Are her conclusions anything more than speculation?

*S*ort out the political implications.

- If the debate over a nomination is all about a justice's ideology, but justices change their views so dramatically once they are on the Court, is lifetime tenure a good idea? Should the debate over a nomination be focused on ideology or on other qualifications?

9.2 No More Mr. Nice Guy

The Supreme Court's Stealth Hard-liner

Jeffrey Toobin, New Yorker

Why We Chose This Piece

In "No More Mr. Nice Guy," the New Yorker's Jeffrey Toobin takes on the question Lith-wick finishes with: what is Chief Justice John Roberts's true ideological nature? The short answer is, don't look for this man to move to the left anytime soon. But the longer answer is nuanced and complicated, as Toobin explores the kind of conservative views Roberts holds. This article is long and complex because of the legal detail, but we like it because it provides a respectful view of the range of ideology on the Court, and even the shades of difference among those who ultimately vote the same way. Read it carefully and absorb the views of Chief Justice Roberts. Can you imagine a conversation between him and President Barack Obama on issues of race or executive power?

When John G. Roberts, Jr., emerges from behind the red curtains and takes his place in the middle of the Supreme Court bench, he usually wears a pair of reading glasses, which he peers over to see the lawyers arguing before him. It's an old-fashioned look for the Chief Justice of the United States, who is fifty-four, but, even with the glasses, there's no mistaking that Roberts is the youngest person on the Court. (John Paul Stevens, the senior Associate Justice, who sits to Roberts's right, is thirty-five years older.) Roberts's face is unlined, his shoulders are broad and ath-letic, and only a few wisps of gray hair mark him as changed in any way from the judge who charmed the Senate Judiciary Committee at his confirmation hearing, in 2005.

On April 29th, the last day of arguments for the Court's current term, the Justices heard Northwest Austin Municipal Utility District No. 1 v. Holder, a critical case about the future of the Voting Rights Act. Congress originally passed the law in 1965, and three years ago overwhelmingly passed its latest reauthorization, rejecting arguments that improvements in race relations had rendered the act unnecessary. Specifically, the bill, signed by President George W. Bush in 2006, kept in place Section 5 of the law, which says that certain jurisdictions, largely in the Old South, have to obtain the approval of the Justice Department before making any changes to their electoral rules, from the location of polling places to the boundaries of congressional districts. A small utility district in Texas challenged that part of the law, making the same argument that members of Congress had just discounted—that this process, known as preclearance, amounted to a form of discrimination against the citizens of the New South.

Roberts said little to the lawyer for the plaintiff, but when Neal K. Katyal, the Dep-uty Solicitor General, took to the lectern to defend the Voting Rights Act, the Chief Justice pounced. "As I understand it, one-twentieth of one per cent of the submissions

---

Selection published: May 25, 2009

are not precleared," Roberts said. "That, to me, suggests that they are sweeping far more broadly than they need to to address the intentional discrimination under the Fifteenth Amendment"—which guarantees the right to vote regardless of race.

"I disagree with that, Mr. Chief Justice," Katyal said. "I think what it represents is that Section 5 is actually working very well—that it provides a deterrent." According to Katyal, the fact that the Justice Department cleared almost all electoral changes proved, in effect, that the South had been trained, if not totally reformed.

Roberts removed his glasses and stared down at Katyal. "That's like the old elephant whistle," he said. "You know, 'I have this whistle to keep away the elephants.' You know, well, that's silly. 'Well, there are no elephants, so it must work.'"

Roberts was relentless in challenging Katyal: "So your answer is that Congress can impose this disparate treatment forever because of the history in the South?"

"Absolutely not," Katyal said.

"When can they—when do they have to stop?"

"Congress here said that twenty-five years was the appropriate reauthorization period."

"Well, they said five years originally, and then another twenty years," Roberts said, referring to previous reauthorizations of the act. "I mean, at some point it begins to look like the idea is that this is going to go on forever."

And this, ultimately, was the source of Roberts's frustration—and not just in this case. In a series of decisions in the past four years, the Chief Justice has expressed the view that the time has now passed when the Court should allow systemic remedies for racial discrimination. The previous week, the Court heard a challenge by a group of white firefighters in New Haven who were denied promotions even though they had scored better than black applicants on a test. Roberts was, if anything, even more belligerent in questioning the lawyer defending the city. "Now, why is this not intentional discrimination?" he asked. "You are going to have to explain that to me again, because there are particular individuals here," he said. "And they say they didn't get their jobs because of intentional racial action by the city." He added, "You maybe don't care whether it's Jones or Smith who is not getting the promotion," he said. "All you care about is who is getting the promotion. All you care about is his race."

When Antonin Scalia joined the Court, in 1986, he brought a new gladiatorial spirit to oral arguments, and in subsequent years the Justices have often used their questions as much for campaign speeches as for requests for information. Roberts, though, has taken this practice to an extreme, and now, even more than the effervescent Scalia, it is the Chief Justice, with his slight Midwestern twang, who dominates the Court's public sessions.

Roberts's hard-edged performance at oral argument offers more than just a rhetorical contrast to the rendering of himself that he presented at his confirmation hearing. "Judges are like umpires," Roberts said at the time. "Umpires don't make the rules. They apply them. The role of an umpire and a judge is critical. They make sure everybody plays by the rules. But it is a limited role. Nobody ever went to a ballgame to see the umpire." His jurisprudence as Chief Justice, Roberts said, would be characterized by "modesty and humility." After four years on the Court, however, Roberts's record is not that of a humble moderate but, rather, that of a doctrinaire conservative. The kind of humility that Roberts favors reflects a view that the Court should almost always

165

defer to the existing power relationships in society. In every major case since he became the nation's seventeenth Chief Justice, Roberts has sided with the prosecution over the defendant, the state over the condemned, the executive branch over the legislative, and the corporate defendant over the individual plaintiff. Even more than Scalia, who has embodied judicial conservatism during a generation of service on the Supreme Court, Roberts has served the interests, and reflected the values, of the contemporary Republican Party.

Two days after the argument in the Voting Rights Act case, David H. Souter announced his resignation, giving President Barack Obama his first chance to nominate a Justice to the Court. The first Democratic nominee to the Court in fifteen years will confront what is now, increasingly, John Roberts's Court. Along with Scalia, Clarence Thomas, Samuel A. Alito, Jr., and (usually) Anthony Kennedy, the majority of the Court is moving right as the rest of the country—or, at least, the rest of the federal government—is moving left. At this low moment in the historical reputation of George W. Bush, his nominee for Chief Justice stands in signal contrast to what appears today to be a failed and fading tenure as President. Roberts's service on the Court, which is, of course, likely to continue for decades, offers an enduring and faithful reflection of the Bush Presidency.

The Justices of the Supreme Court, as a rule, spare themselves unnecessary tedium. Their public hearings are lean and to the point; they hear lawyers' arguments and, later, announce their decisions. Still, one relic of more leisurely times remains. Several times a month, before the start of the day's oral arguments, the Justices allow attorneys to be sworn in as members of the Supreme Court bar in person, a process that can take fifteen minutes. (Most lawyers now conduct the swearing-in process by mail.) Rehnquist barely tolerated the practice, rushing through it and mumbling the names, and several colleagues (notably Souter) display an ostentatious boredom that verges on rudeness.

John Roberts, in contrast, welcomes each new lawyer with a smile, and when fathers or mothers put forth their lawyer children for admission—a tradition of sorts at the Court—the Chief makes sure to acknowledge "your son" and "your daughter" on the record. Everyone beams. It's a small thing, of course, but just one example of Roberts's appealing behavior in public, much as the nation viewed it during his testimony before the Judiciary Committee. At the time, Senator Dick Durbin, an Illinois Democrat who voted against Roberts's confirmation, nonetheless observed that he was so ingratiating that he had "retired the trophy" for performance by a judicial nominee. When, early in his tenure, a light bulb exploded in the courtroom in the middle of a hearing, Roberts quipped, "It's a trick they play on new Chief Justices all the time." Laughter broke the tension.

Roberts was born in Buffalo on January 27, 1955, and raised in northern Indiana, where his father was an executive with a steel company and his mother a homemaker. (He has three sisters.) Jackie, as he was known, was educated at Catholic schools, and graduated from La Lumiere, at the time an all-boys parochial boarding school in LaPorte. He was the classic well-rounded star student—valedictorian and captain of the football team. He went on to Harvard, majored in history, and graduated in three years, summa cum laude.

At Harvard Law School, Roberts continued to excel, in an even more competitive atmosphere. "He was extremely smart," said Laurence Tribe, the liberal scholar who taught Roberts constitutional law and grew to know him through his work on the *Law Review*. "He was really very good at being thoughtful and careful and not particularly conspicuous. He was very lawyerly, even as a law student." In the mid-seventies, the atmosphere at Harvard still reflected the tumult of the sixties. Roberts stood out as a conservative, though not a notably intense one. "On the *Law Review*, John was the managing editor, so that meant he gave us our work assignments every day," Elizabeth Geise, who was a year behind Roberts in law school, said. "He was very honest, straightforward, lot of integrity, fair. He was conservative, and we all knew that. That was unusual in those days. You couldn't think of a guy who was a straighter arrow." After graduating magna cum laude, in 1979, Roberts first clerked for Henry J. Friendly, of the federal appeals court in New York, who was legendary for his scholarship and erudition, but was not known as an especially partisan figure.

From New York, Roberts moved to the Supreme Court, where he became a clerk for Associate Justice William H. Rehnquist, and it was in Washington that his political education began. Rehnquist, appointed by Richard Nixon in 1972, was, in his first decade as a Justice, almost a fringe right-wing figure on the Court, which was then dominated by William J. Brennan, Jr. But Ronald Reagan's election to the Presidency, which took place just a few months into Roberts's clerkship, lifted Rehnquist to power and, more broadly, gave flight to the conservative legal movement.

At that early stage of the Reagan era, conservatives had a problem, because there were no institutions where like-minded lawyers could be nurtured; the Federalist Society, the conservative legal group, was not founded until 1982. "Roberts got a lot of attention because he clerked for Rehnquist," said Steven Teles, a professor of political science at Johns Hopkins and the author of "The Rise of the Conservative Legal Movement." "Without the Federalist Society, there were not a lot of other ways for the Administration to make sure that they were getting true conservatives. The Rehnquist clerkship marked Roberts as someone who could be trusted."

As a former law clerk to Rehnquist, not to mention his immediate successor as Chief Justice, Roberts was an obvious choice to deliver the annual lecture named for Rehnquist at the University of Arizona law school in February. Roberts is a gifted public speaker—relaxed, often funny, sometimes self-deprecating—and he began his speech with a warm remembrance of his mentor. Like Barack Obama, Roberts can make reading from a prepared text look almost spontaneous. "I first met William Rehnquist more than twenty-eight years ago," he told the audience in Tucson. "The initial meeting left a strong impression on me. Justice Rehnquist was friendly and unpretentious. He wore scuffed Hush Puppy shoes. That was my first lesson. Clothes do not make the man. The Justice sported long sideburns and Buddy Holly glasses long after they were fashionable. And he wore loud ties that I am confident were never fashionable."

Before long, though, Roberts steered away from nostalgic reverie and into constitutional controversy. He maintained his relaxed and conversational cadence, but his words reflected a sharply partisan world view. "When Justice Rehnquist came onto the Court, I think it's fair to say that the practice of constitutional law—how constitutional law was made—was more fluid and wide-ranging than it is today, more in the realm of political science," Roberts said. "Now, over Justice Rehnquist's time on the Court, the method of analysis and argument shifted to the more solid grounds of legal arguments—what are the texts of the statutes involved, what precedents control. Rehnquist, a student both of political science and the law, was significantly responsible for that seismic shift." Rehnquist joined the Court toward the end of its liberal heyday—the era when the Justices expanded civil-rights protections for minorities, established new barriers between church and state, and, most famously, recognized a constitutional right to abortion for women. This period, in Roberts's telling, was the bad old days.

These sentiments reflect a common view for conservatives like Roberts. "There really was a sense at the time among the lawyers in his Administration that Reagan had a mandate for comprehensive change in the nature of government," Teles said. "They thought a lot of what the liberals had done in creating, say, affirmative action was simply interest-group politics and not really 'law' at all, and it was their job to restore professionalism to the legal profession in government."

"I heard about John, and I immediately tried to hire him," Charles Fried, the Harvard law professor who was Reagan's second Solicitor General, said. Kenneth Starr, who was chief of staff to William French Smith, Reagan's Attorney General, had hired Roberts as a special assistant to Smith. Roberts then went to work at the White House, as an associate counsel.

All the lawyers who worked for Reagan were, in some general sense, conservative, but there is a difference between those, like Roberts, who came of age during Reagan's first term in office and those who prospered in his second. "The Department of Justice in the first term was full of serious, principled people," Teles said. "They didn't see themselves as part of the Christian right, or even necessarily part of a larger political movement, but they did think of themselves as real lawyers who were reacting to what they thought of as the excesses of liberalism." They believed, Teles said, "in what they called judicial restraint and strict constructionism. Roberts comes out of this world." Liberal critics, in turn, regard this view as unduly deferential to the status quo and thus a kind of abdication of the judicial role.

The legal philosophy of Edwin Meese III, which promoted an "originalist" view of the Constitution, dominated Reagan's second term. Originalists, whose ranks now include Scalia and Thomas, believe that the Constitution should be interpreted in line with the intentions and beliefs of its framers. "John was not part of the Meese crowd," one lawyer who worked with Roberts in the Reagan years said. "They cared more about a strict separation of powers, and even some limitations on executive and government power."

Originalists and judicial-restraint conservatives generally reach similar conclusions on legal issues, but their reasoning differs. Both, for example, believe that the Constitution does not protect a woman's right to abortion. "An originalist on abortion would say that at the time of the Constitution, or of the adoption of the Fourteenth Amendment, abortion was prohibited, and that's it," Akhil Reed Amar, a professor at Yale Law School, said. "A conservative like Roberts, on the other hand, wouldn't look immediately at the question of whether all abortions should be outlawed, but examine the specific restriction on abortion rights at issue in the case and probably uphold it. He'd avoid the culture-war rhetoric and gradually begin cutting back on abortion rights without making lots of noise about getting rid of it altogether." In 2007, Roberts joined Kennedy's opinion that followed this approach in upholding a federal anti-abortion law. The Court's two originalists, Scalia and Thomas, wrote a separate concurring opinion in that case, urging, as they had before, that Roe v. Wade be overturned once and for all.

In documents from the Reagan era that were made public during Roberts's confirmation hearing, the young lawyer emerges as a loyal (and low-level) foot soldier in the Reagan revolution. On issues where there was disagreement within the Administration, Roberts's memos generally show him supporting the more conservative position, especially on matters of race and civil rights. Roberts said that affirmative action required the "recruiting of inadequately prepared candidates," and sought a narrow scope for Title IX, the law that mandates equal rights for men and women in educational settings. In 1981, Roberts wrote that a revision of the Voting Rights Act would "establish essentially a quota system for electoral politics by creating a right to proportional racial representation." (Reagan signed the revision anyway.)

Roberts's reputation soared in his White House years. "He was already on that superstar trajectory," said Henny Wright, a lawyer, now living in Dallas, who became friends with Roberts in Washington at the time. "He was pretty much like he is today, except without the bald spot. Extremely attractive, in every sense of the word. He's smart, he's funny, he's gregarious, he's good-looking. In those days, he was never too busy to play a round of golf. He's not a very good golfer, but, unlike a lot of golfers, he doesn't let that ruin his day or your day." Roberts's wit even came through in the usually stultifying format of the interoffice memo. In 1983, Fred Fielding, the White House counsel, asked Roberts to evaluate a proposal then in circulation to create a kind of super appeals court to assist the Supreme Court with its ostensibly pressing workload. In response, Roberts noted, "While some of the tales of woe emanating from the court are enough to bring tears to the eyes, it is true that only Supreme Court justices and schoolchildren are expected to and do take the entire summer off."

With the completion of oral arguments in the Voting Rights Act case, the Court has now entered the most contentious weeks of its year. The Justices almost always save their most controversial cases for the end of the term, and this year tensions may run higher than usual. For starters, the Supreme Court Building is now in the sixth year of a renovation—the first since it was dedicated, in 1935—that has forced each of the Justices to move to temporary chambers. The Justices do not take kindly to such disruptions, especially because they are now, by historical standards, a very old Court. John Paul Stevens just turned eighty-nine, and four Justices (Ruth Bader Ginsburg, Scalia, Kennedy, and Stephen Breyer) are in their seventies. The renovation project will also involve closing the entrance to the Court at the top of its iconic front steps—a change that is said to be a security measure but that several Justices regard as a distressing symbol. Souter's impending departure, and unknown replacement, is another source of anxiety.

The substance of the Court's work, of course, contributes most to the strains among the Justices. The Chief Justice has not yet embraced one particular judicial principle as his special interest—in the way that Rehnquist chose federalism and states' rights—but Roberts is clearly moved by the subject of race, as illustrated by his combative performance during the Texas and New Haven arguments. His concerns reflect the views that prevailed at the Reagan White House: that the government should ignore historical or even continuing inequities and never recognize or reward individuals on the basis of race. In a recent case, a majority of the Justices applied a provision of the Voting Rights Act to reject part of a Texas redistricting plan that was found to hurt Hispanic voters. Roberts dissented from that decision, writing, in an unusually direct expression of disgust, "It is a sordid business, this divvying us up by race."

Race was also at the center of the most important opinion so far in his career as Chief Justice—a case that also displayed his pugnacious style in oral argument. Parents Involved in Community Schools v. Seattle School District No. 1 concerned a challenge to the city's racial-integration plan. The Seattle plan assigned students to schools based on a variety of factors, including how close the student lived to the school and whether siblings already attended, but the goal of maintaining racial diversity was considered as well. At the oral argument, on December 4, 2006, the Chief Justice tore into Michael F. Madden, the lawyer for the Seattle school district.

"You don't defend the choice policy on the basis that the schools offer education to everyone of the same quality, do you?" he asked, and Madden said that he did defend it on those grounds.

"How is that different from the 'separate but equal' argument?" Roberts went on. "In other words, it doesn't matter that they're being assigned on the basis of their race because they're getting the same type of education."

"Well, because the schools are not racially separate," the lawyer said. "The goal is to maintain the diversity that existed within a broad range in order to try to obtain the benefits that the educational research shows flow from an integrated education."

Roberts wouldn't let the issue go. "Well, you're saying every—I mean, everyone got a seat in Brown as well; but, because they were assigned to those seats on the basis of race, it violated equal protection. How is your argument that there's no problem here because everybody gets a seat distinguishable?"

"Because segregation is harmful," Madden said. "Integration, as this Court has recognized…has benefits."

In the Seattle case, the Court ruled by a five-to-four vote that the integration plan did indeed violate the equal-protection clause of the Constitution, and Roberts assigned himself the opinion. The Chief Justice said that the result in the Seattle case was compelled by perhaps the best-known decision in the Court's history, Brown v. Board of Education. In that ruling, in 1954, the Court held that school segregation was unconstitutional and rejected the claim that segregated schools were "separate but equal." In Roberts's view, there was no legal difference between the intentionally segregated public schools of Topeka, Kansas, at issue in Brown, and the integration plan in Seattle, five decades later. In the most famous passage so far of his tenure as Chief Justice, Roberts wrote, "The way to stop discrimination on the basis of race is to stop discriminating on the basis of race."

Roberts's opinion drew an incredulous dissent from Stevens, who said that the Chief Justice's words reminded him of "Anatole France's observation" that the "majestic equality" of the law forbade "rich and poor alike to sleep under bridges, to beg in the streets, and to steal their bread." For dozens of years, the Court had drawn a clear distinction between laws that kept black students out of white schools (which were forbidden) and laws that directed black and white students to study together (which were allowed); Roberts's decision sought to eliminate that distinction and, more gener-ally, called into question whether any race-conscious actions by government were still constitutional. "It is my firm conviction that no Member of the Court that I joined in 1975 would have agreed with today's decision," Stevens concluded.

In Roberts's first term, when Alito also joined the Court, there were fewer controver-sial cases than usual, as well as an apparent effort by the Justices to reach more unanimous decisions. But the Seattle case came down on June 28, 2007, which was the last day of Roberts's second full term as Chief Justice and a year of routs for liber-als on the Court. That same day, the Justices overturned a ninety-six-year-old prece-dent in antitrust law and thus made it harder to prove collusion by corporations. Also that year they upheld the federal Partial Birth Abortion Ban Act, in Kennedy's opinion, even though the Court had rejected a nearly identical law just seven years earlier. The case of Ledbetter v. Goodyear, brought by a sympathetic grandmother who had been paid far less than men doing the same work at the tire company, became a political flashpoint because the conservative majority, in an opinion by Alito, imposed seem-ingly insurmountable new burdens on plaintiffs in employment-discrimination law-suits. (Ginsburg, in an unusual move, read her dissent from the bench.) In all these cases, Roberts and Alito joined with Scalia, Clarence Thomas, and Kennedy to make the majority. On this final day, Breyer offered an unusually public rebuke to his new colleagues. "It is not often in the law that so few have so quickly changed so much," Breyer said.

Roberts's sure-handed sense of public relations has deserted him only once during his tenure so far. The Chief Justice, as the leader of the federal judiciary, is obligated to prepare an annual report, which historically has been a fairly anodyne document—a set of modest requests to Congress, like faster confirmation of judges or new construc-tion funds for courthouses. In 2006, however, Roberts devoted his entire report to arguing for raises for federal judges, and he even went so far as to call the status quo on salaries a "constitutional crisis." Most federal judges are paid a hundred and sixty-nine thousand dollars, and at that point they had not had a real raise in fifteen years. This request to Congress was universally popular among Roberts's colleagues, who were long used to watching their law clerks exceed their own salaries in their first year of private practice.

Congress, however, snubbed the Chief Justice. Six-figure salaries, lifetime tenure, and the opportunity to retire at full pay did not look inadequate to the elected officials, who make the same amount as judges and must face ordinary voters. Roberts's blind-ness on the issue may owe something to his having inhabited a rarefied corner of Washington for the past three decades.

In 1986, after his service in the Reagan White House, Roberts went to the Washing-ton law firm of Hogan & Hartson, where he developed a successful practice as an appellate advocate. "John's a very, very conservative fellow, and I'm the opposite, but that was never a problem for us," E. Barrett Prettyman, Jr., a longtime partner at the firm and a co-counsel with Roberts on dozens of cases, said. "Our work was mostly corporate, some criminal, a few individuals as clients. The key to his success was that he was very clear, very articulate, and never confusing."

When George H. W. Bush won the Presidency, in 1988, his new Solicitor General, Kenneth Starr, hired Roberts again, this time as his principal deputy. Near the end of the first Bush's term, Roberts was nominated to the United States Court of Appeals for the D.C. Circuit, but Democrats in the Senate, sensing a victory in the approaching 1992 election, refused to let him come up for a vote. So, for Bill Clinton's eight years in office, Roberts went back to Hogan & Hartson, where, according to his financial-disclosure forms, he made more than a million dollars a year. In 1996, Roberts, then forty-one, married Jane Sullivan, a fellow-lawyer, also in her forties, who now works as a legal recruiter. In 2000, they adopted two children, who are both now eight years old.

While at Hogan, Roberts became a lunchtime regular at the table of J. William Fulbright, the former Arkansas senator, in the firm's cafeteria. Fulbright was affiliated with Hogan from the time of his departure from office, in 1974, until his death, in 1995, and he presided over a salon of sorts for partners with an interest in politics. "It was a politically diverse group, and they'd just get together and talk about the issues of the day," David Leitch, who was also a partner at Hogan, said. "John is interested in political issues, he is interested in the process of politics. He used to like to handicap elections." Roberts took a direct role in the contested 2000 election, travelling to Tallahassee to assist George W. Bush's legal team in the recount litigation. He was rewarded for his efforts the following year, when Bush, like his father before him, nominated Roberts to the D.C. Circuit. He was confirmed two years later, and he served there until Bush chose him for the Supreme Court.

In one respect, Roberts's series of prestigious jobs all amounted to doing the same thing for more than twenty years—reading and writing appellate briefs and, later, appellate decisions. During the heart of his career, Roberts's circle of professional peers consisted entirely of other wealthy and accomplished lawyers. In this world, a hundred and sixty-nine thousand dollars a year might well look like an unconscionably low wage. "Some judges have actually left the bench because they could make more money in private practice, and some Justices have complained privately about how it's almost impossible to educate your family on that kind of money," Prettyman said. "You don't want an unhappy court, judges who are worried about their salaries. John saw that."

Roberts's career as a lawyer marked him in other ways as well. In private practice and in the first Bush Administration, a substantial portion of his work consisted of representing the interests of corporate defendants who were sued by individuals. For example, shortly before Roberts became a judge, he successfully argued in the Supreme Court that a woman who suffered from carpal-tunnel syndrome could not win a recovery from her employer, Toyota, under the Americans with Disabilities Act. Likewise, Roberts won a Supreme Court ruling that the family of a woman who died in a fire could not use the federal wrongful-death statute to sue the city of Tarrant, Alabama. In a rare loss in his thirty-nine arguments before the Court, Roberts failed to persuade the Justices to uphold a sixty-four-million-dollar fine against the United Mine Workers, which was imposed by a Virginia court after a strike.

One case that Roberts argued during his tenure in the Solicitor General's office in George H. W. Bush's Administration, Lujan v. National Wildlife Federation, seems to have had special resonance for him. The issue involved the legal doctrine known as "standing"—one of many subjects before the Supreme Court that appear to be just procedural in nature but are in fact freighted with political significance. "One of the distinctive things about American courts is that we have all these gatekeeper provisions that keep courts from getting involved in every single dispute," Samuel Issacharoff, a professor at New York University School of Law, says. "The doctrine of standing says that you only want lawsuits to proceed if the plaintiffs are arguing about a real injury done to them, not simply that they want to be heard on a public-policy question." Liberals and conservatives have been fighting over standing for decades. "Standing is a technical legal doctrine, but it is shorthand for whether courts have a role in policing the conduct of government," Issacharoff says. "Typically, the public-interest advocates, usually on the liberal side of the spectrum, favor very loose standing doctrines, and people who want to protect government from scrutiny, who tend to be on the conservative side, want to require more and more specific standing requirements."

Lujan v. National Wildlife Federation was one of the Rehnquist Court's most important standing cases. The environmental group had challenged the Reagan Administration's effort to make as much as a hundred and eighty million acres of federal land available for mining. In an argument before the Court on April 16, 1990, Roberts said that the mere allegation that a member of the National Wildlife Federation used land "in the vicinity" of the affected acres did not entitle the group to standing to bring the case. "That sort of interest was insufficient to confer standing, because it was in no way distinct from the interest any citizen could claim, coming in the courthouse and saying, 'I'm interested in this subject,'" Roberts told the Justices. By a vote of five to four, the Justices agreed with Roberts and threw out the case. According to Issacharoff, "Lujan was the first big case that said, Just because you are really devoted to a cause like the environment, that doesn't mean we are going to let you into the courthouse."

As a lawyer and now as Chief Justice, Roberts has always supported legal doctrines that serve a gatekeeping function. In DaimlerChrysler v. Cuno, a group of taxpayers in Toledo, Ohio, went to court to challenge local tax breaks that were given to the carmaker to expand its operations in the city; the Supreme Court held that the plaintiffs lacked standing. In a broadly worded opinion that relied in part on the Lujan case, Roberts suggested that most state and local activities were off limits to challenge from taxpayers. "Affording state taxpayers standing to press such challenges simply because their tax burden gives them an interest in the state treasury," Roberts wrote, "would interpose the federal courts as virtually continuing monitors of the wisdom and soundness of state fiscal administration, contrary to the more modest role Article III envisions for federal courts." As usual with Roberts's jurisprudence, the citizen plaintiffs were out of luck.

In the past four years, Roberts and Scalia, while voting together most of the time, have had a dialogue of sorts about how best to address the Court's liberal precedents. For example, Roberts wrote a narrow opinion in 2007 holding that the McCain-Feingold campaign-finance law did not apply to certain political advertisements in Wisconsin. Scalia agreed with Roberts's conclusion in the case, but he said that the Chief Justice should have gone farther and declared the whole law unconstitutional, on free-speech grounds. Scalia insisted that Roberts was just being coy, that his opinion had in fact overruled an earlier ruling that upheld the campaign-finance law, but that he wouldn't come out and say it. "This faux judicial restraint is judicial obfuscation," Scalia wrote.

In a case about the free-speech rights of students, Roberts wrote the opinion approving the suspension of a high-school student in Alaska for holding a sign that said "BONG HiTS 4 JESUS" on a street off school grounds. The Chief Justice said the school had the right to "restrict student speech at a school event, when that speech is reasonably viewed as promoting illegal drug use." Thomas, characteristically, wrote a concurring opinion urging the Court to go farther and hold that students have no First Amendment rights at all. But the larger point remained that Roberts, Scalia, and Thomas voted together in that case, as they do virtually all the time. "These kinds of distinctions among the conservatives are just angels-on-the-head-of-a-pin stuff," says Theodore B. Olson, the former Solicitor General, who remains a frequent advocate before the Court. "Roberts is just what he said he would be in his hearing—a judge who believes in humility and judicial restraint." Like the other conservatives, for instance, Roberts has been a consistent supporter of death sentences, and he wrote the Court's opinion holding that lethal injection does not amount to the sort of cruel and unusual punishment prohibited by the Eighth Amendment. Many liberals, too, feel that Roberts is far more similar to his conservative colleagues than he appeared to be at the time of his confirmation hearing. According to Harvard's Laurence Tribe, "The Chief Justice talks the talk of moderation while walking the walk of extreme conservatism."

On issues of Presidential power, Roberts has been to Scalia's right—a position that's in keeping with his roots in the Reagan Administration. "John was shaped by working at the White House, where you develop a mind-set of defending Presidential power," the lawyer who worked with Roberts in the Reagan years said. Just a few days before Bush appointed Roberts to the Supreme Court, in 2005, Roberts joined an opinion on the D.C. Circuit in Hamdan v. Rumsfeld that upheld the Bush Administration's position on the treatment of detainees at Guantánamo Bay. (With Roberts recused from the case, the Supreme Court overruled that decision in 2006, by a five-to-three vote, with Kennedy joining the liberals.) Scalia has occasionally shown a libertarian streak, but Roberts, true to his White House past, has consistently voted to uphold the prerogatives of the executive, especially the military, against the other branches. Last year, Roberts dissented from Kennedy's opinion for a five-to-four Court in Boumediene v. Bush, which held that the Military Commissions Act of 2006 violated the rights of Guantánamo detainees. Roberts saw the case as mostly a contest between the executive branch and the rest of the federal government. "Today the Court strikes down as inadequate the most generous set of procedural protections ever afforded aliens detained by this country as enemy combatants," Roberts wrote in his dissent. "One cannot help but think...that this decision is not really about the detainees at all, but about control of federal policy regarding enemy combatants."

Roberts's solicitude for the President and the military extends to lower-profile cases as well. In Winter v. National Resources Defense Council, the question was whether the Navy had to comply with a federal environmental law protecting dolphins and other wildlife while conducting submarine exercises off California. Roberts said no. "We do not discount the importance of plaintiffs' ecological, scientific, and recreational interests in marine mammals," the Chief Justice wrote. "Those interests, however, are plainly outweighed by the Navy's need to conduct realistic training exercises to ensure that it is able to neutralize the threat posed by enemy submarines." Though Roberts was writing for only a five-to-four majority, he added, "Where the public interest lies does not strike us as a close question."

On the morning of January 20th, the Supreme Court held a small reception for the Justices and their guests before they all headed across First Street to the Capitol for the Inauguration of Barack Obama. Friends present say that Roberts was nervous that morning. He was used to appearing before crowds, of course, but this was the first time that he would be performing the most public of the Chief Justice's duties—administering the Presidential oath of office—and the audience, in person and by broadcast, would be in the many millions. In keeping with his perfectionist nature, Roberts had rehearsed the oath ceremony and had long since committed the words to memory.

Through intermediaries, Roberts and Obama had agreed how to divide the thirty-five-word oath for the swearing in. Obama was first supposed to repeat the clause "I, Barack Hussein Obama, do solemnly swear." But, when Obama heard Roberts begin to speak, he interrupted Roberts before he said "do solemnly swear." This apparently flustered the Chief Justice, who then made a mistake in the next line, inserting the word "faithfully" out of order. Obama smiled, apparently recognizing the error, then tried to follow along. Roberts then garbled another word in the next passage, before correctly reciting, "preserve, protect, and defend the Constitution of the United States."

At the lunch in the Capitol that followed, the two men apologized to each other, but Roberts insisted that he was the one at fault. For the day, Roberts lost some of his customary equanimity as he brooded about making such a public mistake. (He went to the White House the next day, and the oath was repeated, correctly, to forestall any challenges to its legality.) Since then, Roberts has put the embarrassment behind him and even made it the subject of a little humor at his own expense. On January 26th, he presided over the installation of the new leader of the Smithsonian Institution. "Those of you who have read it will see from the program that the Smithsonian some time ago adopted the passing of a key in lieu of the administration of an oath," Roberts said. "I don't know who was responsible for that decision. But I like him."

Still, the flubbed oath will always link Roberts and Obama, whose lives reflect considerable similarities as well as major differences. They belong to roughly the same generation—Roberts is six years older—and received similar educations. Roberts and Obama graduated from Harvard Law School in 1979 and 1991, respectively—Obama had taken time off to work as a community organizer in Chicago—and both served on the *Law Review*. (Obama was president, the top position; Roberts, in his capacity as managing editor, was just below that.) They share an even-tempered disposition, obvious but unshowy intelligence, and fierce ambition leavened by considerable charm.

But the distinctions between these two men are just as apparent. Obama is the first President in history to have voted against the confirmation of the Chief Justice who later administered his oath of office. In his Senate speech on that vote, Obama praised Roberts's intellect and integrity and said that he would trust his judgment in about ninety-five per cent of the cases before the Supreme Court. "In those five per cent of hard cases, the constitutional text will not be directly on point. The language of the statute will not be perfectly clear. Legal process alone will not lead you to a rule of decision," Obama said. "In those circumstances, your decisions about whether affirmative action is an appropriate response to the history of discrimination in this country or whether a general right of privacy encompasses a more specific right of women to control their reproductive decisions...the critical ingredient is supplied by what is in the judge's heart." Obama did not trust Roberts's heart. "It is my personal estimation that he has far more often used his formidable skills on behalf of the strong in opposition to the weak," the Senator said. The first bill that Obama signed as President was known as the Lilly Ledbetter Fair Pay Act; it specifically overturned the interpretation of employment law that Roberts had endorsed in the 2007 case.

In a way, Obama offers a mirror image of the view of the Supreme Court that Roberts presented in his tribute to Rehnquist in Tucson. To Obama, what Roberts called the "solid grounds of legal arguments" was only the beginning of constitutional interpretation, not the end. In his statement announcing Souter's resignation, on May 1st, the President defined the qualities he was looking for in a Justice in a very different way from Roberts's description of Rehnquist. "I will seek someone who understands that justice isn't about some abstract legal theory or footnote in a casebook. It is also about how our laws affect the daily realities of people's lives—whether they can make a living and care for their families; whether they feel safe in their homes and welcome in their own nation," Obama said. "I view that quality of empathy, of understanding and identifying with people's hopes and struggles, as an essential ingredient for arriving at just decisions and outcomes."

The differences between Roberts and Obama include such issues as abortion and affirmative action, but they extend beyond such familiar legal battlegrounds to what Roberts called, in his Tucson speech, "the nature of the Court itself." "When Justice Rehnquist went on the Court, a minority of the Justices had been former federal judges," Roberts observed. "Today, for the first time in its history, every member of the Court was a federal court-of-appeals judge before joining the Court—a more legal perspective, and less of a policy perspective."

Obama does not regard the all-former-judge makeup of the Supreme Court as an unalloyed virtue. "The obvious sources of candidates have been people already on the bench and people who are distinguished academic legal scholars and teachers," Gregory Craig, the White House counsel, told me in February. "But he's also looking for lawyers who have been public defenders or prosecutors, or representing points of view with respect to immigration or the Innocence Project. He doesn't think you have to be a member of the circuit courts of appeals to be on the Supreme Court." Obama has spoken fondly of Earl Warren, the fourteenth Chief Justice, who came to the Court from the governorship of California.

When Vice-President Biden publicly mocked Roberts about his gaffe at a ceremony shortly after the Inauguration, Obama shot him a scathing look of rebuke. (Biden later called Roberts to apologize.) Still, there is no disputing that the President and the Chief Justice are adversaries in a contest for control of the Court, and that both men come to that battle well armed. Obama has at most one more chance to take the oath of office, and Roberts will probably have a half-dozen more opportunities to get it right. But each time Roberts walks down the steps of the Capitol to administer the oath, he may well be surrounded—and eventually outvoted—by Supreme Court colleagues appointed by Barack Obama.

*C*onsider the source and the audience.

- Toobin is writing for the *New Yorker* audience—a sophisticated, educated, and most likely liberal group of readers. Toobin himself seems to be more liberal than not. Does that mean that his analysis of Roberts's views is suspect? Would a conservative writer present Roberts's views differently?
- Toobin is himself a graduate of Harvard Law, where he was a member of its *Law Review*. Does the fact that he has a legal background and can rely on his readers to be well-educated mean that you approach the article differently than you might a similar piece in a more mass-oriented magazine like *Time* or *Newsweek*?

*L*ay out the argument, the values, and the assumptions.

- What views does Toobin attribute to Roberts, and why does he think they aren't consistent with "Mr. Nice Guy?" What does that tell you about Toobin's own views?
- What is the difference between Roberts's brand of conservatism and that of Justices Scalia and Thomas? Does Toobin think it makes much practical difference on the Court?
- Toobin says President Obama's Court might be the mirror image of Roberts's. How so?

*U*ncover the evidence.

- Toobin relies partly for his claims on the opinions of observers of Chief Justice Roberts, but his primary source is Roberts's own words, whether in speeches, in legal opinions, or in oral arguments before the Court. Is that persuasive to you? What evidence might be more persuasive?

*E*valuate the conclusion.

- Toobin's argument is complex, but his conclusions might be summarized as a caution to readers not to be fooled by Roberts's smiling face, partly because Toobin seems to agree with Obama's view that Roberts is more likely to side with the strong rather than the weak, or as Toobin says, he defers to existing power relationships in society. Is that conclusion borne out by Justice Roberts's legal opinions and arguments?
- If you could ask Roberts, do you think he would disagree with Toobin's conclusions?

*S*ort out the political implications.

- Toobin imagines a Court led by Roberts but peopled in part by Obama's appointees. Obama's first appointee was Sonia Sotomayor. How do you think her behavior on the Court will compare to Roberts's?
- Toobin also implies that Roberts presented himself one way during his Senate confirmation hearings but behaves in a slightly different way on the Court. Did Roberts misrepresent himself, or was he merely cagey? Can the Senate find out with accuracy what is in the mind of presidential nominees?

9.3 Whose Identity Politics?

Eugene Robinson, Washington Post

Why We Chose This Piece

Long before her nomination by President Barack Obama to the Supreme Court, Sonia Sotomayor wrote that her identity as a "wise Latina" would help her reach better conclusions than, presumably, those who were not wise, female, or Hispanic. Just what she meant by this remark was the hot topic during her confirmation hearings, with Republican senators asking her repeatedly whether this implied a racial bias on her part. Democrats, on the other hand, were not worried by the remark, and seemed stymied by the idea that her background would not color her views of the world in some critical ways. Sotomayor, for her part, insisted that her identity would not change the way she viewed or applied the law.

In this article, the Washington Post's *Eugene Robinson, who won a Pulitzer Prize for his columns written during the 2008 presidential campaign, argues that all people, no matter what their race, ethnicity, and gender, are influenced by their backgrounds. Writing in the middle of Sotomayor's confirmation hearings, Robinson unpacks the notion of identity politics, querying why only people of color and women are accused of practicing it. We chose this piece because Robinson raises an obvious and important question: is it ever possible to set aside one's experiences and background and be truly neutral?*

The only real suspense in the confirmation hearings for Supreme Court nominee Sonia Sotomayor is whether the Republican Party will persist in tying its fortunes to an anachronistic claim of white male exceptionalism and privilege.

Republicans' outrage, both real and feigned, at Sotomayor's musings about how her identity as a "wise Latina" might affect her judicial decisions is based on a flawed assumption: that whiteness and maleness are not themselves facets of a distinct identity. Being white and male is seen instead as a neutral condition, the natural order of things. Any "identity"—black, brown, female, gay, whatever—has to be judged against this supposedly "objective" standard.

Thus it is irrelevant if Justice Samuel A. Alito Jr. talks about the impact of his background as the son of Italian immigrants on his rulings—as he did at his confirmation hearings—but unforgivable for Sotomayor to mention that her Puerto Rican family history might be relevant to her work. Thus it is possible for Sen. Jeff Sessions (R-Ala.) to say with a straight face that heritage and experience can have no bearing on a judge's work, as he posited in his opening remarks yesterday, apparently believing that

Selection published: June 14, 2009

the white male justices he has voted to confirm were somehow devoid of heritage and bereft of experience.

The whole point of Sotomayor's much-maligned "wise Latina" speech was that everyone has a unique personal history—and that this history has to be acknowledged before it can be overcome. Denying the fact of identity makes us vulnerable to its most pernicious effects. This seems self-evident. I don't see how a political party that refuses to accept this basic principle of diversity can hope to prosper, given that soon there will be no racial or ethnic majority in this country.

Yet the Republican Party line assumes a white male neutrality against which Sotomayor's "difference" will be judged. Sessions was accusatory in quoting Sotomayor as saying, in a speech years ago, that "I willingly accept that we who judge must not deny the differences resulting from experience and heritage, but attempt...continuously to judge when those opinions, sympathies and prejudices are appropriate."

This is supposed to be a controversial statement? Only, I suppose, if you assume that there are judges who have no opinions, sympathies or prejudices—or, perhaps, that the opinions, sympathies and prejudices of the first Hispanic nominee to the Supreme Court are somehow especially problematic.

There is, after all, a context in which these confirmation hearings take place: The nation continues to take major steps toward fulfilling the promise of its noblest ideals. Barack Obama is our first African American president. Sonia Sotomayor would be only the third woman, and the third member of a minority group, to serve on the nation's highest court. Aside from these exceptions, the White House and the Supreme Court have been exclusively occupied by white men—who, come to think of it, are also members of a minority group, though they certainly haven't seen themselves that way.

Judging from Monday's hearing, some Republican senators are beginning to notice this minority status—and seem a bit touchy about it. Sen. Lindsey O. Graham (R-S.C.) was more temperate in his remarks than most of his colleagues, noting that Obama's election victory ought to have consequences and hinting that he might vote to confirm Sotomayor. But when he brought up the "wise Latina" remark, as the GOP playbook apparently required, Graham said that "if I had said anything remotely like that, my career would have been over."

That's true. But if Latinas had run the world for the last millennium, Sotomayor's career would be over, too. Pretending that the historical context doesn't exist—pretending that white men haven't enjoyed a privileged position in this society—doesn't make that context go away.

Yes, justice is supposed to be blind. But for most of our nation's history, it hasn't been—and women and minorities are acutely aware of how our view of justice has evolved, or been forced to evolve. Women and minorities are also key Democratic Party constituencies, and if the Republican Party is going to be competitive, it can't be seen as the party of white male grievance—especially in what is almost certainly a lost cause. Democrats, after all, have the votes to confirm Sotomayor.

"Unless you have a complete meltdown, you're going to get confirmed," Graham told the nominee. He was right—Republicans probably can't damage her. They can only damage themselves.

*C*onsider the source and the audience.

- The *Washington Post* is a national newspaper with a particular focus on Washington insider politics. While its editorial pages frequently take a conservative stance, Robinson himself is more liberal. Why is his argument here one that would be identified as "liberal?"
- Robinson's tone is one of bemusement that white Republican senators could possibly think that they have not been shaped by their own backgrounds. He is an African American; how would his experience of the world differ from theirs? How might their different perspectives shape their respective views on this?

*L*ay out the argument, the values, and the assumptions.

- Robinson makes no bones about his values here. He thinks people cannot help but be influenced by their backgrounds, and he doesn't see that as necessarily a bad thing. He does think they should try to rise beyond it, though. How?
- What does Robinson think the Republican white males in the Senate need to do to get beyond their own backgrounds and identities?

*U*ncover the evidence.

- Does Robinson have any evidence for his claim that white maleness is an identity of its own and that some white males treat their identity as an objective slate rather than as a rich and textured background? Does he need any? What would it be?

*E*valuate the conclusion.

- Robinson is making an obvious claim—for most of our history, white males have held the reins of power. But his less obvious point is that that doesn't mean that the white male perspective is "a neutral condition, the natural order of things." Is this true?
- What do you think of the conclusion that a self-aware Latina, who recognizes the impact her experiences have had on her views, has a better chance of making an objective decision than a white male who might be unaware of the impact of his background on his perspective?

*S*ort out the political significance.

- Robinson does not condemn all white males here. His focus is on the very narrow group of white Republican senators who were challenging Sotomayor's objectivity without questioning their own. He thinks their attitude spells trouble for the Republican Party. Why?

9.4 Obstruction of Judges

Jeffrey Rosen, New York Times Magazine

Why We Chose This Piece

The Constitution gives the Senate the job of approving presidential nominees to the federal judiciary from the Supreme Court on down. This article is about the growing trend in the past twenty years for senators to subject nominees to the federal appeals courts to the same stringent ideological tests that they have been applying to Supreme Court nominees since the 1970s. The result of this practice is that when the president and the majority party in the Senate are from different parties, many nominees can be blocked based on questions such as whether the Constitution should be read strictly or flexibly and whether judges should take an active role in overturning the laws of legislatures and making policy.

Are such concerns relevant at the appellate level? Are there "litmus tests" that should be given to potential judges? What are the consequences of using them? Interestingly, one of the judges that Rosen focuses on in this article is John Roberts, who has since become Chief Justice of the United States. If he had known that would happen, would Rosen have written this article differently?

Allen Snyder and John Roberts are two of the most respected appellate lawyers in Washington. They were at the top of their classes at Harvard Law School, and they went on to clerk for Justice William Rehnquist on the Supreme Court. Both ended up at the glamorous law firm Hogan & Hartson, where they became partners as well as friends, advising each other about ethical issues and preparing each other for arguments before the Supreme Court. In recognition of their exceptional talents, they were nominated by the president to sit on the U.S. Court of Appeals for the District of Columbia Circuit, widely viewed as the second most important court in the nation.

Roberts, a Republican, was nominated by the first President Bush; Snyder, a Democrat, was nominated by President Clinton. But neither nominee made it through the Senate, and together they stand as examples—call them exhibits A and B—of a crisis that has paralyzed the judicial nomination process for more than a decade. Roberts was nominated by Bush in January 1992. The Senate, controlled at the time by the Democrats, refused to give him a hearing, and his nomination lapsed with Bush's defeat that November. In September 1999, Clinton nominated Snyder; the Senate, back in the hands of Republicans, refused to bring his nomination to a vote. Last May, the second President Bush renominated Roberts to the seat he was denied a decade ago—but just when Senate Republicans were on the verge of scheduling a hearing, James Jeffords of Vermont renounced the G.O.P., and the Democrats took control once

---

Selection published: August 11, 2002

again. Now more than a year has passed since Roberts's second nomination, and the Judiciary Committee has still not scheduled a hearing and is in no rush to do so. "I can't tell you," Senator Charles Schumer said when I asked if Roberts would get a hearing. "I think it's the intention to have hearings on most of the nominees, although we're not going to be stampeded. What the ideologues want to do is stampede us."

The confirmation process for federal judges is in something of a meltdown. Appellate nominations are now provoking a level of partisan warfare that used to be reserved for the Supreme Court. In a fit of recriminations, Democrats and Republicans are blaming each other for changing the rules of the game. James Buckley, a former judge on the D.C. Circuit, recently wrote an op-ed column in *The Wall Street Journal* accusing Senate Democrats of "obstruction of justice" for refusing to grant hearings to President Bush's appellate nominees. "This extraordinary inaction is having a significant effect on the court's ability to handle its workload," he wrote. Democrats made identical charges against Republicans during the Clinton years.

Already this year the Democrats have rejected one Bush nominee, Charles Pickering, and are now trying to defeat another, Priscilla Owen, largely because of concerns about *Roe v. Wade*. And the recent decision by a federal appeals court in California striking down the Pledge of Allegiance has only fanned the partisan flames. "This highlights what the fight over federal judges is all about," said the Senate minority leader, Trent Lott.

Despite the suggestion of Republicans, the federal appeals courts are not yet paralyzed by the slowdown of the confirmation process, which began during the first Bush administration. The U.S. Court of Appeals for the D.C. Circuit, which had 12 judges at its peak, has been able to function with four standing vacancies. (Indeed, Republicans argued during the Clinton years that the court had too little work to occupy 10 judges.) And the Pledge of Allegiance decision—written by a Nixon appointee—will almost certainly be reversed.

Like the fight over abortion, however, the Pledge of Allegiance decision is a symptom of a broader dysfunction in American politics: the legalization of the culture wars. That phenomenon, which is at the heart of the breakdown of the confirmation process, has its roots in the 1980's, when an army of interest groups on the left and on the right were created to lobby the courts for victories over cultural disputes that each side was unable to win in the legislatures. Right-wing groups resolved to use the courts to restrict Congress's power to pass anti-discrimination laws, affirmative action and environmental regulations, while left-wing groups pledged to extend the logic of *Roe v. Wade* to protect gay rights, the right to die and other forms of personal autonomy.

These groups cut their teeth on Supreme Court nominations, especially the conflagrations over Robert Bork and Clarence Thomas. But now there hasn't been a Supreme Court vacancy for eight years—the longest period since the beginning of the 19th century. Biding their time until the next Supreme Court explosion, the interest groups have been working to justify their continued existence by turning their vast screening machinery on the lower federal courts. Both sides have urged sympathetic senators to treat each nominee to the federal appellate courts as a Supreme Court justice in miniature, and to ask the nominees not merely whether they would follow Supreme Court precedents like *Roe v. Wade* but also whether they personally agree with them.

This strategy makes no sense. Unlike Supreme Court justices, lower-court judges are required to apply Supreme Court precedents, rather than second-guess them. By treating every appellate-court nomination as a dress rehearsal for a Supreme Court battle to come, the Senate and the interest groups have created the misleading impression that lower-court judges are more polarized and less constrained than they actually are. In fact, on the best functioning appellate courts, there are clear right and wrong answers in most cases that judges, Democrats and Republicans alike, can identify after careful study of the complicated facts and relevant precedents. By subjecting lower-court nominees to brutalizing confirmation hearings in the Supreme Court style, the Senate is contributing to the Clarence Thomas syndrome, which occurs when a judge is so scarred and embittered by his confirmation ordeal that he becomes radicalized on the bench, castigating his opponents and rewarding his supporters. In short, by exaggerating the stakes in the lower-court nomination battles, interest groups on both sides may be encouraging the appointment of judges who will fulfill their worst fears.

As a case study in the way that nominees on both sides are being caricatured by the confirmation process, I arranged to meet with Allen Snyder and with John Roberts. Snyder, who is 56, is based at home these days; after his nomination died in the Senate in 2000, he resigned his partnership at Hogan and took early retirement.

Quiet and mild-mannered, Snyder exudes moderation and weighs his words carefully. But he is clearly still frustrated by the fact that the opposition to him was almost entirely masked. "As a nominee, you get virtually no information as to what's going on," he said in a conversation at Hogan & Hartson. "I got a call the afternoon before that I was getting a hearing the very next morning." Snyder's hearing in May 2000, eight months after he was nominated, was something of a lovefest. Though he was nominated by Clinton, he had the support of several influential conservatives, including his former boss, Chief Justice Rehnquist, and Robert Bork, who worked with him on behalf of Netscape in the Justice Department's suit against Microsoft. At the hearing, whose chairman was Senator Arlen Specter of Pennsylvania, Snyder proclaimed his devotion to judicial restraint. "Senator Specter congratulated me on how well things had gone and told me he was confident I would be confirmed and told me I would be a great judge," Snyder recalls. "And then the committee never took a vote."

A week after the hearing, *The Wall Street Journal* wrote a vicious editorial attacking Senator Orrin Hatch for having granted Snyder a hearing in the first place. Titled "A G.O.P. Judicial Debacle?" the editorial's only charge against Snyder was that he served as a lawyer for Bruce Lindsey, President Clinton's White House counsel. Calling the nomination Snyder's reward for "counseling the consigliere," the editorial pointed out that "conservatives still hold a 6-4 ideological edge on the D.C. Circuit on most issues" and that Snyder's confirmation might mean "a 5-5 split that could haunt the first year of a Bush Presidency." Blaming the Democrats for having "established a precedent for sitting on election-year nominees" by denying a hearing to John Roberts in 1992, the editorial concluded, "If Senator Hatch lacks the backbone, we suspect the nomination could still be stopped with the right phone call—to Senate Majority Leader Trent Lott from George W. Bush." Shortly after, Snyder was told that Lott had decided to kill his nomination.

"I think what happened to John Roberts and others caused there to be a sense of payback," Snyder says.

A few days after meeting Snyder, I returned to the 13th floor of Hogan & Hartson to meet Roberts. If Snyder is quiet and gently formal, Roberts, 47, is boyish and ebullient. Although he felt frustrated and out-of-sorts during the wait for a hearing during his first nomination, now, during his second, he is 10 years older and resolved to be more patient, fully aware of the uncertainties ahead. The Democrats have not yet decided whether they will give Roberts a hearing. And even if he does get a hearing, his candidacy has been thrown into further question by the Democrats' decision to make each confirmation a referendum on a single case: *Roe v. Wade*.

In 1990, when he was a deputy solicitor general, Roberts signed a brief in a case about abortion financing that included a footnote calling for *Roe v. Wade* to be overturned, the Bush administration's official position at the time. "I think that raises very serious questions about where he is on this issue," I was told by Kate Michelman, the head of the National Abortion and Reproductive Rights Action League. Was it really fair, I asked, to hold Roberts accountable for defending the Bush administration's position, which was after all his job? "I think Roberts is going to have to speak directly as to whether or not he believes that the Constitution protects the right to choose," Michelman replied, "and if not, then I think he should not sit on the bench."

Michelman's challenge—that all Bush's judicial nominees must swear a loyalty oath not merely to accept *Roe* but personally to embrace it—is one that several Democratic senators on the Judiciary Committee have taken up. Several of the Democrats say they are haunted by the example of Clarence Thomas, who swore at his confirmation hearing that he believed that the Constitution protects a right to privacy and then promptly voted to overturn *Roe v. Wade*. To avoid a repeat of this, Senate Democrats have decided to ask nominees not merely whether they would apply *Roe v. Wade* in the future but whether they have questioned it in the past.

In the case of Priscilla Owen, a nominee to the federal appeals court in Texas, the Democrats' concerns are arguably justified: even President Bush's White House counsel, Alberto Gonzales, called Owen's attempt to narrow a Texas law allowing minors to have abortions without their parents' consent "an unconscionable act of judicial activism" when he was a colleague of Owen's in Texas. But the Democrats have also opposed other nominees who had no clear judicial record on abortion. During the confirmation hearing earlier this year for Charles Pickering, whom the Judiciary Committee ultimately rejected, Senator Maria Cantwell of Washington State pressed Pickering to explain where, precisely, he found a right to privacy in the Constitution. "My personal view is immaterial and irrelevant," Pickering responded, adding that he would follow *Roe v. Wade*. (The exchange shook a conservative friend of mine. "She wanted to know what was in Pickering's soul," he marveled.)

Many lawyers and law professors—on both sides of the abortion issue, Democratic as well as Republican—view *Roe* as a loosely reasoned decision that failed to explain convincingly why the Constitution protects the right to choose during the first trimester of pregnancy. Nevertheless, after the Supreme Court reaffirmed *Roe* in 1992, not even the most conservative lower-court judge in the country has refused to apply it for a simple reason: lower-court judges are required to follow Supreme Court precedents whether they like them or not.

By putting abortion at the center of the lower-court nomination battles, the Democrats seem more interested in placating liberal interest groups than in examining the issues that the lower-court judges actually decide. "Kate Michelman is very helpful to us in identifying problems with nominees," says a Democratic Senate staff member, "and in deciding who is vulnerable."

But the Democrats' extremism on the abortion question is matched by the extremism of the right. The man who has been called the leading judicial attack dog on the right is Thomas Jipping. He recently moved from the Free Congress Foundation to a group called the Concerned Women for America, whose mission is to "bring Biblical principles into all levels of public policy." This means outlawing abortion, promoting school prayer and fighting all pornography and obscenity. Jipping defines a judicial activist as anyone who accepts three decades of Supreme Court precedent in abortion cases. "This entire abortion area is just an exercise in judicial invention," he told me. "I have not heard of a Clinton nominee who embraced judicial restraint."

Taking an even more combative view of the culture wars, Robert Bork, the rejected Supreme Court nominee, recently wrote a polemic in *The New Criterion* urging conservatives to relitigate the entire 20th century. Describing a pitched battle between the "traditionalists" and the "emancipationists," Bork wrote that the courts, and especially the Supreme Court, are "the enemy of traditional culture," in areas including "speech, religion, abortion, sexuality, welfare, public education and much else." "It is not too much to say," Bork argued, "that the suffocating vulgarity of popular culture is in large measure the work of the court."

Bork is living in a dystopian time warp. As sociologists like Alan Wolfe and Francis Fukuyama have demonstrated, social conservatives largely lost the culture wars in the 1990's not because of the Supreme Court but because of MTV, the Internet, the expansion of sexual equality and other democratizing forces of popular culture. Nevertheless, because a minority of extreme Republican and Democratic interest groups and judges refuse to accept the Supreme Court's relatively moderate compromises on abortion and religion, our confirmation battles continue to be fought over the most extreme positions in the culture wars, which the American people have already rejected.

This is particularly true on the court to which Roberts and Snyder were nominated. The U.S. Court of Appeals for the D.C. Circuit hasn't heard an important abortion-rights case in living memory. Instead, the D.C. Circuit focuses on the less sexy but no less important issues concerning the limitations of federal power and the boundaries of the regulatory state. There is a pitched battle among liberal and conservative judges, from the Supreme Court on down, about whether the Constitution imposes meaningful limits on Congress's ability to regulate the environment, the workplace and affirmative action. Here it is the Republicans who want to use the courts to strike down laws passed by legislatures and the Democrats who are defending judicial restraint. For this reason, Senator Schumer has vowed to ask all Bush nominees what they think of the Supreme Court's recent decisions limiting the scope of federal power. Schumer argues plausibly that since President Clinton, by and large, appointed moderate rather than extremist Democrats to the appellate courts, the Senate should ensure balance by screening out extremist Republicans.

Asking the nominees their views about federalism is a more appropriate way of smoking out extremists than grilling them about *Roe v. Wade*. But even when it comes to the debates over federalism, the D.C. Circuit today is far less polarized than the confirmation battles it has ignited might suggest. Eleven years ago, when I was a law clerk for Abner Mikva, then the chief judge of the D.C. Circuit, the liberal and conservative judges were at one another's throats. On the left and on the right, a few of the judges had strong ideological agendas and aggressive personalities, and this combination led them to fight constantly over internecine issues.

Over the past decade, however, the personalities on both the D.C. Circuit and the legal landscape in America have mellowed. Many of the most bruising legal battles in the culture wars have been settled by the Supreme Court: now that the justices have significantly restricted the discretion of lower courts in cases involving criminals' rights, for example, there is far less for lower-court judges to fight about. In fact, an alliance between libertarian Republicans and libertarian Democrats has produced important victories for privacy and free expression since Sept. 11.

Moreover, President Clinton's appointments to the D.C. Circuit have won the respect of their conservative colleagues for their personal as well as their judicial moderation. Because the judges now trust one another enough to reason together, fewer than 3 percent of the cases between 1995 and 2001 provoked any dissenting opinions at all. In an impressive sign of the court's bipartisanship and mutual trust, all seven judges joined together last June to find Microsoft liable for antitrust violations.

Federal courts, as it happens, are very much like university faculties: small groups of prima donnas, often with too much time on their hands, whose political dynamics can be shaped as much by personalities as by reasoned arguments. On a small court, the addition of one or two disruptive figures can change the dynamics of the entire group, causing Democrats and Republicans to gravitate toward increasingly extreme positions in order to signal their allegiance to one side or the other. Once a court has been polarized, moreover, it can easily deteriorate into a group of squabbling children. The U.S. Court of Appeals for the Sixth Circuit demonstrated this tendency in its recent opinion upholding the University of Michigan Law School's affirmative action program. One of the dissenting judges published a remarkable appendix accusing the chief judge of having cherry-picked the judges on an earlier panel to reach a predetermined result.

The D.C. Circuit at the moment is one of the best-functioning courts in the country. It would be bad for the law and bad for the future of the regulatory state if President Bush's successful nominees were so embittered by their confirmation ordeals that, like Clarence Thomas, they arrived on the court in the mood for pay back. Instead of flyspecking their views about *Roe v. Wade* therefore, it would make more sense for the Senate to explore whether nominees like John Roberts have the judicial temperament and personal humility to defer to Congress and to apply the Supreme Court's precedents. Judicial temperament is often hard to predict; but for what it's worth, I was struck in a wide-ranging conversation by Roberts's sense of humor, apparent modesty and above all his Jimmy Stewart—like reverence for the ideal of law shaped by reasoned argument rather than by ideology. "If I were inclined to do something that I would find politically satisfying and that I didn't feel I could adequately defend in an opinion," Roberts told me, "it would embarrass me to put that out in front of" the Clinton appointees on the court, whom he has known for years and respects.

After talking to Roberts and Snyder, in fact, I had the impression that they would agree in more cases than they disagreed, and that both had the sheer legal ability that sometimes distinguishes judges who care about working to identify the right answer from those who are driven by ideological agendas.

"John is one of the most brilliant minds in this or probably any other city, and he clearly meets anybody's tests for qualifications and legal background," Snyder says.

"I can't see much difference in terms of how Allen and I would approach cases," Roberts says. "He thinks there is an answer, and the harder you work, the more likely you are to get it, and to get it right. I think we share that." The Senate—and the nation—may never find that out.

Consider the source and the audience.

- This article appeared in the *New York Times Magazine*. Although Rosen is the legal writer for the *New Republic*, a liberal opinion magazine, the *Times* serves a more general audience. How is this fact reflected in Rosen's tone and conclusions?

Lay out the argument, the values, and the assumptions.

- What is Rosen's main goal here? What kind of tone would he like to see on courts such as the U.S. Court of Appeals for the D.C. Circuit?
- Why does he think that tone is in danger?
- How does he think it can be preserved?

Uncover the evidence.

- What different kinds of evidence does Rosen assemble to make his case? Is it a persuasive combination? What if Snyder and Roberts were less likable guys and more ideologically extreme? Would that have damaged Rosen's argument?

Evaluate the conclusion.

- Who does Rosen hold responsible for the way judicial confirmations do or do not proceed today? Is he right?

Sort out the political implications.

- If the trend discussed by Rosen continues, what is it likely to mean for our court system? Does the fact that Roberts is now chief justice mean that the trend is over?
- Why do senators listen to interest groups anyway? Can that be changed? How?

9.5 *Federalist* No. 78

Alexander Hamilton, The Federalist Papers

Why We Chose This Piece

Thus far we have read a number of articles that deal with the increasing power and political nature of the courts. Yet, as we noted in the introduction to this chapter, Hamilton claimed that the judiciary would be the least dangerous branch of government because it was the least powerful. Have things changed, or could we have anticipated the power of today's courts from Hamilton's own arguments?

This essay is fascinating, but it needs careful reading—several subarguments require some unraveling before we can be clear about Hamilton's thesis. The basic task he undertakes here is to justify why judges in federal courts should be appointed to hold their offices on good behavior—essentially that they be appointed for life unless they do something really wrong. (The conditions for impeaching a judge are the same as for impeaching a president—the commitment of high crimes and misdemeanors.) Hamilton first declares that the judiciary is the least powerful branch of the federal government, seeming to suggest that giving lifetime appointments to an institution that is not very powerful is not all that threatening in the first place. Then he embarks on a far more controversial argument. Federal judges require lifetime tenure to keep them politically independent from the other two branches not because they are not powerful but because they are the only ones who hold in their hands the power to determine if the laws of Congress violate the will of the people as expressed in the Constitution. Does Hamilton's famous justification of judicial review, a power that does not appear in the Constitution itself, contradict any aspect of what he said about the judiciary's being the weakest branch of government?

To the People of the State of New York: WE PROCEED now to an examination of the judiciary department of the proposed government. In unfolding the defects of the existing Confederation, the utility and necessity of a federal judicature have been clearly pointed out. It is the less necessary to recapitulate the considerations there urged, as the propriety of the institution in the abstract is not disputed; the only questions which have been raised being relative to the manner of constituting it, and to its extent. To these points, therefore, our observations shall be confined.

The manner of constituting it seems to embrace these several objects: Ist. The mode of appointing the judges. 2d. The tenure by which they are to hold their places. 3d. The partition of the judiciary authority between different courts, and their relations to each other.

Selection published: May 28, 1788

First. As to the mode of appointing the judges; this is the same with that of appointing the officers of the Union in general, and has been so fully discussed in the two last numbers, that nothing can be said here which would not be useless repetition.

Second. As to the tenure by which the judges are to hold their places; this chiefly concerns their duration in office; the provisions for their support; the precautions for their responsibility.

According to the plan of the convention, all judges who may be appointed by the United States are to hold their offices DURING GOOD BEHAVIOR; which is conformable to the most approved of the State constitutions and among the rest, to that of this State. Its propriety having been drawn into question by the adversaries of that plan, is no light symptom of the rage for objection, which disorders their imaginations and judgments. The standard of good behavior for the continuance in office of the judicial magistracy, is certainly one of the most valuable of the modern improvements in the practice of government. In a monarchy it is an excellent barrier to the despotism of the prince; in a republic it is a no less excellent barrier to the encroachments and oppressions of the representative body. And it is the best expedient which can be devised in any government, to secure a steady, upright, and impartial administration of the laws.

Whoever attentively considers the different departments of power must perceive, that, in a government in which they are separated from each other, the judiciary, from the nature of its functions, will always be the least dangerous to the political rights of the Constitution; because it will be least in a capacity to annoy or injure them. The Executive not only dispenses the honors, but holds the sword of the community. The legislature not only commands the purse, but prescribes the rules by which the duties and rights of every citizen are to be regulated. The judiciary, on the contrary, has no influence over either the sword or the purse; no direction either of the strength or of the wealth of the society; and can take no active resolution whatever. It may truly be said to have neither FORCE nor WILL, but merely judgment; and must ultimately depend upon the aid of the executive arm even for the efficacy of its judgments.

This simple view of the matter suggests several important consequences. It proves incontestably, that the judiciary is beyond comparison the weakest of the three departments of power;[1] that it can never attack with success either of the other two; and that all possible care is requisite to enable it to defend itself against their attacks. It equally proves, that though individual oppression may now and then proceed from the courts of justice, the general liberty of the people can never be endangered from that quarter; I mean so long as the judiciary remains truly distinct from both the legislature and the Executive. For I agree, that "there is no liberty, if the power of judging be not separated from the legislative and executive powers."[2] And it proves, in the last place, that as liberty can have nothing to fear from the judiciary alone, but would have every thing to fear from its union with either of the other departments; that as all the effects of such a union must ensue from a dependence of the former on the latter, notwithstanding a nominal and apparent separation; that as, from the natural feebleness of the judiciary, it is in continual jeopardy of being overpowered, awed, or influenced by its coordinate branches; and that as nothing can contribute so much to its firmness and independence as permanency in office, this quality may therefore be justly regarded as an indispensable ingredient in its constitution, and, in a great measure, as the citadel of the public justice and the public security.

The complete independence of the courts of justice is peculiarly essential in a limited Constitution. By a limited Constitution, I understand one which contains certain specified exceptions to the legislative authority; such, for instance, as that it shall pass no bills of attainder, no ex-post-facto laws, and the like. Limitations of this kind can be preserved in practice no other way than through the medium of courts of justice, whose duty it must be to declare all acts contrary to the manifest tenor of the Constitution void. Without this, all the reservations of particular rights or privileges would amount to nothing.

Some perplexity respecting the rights of the courts to pronounce legislative acts void, because contrary to the Constitution, has arisen from an imagination that the doctrine would imply a superiority of the judiciary to the legislative power. It is urged that the authority which can declare the acts of another void, must necessarily be superior to the one whose acts may be declared void. As this doctrine is of great importance in all the American constitutions, a brief discussion of the ground on which it rests cannot be unacceptable.

There is no position which depends on clearer principles, than that every act of a delegated authority, contrary to the tenor of the commission under which it is exercised, is void. No legislative act, therefore, contrary to the Constitution, can be valid. To deny this, would be to affirm, that the deputy is greater than his principal; that the servant is above his master; that the representatives of the people are superior to the people themselves; that men acting by virtue of powers, may do not only what their powers do not authorize, but what they forbid.

If it be said that the legislative body are themselves the constitutional judges of their own powers, and that the construction they put upon them is conclusive upon the other departments, it may be answered, that this cannot be the natural presumption, where it is not to be collected from any particular provisions in the Constitution. It is not otherwise to be supposed, that the Constitution could intend to enable the representatives of the people to substitute their WILL to that of their constituents. It is far more rational to suppose, that the courts were designed to be an intermediate body between the people and the legislature, in order, among other things, to keep the latter within the limits assigned to their authority. The interpretation of the laws is the proper and peculiar province of the courts. A constitution is, in fact, and must be regarded by the judges, as a fundamental law. It therefore belongs to them to ascertain its meaning, as well as the meaning of any particular act proceeding from the legislative body. If there should happen to be an irreconcilable variance between the two, that which has the superior obligation and validity ought, of course, to be preferred; or, in other words, the Constitution ought to be preferred to the statute, the intention of the people to the intention of their agents.

Nor does this conclusion by any means suppose a superiority of the judicial to the legislative power. It only supposes that the power of the people is superior to both; and that where the will of the legislature, declared in its statutes, stands in opposition to that of the people, declared in the Constitution, the judges ought to be governed by the latter rather than the former. They ought to regulate their decisions by the fundamental laws, rather than by those which are not fundamental.

This exercise of judicial discretion, in determining between two contradictory laws, is exemplified in a familiar instance. It not uncommonly happens, that there are two statutes existing at one time, clashing in whole or in part with each other, and neither of them containing any repealing clause or expression. In such a case, it is the province of the courts to liquidate and fix their meaning and operation. So far as they can, by any fair construction, be reconciled to each other, reason and law conspire to dictate that this should be done; where this is impracticable, it becomes a matter of necessity to give effect to one, in exclusion of the other. The rule which has obtained in the courts for determining their relative validity is, that the last in order of time shall be preferred to the first. But this is a mere rule of construction, not derived from any positive law, but from the nature and reason of the thing. It is a rule not enjoined upon the courts by legislative provision, but adopted by themselves, as consonant to truth and propriety, for the direction of their conduct as interpreters of the law. They thought it reasonable, that between the interfering acts of an EQUAL authority, that which was the last indication of its will should have the preference.

But in regard to the interfering acts of a superior and subordinate authority, of an original and derivative power, the nature and reason of the thing indicate the converse of that rule as proper to be followed. They teach us that the prior act of a superior ought to be preferred to the subsequent act of an inferior and subordinate authority; and that accordingly, whenever a particular statute contravenes the Constitution, it will be the duty of the judicial tribunals to adhere to the latter and disregard the former.

It can be of no weight to say that the courts, on the pretense of a repugnancy, may substitute their own pleasure to the constitutional intentions of the legislature. This might as well happen in the case of two contradictory statutes; or it might as well happen in every adjudication upon any single statute. The courts must declare the sense of the law; and if they should be disposed to exercise WILL instead of JUDGMENT, the consequence would equally be the substitution of their pleasure to that of the legislative body. The observation, if it prove any thing, would prove that there ought to be no judges distinct from that body.

If, then, the courts of justice are to be considered as the bulwarks of a limited Constitution against legislative encroachments, this consideration will afford a strong argument for the permanent tenure of judicial offices, since nothing will contribute so much as this to that independent spirit in the judges which must be essential to the faithful performance of so arduous a duty.

This independence of the judges is equally requisite to guard the Constitution and the rights of individuals from the effects of those ill humors, which the arts of designing men, or the influence of particular conjunctures, sometimes disseminate among the people themselves, and which, though they speedily give place to better information, and more deliberate reflection, have a tendency, in the meantime, to occasion dangerous innovations in the government, and serious oppressions of the minor party in the community. Though I trust the friends of the proposed Constitution will never concur with its enemies,[3] in questioning that fundamental principle of republican government, which admits the right of the people to alter or abolish the established Constitution, whenever they find it inconsistent with their happiness, yet it is not to be inferred from this principle, that the representatives of the people, whenever a momentary inclination happens to lay hold of a majority of their constituents, incompatible with the provisions in the existing Constitution, would, on that account, be justifiable in a violation of those provisions; or that the courts would be under a greater obligation to connive at infractions in this shape, than when they had proceeded wholly from the cabals of the representative body. Until the people have, by some solemn and authoritative act, annulled or changed the established form, it is binding upon themselves collectively, as well as individually; and no presumption, or even knowledge, of their sentiments, can warrant their representatives in a departure from it, prior to such an act. But it is easy to see, that it would require an uncommon portion of fortitude in the judges to do their duty as faithful guardians of the Constitution, where legislative invasions of it had been instigated by the major voice of the community.

But it is not with a view to infractions of the Constitution only, that the independence of the judges may be an essential safeguard against the effects of occasional ill humors in the society. These sometimes extend no farther than to the injury of the private rights of particular classes of citizens, by unjust and partial laws. Here also the firmness of the judicial magistracy is of vast importance in mitigating the severity and confining the operation of such laws. It not only serves to moderate the immediate mischiefs of those which may have been passed, but it operates as a check upon the legislative body in passing them; who, perceiving that obstacles to the success of iniquitous intention are to be expected from the scruples of the courts, are in a manner compelled, by the very motives of the injustice they meditate, to qualify their attempts. This is a circumstance calculated to have more influence upon the character of our governments, than but few may be aware of. The benefits of the integrity and moderation of the judiciary have already been felt in more States than one; and though they may have displeased those whose sinister expectations they may have disappointed, they must have commanded the esteem and applause of all the virtuous and disinterested. Considerate men, of every description, ought to prize whatever will tend to beget or fortify that temper in the courts: as no man can be sure that he may not be to-morrow the victim of a spirit of injustice, by which he may be a gainer to-day. And every man must now feel, that the inevitable tendency of such a spirit is to sap the foundations of public and private confidence, and to introduce in its stead universal distrust and distress.

That inflexible and uniform adherence to the rights of the Constitution, and of individuals, which we perceive to be indispensable in the courts of justice, can certainly not be expected from judges who hold their offices by a temporary commission. Periodical appointments, however regulated, or by whomsoever made, would, in some way or other, be fatal to their necessary independence. If the power of making them was committed either to the Executive or legislature, there would be danger of an improper complaisance to the branch which possessed it; if to both, there would be an unwillingness to hazard the displeasure of either; if to the people, or to persons chosen by them for the special purpose, there would be too great a disposition to consult popularity, to justify a reliance that nothing would be consulted but the Constitution and the laws.

There is yet a further and a weightier reason for the permanency of the judicial offices, which is deducible from the nature of the qualifications they require. It has been frequently remarked, with great propriety, that a voluminous code of laws is one of the inconveniences necessarily connected with the advantages of a free government.

To avoid an arbitrary discretion in the courts, it is indispensable that they should be bound down by strict rules and precedents, which serve to define and point out their duty in every particular case that comes before them; and it will readily be conceived from the variety of controversies which grow out of the folly and wickedness of mankind, that the records of those precedents must unavoidably swell to a very considerable bulk, and must demand long and laborious study to acquire a competent knowledge of them. Hence it is, that there can be but few men in the society who will have sufficient skill in the laws to qualify them for the stations of judges. And making the proper deductions for the ordinary depravity of human nature, the number must be still smaller of those who unite the requisite integrity with the requisite knowledge. These considerations apprise us, that the government can have no great option between fit character; and that a temporary duration in office, which would naturally discourage such characters from quitting a lucrative line of practice to accept a seat on the bench, would have a tendency to throw the administration of justice into hands less able, and less well qualified, to conduct it with utility and dignity. In the present circumstances of this country, and in those in which it is likely to be for a long time to come, the disadvantages on this score would be greater than they may at first sight appear; but it must be confessed, that they are far inferior to those which present themselves under the other aspects of the subject.

Upon the whole, there can be no room to doubt that the convention acted wisely in copying from the models of those constitutions which have established GOOD BEHAVIOR as the tenure of their judicial offices, in point of duration; and that so far from being blamable on this account, their plan would have been inexcusably defective, if it had wanted this important feature of good government. The experience of Great Britain affords an illustrious comment on the excellence of the institution.

Notes

1. The celebrated Montesquieu, speaking of them, says: "Of the three powers above mentioned, the judiciary is next to nothing." *Spirit of Laws*, vol. I., page 186.
2. Idem, page 181.
3. Vide "Protest of the Minority of the Convention of Pennsylvania," Martin's Speech, etc.

*C*onsider the source and the audience.

- Hamilton is writing to audiences who are skeptical of the power in the new Constitution he wants them to ratify. Article III of the Constitution, setting out the judiciary, is among the briefest and least specific of the constitutional provisions precisely because so many people objected to a strong and powerful federal court system. How is this factor likely to shape the arguments he makes here?

*L*ay out the argument, the values, and the assumptions.

- We know from a variety of sources that Hamilton was an advocate of a strong federal government. In this essay, how does he balance his own preferences with the necessity to persuade people who fear a strong government?
- What are Hamilton's major arguments for lifetime tenure of federal judges?

- Why does he think that judicial review does not unduly elevate the Court over the legislature?
- How does he think judges can be kept from exercising their will rather than their judgment?

*U*ncover the evidence.

- Does Hamilton provide any evidence to support his arguments? What are the advantages and limitations of relying on logic and rhetoric to support one's arguments?

*E*valuate the conclusion.

- Hamilton believes that there "can be no room to doubt" that federal judges should be appointed for life, and he incidentally believes that it is okay to give them the power to strike down the laws passed by Congress if they do not, in their judgment, conform to the Constitution. Has he made his case?
- Is his argument consistent with his initial contention that the courts will constitute the least dangerous and weakest branch of government?

*S*ort out the political implications.

- In what ways does judicial politics today depart from Hamilton's plan? Is the judiciary truly independent of the other two branches? Does politics intrude, despite Hamilton's precaution of providing lifetime tenure?
- What would Hamilton think about the Supreme Court's ruling in *Bush v. Gore?*

10 ★ ★ ★

Public Opinion

How much should public opinion count in a democracy? Do we want our representatives to be slaves to what we say we want? Do we think they should ignore us and steer their own course? When Bill Clinton was running for president, he was nicknamed "Slick Willie" for his practice of changing his issue stances according to the polls. Eight years later, George W. Bush promised that his administration would not be run by pollsters because, he said, true leaders make up their own minds and are not swayed by public opinion. The difference in these two leadership styles boils down to a difference over a fundamental question of democracy: Should what citizens think matter to their representatives, or should those representatives follow their own judgment and consciences?

People who support Bush's view on this issue claim that citizens are too ignorant, busy, or irrational to have opinions of the quality that we want represented in government, and that our representatives are better qualified to know what we want. Opponents of that view claim that no one is better qualified than the American public to decide what Americans want, and that the essence of democracy is responsiveness to public opinion. Many social scientists claim that even though people are busy and do not focus on politics on a daily basis, they still gather enough information to make informed choices about the things that affect their interests.

Regardless of whether they think public opinion ought to matter, most politicians act as if it does matter. Elected officials, after all, have to contend with what the public thinks during elections, even if they disregard polls at other times. And, as it turns out, few politicians disregard polls altogether.

Indeed, nationwide, pollsters have gotten into the habit of asking Americans what they think about a variety of issues, and they have scientifically honed the instruments with which they measure opinions. They do this for lots of reasons: Marketers want to find out what consumers want to buy, politicians want to know what voters want them to do, and everyday Americans want to know what their neighbors and colleagues are up to. There is no denying that, in American politics today, polling is big business.

The articles in this chapter illustrate the debates surrounding the role of public opinion polls in democratic governance. An article from *The American Spectator*, a conservative opinion journal, laments the ignorance of the American public on a host of issues and is pessimistic about its effect on public policy. The second article, from *The Economist*, discusses the difficulty that pollsters had in obtaining accurate preelection polls in the 2008 presidential election. In the fourth piece, Mark Mellman, a Democratic pollster, questions the interpretation of a recent poll on Americans' views on abortion. The fourth piece, from *Washington Monthly*, an investigative, anti-establishment journal, Joshua Green compares the polling efforts of Presidents Bill Clinton and George W. Bush. Finally, we turn to George Gallup, the father of opinion polling in America, for the classic defense of public opinion's role in democratic government.

 10.1 Party On, Dudes!

Ignorance Is the Curse of the Information Age

Matthew Robinson, The American Spectator

Why We Chose This Piece

One of the great debates among scholars of public opinion is whether the American public is informed regarding politics and policy. If not, then public opinion polls may measure nothing but a bunch of noise. The author of this article is clear where he stands in the debate. Matthew Robinson bemoans the ignorance of the American public and its general unfitness for the task of self-governance. In a way, he is writing about all of us. As you read the article, poll yourself. Do you think the Constitution guarantees you a job? Do you know who Alexander Hamilton is? Can you identify the Chief Justice of the U.S. Supreme Court? Do you know what DNA is? Do you know who won the battle of Yorktown? Can you correctly estimate the proportion of the U.S. population that is homeless or the number of abortions performed every year?

Also, ask yourself whether these kinds of questions matter. If you don't know who won the battle of Yorktown, does that mean you don't have a well-thought out position on abortion? If you have forgotten who exactly Alexander Hamilton was, does that mean that you can't cast an informed vote in a presidential election? In other words, how important is this kind of knowledge to our ability to formulate opinions on public matters and to understand our own political interests? If we do not match the democratic ideal of interested and informed citizens, should our opinions count?

Almost any look at what the average citizen knows about politics is bound to be discouraging. Political scientists are nearly unanimous on the subject of voter ignorance. The average American citizen not only lacks basic knowledge but also holds beliefs that are contradictory and inconsistent. Here is a small sample of what Americans "know":

Selection published: March/April 2002

Nearly one-third of Americans (29 percent) think the Constitution guarantees a job. Forty-two percent think it guarantees health care. And 75 percent think it guarantees a high school education.

Forty-five percent think the communist tenet "from each according to his abilities, to each according to his needs" is part of the U.S. Constitution.

More Americans recognize the Nike advertising slogan "Just Do It" than know where the right to "life, liberty, and the pursuit of happiness" is set forth (79 percent versus 47 percent). 90 percent know that Bill Gates is the founder of the company that created the Windows operating system. Just over half (53 percent) correctly identified Alexander Hamilton as a Founding Father.

Fewer than half of adults (47 percent) can name their own Representative in Congress. Fewer than half of voters could identify whether their congressman voted for the use of force in the Persian Gulf War.

Just 30 percent of adults could name Newt Gingrich as the congressman who led Republican congressional candidates in signing the Contract with America. Six months after the GOP took Congress, 64 percent admitted they did not know.

A 1998 poll by the Pew Research Center for the People and the Press showed that 56 percent of Americans could not name a single Democratic candidate for president; 63 percent knew the name "Bush," but it wasn't clear that voters connected the name to George W. Bush.

According to a January 2000 Gallup poll, 66 percent of Americans could correctly name Regis Philbin when asked who hosts *Who Wants to Be a Millionaire*, but only 6 percent could correctly name Dennis Hastert when asked to name the Speaker of the House of Representatives in Washington.

Political scientists Michael X. Delli Carpini and Scott Keeter studied 3,700 questions surveying the public's political knowledge from the 1930's to the present. They discovered that people tend to remember or identify trivial details about political leaders, focusing on personalities or simply latching onto the policies that the press plays up. For example, the most commonly known fact about George Bush while he was president was that he hated broccoli, and during the 1992 presidential campaign, although 89 percent of the public knew that Vice President Quayle was feuding with the television character Murphy Brown, only 19 percent could characterize Bill Clinton's record on the environment.

Their findings demonstrate the full absurdity of public knowledge: More people could identify Judge Wapner (the longtime host of the television series *The People's Court*) than could identify Chief Justices Warren Burger or William Rehnquist. More people had heard of John Lennon than of Karl Marx. More Americans could identify comedian-actor Bill Cosby than could name either of their U.S. senators. More people knew who said, "What's up, Doc," "Hi ho, Silver," or "Come up and see me sometime" than "Give me liberty or give me death," "The only thing we have to fear is fear itself," or "Speak softly and carry a big stick." More people knew that Pete Rose was accused of gambling than could name any of the five U.S. senators accused in the late 1980s of unethical conduct in the savings and loan scandal.

In 1986, the National Election Survey found that almost 24 percent of the general public did not know who George Bush was or that he was in his second term as vice president of the United States. "People at this level of inattentiveness can have only the haziest idea of the policy alternatives about which pollsters regularly ask, and such ideas as they do have must often be relatively innocent of the effects of exposure to elite discourse," writes UCLA political science professor John R. Zaller.

All of this would appear to be part of a broader trend of public ignorance that extends far beyond politics. Lack of knowledge on simple matters can reach staggering levels. In a 1996 study by the National Science Foundation, fewer than half of American adults polled (47 percent) knew that the earth takes one year to orbit the sun. Only about 9 percent could describe in their own words what a molecule is, and only 21 percent knew what DNA is.

Esoteric information? That's hard to say. One simple science-related question that has grown to have major political importance is whether police ought to genetically tag convicted criminals in the hopes of linking them to unsolved crimes. In other words, should police track the DNA of a convicted burglar to see if he is guilty of other crimes? Obviously issues of privacy and government power are relevant here. Yet how can a poll about this issue make sense if the citizenry doesn't understand the scientific terms of debate? Asking an evaluative question seems pointless.

The next generation of voters—those who will undoubtedly be asked to answer even tougher questions about politics and science—are hardly doing any better on the basics. A 2000 study by the American Council of Trustees and Alumni found that 81 percent of seniors at the nation's fifty-five top colleges scored a D or F on high school-level history exams. It turns out that most college seniors—including those from such elite universities as Harvard, Stanford, and the University of California—do not know the men or ideas that have shaped American freedom. Here are just a few examples from *Losing America's Memory: Historical Illiteracy in the 21st Century*, focusing on people's lack of knowledge about our First Citizen—the man whose respect for the laws of the infant republic set the standard for virtue and restraint in office.

Barely one in three students knew that George Washington was the American general at the battle of Yorktown—the battle that won the war for independence.

Only 42 percent could identify Washington with the line "First in war, first in peace, first in the hearts of his countrymen."

Only a little more than half knew that Washington's farewell address warned against permanent alliances with foreign governments.

And when it comes to actually explaining the ideas that preserve freedom and restrain government, the college seniors performed just as miserably.

More than one in three were clueless about the division of power set forth in the U.S. Constitution.

Only 22 percent of these seniors could identify the source of the phrase "government of the people, by the people, and for the people" (from Lincoln's Gettysburg Address).

Yet 99 percent of college seniors knew the crude cartoon characters Beavis and Butthead, and 98 percent could identify gangsta rapper Snoop Doggy Dogg.

Apparent ignorance of basic civics can be especially dangerous. Americans often "project" power onto institutions with little understanding of the Constitution or the law. Almost six of ten Americans (59 percent) think the president, not Congress, has the power to declare war. Thirty-five percent of Americans believe the president has the power to adjourn Congress at his will. Almost half (49 percent) think he has the power to suspend the Constitution (49 percent). And six in ten think the chief executive appoints judges to the federal courts without the approval of the Senate.

Some political scientists charge that American ignorance tends to help institutions and parties in power. That is hardly the active vigilance by the citizenry that the founders advocated. Political scientists continue to debate the role of ignorance and the future of democracy when voters are so woefully ignorant. As journalist Christopher Shea writes, "Clearly, voter ignorance poses problems for democratic theory: Politicians, the representatives of the people, are being elected by people who do not know their names or their platforms. Elites are committing the nation to major treaties and sweeping policies that most voters don't even know exist."

Professors Delli Carpini and Keeter discovered, for example, that most Americans make fundamental errors on some of the most contested and heavily covered political questions. "Americans grossly overestimate the average profit made by American corporations, the percentage of the U.S. population that is poor or homeless, and the percentage of the world population that is malnourished," they write. "And, despite twelve years of antiabortion administrations, Americans substantially underestimate the number of abortions performed every year."

With most voters unable to even name their congressperson or senators during an election year, the clear winner is the establishment candidate. Studies by Larry Bartels at Princeton University show that mere name recognition is enough to give incumbents a 5-percentage-point advantage over challengers: Most voters in the election booth can't identify a single position of the incumbent, but if they've seen the candidate's name before, that can be enough to secure their vote. (In many cases, voters can't even recognize the names of incumbents.)

Media polls are typically searching in vain for hard-nosed public opinion that simply isn't there. Polls force people to say they are leaning toward a particular candidate, but when voters are asked the more open-ended question "Whom do you favor for the presidency?" the number of undecided voters rises. The mere practice, in polling, of naming the candidates yields results that convey a false sense of what voters know. When Harvard's "Vanishing Voter Project" asked voters their presidential preferences without giving the names of candidates, they routinely found that the number of undecided voters was much higher than in media polls. Just three weeks before the 2000 election, 14 percent of voters still hadn't made up their minds.

Even when polling covers subjects on which a person should have direct knowledge, it can yield misleading results because of basic ignorance. The non-partisan Center for Studying Health System Change (HSC) found that how people rate their health care is attributable to the type of plan they *think* they are in more than their actual health insurance. The center asked twenty thousand privately insured people what they thought of their coverage, their doctor, and their treatment. But instead of just taking their opinions and impressions, the center also looked at what coverage each respondent actually had.

Nearly a quarter of Americans misidentified the coverage they had. Eleven percent didn't know they were in an HMO, and another 13 percent thought they were in an HMO but were *not*. Yet when people believed they were in a much-maligned HMO (even when they actually had another kind of insurance), their perceived satisfaction with their health care was lower than that of people who believed they had non-HMO coverage (even when they were in an HMO). Similarly, on nearly all ten measures studied by the center, those HMO enrollees who thought they had a different kind of insurance gave satisfaction ratings similar to those who actually had those other kinds of insurance.

Once center researchers adjusted for incorrect self-identification, the differences between HMO and non-HMO enrollees nearly vanished. Even on something as personal as health care, citizens display a striking and debilitating ignorance that quietly undermines many polling results.

After looking at the carnage of polls that test voter knowledge rather than impressions, James L. Payne concluded in his 1991 book *The Culture of Spending*:

> *Surveys have repeatedly found that voters are remarkably ignorant about even simple, dramatic features of the political landscape. The vast majority of voters cannot recall the names of congressional candidates in the most recent election; they cannot use the labels "liberal" and "conservative" meaningfully; they do not know which party controls Congress; they are wildly wrong about elementary facts about the federal budget; and they do not know how their congressmen vote on even quite salient policy questions. In other words, they are generally incapable of rewarding or punishing their congressman for his action on spending bills.*

Ignorance of basic facts such as a candidate's name or position isn't the only reason to question the efficacy of polling in such a dispiriting universe. Because polls have become "players in the political process," their influence is felt in the policy realm, undercutting efforts to educate because they assume respondents' knowledge and focus on the horse race. Is it correct to say that Americans oppose or support various policies when they don't even have a grasp of basic facts relating to those policies? For instance, in 1995, GrassRoots Research found that 83 percent of those polled underestimated the average family's tax burden. Taxes for a four-person family earning $35,000 are 54 percent higher than most people think. Naturally when practical-minded Americans look at political issues, their perceptions of reality influence which solutions they find acceptable. If they perceive that there are fewer abortions or lower taxes than there really are, these misperceptions may affect the kinds of policy prescriptions they endorse. They might change their views if introduced to the facts. In this sense, the unreflective reporting on public opinion about these policy issues is deceptive.

The Wall Street Journal editorial page provides another example of how ignorance affects public debate. Media reports during the 1995 struggle between the Republicans in Congress and the Clinton White House continually asserted that the public strongly opposed the GOP's efforts to slow the growth of Medicare spending. A poll by Public Opinion Strategies asked one thousand Americans not what they felt but what they actually *knew* about the GOP plan. Twenty-seven percent said they thought the GOP would cut Medicare spending by $4,000 per recipient. Almost one in four (24 percent) said it would keep spending the same. Another 25 percent didn't know. Only 22 percent knew the correct answer: The plan would increase spending to $6,700 per recipient.

Public Opinion's pollsters then told respondents that true result of the GOP plan and explained: "[U]nder the plan that recently passed by Congress, spending on

Medicare will increase 45 percent over the next seven years, which is twice the projected rate of inflation." How did such hard facts change public opinion about Medicare solutions? Six of ten Americans said that the GOP's proposed Medicare spending was too *high*. Another 29 percent said it was about right. Only 2 percent said it was too *low*.

Indeed polling and the media may gain their ability to influence results from voter ignorance. When a polling question introduces new facts (or any facts at all), voters are presented with a reframed political issue and thus may have a new opinion. Voters are continually asked about higher spending, new programs, and the best way to solve social ills with government spending. But how does the knowledge base (or lack of knowledge) affect the results of a polling question? That is simply unknown. When asked in a June 2000 *Washington Post* poll how much money the federal government gives to the nation's public schools, only 31 percent chose the correct answer. Although only 10 percent admitted to not knowing the correct answer, fully 60 percent of registered voters claimed they knew but were wrong. Is there any doubt that voters' knowledge, or lack thereof, affects the debate about whether to raise school spending to ever higher levels?

Reporters often claim that the public supports various policies, and they use such sentiment as an indicator of the electoral prospects of favored candidates. But this, too, can be misleading. Take, for instance, the results of a survey taken by The Polling Company for the Center for Security Policy about the Strategic Defense Initiative. Some 54 percent of respondents thought that the U.S. military had the capability to destroy a ballistic missile before it could hit an American city and do damage. Another 20 percent didn't know or refused to answer. Only 27 percent correctly said that the U.S. military could not destroy a missile.

What's interesting is that although 70 percent of those polled said they were concerned about the possibility of ballistic missile attack, the actual level of ignorance was very high. The Polling Company went on to tell those polled that "government documents indicate that the U.S. military cannot destroy even a single incoming missile." The responses were interesting. Nearly one in five said they were "shocked and angry" by the revelation. Another 28 percent said they were "very surprised," and 17 percent were "somewhat surprised." Only 22 percent said they were "not surprised at all." Finally 14 percent were "skeptical because [they] believe that the documents are inaccurate."

Beyond simply skewing poll results, ignorance is actually amplified by polling. Perhaps the most amazing example of the extent of ignorance can be found in Larry Sabato's 1981 book *The Rise of Political Consultants*. Citizens were asked: "Some people say the 1975 Public Affairs Act should be repealed. Do you agree or disagree that it should be repealed?" Nearly one in four (24 percent) said they wanted it repealed. Another 19 percent wanted it to remain in effect. Fifty-seven percent didn't know what should be done. What's interesting is that there was no such thing as the 1975 Public Affairs Act. But for 43 percent of those polled, simply asking that question was enough to create public opinion.

Ignorance can threaten even the most democratic institutions and safeguards. In September 1997, the Center for Media and Public Affairs conducted one of the largest surveys ever on American views of the Fourth Estate. Fully 84 percent of Americans

are willing to "turn to the government to require that the news media give equal coverage to all sides of controversial issues." Seven in ten back court-imposed fines for
inaccurate or biased reporting. And just over half (53 percent) think that journalists
should be licensed. Based on sheer numbers—in the absence of the rule of law and
dedication to the Bill of Rights—there is enough support to put curbs on the free
speech that most journalists (rightly) consider one of the most important bulwarks of
liberty.

In an era when Americans have neither the time nor the interest to track politics
closely, the power of the pollster to shape public opinion is almost unparalleled when
united with the media agenda.

For elected leaders, voter ignorance is something they have to confront when they
attempt to make a case for new policies or reforms. But for the media, ignorance isn't
an obstacle. It's an opportunity for those asking the questions—whether pollster or
media polling director—to drive debate. As more time is devoted to media pundits,
journalists, and pollsters, and less to candidates and leaders, the effect is a negative
one: Public opinion becomes more important as arbiter for the chattering classes. But
in a knowledge vacuum, public opinion also becomes more plastic and more subject
to manipulation, however well intentioned.

Pollsters often try to bridge the gap in public knowledge by providing basic definitions of terms as part of their questions. But this presents a new problem: By writing
the questions, pollsters are put in a position of power, particularly when those questions will be used in a media story. The story—if the poll is the story—is limited by the
questions asked, the definitions supplied, and the answers that respondents are given
to choose from.

The elevation of opinion without context or reference to knowledge exacerbates a
problem of modern democracies. Self-expression may work in NEA-funded art, but it
robs the political process of the communication and discussion that marries compromise with principle. Clearly "opinion" isn't the appropriate word for the melange of
impressions and sentiment that are presented as the public's beliefs in countless newspaper and television stories. If poll respondents lack a solid grasp of the facts, surveys
give us little more than narcissistic opinion.

As intelligent and precise thinking declines, all that remains is a chaos of ideologies
in which the lowest human appetites rule. In her essay "Truth and Politics," historian
Hannah Arendt writes: "Facts inform opinions, and opinions, inspired by different
interests and passions, can differ widely and still be legitimate as long as they respect
factual truth. Freedom of opinion is a farce unless factual information is guaranteed
and facts themselves are not in dispute."

If ignorance is rife in a republic, what do polls and the constant media attention to
them do to deliberative democracy? As Hamilton put it, American government is based
on "reflection and choice." Modern-day radical egalitarians—journalists and pollsters
who believe that polls are the definitive voice of the people—may applaud the ability
of the most uninformed citizen to be heard, but few if any of these champions of polling ever write about or discuss the implications of ignorance to a representative democracy. This is the dirtiest secret of polling.

Absent from most polling stories is the honest disclosure that American ignorance
is driving public affairs. Basic ignorance of civic questions gives us reason to doubt the

veracity of most polls. Were Americans armed with strongly held opinions and well-grounded knowledge of civic matters, they would not be open to manipulation by the wording of polls. This is one of the strongest reasons to question the effect of polls on representative government.

Pollsters assume and often control the presentation of the relevant facts. As a blunt instrument, the pollster's questions fail to explore what the contrary data may be. This is one reason that public opinion can differ so widely from one poll to another. When the citizens of a republic lack basic knowledge of political facts and cannot process ideas critically, uninformed opinion becomes even more potent in driving people. Worse, when the media fail to think critically about the lines of dispute on political questions, polls that are supposed to explore opinion will simplify and even mislead political leaders as well as the electorate.

When the media drive opinion by constant polling, the assumption of an educated public undermines the process of public deliberation that actually educates voters. Ideas are no longer honed, language isn't refined, and debate is truncated. The common ground needed for compromise and peaceful action is eroded because the discussion about facts and the parameters of the question are lost. In the frenzy to judge who wins and who loses, the media erode what it is to be a democracy. Moments of change become opportunities for spin, not for new, bold responses to the exigencies of history.

Not only are polls influenced, shaped, and even dominated by voter ignorance, but so is political debate. The evidence shows that ignorance is being projected into public debate because of the pervasiveness of polls. Polls are leading to the democratization of ignorance in the public square by ratifying ill-formed opinions, with the march of the mob instigated by an impatient and unreflective media. Polls—especially in an age marked by their proliferation—are serving as broadcasting towers of ignorance.

Political science professor Rogan Kersh notes, "Public ignorance and apathy toward most policy matters have been constant (or have grown worse) for over three decades. Yet the same period has seen increasing reliance on finely tuned instruments for measuring popular opinion, and more vigorous applications of the results in policy making." And here is the paradox in the Age of Polls: Pollsters and political scientists are still unclear about the full consequences of running a republic on the basis of opinion polls. The cost of voter ignorance is high, especially in a nation with a vast and sprawling government that, even for the most plugged-in elites, is too complicated to understand. Media polling that does not properly inform viewers and readers of its limitations serves only to give the facade of a healthy democracy, while consultants, wordsmiths, and polling units gently massage questions, set the news agenda, and then selectively report results. It is like the marionette player who claims (however invisible the strings) that the puppet moves on his own.

*C*onsider the source and the audience.

- Robinson is an editor at *The American Spectator,* a conservative opinion journal. How might the conservative nature of the journal affect the evaluation of public opinion presented here?

L̲ay out the argument, the values, and the assumptions.

- What is Robinson's view of how democracy should work? Is there a place for public opinion polls in his view? For voting? What views should be represented?
- Robinson believes that American public discourse is in trouble because of unscrupulous pollsters, shoddy journalism, and ignorant voters. Are polls influenced by voter ignorance, or is voter ignorance a product of manipulative polls?
- Does Robinson show a link between voter ignorance and bad public policy? Do voters need the information he believes they don't have in order to make sound political decisions?

U̲ncover the evidence.

- Robinson's chief concern is voter ignorance, and he cites a lot of poll evidence and scholarly opinion to illustrate it. Do we need to know anything more about the polling evidence he cites in order to evaluate it?
- Does Robinson provide evidence that voter ignorance and irresponsible polling actually drive public affairs?

E̲valuate the conclusion.

- Robinson makes a number of observations about the American voter. Are the conclusions he draws from them clear? Do they necessarily follow from his assumptions and evidence?

S̲ort out the political implications.

- If Robinson were writing the rules, what role would the American public play in U.S. government? What role would the media play?

 10.2 In Poll Position

Opinion Polls Show That Barack Obama Is Comfortably Ahead in the Race to Be President. Are They Right?

The Economist

Why We Chose This Piece

> *During presidential elections, Americans are obsessed with so-called horse-race polls that show what the result of the election would be if it were held at the time the poll was conducted. Never was this more true than during the 2008 presidential election. However, people often accept the results of these polls as being true without scratching below the surface and investigating questions such as, How was the poll conducted? Who was*

Selection published: October 17, 2008

included in the survey? What was the margin of error? The answers to these questions often influence how one should interpret the results.

The subject of poll accuracy is especially pertinent in the shadow of the 2008 presidential election. Preelection polls regularly showed that Barack Obama led John McCain, but, as this article makes clear, there was a great deal of debate about whether these polls were correct. Trying to determine who will win an election seems relatively straightforward. You simply ask people who they will vote for and tally the results. In reality, however, the process is far more complex. We include this article because it exposes you to issues that people should think about as they digest poll results.

Everyone knows that opinion polls give Barack Obama a lead in the race to the White House. But by how much? On Wednesday October 15th one poll (by CBS and the New York Times) suggested that the Democrat had an advantage of 14 points over John McCain. With little more than two weeks to go, the Republican could never overcome such a deficit, barring an act of God. But another poll published on the same day had Mr Obama leading by just three points, within the poll's margin of error.

Polling has always mixed art and science: at least one of those polls this week, and perhaps both, is wrong. During the primary season, especially on the Democratic side, many pollsters missed their targets by a mile, for example by predicting that Mr Obama would win comfortably in New Hampshire, only for Hillary Clinton to triumph.

This year has presented unusual challenges, largely because of Mr Obama. One difficulty is turnout. Traditionally, pollsters know that youngsters are less likely to turn out, and blacks too. But the youthful and black Mr Obama has brought both groups out in large numbers, getting them to register, to attend rallies and, during the primary season, to cast votes. Pollsters struggled to keep up. For example, in the black-heavy states of the south, Mr Obama was expected to win comfortably. Instead, he won overwhelmingly, and the big margins brought him crucial delegates.

Then there is the much-discussed "Bradley effect." Many experts still think that white voters will tell pollsters that they might vote for Mr Obama, but secret racism, concealed for embarrassment, will have them voting for Mr McCain instead. No such across-the-board effect could be seen in the primaries, as, in most states, he outperformed the polls. Where he struggled in the primaries, however, could be important for the presidential election: he did worse than his polls in Rust Belt and Appalachian states. A few of those remain in the balance; Ohio, in particular, broke heavily away from Mr Obama in the primaries, even more so than polls predicted.

Pollsters are also flummoxed by the question of how to count voters who use only mobile phones. Most polling is done over fixed-line phones, but a growing number of Americans have only a mobile telephone. These tend to be younger, technologically savvy and urban types, who are probably inclined to favour Mr Obama. Although pollsters try to correct for this in their models, it is impossible to know how significant the problem is, as phone-owning habits are changing fast. More polls do include a sampling of mobile-phone respondents and these seem to show a marked leaning towards Mr Obama. But this does not mean that those pollsters have the right mix of phone-owners in their sample.

A last factor is turnout operations. A candidate may lag in the polls, but have a crack organisation that will be more successful at getting its supporters to the polling station on election day. George Bush is widely credited with a powerful machine that helped him to win a close race in 2004, when many factors (including a worsening war in Iraq) weighed him down.

Assessing these factors together makes it even harder to predict how the polls might be getting the details wrong. The fact that Mr Obama, mostly, outdid his poll-ratings in the course of the primary race is encouraging for the Democrat. But as Mr McCain was involved in a relatively short primary race, there is no comparable data for him.

Some current information may provide a clue. One pollster, SurveyUSA, has been tracking early voters in states that permit voting before election day. The results so far show Mr Obama beating Mr McCain by larger margins among early-voters than is suggested by opinion polls in the same states. For example in Ohio opinion polls give Mr Obama a lead of a few percentage points, but among those who have already voted he has a lead of about 18 points. Early voting is not necessarily an accurate guide to the eventual result, as the most partisan are likely to vote early, with important swing voters deciding later. But, again, Mr Obama has reason to cheer. Older voters are also fond of casting their ballots early, and one might expect the elderly to lean in favour of the Republican candidate. So far, however, Mr Obama appears to be doing better.

Mr McCain can take some solace. The gap between candidates usually narrows nearer to polling day. He is finding a more convincing message on the economy and on his differences with Mr Obama. And fears about the economy may now be priced into the polls, so worse news may not damage Mr McCain any further. But he must work to change the polls, not just hope they are wrong. If they are right, on average, Mr McCain is set to lose. And if they are wrong in most of the quantifiable ways that can be examined—the Bradley effect, mobile-onlys and so on—Mr McCain may possibly lose in a landslide.

*C*onsider the source and the audience.

- *The Economist* is a weekly international magazine devoted to covering business and political news around the world. One particularly interesting aspect of *The Economist* is that all of its articles are written anonymously. Does this matter?
- Why would an international audience be interested in the accuracy of preelection polls for a presidential election in the United States?

*L*ay out the argument, the values, and the assumptions.

- How did the presence of Barack Obama as one of the two major-party presidential candidates complicate the job of pollsters?
- How did an increase in the number of mobile phones complicate the job of pollsters?

*U*ncover the evidence.

- The author uses polls from the primary season as a gauge regarding the accuracy of the general election polls. How might primary and general election polls be comparable? How might they be different?
- The author also discusses a poll of early voters (people who cast their ballots before Election Day). What insight might polls of early voters provide regarding the accuracy of the preelection

polls and the outcome of the election? Why might relying on early voters be problematic for gauging who will win?

*E**valuate the conclusion.***

- The argument made in this article is easy to evaluate. Did the concerns about the accuracy of preelection polls come to fruition?

*S**ort out the political implications.***

- Does it matter if preelection polls are accurate? What might happen if the preelection polls do not correctly predict the winner?
- Do preelection polls serve an important purpose, or do they simply have entertainment value for the public? How might campaigns view preelection polls differently than the public does?

10.3 Pro-Life and Pro-Choice

Mark Mellman, TheHill.com

Why We Chose This Piece

It seems like hundreds of polls are released every day that tell people how Americans feel about numerous issues. Interpreting those poll results can be hard work. It is easy to simply accept the results of the polls at face value, but sometimes you need to dig a little deeper to understand what—if anything—the poll results actually mean.

Here, Mark Mellman, a Democratic pollster, questions the interpretation of a Gallup poll probing Americans' opinions on abortion. We chose this piece because, unlike Matthew Robinson, the author of the first selection in this chapter, Mellman wants you to be critical of polls, not skeptical of them. He is, after all, a pollster, and he believes that when polls are implemented correctly, they can provide valuable information. Also, the focus of the article is abortion, a highly salient, emotionally charged issue. Yet even on an issue such as abortion, results may differ based on how the question is asked. Finally, Mellman's critique is interesting because Gallup isn't some ragtag polling operation. It is considered by many to be the granddaddy of polling organizations. Indeed, the namesake of the organization, and also the author of the last piece in this chapter, is thought of as the father of opinion polling in America. Gallup is an organization that has credibility; as a result, people may be willing to accept its poll results as fact, something that Mellman clearly believes is problematic.

Obtaining meaningful poll results requires asking meaningful questions. It seems obvious, but too often this basic rule is observed in the breech.

Selection published: May 19, 2009

Typically, after some useless result escapes into the ether, reporters and interest groups proceed to spin some new theory of public opinion based on faulty analysis of a meaningless question.

Last week's Gallup poll on abortion followed this oft-repeated pattern. Gallup confined itself to reporting the accurate, if misleading, result—"51 percent of Americans call[ing] themselves 'pro-life' on the issue of abortion and 42 percent 'pro-choice.' This is the first time a majority of U.S. adults have identified themselves as pro-life since Gallup began asking this question in 1995."

A Wall Street Journal blog twisted the result to suggest a substantive interpretation not in evidence—"A majority of Americans now say they oppose abortion rights, according to a Gallup poll released today." Leave it to those who want to make all abortions illegal to move way beyond the facts, citing the poll results as proof the anti-abortion cause "is a vibrant, growing, youthful movement."

What did these Gallup results actually reveal about American public opinion? Damn little.

First, as Professor Charles Franklin points out, the sample for this particular Gallup poll was much more Republican than most others Gallup has done, leading more respondents to identify themselves as "pro-life."

More problematic is the language itself. While the political class readily identifies with words like "pro-choice" and "pro-life," many voters do not. In a large national survey we conducted, fewer than half of respondents defined the term "pro-choice" in a way even remotely connected to the abortion debate. Only 28 percent made explicit reference to abortion in their response. Another 20 percent offered a vague definition, usually about trusting women.

Half, however, were not even close. "Having the choice to change your mind if you want to—about anything." "The choice to live, the choice to die." "Choosing your religion for me." Thus, questions asking voters to embrace one of these labels are not necessarily even tapping into the abortion debate, because so few know what the terms mean.

In addition, accepting one of those labels does not necessarily relate to real public policy choices in any meaningful way. For instance, in our survey, nearly a third of those who called themselves "pro-life" reject the view that "the government should pass more laws restricting the availability of abortions," saying instead "the government should not interfere with a woman's access to abortion." Would anti-choice leaders hold up as one of their own a politician who opposed laws restricting abortion?

That is exactly where the American people are—by 62 percent to 27, voters oppose additional legal restrictions on the availability of abortion.

Roe v. Wade is at the heart of the public policy debate. A week after Gallup's poll, CNN and Opinion Research Corp. defined the decision this way: "The 1973 Roe v. Wade decision established a woman's constitutional right to an abortion at least in the first three months of pregnancy." Sixty-eight percent wanted to keep Roe in place—hardly the position of those celebrating Gallup's result. Just 30 percent supported overturning Roe.

In short, the data tell us Americans oppose government restrictions on abortion and want to keep Roe in place, while identifying themselves as pro-life—a term many do not understand.

Useful poll questions on public policy meet at least two key criteria. They use words and concepts respondents understand and they employ categories that reflect the real terms of the debate. Asking people whether they are "pro-choice" or "pro-life" meets neither of those criteria and therefore does more to obscure the debate than to illuminate it.

*C*onsider the source and the audience.

- Does the fact that Mellman is a Democratic pollster matter? How might his background affect his argument?

*L*ay out the argument, the values, and the assumptions.

- Why does Mellman believe the result of the Gallup poll is "misleading?" What problems does Mellman have with the question Gallup asked?
- Is it just the Gallup organization that he is critical of or someone or something else?

*U*ncover the evidence.

- How does Mellman demonstrate that the results are misleading?

*E*valuate the conclusion.

- What does Mellman ultimately conclude regarding where Americans stand on the issue of abortion? How does he know this?

*S*ort out the political implications.

- Poll results are often reported in the media with little context or information regarding how the poll was conducted. Why might this be problematic?
- Is it important in a democracy that the public have confidence in poll results?

 ## 10.4 The Other War Room

Joshua Green, Washington Monthly

Why We Chose This Piece

At first glance, it might appear odd to be reading an article about how pollsters were used by two former presidents, one of whom was president while many of you were still in elementary school. However, we include this article because it provides not only clear insight into two very different presidential approaches to polling the public, but also two different views of presidential leadership. The article remains as relevant today as it was at the time it was written, early in George W. Bush's first term.

Selection published: April 2002

Bill Clinton was famous for his polling activities, and he was often accused by his opponents of being too "poll driven"—that is, willing to change his policies according to what his pollsters told him the American people wanted to hear. George W. Bush ran for president, in part, on his independence from polls in formulating policy stances. This article doesn't dispute that fact, but it argues that Bush used polls, too, just in a different way.

Although it is still early in President Barack Obama's term, we know that he has polled slightly more than Bush and slightly less than Clinton. His pollsters tend to remain out of the public eye, and his political advisors, not Obama himself, appear to digest the poll results. As you read the article, ask yourself whether Obama's use of polling and leadership style are more in line with Clinton's or Bush's? Or do they fall somewhere in between?

On a Friday afternoon late last year, press secretaries from every recent administration gathered in the Ward Room of the White House at the invitation of Ari Fleischer, press secretary to President Bush. There was no agenda. It was just one of those unexpectedly nice things that seemed to transpire during the brief period after September 11 when people thought of themselves as Americans first and Democrats and Republicans second. Over a lunch of crab cakes and steak, Republicans such as Fleischer and Marlin Fitzwater traded war stories with Joe Lockhart, Mike McCurry, and assorted other Democrats. Halfway through lunch, President Bush dropped by unexpectedly and launched into an impromptu briefing of his own, ticking off the items on his agenda until he arrived at the question of whether it was preferable to issue vague warnings of possible terrorist threats or to stay quietly vigilant so as not to alarm people. At this point, former Clinton press secretary Dee Dee Myers piped up, "What do the poll numbers say?" All eyes turned to Bush. Without missing a beat, the famous Bush smirk crossed the president's face and he replied, "In this White House, Dee Dee, we don't poll on something as important as national security."

This wasn't a stray comment, but a glimpse of a larger strategy that has served Bush extremely well since he first launched his campaign for president—the myth that his administration doesn't use polling. As Bush endlessly insisted on the campaign trail, he governs "based upon principle and not polls and focus groups."

It's not hard to understand the appeal of this tactic. Ever since the Clinton administration's well-noted excesses—calling on pollsters to help determine vacation spots and family pets—polling has become a kind of shorthand for everything people dislike about Washington politics. "Pollsters have developed a reputation as Machiavellian plotters whose job it is to think up ways to exploit the public," says Andrew Kohut, director of the Pew Research Center for the People and the Press. Announcing that one ignores polls, then, is an easy way of conveying an impression of leadership, judgment, and substance. No one has recognized and used this to such calculated effect as Bush. When he announced he would "bring a new tone to Washington," he just as easily could have said he'd banish pollsters from the White House without any loss of effect. One of the most dependable poll results is that people don't like polling.

But in fact, the Bush administration is a frequent consumer of polls, though it takes extraordinary measures to appear that it isn't. This administration, unlike Clinton's, rarely uses poll results to ply reporters or congressional leaders for support. "It's rare to even hear talk of it unless you give a Bush guy a couple of drinks," says one White House reporter. But Republican National Committee filings show that Bush actually uses polls much more than he lets on, in ways both similar and dissimilar to Clinton. Like Clinton, Bush is most inclined to use polls when he's struggling. It's no coincidence that the administration did its heaviest polling last summer, after the poorly received rollout of its energy plan, and amid much talk of the "smallness" of the presidency. A *Washington Monthly* analysis of Republican National Committee disbursement filings revealed that Bush's principal pollsters received $346,000 in direct payments in 2001. Add to that the multiple boutique polling firms the administration regularly employs for specialized and targeted polls and the figure is closer to $1 million. That's about half the amount Clinton spent during his first year; but while Clinton used polling to craft popular policies, Bush uses polling to spin unpopular ones— arguably a much more cynical undertaking.

Bush's principal pollster, Jan van Lohuizen, and his focus-group guru, Fred Steeper, are the best-kept secrets in Washington. Both are respected but low-key, proficient but tight-lipped, and, unlike such larger-than-life Clinton pollsters as Dick Morris and Mark Penn, happy to remain anonymous. They toil in the background, poll-testing the words and phrases the president uses to sell his policies to an often-skeptical public; they're the Bush administration's Cinderella. "In terms of the modern presidency" says Ron Faucheux, editor of *Campaigns & Elections*, "van Lohuizen is the lowest-profile pollster we've ever had." But as Bush shifts his focus back toward a domestic agenda, he'll be relying on his pollsters more than ever.

Bush's Brain

On the last day of February, the Bush administration kicked off its renewed initiative to privatize Social Security in a speech before the National Summit on Retirement Savings in Washington, D.C. Rather than address "Social Security," Bush opted to speak about "retirement security." And during the brief speech he repeated the words "choice" (three times), "compound interest" (four times), "opportunity" (nine times) and "savings" (18 times). These words were not chosen lightly. The repetition was prompted by polls and focus groups. During the campaign, Steeper honed and refined Bush's message on Social Security (with key words such as "choice," "control," and "higher returns"), measuring it against Al Gore's attack through polls and focus groups ("Wall Street roulette," "bankruptcy" and "break the contract"). Steeper discovered that respondents preferred Bush's position by 50 percent to 38 percent, despite the conventional wisdom that tampering with Social Security is political suicide. He learned, as he explained to an academic conference last February, that "there's a great deal of cynicism about the federal government being able to do anything right, which translated to the federal government not having the ability to properly invest people's Social Security dollars." By couching Bush's rhetoric in poll-tested phrases that reinforced this notion, and adding others that stress the benefits of privatization, he was able to capitalize on what most observers had considered to be a significant political disadvantage. (Independent polls generally find that when fully apprised of Bush's plan, including the risks, most voters don't support it.)

This is typical of how the Bush administration uses polls: Policies are chosen beforehand, polls used to spin them. Because many of Bush's policies aren't necessarily popular with a majority of voters, Steeper and van Lohuizen's job essentially consists of finding words to sell them to the public. Take, for instance, the Bush energy plan. When administration officials unveiled it last May, they repeatedly described it as "balanced" and "comprehensive," and stressed Bush's "leadership" and use of "modern" methods to prevent environmental damage. As *Time* magazine's Jay Carney and John Dickerson revealed, van Lohuizen had poll-tested pitch phrases for weeks before arriving at these as the most likely to conciliate a skeptical public. (Again, independent polls showed weak voter support for the Bush plan.) And the "education recession" Bush trumpeted throughout the campaign? Another triumph of opinion research. Same with "school choice," the "death tax," and the "wealth-generating private accounts" you'll soon hear more about when the Social Security debate heats up. Even the much-lauded national service initiative Bush proposed in his State of the Union address was the product of focus grouping. Though publicly Bush prides himself on never looking in the mirror (that's "leadership"), privately, he's not quite so secure. His pollsters have even conducted favorability ratings on Ari Fleischer and Karen Hughes.

Bush's public opinion operation is split between Washington, D.C., where van Lohuizen's firm, Voter/Consumer Research, orchestrates the primary polling, and Southfield, Mich., where Steeper's firm, Market Strategies, runs focus groups. What the two have in common is Karl Rove. Like many in the administration, Steeper was a veteran of the first Bush presidency, and had worked with Rove on campaigns in Illinois and Missouri. Van Lohuizen has been part of the Bush team since 1991, when Rove hired him to work on a campaign to raise the local sales tax in Arlington, Texas, in order to finance a new baseball stadium for Bush's Texas Rangers.

Like previous presidential pollsters, van Lohuizen also serves corporate clients, including Wal-Mart, Qwest, Anheuser-Busch, and Microsoft. And like his predecessors, this presents potential conflicts of interest. For example, van Lohuizen polls for Americans for Technology Leadership, a Microsoft-backed advocacy group that commissioned a van Lohuizen poll last July purporting to show strong public support for ending the government's suit against the company. At the time, Bush's Justice Department was deciding to do just that. Clinton pollster Mark Penn also did work for Microsoft and Clinton took heat for it. Bush has avoided criticism because few people realize he even *has* a pollster.

The nerve center of the Bush polling operation is a 185-station phone bank in Houston through which van Lohuizen conducts short national polls to track Bush's "attributes," and longer polls on specific topics about once a month. These are complemented by Steeper's focus groups.

One real difference between Bush and Clinton is that, while Clinton was the first to read any poll, Bush maintains several degrees of separation from his pollsters. Both report to Matthew Dowd, the administration's chief of polling, stationed at the RNC, who then reports to Rove. "Rove is a voracious consumer of polls," says a Republican pollster. "He gets it, sifts through it, analyzes it, and gives the president the bottom line." In other words, when it comes to polling, Rove serves as Bush's brain.

Poll Vault

The practice of presidents poll-testing their message dates back to John F. Kennedy, who wished to pursue a civil rights agenda but knew that he would have to articulate it in words that the American public in the 1960s would accept. Alarm about being known to use polls is just as old. Kennedy was so afraid of being discovered that he kept the polling data locked in a safe in the office of his brother, the attorney general. Lyndon Johnson polled more heavily than Kennedy did and learned, through polling, that allowing Vietnam to become an issue in 1964 could cost him re-election. Richard Nixon brought polling—and paranoia over polling—to a new level, believing that his appeal to voters was his reputation as a skilled policymaker, and that if people discovered the extent to which he was polling, they would view him as "slick" and desert him. So he kept his poll data in a safe in his home. But though presidents considered it shameful, polling became an important tool for governing well. Nixon was smart enough to make good use of his polls, once opting to ban oil drilling off the California coast after polling revealed it to be highly unpopular with voters. Jimmy Carter's pollster, Pat Caddell, was the first rock-star pollster, partying with celebrities and cultivating a high-profile image as the president's Svengali (an image considerably tarnished when Caddell's polling for another client, Coca-Cola, became the rationale for the disastrous "New Coke" campaign in the 1980s).

Ronald Reagan polled obsessively throughout his presidency. His pollster, Richard Wirthlin, went so far as to conduct them "before Reagan was inaugurated, while he was being inaugurated, and the day after he was inaugurated," says an administration veteran. He was the first to use polls to sell a right-wing agenda to the country, but he knew enough to retreat when polls indicated that he couldn't win a fight. (Wirthlin's polls convinced Reagan not to cut Social Security, as he'd planned.) By contrast, his successor, George H. W. Bush, practically eschewed polls altogether. "There was a reaction against using polls because they reacted against everything Reagan," says Ron Hinckley, a Bush pollster. "They wanted to put their own name on everything. But their efforts to not be like Reagan took them into a framework of dealing with things that ultimately proved fatal." Indeed, in his first two years in office, Bush is said to have conducted just two polls. Even at Bush's highest point—after the Gulf War, when his approval rating stood at 88 percent—Hinckley says that his economic numbers were in the 40s. "We were in a hell of a lot of trouble," he says, "and nobody wanted to listen."

Bill Clinton, of course, polled like no other president. In addition to polling more often and in greater detail than his predecessors, he put unprecedented faith in his pollsters, elevating them to the status of senior advisers. His tendency to obsess over polls disconcerted even those closest to him, and his over-reliance on polls led to some devastating errors, such as following a Morris poll showing that voters wouldn't accept a candid acknowledgment of his relationship with Monica Lewinsky. But the truth about Clinton's use of polls is more nuanced than is generally understood.

Early in his administration, Clinton drifted away from the centrist agenda he campaigned on and staked out policy positions that appealed to his base. Like Reagan, he polled on how best to sell them to the American people. Healthcare reform is the most instructive example. Describing Clinton's handling of healthcare reform in their book *Politicians Don't Pander: Political Manipulation and the Loss of Democratic Responsiveness*, political scientists Lawrence R. Jacobs and Robert Y. Shapiro conclude: "The fundamental political mistake committed by Bill Clinton and his aides was in grossly overestimating the capacity of a president to 'win' public opinion and to use public support as leverage to overcome known political obstacles—from an ideologically divided Congress to hostile interest groups." The authors call this kind of poll-tested message "crafted talk." Clinton learned its shortcomings firsthand and modified his subsequent use of polls. He fired his pollster, Stanley Greenberg, in favor of centrist pollsters such as Dick Morris and Mark Penn. Though widely ridiculed for it in the press, after the disastrous midterm elections in 1994, Clinton began responding to voters' wishes, moving toward the political center.

Oftentimes these were largely symbolic nuggets like supporting school uniforms or choosing Christopher Reeve to speak at the 1996 Democratic National Convention (Reeve outpolled Walter Cronkite and John F. Kennedy, Jr.). But they also included important policies such as reforming welfare, balancing the budget, and putting 100,000 new police officers on the streets. Many of these centrist policies initially met strong resistance from congressional Democrats, the agencies, and interest groups, as well as liberals within the White House. But the fact that the policies polled well became a powerful tool of persuasion for Clinton and his centrist aides to use. Nor was Clinton afraid to act in spite of the polls, which he did on Bosnia, Haiti, the Mexican bailout, and affirmative action. Indeed, according to senior aides, it was forbidden to discuss foreign policy in the weekly polling meeting Clinton held in the White House residence. (Although, in a priceless irony, Clinton was sufficiently worried about appearing to be poll-driven that Morris drafted a list for him of the "unpopular actions you have taken despite polls.")

"The Circle Is Tight"

When George W. Bush launched his campaign for president, he did so with two prevailing thoughts in mind: to avoid his father's mistakes and to distinguish himself from Bill Clinton. To satisfy the first, Bush needed a tax cut to rival the one being offered by Steve Forbes, at the time considered Bush's most formidable rival for the GOP nomination. But to satisfy the second, Bush needed to engage in some tricky maneuvering. A van Lohuizen poll conducted in late 1998 showed tax cuts to be "the least popular choice" on his agenda among swing voters. So Bush faced a dilemma: He had to sell Americans a tax cut most didn't want, using a poll-crafted sales pitch he didn't want them to know about. In speeches, Bush started listing the tax cut after more popular items like saving Social Security and education. In March 2001, with support still flagging, he began pitching "tax cuts and debt relief" rather than just tax cuts—his polling showed that the public was much more interested in the latter. After plenty of creative math and more poll-tested phrases, Bush's tax cut finally won passage (a larger one, in fact, than he'd been offering in '98).

In a way, Bush's approach to polling is the opposite of Clinton's. He uses polls but conceals that fact, and, instead of polling to ensure that new policies have broad public support, takes policies favored by his conservative base and polls on how to make them seem palatable to mainstream voters. This pattern extends to the entire administration. Whereas Clinton's polling data were regularly circulated among the staff, Bush limits his to the handful of senior advisers who attend Rove's "strategy meetings." According to White House aides, the subject is rarely broached with the president or at other senior staff meetings. "The circle is tight," Matthew Dowd, Bush's chief of polling, testifies. "Very tight." As with Kennedy and Nixon, the Bush administration keeps its polling data under lock and key. Reagan circulated favorable polling data widely among congressional Republicans in an effort to build support. Clinton did likewise and extended this tactic to the media, using polls as political currency to persuade reporters that he was on the right side of an issue. "You don't see it like you did in the Dick Wirthlin days," says a top Republican congressman. "The White House pollster won't meet with the caucus to go through poll data. It just doesn't happen." Says a White House reporter, "The Clinton folks couldn't wait to call you up and share polling data, and Democratic pollsters who worked for the White House were always calling you to talk about it. But there's a general dictate under Bush that they don't use polls to tell them what to think." This policy extends to the president's pollsters, who are discouraged from identifying themselves as such. The strategy seems to be working. A brief, unscientific survey of White House reporters revealed that most couldn't name van Lohuizen as the Bush's primary pollster (most guessed Dowd, who doesn't actually poll). For his part, van Lohuizen sounded genuinely alarmed when I contacted him.

Crafted Talk

It's no mystery why the Bush administration keeps its polling operation in a secure, undisclosed location. Survey after survey shows that voters don't want a president slavishly following polls—they want "leadership" (another word that crops up in Bush's speeches with suspicious frequency). So it's with undisguised relish that Dowd tells me, "It was true during the campaign, it's true now. We don't poll policy positions. Ever."

But voters don't like a president to ignore their desires either. One of the abiding tensions in any democracy is between the need for leaders to respond to public opinion but also to be willing to act in ways that run counter to it. Good presidents strike the right balance. And polls, rightly used, help them do it.

But used the wrong way, polls become a way to cheat the system and evade this tension altogether. As Jacobs and Shapiro explain in *Politicians Don't Pander*, with the exception of the latter Clinton years, presidents since 1980 have increasingly used polls to come up with the "crafted talk" that makes their partisan, interest-group-driven policies seem more mainstream than they really are. Consider the Republican stimulus plan unveiled last winter: So heavily did it tilt toward corporate interests that focus group participants refused to believe that it was real—yet Bush pitched it for months as a "jobs" package.

Presidents, of course, must occasionally break with public opinion. But there's a thin line between being principled and being elitist. For many years, Democrats hurt themselves and the country by presuming they knew better than voters when it came to things like welfare, crime, and tax increases. Clinton used polling to help Democrats break this habit. Bush is more intent on using it to facilitate the GOP's own peculiar political elitism—the conviction that coddling corporations and cutting taxes for the rich will help the country, regardless of the fact that a majority of voters disagree.

Bush's attempt to slip a conservative agenda past a moderate public could come back to hurt him, especially now that his high approval ratings might tempt him to overreach. Recent history shows that poll-tested messages are often easy to parry. During the debate over Clinton's healthcare plan, for instance, Republican opponents launched their own poll-tested counterattack, the famous "Harry and Louise" ads, which were broadcast mainly on airport cable networks such as "CNN Airport" where well-traveled congressmen would be sure to spot them and assume they were ubiquitous. Because lawmakers and voters never fully bought Clinton's policy, it couldn't withstand the carefully tested GOP rebuttal.

A similar fate befell the GOP when it took over Congress in 1995, after campaigning on a list of promises dubbed the "Contract With America." As several pollsters and political scientists have since pointed out, the Contract's policies were heavily geared toward the party's conservative base but didn't register with voters—things like corporate tax cuts and limiting the right to sue. The GOP's strategy was to win over the press and the public with poll-tested "power phrases." Education vouchers, for instance, were promoted as a way of "strengthening rights of parents in their children's education," and Republicans were instructed by RNC chairman Haley Barbour to repeat such phrases "until you vomit." But when it came to proposals such as cutting Medicare, Republicans discovered that their confidence in being able to move public opinion—"preserving" and "protecting" Medicare—was misplaced. Clinton successfully branded them as "extremists," and this proposal, along with many of the Contract's provisions, never made it beyond the House.

Like so many other Republican ideas, Barbour's has been reborn under Bush. "What's happened over time is that there's a lot more polling on spin," says Jacobs. "That's exactly where Bush is right now. He's not polling to find out issues that the public supports so that he can respond to their substantive interests. He's polling on presentation. To those of us who study it, most of his major policy statements come off as completely poll concocted." Should this continue, the administration that condemns polling so righteously may not like what the polls wind up saying.

Consider the source and the audience.

- *The Washington Monthly* is an independent investigative political journal that prides itself on its ability to take on both liberals and conservatives, and whose mission statement makes clear its goal of influencing Washington insiders. How does this article fit that profile?

Lay out the argument, the values, and the assumptions.

- What does Green believe the role of public opinion ought to be in a democracy? How does he differ here from Matthew Robinson (the author of the first article in this chapter)?
- When should a president listen to public opinion, and when should he not? What role can polls play here?
- Is there a legitimate way for politicians to use public opinion and an illegitimate one?

Uncover the evidence.

- Where does Green go to investigate public opinion gathering in the Bush administration? Given how "tight the circle is," how can he know what he claims to know?
- Whether or not Bush uses polls is a matter for factual investigation. What kind of evidence does Green rely on to support his claim that Bush uses polls to "spin" policy stances he has already taken and make them palatable to the public?

E*valuate the conclusion.*

- What are the differences between Green's and Robinson's conclusions? What role does each think public opinion plays in policymaking, and who does each hold responsible for the manipulation of public opinion?
- Is Green right in saying that those who manipulate public opinion to advance a more extreme ideological agenda will be vulnerable to attack from moderate opponents more in tune with the public?

S*ort out the political implications.*

- What does it mean for the future of democracy if more polls are being done to "spin" policy than to create and direct it?

 ## 10.5 Will the Polls Destroy Representative Democracy?

George Horace Gallup and Saul Forbes Rae, The Pulse of Democracy

Why We Chose This Piece

> *This selection is a concluding chapter of a book that polling pioneer George Horace Gallup coauthored about the role of polls in democracy. We include it because, counter to some of the articles we have read in this chapter, this is a classic statement of confidence in the American people particularly, and in the central role of public opinion in a democracy generally. Gallup's book was written in 1940. Are his arguments still relevant today?*

A nother accusation leveled at the modern polls is based on the assumption that they intensify the "band-wagon" instinct in legislators and undermine the American system of representative government. "Ours is a representative democracy," a newspaper editorial suggested soon after the polls had become prominent in 1936, "in which it is properly assumed that those who are chosen to be representatives will think for themselves, use their best judgment individually, and take the unpopular side of an argument whenever they are sincerely convinced that the unpopular side is in the long run in the best interests of the country."

The point has been made more recently by a student of public opinion. "If our representatives were told," it has been written, "that 62% of the people favored payment of the soldier's bonus or 65% favored killing the World Court Treaty, the desire of many of them to be re-elected would lead them to respond to such statistics by voting for or against a measure not because they considered it wise or stupid but because they wanted to be in accord with what was pictured to them as the will of the electorate."[1]

Selection published: 1940

Beyond such criticisms, and at the root of many objections to the polls of public opinion, lies a fundamental conflict between two opposed views of the democratic process and what it means. This conflict is not new—it is older than American political theory itself. It concerns the relationship between representative government and direct democracy, between the judgments of small exclusive groups and the opinions of the great mass of the people. Many theorists who criticize the polls do so because they fear that giving too much power to the people will reduce the representative to the role of rubber stamp. A modern restatement of this attitude may be found in an article written by Colonel O. R. Maguire in the November, 1939, issue of the *United States Law Review.*[2]

Colonel Maguire quotes James Madison: "...pure democracies...have ever been spectacles of turbulence and contention; have ever been found incompatible with personal security or the rights of property; and have in general been as short in their lives as they have been violent in their deaths."

To support these statements made by an eighteenth-century conservative who feared the dangers of "too much democracy," Maguire insists that the ordinary man is incapable of being a responsible citizen, and leans heavily on the antidemocratic psychological generalizations of Ross, Tarde, and Le Bon. He follows James Madison and the English Conservative, Edmund Burke, in upholding the conception of representative government under which a body of carefully chosen, disinterested public representatives "whose wisdom may best discern the true interest of their country, and whose patriotism and love of justice will be least likely to sacrifice it to temporary or partial considerations," interpret the real will of the people. Under such conditions, it is argued, "it may well happen that the public voice, pronounced by the representatives of the people, will be more consonant to the public good than if pronounced by the people themselves, convened for that purpose." The polls are condemned because, in his view, they invite judgments on which the people are ignorant and ill-informed, on which discussion must be left to representatives and specialists. Finally, a grim picture is drawn of the excesses that will follow the growth of "direct democracy": "...the straw ballot will undermine and discourage the influence of able and conscientious public men and elevate to power the demagogue who will go to the greatest extremes in taking from those who have and giving to those who have not, until there has been realized the prophecy of Thomas Babington Macaulay that America will be as fearfully plundered from within by her own people in the twentieth century as Rome was plundered from without by the Gauls and Vandals."

This case against government by public opinion reveals suspicion not only of the public-opinion surveys, but also of the mass of the people. By and large, the thesis that the people are unfit to rule, and that they must be led by their natural superiors—the legislators and the experts—differs only in degree, and not in essence, from the view urged by Mussolini and Hitler that the people are mere "ballot cattle," whose votes are useful not because they represent a valuable guide to policy, but merely because they provide "proof" of the mass support on which the superior regime is based. It must not be forgotten that the dictators, too, urge that the common people, because of their numbers, their lack of training, their stupidity and gullibility, must be kept as far away as possible from the elite whose task it is to formulate laws for the mass blindly to obey.

Many previous statements and charges of just this kind can be found throughout history. Every despot has claimed that the people were incapable of ruling themselves, and by implication decided that only certain privileged leaders were fit for the legislative task. They have argued that "the best" should rule—but at different times and in different places the judgments as to who constituted "the best" have been completely contradictory. In Burke's England or Madison's America, it was the peerage or the stable wealthier classes—"the good, the wise, and the rich." In Soviet Russia, the representatives of the proletariat constitute "the best."

But the history of autocracy has paid eloquent testimony to the truth of Lord Acton's conclusion that "Power corrupts—absolute power corrupts absolutely." The possible danger of what has been called "the never-ending audacity of elected persons" emphasizes the need for modifying executive power by the contribution of the needs and aspirations of the common people. This is the essence of the democratic conception: political societies are most secure when deeply rooted in the political activity and interest of the mass of the people and least secure when social judgment is the prerogative of the chosen few.

The American tradition of political thought has tried to reconcile these two points of view. Since the beginning of the country's history, political theorists have disagreed on the extent to which the people and their opinions could play a part in the political decision.

"Men by their constitutions," wrote Jefferson, "are naturally divided into two parties: 1.—Those who fear and distrust the people and wish to draw all powers from them into the hands of the higher classes; 2.—Those who identify themselves with the people, have confidence in them, cherish and consider them as the most wise depository of the public interests."[3] Jefferson himself believed that the people were less likely to misgovern themselves than any small exclusive group, and for this reason urged that public opinion should be the decisive and ultimate force in American politics.

His opponents have followed Alexander Hamilton, whose antidemocratic ideas provide an armory for present-day conservatives. "All communities divide themselves into the few and the many," Hamilton declared. "The first are the rich and well-born, the others are the mass of the people. The voice of the people has been said to be the Voice of God; and however generally this maxim has been quoted and believed, it is not true in fact. The people seldom judge or determine right." Those who have followed the Federalist philosophy have largely been concerned with the liberties and property of the minority and have continually urged the necessity of building checks against the people's power.

Those who favor rule of "the best," through the gifted representative, and those who desire to give the common people more power are frequently at loggerheads because their arguments do not meet each other. The need exists to find the right balance between the kind of mass judgments and comments obtained by the public-opinion polls and the opinions of legislators. Both extreme views contain a kernel of truth. No one would deny that we need the best and the wisest in the key positions of our political life. But the democrat is right in demanding that these leaders be subject to check by the opinions of the mass of the people. He is right in refusing to let these persons rule irresponsibly. For in its most extreme form, the criticism that opposes any effort, like the modern polls, to make the people more articulate, that inveighs against the perils of a "direct democracy," leads directly to antidemocratic government. If it is argued that legislators understand better than the people what the people want, it is but a short step to give legislators the power to decree what the people *ought* to want. Few tendencies could be more dangerous. When a special group is entrusted with the task of determining the values for a whole community, we have gone a long way from democracy, representative or any other kind.

The debate hinges to some extent on which particular theory of the representatives' role is accepted. There is the view which the English Conservative, Edmund Burke, advanced in the eighteenth century to the electors of Bristol: "His unbiased opinion, his mature judgment, his enlightened conscience, he ought not to sacrifice to you; to any man, or to any set of men living. These he does not derive from your pleasure. They are a trust from Providence, for the abuse of which he is deeply answerable. Your representative owes you, not his industry only, but his judgment; and he betrays instead of serving you, if he sacrifices it to your opinion." This view has been restated more sharply in the words of the Southern Senator who is reported to have told a state delegation: "Not for hell and a brown mule will I bind myself to your wishes." But, on the other hand, it must be remembered that the electors of Bristol rejected Burke after his address, and that there are many in our own day who take the view that one of the legislator's chief tasks in a democracy must be to "represent."

Unless he is to be the easy prey of special interests and antisocial pressure, he must have access to the expression of a truly "public" opinion, containing the views of all the groups in our complex society. For free expression of public opinion is not merely a right which the masses are fortunate to possess—it is as vital for the leaders as for the people. In no other way can the legislators know what the people they represent want, what kinds of legislation are possible, what the people think about existing laws, or how serious the opposition may be to a particular political proposal. A rigid dictatorship, or any organization of political society which forbids the people to express their own attitudes, is dangerous not only to the people, but also to the leaders themselves, since they never know whether they are sitting in an easy chair or on top of a volcano. *People who live differently think differently*. In order that their experience be incorporated into political rules under which they are to live, their thinking must be included in the main body of ideas involved in the process of final decisions. That is why the surveys take care to include those on relief as well as those who draw their income from investments, young as well as old, men and women of all sorts from every section of the country, in the sample public.

Another form which the case against the people takes is the argument that we are living today in a society so complex and so technical that its problems cannot be trusted to the people or their representatives, but must be turned over to experts. It has been urged that only those who know *how* to legislate should have the power of decreeing what type of legislation *ought* to exist. The Technocracy movement put this view squarely before the American public. If it is true, it means that the kind of mass value judgments secured by the polls and surveys is quite useless in political life. It means that the people and their representatives must abdicate before the trained economist, the social worker, the expert in public finance, in tariffs, in rural problems, in foreign affairs. These learned persons, the argument runs, are the only ones who know and understand the facts, therefore, they alone are competent to decide on matters of policy.

There is something tempting about the view that the people should be led by an aristocracy of specialists. But Americans have learned something from the experience of the past decade. They have learned, in the first place, that experts do not always agree about the solutions for the ills of our times. "Ask six economists their opinion on unemployment," an English wag has suggested, "and you will get seven different answers—two from Mr. John Maynard Keynes."

The point is obviously exaggerated. Certainly today a vast body of useful, applicable knowledge has been built up by economists and other specialists—knowledge which is sorely needed to remedy the ills of our time. But all that experts can do, even assuming we can get them to agree about what need be done, is to tell *how* we can act.

The objectives, the ends, the basic values of policy must still be decided. The economist can suggest what action is to be taken if a certain goal is to be reached. He, speaking purely as an economist, cannot say what final goal *should* be reached. The lawyer can administer and interpret the country's laws. He cannot say what those laws should be. The social worker can suggest ways of aiding the aged. He cannot say that aiding aged persons is desirable. The expert's function is invaluable, but its value lies in judging the means—not the ends—of public policy.

Thus the expert and his techniques are sorely needed. Perhaps Great Britain has gone even further than the United States in relating expert opinion to democratic government. The technique of the Royal Commission, and the other methods of organizing special knowledge, are extremely valuable ways of focusing the attention of the general public on specific evils and on solutions of them. In these Commissions, expert opinion is brought to bear, and opportunities for collective deliberation are created for those with special knowledge of political and economic questions. But even these Royal Commissions must remain ineffective until the general public has passed judgment on whether or not their recommendations should be implemented into legislation.

As a corollary of this view that expert opinion can bear only on specific questions of means, on the technical methods by which solutions are to be achieved, we must agree that most people do not and, in the nature of things, cannot have the necessary knowledge to judge the intimate details of policy. Repeated testing by means of the poll technique reveals that they cannot be expected to have opinions or intelligent judgments about details of monetary policy, of treaty making, or on other questions involving highly specialized knowledge. There are things which cannot be done by public opinion, just as there are things which can only be done by public opinion. "The people who are the power [sic] entitled to say what they want," Bryce wrote, "are less qualified to say how, and in what form, they are to obtain it; or in other words, public opinion can determine ends, but is less fit to examine and select means to those ends."[4]

All this may be granted to the critics. But having urged the need for representatives and experts, we still need to keep these legislators and experts in touch with the public and its opinions. We still have need of declarations of attitudes from those who live under the laws and regulations administered by the experts. For only the man on relief can tell the administrator how it feels to be on relief. Only the small businessman can express his attitude on the economic questions which complicate his existence. Only women voters can explain their views on marriage and divorce. Only all these groups, taken together, can formulate the general objectives and tendencies which their experience makes them feel would be best for the common welfare. For the ultimate values of politics and economics, the judgments on which public policy is based, do not come from special knowledge or from intelligence alone. *They are compounded from the day-to-day experience of the men and women who together make up the society we live in.*

That is why public-opinion polls are important today. Instead of being attempts to sabotage representative government, kidnap the members of Congress, and substitute the taxi driver for the expert in politics, as some critics insist, public-opinion research is a necessary and valuable aid to truly representative government. The continuous studies of public opinion will merely *supplement*, not destroy, the work of representatives. What is evident here is that representatives will be better able to represent if they have an accurate measure of the wishes, aspirations, and needs of different groups within the general public, rather than the kind of distorted picture sent them by telegram enthusiasts and overzealous pressure groups who claim to speak for all the people, but actually speak only for themselves. Public-opinion surveys will provide legislators with a new instrument for estimating trends of opinion, and minimize the chances of their being fooled by clamoring minorities. For the alternative to these surveys, it must be remembered, is not a perfect and still silence in which the Ideal Legislator and the Perfect Expert can commune on desirable policies. It is the real world of competing pressures, vociferous demonstrations, and the stale cries of party politics.

Does this mean that constant soundings of public opinion will inevitably substitute demagoguery for statesmanship? The contrary is more likely. The demagogue is no unfamiliar object. He was not created by the modern opinion surveys. He thrives, not when the people have power, facts, information, but when the people are insecure, gullible, see and hear only one side of the case. The demagogue, like any propagandist of untruths, finds his natural habitat where there is no method of checking on the truth or falsity of his case. To distinguish demagogues from democratic leaders, the people must know the facts, and must act upon them.

Is this element secured by having no measurement of public opinion, or by having frequent, accurate measurement? When local Caesars rise to claim a large popular support for their plans and schemes, is it not better to be able to refer to some more tangible index of their true status than their own claims and speeches? The poll measurements have, more than once, served in the past to expose the claims of false prophets.

As the polls develop in accuracy, and as their returns become more widely accepted, public officials and the people themselves will probably become more critical in distinguishing between the currents of opinion which command the genuine support of a large section of the public and the spurious claims of the pressure groups. The new methods of estimating public opinion are not revolutionary—they merely supplement the various intuitive and haphazard indices available to the legislator with a direct, systematic description of public opinion. Politicians who introduced the technique of political canvassing and door-to-door surveys on the eve of elections, to discover the voting intentions and opinions of the public in their own districts, can hardly fail to acknowledge the value of canvassing the people to hear their opinions, not only on candidates, but on issues as well. It is simply a question of substituting more precise methods for methods based on impressions. Certainly people knew it was cold long before the invention of the thermometer, but the thermometer has helped them to know exactly how cold it is, and how the temperature varies at different points of time. In the same way, politicians and legislators employed methods for measuring the attitudes of the public in the past, but the introduction of the sampling referendum allows their estimates to be made against the background of tested knowledge.

Will the polls of the future become so accurate that legislators will automatically follow their dictates? If this happened would it mean rule by a kind of "mobocracy"? To the first point, it may be suggested that although great accuracy can be achieved through careful polling, no poll can be completely accurate in every single instance over a long period of time. In every sampling result there is a small margin of error which must never be overlooked in interpreting the results. The answer to the second question depends essentially on the nature of the judgments which people make, and on the competence of the majority to act as a directive force in politics.

There has always been a fear of the majority at the back of the minds of many intelligent critics of the polls. Ever since the time of Alexis de Tocqueville, the phrase, "tyranny of the majority," has been used widely by critics of democratic procedure, fearful lest the sheer weight of numbers should crush intelligent minorities and suppress the criticism that comes from small associations which refuse to conform to the majority view. It has been asserted that the same tendencies to a wanton use of power which exist in a despotism may also exist in a society where the will of the majority is the supreme sovereign power.

What protection exists against this abuse of power by a majority scornful of its weaker critics and intolerant of dissenting opinions? The sages of 1787 were fully aware of the danger, and accordingly created in the Bill of Rights provisions whereby specific guarantees—free speech, free association, and open debate—were laid down to ensure the protection of the rights of dissident minorities.

Obviously, such legal provisions cannot guarantee that a self-governing community will never make mistakes, or that the majority will always urge right policies. No democratic state can ever be *certain* of these things. Our own history provides abundant evidence pointing to the conclusion that the majority can commit blunders, and can become intolerant of intelligent minority points of view. But popular government has never rested on the belief that such things *cannot* happen. On the contrary, it rests on the sure knowledge that they *can* and *do* happen, and further, that they can and do happen in autocracies—with infinitely more disastrous consequences. The democratic idea implies awareness that the people *can* be wrong—but it attempts to build conditions within which error may be discovered and through which truth may become more widely available. It recognizes that people can make crucial mistakes when they do not have access to the facts, when the facts to which they have access are so distorted through the spread of propaganda and half-truths as to be useless, or when their lives are so insecure as to provide a breeding ground for violence and extremes.

It is important to remember that while the seismograph does not create earthquakes, this instrument may one day help to alleviate such catastrophes by charting the place of their occurrence, their strength, and so enabling those interested in controlling the effects of such disasters to obtain more knowledge of their causes. Similarly, the polls do not create the sources of irrationalism and potential chaos in our society. What they can do is to give the people and the legislators a picture of existing tendencies, knowledge of which may save democracy from rushing over the edge of the precipice.

The antidote for "mobocracy" is not the suppression of public opinion, but the maintenance of a free tribunal of public opinion to which rival protagonists can make their appeals. Only in this atmosphere of give-and-take of rival points of view can democratic methods produce intelligent results. "The clash and conflict of argument bring out the strength and weakness of every case," it has been truly said, "and that which is sound tends to prevail. Let the cynic say what he will. Man is not an irrational animal. Truth usually wins in the long run, though the obsessions of self-interest or prejudice or ignorance may long delay its victory."

There is a powerful incentive to expose the forces which prevent the victory of truth, for there is real value in the social judgments that are reached through widespread discussion and debate. Although democratic solutions may not be the "ideally best," yet they have the fundamental merit of being solutions which the people and their representatives have worked out in co-operation. There is value in the method of trial and error, for the only way people will ever learn to govern themselves is by governing themselves.

Thus the faith to which the democrat holds is not found so much in the inherent wisdom of majorities as in the value of rule by the majority principle. The democrat need not depend upon a mystic "general will" continually operating to direct society toward the "good life." He merely has to agree that the best way of settling conflicts in political life is by some settled rule of action, and that, empirically, this lies in the majority principle. For when the majority is finally convinced, the laws are immeasurably more stable than they would be were they carried out in flagrant opposition to its wishes. In the long run, only laws which are backed by public opinion can command obedience.

"The risk of the majority principle," it has been said "is the least dangerous, and the stakes the highest, of all forms of political organization. It is the risk least separable from the process of government itself. When you have made the commonwealth reasonably safe against raids by oligarchies or depredations by individual megalomaniacs; when you have provided the best mechanisms you can contrive for the succession to power, and have hedged both majorities and minorities about with constitutional safeguards of their own devising, then you have done all that the art of politics can ever do. For the rest, insurance against majority tyranny will depend on the health of your economic institutions, the wisdom of your educational process, the whole ethos and vitality of your culture."[5] In short, the democrat does not have to believe that man is infinitely perfectible, or that he is infinitely a fool. He merely has to realize that under some conditions men judge wisely and act decently, while under other conditions they act blindly and cruelly. His job is to see that the second set of conditions never develops, and to maximize the conditions which enable men to govern themselves peacefully and wisely.

The "tyranny of the majority" has never been America's biggest problem. It is as great a danger to contemplate the "tyranny of the minority," who operate under cover of the Bill of Rights to secure ends in the interests of a small group. The real tyranny in America will not come from a better knowledge of how majorities feel about the questions of the day which press for solution. Tyranny comes from ignorance of the power and wants of the opposition. Tyranny arises when the media of information are closed, not when they are open for all to use.

The best guarantee for the maintenance of a vigorous democratic life lies not in concealing what people think, but in trying to find out what their ultimate purposes are, and in seeking to incorporate these purposes in legislation. It demands exposing the weakness of democracy as well as its values. Above all, it is posited on the belief that political institutions are not perfect, that they must be modified to meet changing conditions, and that a new age demands new political techniques.

Notes

1. C. W. Smith, *Public Opinion in a Democracy*, New York, 1939, p. 411.
2. O. R. Maguire, "The Republican Form of Government and the Straw Poll—an Examination," *U.S. Law Review*, November, 1939.
3. Herbert Agar, *Pursuit of Happiness*, p. 42.
4. James Bryce, *The American Commonwealth*, p. 347.
5. Max Lerner, *It Is Later Than You Think*, 1938, p. 111.

Consider the source and the audience.

- Gallup was writing a book to showcase his science of polling and its possibilities. Would that fact affect his message?

Lay out the argument, the values, and the assumptions.

- Gallup and Rae discuss two views of the democratic process. To which of these views do they adhere?
- What is public opinion capable of doing, and what are its limitations?
- What is the worst form of government that Gallup and Rae can imagine? How do they think the monitoring of public opinion can help avert that form of government?

Uncover the evidence.

- From what sources do Gallup and Rae draw the evidence for their argument? Are historical example and philosophical principle sufficient to make their case? Could they offer any kind of empirical evidence?

Evaluate the conclusion.

- Is democracy doomed if it is not based on the public's own determination of what it wants?
- Can public opinion be an effective check on the dangers inherent in democracy?

Sort out the political implications.

- How much democracy would Gallup and Rae favor? What role do they see for polls? What would they think of the uses to which polling is put today?

11

Political Parties

The U.S. Constitution is silent on the subject of political parties, but our founders were not. Madison warned against the dangers of factional divisions among the population in *The Federalist Papers* (see Reading 12.4), and George Washington echoed that warning when he left office after serving two terms as the first president of the new nation (see Reading 11.5). And yet, parties were present in the early days of the republic, and they are present today.

Defined as groups that unite under a common label to control government and to promote their ideas and policies, parties have become an integral part of the American political system. Two parties in particular, the Democrats and the Republicans, have dominated the political scene for approximately 150 years.

Defenders of parties say that they strengthen American democracy, serving to recruit candidates, define their policy agendas, and run their campaigns, as well as providing a link between voters and the people they elect, greater political accountability, and continuity and stability in government. Some people go so far as to say that it is political parties that make democracy possible.[1]

Critics, however, say that parties are captives of special interests, that their divisive partisanship turns off voters, that they narrow voters' political choices, that they provide a haven for corruption, and that they are driven by an untouchable elite. Some critics want to do away with parties altogether; others want to change the rules to empower more parties; still others want to reduce the power of all parties.

The selections in this chapter look at some central issues in the study of political parties. We begin with an article that focuses on recent divisions in the Republican Party, also known as the GOP, between cultural conservatives and more moderate—even liberal—Republicans. The next article, from *The Atlantic*, examines the recent trend of the Millennial Generation to support Barack Obama and the Democratic Party. The author, Ronald Brownstein, argues that this development could portend bad things for the future of the Republican Party. In the third selection, conservative columnist Fred Barnes encourages the GOP to stand up to President Obama's agenda. He argues that doing so will bring the party back to power. Fourth, Kurt Andersen argues in *New York Magazine* that neither major party is acceptable and instead pushes for the creation of a third party. Finally, we look at a classic, George Washington's farewell address, in which he celebrates American government but points out the pitfalls he sees before it, chief of which is the danger of partisan division.

Notes

1. E. E. Schattschneider, *Party Government* (New York: Farrar and Rinehart, Inc., 1942).

 ## 11.1 Yes, Virginia, There Are Liberal Republicans

Robert J. Elisberg, Huffington Post

Why We Chose This Piece

After Barack Obama's victory in 2008 and the Democratic Party's gain in seats in both the House and the Senate, conversation among pundits and politicos centered around what was wrong with the Republican Party and how it would brand itself in the future. This debate emerged well before 2008 with longstanding tensions between fiscal conservatives and cultural conservatives, but it has reached a fever pitch as illustrated by public sparring between conservative Republicans like Rush Limbaugh and moderate Republicans like Colin Powell after the 2008 election. As the Republican Party gears up to challenge Barack Obama in 2012, whether the party should move to the right or the left will be a regular subject of debate. We chose this commentary because the author highlights the controversy over the direction of the party, although he clearly falls on one side of the fence. Why would there be liberal Republicans and conservative Democrats?

Several weeks back, I was talking with a friend who is politically conservative. I praised a recent Obama bill for remarkably getting bi-partisan support, when he cut me off. "Oh, you mean those two women?" he interrupted, with ridicule dripping from his voice. "They're not Republicans. They're Democrats!"

(A quick digression out of fairness. "Those women" was not meant dismissively towards Senators Olympia Snowe and Susan Collins. My friend has a memory like a bad sieve. "Those two women" was the best he could do.)

Anyway, I was certain he was exaggerating—but he wasn't. "Oh, please," he kept scoffing, "they're Democrats."

It was clear that this was something he and his circle had previously settled among themselves. And I realized what the problem was, and it wasn't obstinance or gross stupidity.

Here's the thing, I told him. You've confused being conservative with being Republican. But there are conservative Democrats. And once there were moderate and even liberal Republicans, too. But you've pushed them all out, to the degree that you now

---

Selection published: May 12, 2009

can only recognize a Republican as someone who is conservative. And that's just not the case at all. There are moderate Republicans. And liberal ones.

To my friend's great credit, he stopped a moment, and then actually agreed. Mind you, I have little doubt that the next day this all was forgotten. Putting life into convenient boxes gives too much comforting order, no matter how false. His loss is that the reality would have been so much more rewarding.

You see, time was when the Grand Old Party did, indeed, have grandness to it. When it was a party of mixed views, and moderates and liberals could be seen as actual Republicans, alongside the conservative party elders.

The Republican Party, once upon a time—a time within the life of most people reading this—included among its members such moderates and even liberals as Nelson Rockefeller, Jacob Javits, Margaret Chase Smith, Clifford Case, Mark Hatfield (who co-sponsored with George McGovern an amendment to end the Viet Nam War), Lowell Weicker, Richard Schweiker, Kenneth Keating and John Chafee. Remarkable people all of them, well-worth looking up. They may have been in the minority of their party, but they were trusted and admired voices, helping focus Republican direction.

And most of them now have been blocked out of the memory of today's Republicans, dismissed by a current generation that doesn't consider "those two women" in Maine even to be Republicans.

And so the Republican Party has hounded out officials who've dared not to be conservative. Jim Jeffords left the party. Lincoln Chafee left the party. Arlen Specter left the party. Americans have left the party. Today, only 21 percent of Americans consider themselves Republican. And so, today, there are zero Republicans in the House of Representatives from New England—where the country was founded, by the way. Gone.

And the Republican Party has started to lose the rest of the nation, as well. What has happened is that the Republican Party has become a party of the South. Less a party, in fact, and more a little-tent, religious revival meeting.

By contrast, the Democratic Party ranges from conservative senators like Ben Nelson, Mary Landrieu and Jim Webb—to Ted Kennedy and Barbara Boxer on the liberal wing. With moderates filling the chewy, nougat center. No one would confuse this group—which includes fiscally conservative "Blue Dog Democrats"—of being of a united mind. And the House is even far more mixed. While this often causes consternation within the party, it's also what ultimately gives it a wide exchange of ideas—and ideals.

The result for Republicans is a party so top heavy on the right that John McCain, who long-prided himself as being a self-proclaimed "Maverick," was only able to win the GOP nomination by claiming he always had been a conservative. The result is that "those women"—lifelong Republicans—aren't even viewed as Republicans.

The result is that it wipes out the history—and often impressive history—of the Republican Party.

Today, the party of Abraham Lincoln and Theodore Roosevelt cultivates a divisive, empty demagogue like Sarah Palin, for no reason other than she's conservative, religious, and can see Russia from the beach. Today, the party of Dwight Eisenhower holds Tea Parties and Pizza Parties, dresses up in colonial garb, defends torture, and bows to a radio host.

Today, the Republican Party has forgotten what the Republican Party was founded on, and in doing so, has redefined itself into the ground, as it drives its moderate and liberal members away. The base can deny this all it wants, and wrap itself in its own True Values, but that only confirms the reality.

And if at some point all "those women" and "those men" end up driven away and actually become Democrats, it won't be because the far-right describing them were perceptive, but rather the party created a self-fulfilling prophecy. Because when you push people out of the house, slam the door and lock it, they have nowhere else to go, but rely upon the kindness of the neighbors.

*C*onsider the source and the audience.

- The Huffington Post is a news web site with a liberal bent. Why would its readers be interested in an article such as this one?
- The readers of the Huffington Post tend to be liberal. How might Elisberg's argument or tone change if he were writing for a more conservative outlet? Why would a self-identified Republican write for a predominantly liberal audience?

*L*ay out the argument, the values, and the assumptions.

- According to Elisberg, how has the Republican Party changed over time?
- If the trend that he notes continues, what does he fear will happen to the Republican Party?

*U*ncover the evidence.

- Elisberg is concerned that the Republican Party has become "a party of the South" that has driven away moderates and liberals. How does he show this?

*E*valuate the conclusion.

- Elisberg is convinced that government is better off when parties are ideologically diverse. Do you agree? Why are ideologically diverse parties an improvement over homogeneous parties? What problems might be created by ideologically diverse parties?
- How would conservative Republicans respond to Elisberg's claims?

*S*ort out the political implications.

- If parties were completely polarized (that is, one party entirely liberal and the other entirely conservative), what effect might that have on governing?
- If Republicans continue to alienate moderate and liberal party members, as Elisberg has suggested, what might that mean for the future of the Republican Party? Does the Democratic Party face some of the same concerns?

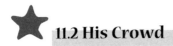

11.2 His Crowd

Ronald Brownstein, The Atlantic

Why We Chose This Piece

The previous article highlights divisions that have emerged in the Republican Party between conservatives and moderate or liberal party members. Here, Ronald Brownstein notes another problem facing the GOP: the fact that young people are moving in large numbers to the Democratic Party. What is it about the Democratic Party that might appeal to young people? What can Republicans do to reverse this trend?

All the controversy about President Obama's upcoming appearance at Notre Dame is overshadowing a larger point about the university commencement tour he began Wednesday night in Arizona: Obama is presenting Democrats an opportunity to establish a lasting and potentially crushing advantage with the Millennial Generation, the largest in American history.

Young voters are not as reflexively Democratic or liberal as many people might think. Since 18-year-olds were granted the vote in 1972, younger voters have often tracked fairly close to the national trend in presidential elections: Ronald Reagan and George H.W. Bush carried them in 1984 and 1988, and they split almost evenly between Al Gore and George W. Bush in 2000.

But over the past three elections, voters under 30 have moved steadily toward the Democrats. In the 2004 presidential race, John Kerry carried 54% of them, compared to only 48% of the country overall. In 2006, Democrats won 60% of voters under 30 in the mid-term House elections, according to the national exit poll. Then in 2008, the bottom fell out for Republicans: against John McCain, Obama won a stunning 66% of voters 18–29. Partially Obama ran so well among young people because so many of them are non-white, and he dominated among non-whites at every age. But the exit polls found Obama also won 54% of white voters under 29; even the younger Bush carried 55% of whites under 30 in each of his two elections.

If anything, Obama's position with the Millennial generation appears even stronger today. Apart from African-Americans, these young people have been Obama's most enthusiastic and consistent supporters in office. In the Gallup tracking polling that's been conducted since January, Obama's approval rating among voters younger than 30 has never fallen below 66%. His approval rating among young voters consistently runs somewhere between six and nine points higher than his overall showing: today, Obama receives positive approval ratings from a dizzying 75% of voters under 30, compared to 66% from the country overall.

Another set of numbers Gallup released earlier this month shows how Obama's strength can bolster his party. Gallup cumulated all of its 123,000 interviews this year to examine party identification in the electorate. Among the Millennial

---

Selection published: May 14, 2009

generation, it found that just 21% identify as Republicans, compared to 36% as Democrats and 34% as independents. "Republicans, for all practical purposes, aren't even on the radar screen with them," says Michael D. Hais, a fellow at the Democratic advocacy group NDN, and co-author of Millennial Makeover, a recent book on the generation.

The enormous advantage among young people for Obama in particular and Democrats in general matters for two reasons. The more immediate is that this generation, which is generally defined as the 93 million people born between 1983 and 2002, will comprise a rapidly increasing share of voters through the next decade. Hais and his co-author, Morley Winograd, also an NDN fellow, have calculated that in 2008, 41% of Millennials were eligible to vote, and they constituted 17% of the electorate. They project that by 2012, 61% of the Millennials will be eligible, and they'll comprise 24% of the electorate; by 2016, the numbers will reach 80% and 30%. By 2020, virtually all of them will be eligible and they could constitute as much as 36% of all voters. If Obama maintains anything near his current strength among Millennials, they will produce a substantially larger vote surplus for him in 2012 than they did in 2008—leaving Republicans a larger deficit to overcome with older voters.

Obama's strength among young people has a second, even more significant, implication: if Republicans cannot reverse it reasonably soon, it could harden into a lasting preference for Democrats in this huge generation. Political scientists and political strategists generally divide into two camps over how partisan allegiances are formed. The lifecycle camp argues that people's views change at different points in their life, with many voters, for instance, becoming more averse to taxes as they acquire families and mortgages. Surely some of that occurs; few people's political preferences are entirely static or so deeply held they cannot be disrupted, at least temporarily, by events.

But probably the dominant camp believes partisan allegiances are forged mostly by the social, economic and political experiences that shape a generation's upbringing. As Winograd and Hais wrote, "Members of the electorate are most easily persuaded when they are young, before their beliefs harden into attitudes they will retain throughout their lives." Kristen Soltis, director of policy research at the Winston Group, a Republican polling firm, has studied young people and politics, and she largely agrees. "I fall into the camp that see it as more generational—that there are period effects that come into play when someone becomes [politically] active, and that colors the way you look at politics throughout your life," she said.

Other numbers from the Gallup polls conducted this year point toward that interpretation. Gallup provided me with their figures breaking out party identification by age on a year-by-year basis. It found unmistakable patterns of allegiance to the two parties that track the most consequential presidencies of recent times.

Democrats did best among voters who turned 18 since George W. Bush took office in 2001 (those now aged 18 through 25). Among those voters, the Democratic Party identification advantage ranged from 14 to 18 percentage points. Democrats also did well, but not quite as well, among those who turned 18 while Bill Clinton was President (those who are now 26 to 33). Among this group, the Democratic Party identification advantage stood at 9 to 12 percentage points. The story was very different in the generation that turned 18 during Ronald Reagan's eight years as president. Those voters (who are now 38 to 45) preferred Democrats over Republicans by only three to nine percentage points. "Those are the Reagan babies," said Winograd.

These striking patterns in attitude underscore the stakes for the two sides through the remainder of Obama's presidency. Soltis says the durability of generational preferences should inspire more urgency among Republicans about the possibility of Obama locking down this cohort for Democrats. She wants the party to emphasize themes of opportunity and to criticize Obama for saddling young people with exploding federal debts. Mostly she wants the party to focus on all the dimensions of its challenge with young people. "We've still got a chance, but it's something that needs to be acted upon quickly," she says.

Winograd and Hais believe Republicans can't do much to detach young voters from Obama if the president is seen as succeeding. In Millennial Makeover, they argue that many of this generation's formative experiences—their diversity, their tolerance of difference, and the patterns of parenting that inclined them to find collective "win-win" solutions—already inclined them toward Democratic beliefs. The perception that Bush failed in the White House reinforced the Millennials' tilt toward Democrats; now Obama, they maintain, has the chance to cement those ties. "They already know that Republicans messed up a la Bush; the question is will Obama turn out to be the successful president they all expect him to be?" Winograd said. The analogy, Winograd and Hais maintain, could be the way Franklin Roosevelt's success built upon Herbert Hoover's failure and created a generation of FDR Democrats that bolstered his party for decades. In the same way, they argue, if Obama succeeds, he "could be the final piece" bonding this generation to Democrats. Of course, if he fails, those bonds could be severely strained, especially since young people have invested so much hope in him.

Either way, it is the lasting loyalty of this mammoth young generation, far more than the dust-up over abortion, that is the real prize at play as Obama begins his first campus tour as president.

*C*onsider the source and the audience.

- *The Atlantic* is a magazine that raises contemporary issues, although it is not likely to be at the top of the Millennial Generation's reading list. Why is this article relevant for people who aren't Millennials?

*L*ay out the argument, the values, and the assumptions.

- Brownstein argues that the Democratic Party has become the party of the Millennial Generation. Why has this generation embraced the Democratic Party?
- Why does Brownstein believe that young people's support of Obama and their movement toward the Democratic Party matters?

*U*ncover the evidence.

- Brownstein provides a significant amount of data to show that young people like Obama and are moving toward the Democratic Party. How might these data be interpreted differently?

*E*valuate the conclusion.

- Has Brownstein convinced you that young people will remain Democrats as they get older? Or is his point something else entirely?

*S*ort out the political implications.

- Unlike some of the authors of other articles in this book, Brownstein makes the political implications of his argument clear. He believes today's young people could become permanent Democrats, which would severely weaken the Republican Party. If that is true, what can Republicans do to reverse this trend? What aspects of the Democratic Party, if any, might not appeal to the Millennial Generation?

 11.3 Be the Party of No

It's the Route to Republican Landslides

Fred Barnes, Weekly Standard

Why We Chose This Piece

The previous two articles raise questions about the future of the Republican Party. Fred Barnes, a columnist for the conservative Weekly Standard, *is likely to believe that the earlier-mentioned problems facing Republicans are exaggerated. Here, he presents his plan for how Republicans can once again return to power.*

We include this piece for two reasons. First, it provides a nice contrast to the earlier readings in this chapter. As you read, ask yourself how Elisberg, the author of the first article, would respond to Barnes's plan? Would Barnes's idea reverse the trend that Brownstein documents in the second article, regarding the Millennial Generation's movement to the Democratic Party? Second, as Barnes makes clear, many in his own party are skeptical of his idea. The article, then, provides an interesting counterargument to traditional views regarding how an out-of-power party should deal with a popular president of the other party.

Republican leaders in Congress have created something called the National Council for a New America (NCNA). It describes itself as "not a Republican-only forum" but one that seeks to "engage people in a discussion to meet common challenges and build a stronger country through common-sense ideas." The expectation—mine, anyway—is those ideas will differ from President Obama's in a way that makes Republicans look fairminded and reasonable. The council's first event at a pizza parlor in Arlington, Virginia, did just that. Mitt Romney and Jeb Bush showed up, media coverage was heavy, and the session was deemed a success.

Selection published: May 18, 2009

Improving the party's image is a worthy cause, but it isn't what Republicans ought to be emphasizing right now. They have a more important mission: to be the party of no. And not just a party that bucks Obama and Democrats on easy issues like releasing Gitmo terrorists in this country, but one committed to aggressive, attention-grabbing opposition to the entire Obama agenda.

Many Republicans recoil from being combative adversaries of a popular president. They shouldn't. Opposing Obama across-the-board on his sweeping domestic initiatives makes sense on substance and politics. His policies—on spending, taxes, health care, energy, intervention in the economy, etc.—would change the country in ways most Americans don't believe in. That's the substance. And a year or 18 months from now, after those policies have been picked apart and exposed and possibly defeated, the political momentum is likely to have shifted away from Obama and Democrats.

This scenario has occurred time and again. Why do you think Democrats won the House and Senate in 2006 and bolstered their majorities in 2008? It wasn't because they were more thoughtful, offered compelling alternatives, or had improved their brand. They won because they opposed unpopular policies of President Bush and exploited Republican scandals in Congress. They were highly partisan and not very nice about it.

If Republicans scan their history, they'll discover unbridled opposition to bad Democratic policies pays off. Those two factors, unattractive policies plus strong opposition, were responsible for the Republican landslides in 1938, 1946, 1966, 1980, and 1994. A similar blowout may be beyond the reach of Republicans in 2010, but stranger things have happened in electoral politics. They'll lose nothing by trying.

Let's look at the five landslides. Republicans were crushed in three straight elections before rebounding in 1938. How come? FDR uncorked his court-packing plan, launched a jihad against disloyal Democrats, and was fairly blamed for a new economic downturn (known as "the depression within the depression"). Republicans piled on and won seven Senate and 81 House seats.

In 1946, the public was fed up with wartime regulations that many Democrats were seeking to retain. Republicans asked, "Had enough?" Voters had.

In 1966, voters reacted adversely to the vast Great Society programs enacted after the Democratic triumph in 1964. Republicans, written off as dead, gained 47 House and four Senate seats, eight governorships, and won the presidency two years later.

Ronald Reagan would, in all likelihood, have defeated President Carter in 1980 on his own merit. But public revulsion at Carter's weak foreign policy and disastrous economic record (double-digit inflation and interest rates) produced a landslide that delivered Republicans the Senate as well. Tough Republican critiques of Carterism had played an indispensable role.

Republicans still pride themselves on the Contract with America—dealing with process issues like a balanced budget amendment and term limits—adopted in the 1994 campaign. It may have helped. But the main reason for the Republican capture of the House and Senate was the agenda of President Clinton: health care, crime, guns, taxes, and a lot more. Republicans dissected Clinton's policies skillfully and relentlessly, particularly turning his health care plan, initially quite popular, into an albatross.

Obama may not be as vulnerable as Clinton was, but his policies are. There's no reason for Republicans to hold back. It's evident now that Obama and the congressional Democrats have no interest in compromise. Their intent is to push far-reaching liberal policies through Congress quickly and with minimal debate. Obama's health care scheme would bring the country one step from a single-payer system. His plan to limit carbon emissions would give the federal government unprecedented power over the economy while emasculating the investors, entrepreneurs, and practically everyone else in the business community.

The Republicans have fertile ground to plow. The public is already dubious of a government-run health insurance plan, the core of Obama-Care. And there's plenty more for Republicans to focus on, including the threat of a government panel that decides which medical practices are covered and which are ostracized. Defeating ObamaCare, given Democratic majorities on Capitol Hill, may be difficult but it's not an impossibility. If Republicans lead the charge, health care providers and consumers are likely to join the active opposition. Otherwise, they'll remain passive.

Obama says his policy to restrict greenhouse gases, known as cap and trade, is "market-based." It isn't. The cap on emissions would be imposed by a government panel. Polls show the majority of Americans disapprove of this. Worse for Obama, Frank Newport, the Gallup boss, says most Americans don't believe global warming poses a serious danger. So why choke off economic growth?

Then there are the unforced errors of the Obama administration to take advantage of. The president's decision to close Gitmo has backfired badly, leaving him with terrorists on his hands and nowhere to put them. The takeover of GM and Chrysler has raised concerns, even in Europe, over the competence and judgment of the Obama team. The American public is lopsidedly against further bailouts of the Big 2.

Republican efforts to escape being tagged the party of no are understandable. The label gives Democrats and the media echo chamber a talking point. Should the NCNA come up with new ideas that spruce up the party's image, that's helpful. The criticism of the council by social conservatives, by the way, is downright counter-productive. Their attacks merely delight Democrats and the press. But no matter how restrained and sensible Republicans sound or how many useful ideas they develop, they're probably stuck with the party of no label. They have more to gain by actually accepting the role and taking on Obama vigorously. If they come to be dubbed the party of no, no, no, a thousand times no, all the better. It will mean they're succeeding.

*C*onsider the source and the audience.

- Barnes is a conservative Republican columnist writing to a conservative audience. Yet, it is clear that he doesn't believe all Republicans will agree with him. Who must he convince? Fellow conservatives? Moderate members of the party? Most Republicans?

*L*ay out the argument, the values, and the assumptions.

- What does Barnes mean when he says the Republican Party should "be the party of no?" Why does he believe that this approach makes sense not only from a policy standpoint, but politically as well?

U*ncover the evidence.*

- Barnes brings in numerous historical examples to support his argument. Is history a persuasive way to make a case? Are the examples he provides relevant to today?
- Barnes writes that "Obama may not be as vulnerable as Clinton was, but his policies are." What evidence does he provide for this claim?

E*valuate the conclusion.*

- Has Barnes convinced you that working against Obama instead of working with Obama is the best way for the Republican Party to revitalize itself and take back power? Can you see any ways in which his plan might backfire?
- Barnes's argument is clearly directed at Republicans. Is it possible, though, that Democrats might agree with Barnes that "being the party of no" is an effective strategy?

S*ort out the political implications.*

- If parties always adopted Barnes's approach, how might this affect governing? Could it lead to more polarized parties? If so, what might be some of the pros and cons of increasingly polarized parties?

11.4 Introducing the Purple Party

Kurt Andersen, New York Magazine

Why We Chose This Piece

One of the topics that regularly drive discussions of political parties in the United States is whether voters need more options. Since the Civil War, the Democratic and Republican Parties have dominated American politics. While third-party movements have emerged over the course of that time, they have rarely been successful. Many Americans, including Kurt Andersen, the author of this article, believe that the two-party system does not give Americans sufficient choice. In this New York Magazine *piece, Andersen "creates" his own party—one that he believes represents the views of more Americans than either of the two major parties. Is it possible for two parties to represent all voters? What might be the benefits of such a system?*

B efore I was old enough to vote, I worked as a volunteer for George McGovern's presidential primary campaign, then voted for him in the November election, then for Carter (twice), then Mondale, Dukakis, Clinton (twice), Gore, and Kerry. I'm nine for nine; I've never voted for a Republican for president, like most people I know—and, I expect, like most New Yorkers.

Selection published: April 24, 2006

However, except for McGovern (I was 18; the Vietnam War was on; his opponent was Richard Nixon), I cast none of those votes very enthusiastically. In the last four mayoral elections, I've voted for the Republican three times—Giuliani in 1993 and 1997, and Bloomberg last fall. Each of those Republican votes felt a little less transgressive and weird.

I don't consider myself a true Democrat. Yet my mayoral votes notwithstanding, I am not now nor have I ever been a Republican, and could never be unless the Lincoln Chafee–Olympia Snowe–John McCain wing of the party were to take decisive control, or hell freezes over. For me, what has happened politically in New York City stays in New York City.

But the thing is, in my political ambivalence I'm not such a freak these days. Fully a third of New Yorkers who voted in the last two elections behaved as I did, voting for Kerry and Bloomberg. Nationally, more and more Americans are clearly disaffected with both big parties. In 2005, for the first time since 1997, the percentages of people telling pollsters they feel generically "very positive" toward the Democrats or Republicans fell to single digits. And antipathy is running at historical highs as well—40 percent negatives for both parties, give or take a few points—which suggests that a huge number of nominal Democrats are voting more against the Bushes and Cheneys (and Santorums and Brownbacks) than they are for the Kerrys and Gores.

Less than a third of the electorate are happy to call themselves Republicans, and only a bit more say they're Democrats—but between 33 and 39 percent now consider themselves neither Democrat nor Republican. In other words, there are more of us than there are of either of them.

What's changed hardly at all over the past 30 years, however, is people's sense of where, in rough terms, they stand ideologically. Almost half of Americans consistently call themselves moderates.

We are people without a party. We open-minded, openhearted moderates are alienated from the two big parties because backward-looking ideologues and p.c. hypocrites are effectively in charge of both. Both are under the sway of old-school clods who consistently default to government intrusion where it doesn't belong—who want to demonize video-game makers and criminalize abortion and hate speech and flag-burning, who are committed to maintaining the status quos of the public schools and health-care system, and who decline to make the hard choices necessary (such as enacting a high gasoline tax or encouraging nuclear energy) to move the country onto a sustainable energy track. Both line up to reject sensible, carefully negotiated international treaties when there's too much sacrifice involved and their special-interest sugar daddies object—the Kyoto Protocol for the Republicans, the Central American Free Trade Agreement for the Democrats.

Some lifelong Republicans (such as my mother) abandoned ship in the nineties when the Evangelicals and right-to-lifers finally loomed too large in her party and Gingrich and company tried to defund public broadcasting and the national cultural endowments. As for us lifelong non-Republicans, we don't want taxes to be any higher than necessary, but the tax-cutting monomania of the GOP these days is grotesque selfishness masquerading as principle—and truly irresponsible, given the free-spending, deficit-ballooning policies it's also pursuing. We are appalled by the half-cynical, half-medieval mistrust and denial of science—the crippling of stem-cell research, the refusal to believe in man-made climate change. And Republicans' ongoing willingness to go racist for political purposes (as Bush's supporters did during the 2000 primaries) is disgusting. Demagoguery is endemic to both parties, but when it comes to exploiting fundamentally irrelevant issues (such as the medical condition of Terri Schiavo), the GOP takes the cake.

Republicans used to brag that theirs was the party of fresh thinking, but who's brain-dead now? All the big new ideas they have trotted out lately—privatizing Social Security, occupying a big country with only 160,000 troops, Middle Eastern democracy as a force-fed contagion—have given a bad name to new paradigms.

As for the Democrats, the Republicans still have a point: Where are the brave, fresh, clear approaches passionately and convincingly laid out? When it comes to reforming entitlements, the Democrats have absolutely refused to step up. Because the teachers unions and their 4 million members are the most important organized faction of its political base, the party is wired to oppose any meaningful experimentation with charter schools or other new modes. Similarly, after beginning to embrace the inevitability of economic globalization in the nineties, and devising ways to minimize our local American pain, the Democrats' scaredy-cat protectionist instincts seem to be returning with a vengeance. On so many issues, the ostensibly "progressive" party's habits of mind seem anything but.

However, what makes so much of the great middle of the electorate most uncomfortable about signing on with the Democratic Party is the same thing that has made them uncomfortable since McGovern—the sense that the anti-military instincts of the left half of the party, no matter how sincere and well meaning, render prospective Democratic presidents untrustworthy as guardians of national security. It's no accident that Bill Clinton was elected and reelected (and Al Gore won his popular majority) during the decade when peace reigned supreme, after the Cold War and before 9/11.

The Bush administration's colossal mismanagement of the occupation of Iraq is not about to make lots of Americans discover their inner pacifist, either. Rather, they will simply crave someone who is sensible, thoughtful, and competent as well as "tough" in his geopolitical m.o. If Iraq is souring most Americans on the Republican brand of dreamy, wishful, recklessly sketchy foreign policy, the result will not and should not be a pendulum swing to its dreamy, wishful, recklessly sketchy left-wing Democratic counterpart.

Wait, wait, the vestigial Democrat in me pleads, Hillary Clinton and Joe Biden are certainly not peace-at-any-price appeasers, and, Howard Dean aside, most of the party bigwigs have strenuously, carefully avoided endorsing a cut-and-run approach in Iraq.

The problem is "strenuously" and "carefully": People know tactical dissembling when they see it, whether it's liberal Democrats hiding their true feelings about military force or Republican Supreme Court nominees hiding their true feelings about abortion law. And Democrats who are sincerely tough-minded on national security are out of sync not only with much of their base but also with one of the party's core brand attributes. The Democrats remain the antiwar party, notwithstanding the post-9/11 growth of the liberal-hawk caucus—just as the Republicans are still the white party, notwithstanding George Bush's manifest friendliness to individual people of color.

So the simple question is this: Why can't we have a serious, innovative, truth-telling, pragmatic party without any of the baggage of the Democrats and Republicans? A real and enduring party built around a coherent set of ideas and sensibility—neither a shell created for a single charismatic candidate like George Wallace or Ross Perot, nor a protest party like the Greens or Libertarians, with no hope of ever getting more than a few million votes in a presidential election. A party that plausibly aspires to be not a third party but the third party—to winning, and governing.

Let the present, long-running duopoly of the Republicans and Democrats end. Let the invigorating and truly democratic partisan flux of the American republic's first century return. Let there be a more or less pacifist, anti-business, protectionist Democratic Party on the left, and an anti-science, Christianist, unapologetically greedy Republican Party on the right—and a robust new independent party of passionately practical progressives in the middle.

It's certainly time. As no less a wise man than Alan Greenspan said last month, the "ideological divide" separating conservative Republicans and liberal Democrats leaves "a vast untended center from which a well-financed independent presidential candidate is likely to emerge in 2008 or, if not then, in 2012."

And it's possible—indeed, for a variety of reasons, more so than it's been in our lifetimes. In 1992, a megalomaniacal kook with no political experience, running in a system stacked powerfully against third parties, won 19 percent of the presidential vote against a moderate Democrat and moderate Republican—and in two states, Perot actually beat one of the major-party candidates. In 1912, former president Teddy Roosevelt, running as a third-party progressive, got more votes than Taft, the Republican nominee. The Republicans, remember, began as a dicey new party until their second nominee, Lincoln, managed to get elected president.

It wouldn't be easy or cheap to create this party. It would doubtless require a rich visionary or two—a Bloomberg, a Steve Jobs, a Paul Tudor Jones—to finance it in the beginning. And since a new party hasn't won the presidency in a century and a half, it would have to struggle for credibility, to convince a critical mass of voters that a vote for its candidates would be, in the near term, an investment in a far better political future and not simply a wasted ballot.

Is this a quixotic, wishful conceit of a few disgruntled gadflies? Sure. This is only a magazine; we're only writers. But the beautiful, radical idea behind democracy was government by amateurs. As the historian Daniel J. Boorstin wrote, "An enamored amateur need not be a genius to stay out of the ruts he has never been trained in." We have a vision if not a true platform, sketches for a party if not quite a set of blueprints. Every new reality must start with a set of predispositions, a scribbled first draft, an earnest dream of the just possibly possible. In our amateur parlor-game fashion we are very serious about trying to get the conversation started, and moving in the right direction.

And New York, as it happens, is the ideal place to give birth to such a movement. This city's spirit—clear-sighted, tough-minded, cosmopolitan, hardworking, good-humored, financially acute, tolerant, romantic—should infuse the party. Despite our lefty reputation, for a generation now this city's governance has tended to be strikingly

239

moderate, highly flexible rather than ideological or doctrinaire. While we have a consistent and overwhelming preference for Democratic presidential candidates, for 24 of the past 28 years the mayors we have elected—Koch, Giuliani, Bloomberg—have been emphatically independent-minded moderates whose official party labels have been flags of convenience. (And before them, there was John Lindsay—elected as a Republican and reelected as an independent before becoming an official Democrat in order to run for president.) Moreover, New York's stealth-independent-party regime has worked: bankruptcy avoided, the subways air-conditioned and graffiti-free, crime miraculously down, the schools reorganized and beginning to improve.

We're certainly not part of red-state America, but when push comes to shove we are really not blue in the D.C.–Cambridge–Berkeley–Santa Monica sense. We are, instead, like so much of the country, vividly purple. And so—for now—we'll call our hypothetical new entity the Purple Party.

"Centrist" is a bit of a misnomer for the paradigm we envision, since that suggests an uninspired, uninspiring, have-it-both-ways, always-split-the-difference approach born entirely of political calculation. And that's because one of the core values will be honesty. Not a preachy, goody-goody, I'll-never-lie-to-you honesty of the Jimmy Carter type, but a worldly, full-throated and bracing candor. The moderation will often be immoderate in style and substance, rather than tediously middle-of-the-road. Pragmatism will be an animating party value—even when the most pragmatic approach to a given problem is radical.

Take health care. The U.S. system requires a complete overhaul, so that every American is covered, from birth to death, whether he is employed or self-employed or unemployed. What?!? Socialized medicine? Whatever. Half of our medical costs are already paid by government, and the per capita U.S. expenditure ($6,280 per year) is nearly twice what the Canadians and Europeans and Japanese pay—suggesting that we could afford to buy our way out of the customer-service problems that afflict other national health systems. Beyond the reformist virtues of justice and sanity, our party would make the true opportunity-society argument for government-guaranteed universal health coverage: Devoted as the Purple Party is to labor flexibility and entrepreneurialism, we want to make it as easy as possible for people to change jobs or quit to start their own businesses, and to do that we must break the weirdly neo-feudal, only-in-America link between one's job and one's medical care.

But the Purple Party wouldn't use its populist, progressive positions on domestic issues like health to avoid talking about military policy, the way Democrats tend to do. We would declare straight out that, alas, the fight against Islamic jihadism must be a top-priority, long-term, and ruthless military, diplomatic, and cultural struggle.

We would be unapologetic in our support of a well-funded military and (depoliticized) intelligence apparatus, and the credible threat of force as a foreign policy tool. We would seldom accuse Democrats of being dupes and wimps or Republicans of being fearmongers and warmongers—but we would have the guts and the standing to do both.

And as we defend our country and civilization against apocalyptic religious fanatics for whom politics and religious belief are one and who consider America irredeemably heathen, we will be especially keen about adhering to the Founders' (and, for that matter, Christ's) ideal concerning the separation of religion and politics—to render to government the things that are its and to God the things that are his. Our party will enthusiastically embrace people of all religious beliefs, but we will never claim special divine virtue for our policies—we'll leave that to the Pat Robertsons and Osama bin Ladens. Where to draw the line is mostly a matter of common sense. Public reminders to honor one's parents and love one's neighbor, and not to lie, steal, or commit adultery or murder? Fine. Genesis taught as science in public schools, and government cosmologists forced by their PR handlers to give a shout-out to creationism? No way. Kids who want to wear crucifixes or yarmulkes or head scarves to those same schools? Sure, why not? And so on.

Our new party will be highly moral (but never moralistic) as well as laissez-faire. In other words, the Purple Party will be both liberal and American in the old-fashioned senses.

So: Are you in?

*C*onsider the source and the audience.

- Andersen is writing for *New York Magazine*, a magazine intended primarily for New Yorkers. He often writes as though he is speaking directly to New Yorkers. Does his argument seem to be one that would resonate only with New Yorkers, or does it have a broader appeal?

*L*ay out the argument, the values, and the assumptions.

- What does Andersen see as being wrong with the two major parties?
- In Andersen's eyes, what would a centrist party stand for?

*U*ncover the evidence.

- Much of Andersen's argument is about his personal experience with the parties. What evidence does he provide that others might agree with him?

*E*valuate the conclusion.

- Does Andersen successfully make the case for a third party? Would his specific party have broad appeal?
- How would members of the Democratic and Republican Parties respond to Andersen's criticisms of them?
- Andersen was writing toward the end of the Bush presidency. Do you think the election of Barack Obama has made him any less supportive of the need for a third party?

*S*ort out the political implications.

- How would American politics change if a viable third party like the one Andersen proposes existed?
- What challenges would such a party face?

11.5 Farewell Address

George Washington

Why We Chose This Piece

> *On the brink of leaving office, President George Washington prepared this address to the nation he had led since its birth. Eager to retire (this address was originally intended to mark his departure four years earlier but he was persuaded to stay on), he was also anxious to point out to the young nation where danger might lie in its future. Chief among his concerns were political parties, fiscal responsibility, and foreign policy.*
>
> *Here we excerpt Washington's remarks with respect to parties since, contrary to many modern observers, he saw party as an evil influence on politics and government. Like his colleague James Madison, who with Alexander Hamilton helped prepare earlier drafts of this address, he feared factional forces that would divide the nation against itself. The founders had tried to keep parties out of their new Constitution, and Washington was concerned that geographical and ideological divisions were admitting them through the back door. They had the potential, he believed, to spell doom for the fledgling republic. That the republic still stands is not to say that his argument has no merit, for many of his concerns find an echo in present-day politics.*

F riends and Citizens:

The period for a new election of a citizen to administer the executive government of the United States being not far distant, and the time actually arrived when your thoughts must be employed in designating the person who is to be clothed with that important trust, it appears to me proper, especially as it may conduce to a more distinct expression of the public voice, that I should now apprise you of the resolution I have formed, to decline being considered among the number of those out of whom a choice is to be made...

The impressions with which I first undertook the arduous trust were explained on the proper occasion. In the discharge of this trust, I will only say that I have, with good intentions, contributed towards the organization and administration of the government the best exertions of which a very fallible judgment was capable. Not unconscious in the outset of the inferiority of my qualifications, experience in my own eyes, perhaps still more in the eyes of others, has strengthened the motives to diffidence of myself; and every day the increasing weight of years admonishes me more and more that the shade of retirement is as necessary to me as it will be welcome. Satisfied that if any circumstances have given peculiar value to my services, they were temporary,

---

Selection delivered: September 17, 1796

I have the consolation to believe that, while choice and prudence invite me to quit the political scene, patriotism does not forbid it…

Here, perhaps, I ought to stop. But a solicitude for your welfare, which cannot end but with my life, and the apprehension of danger, natural to that solicitude, urge me, on an occasion like the present, to offer to your solemn contemplation, and to recommend to your frequent review, some sentiments which are the result of much reflection, of no inconsiderable observation, and which appear to me all-important to the permanency of your felicity as a people. These will be offered to you with the more freedom, as you can only see in them the disinterested warnings of a parting friend, who can possibly have no personal motive to bias his counsel. Nor can I forget, as an encouragement to it, your indulgent reception of my sentiments on a former and not dissimilar occasion.

Interwoven as is the love of liberty with every ligament of your hearts, no recommendation of mine is necessary to fortify or confirm the attachment.

The unity of government which constitutes you one people is also now dear to you. It is justly so, for it is a main pillar in the edifice of your real independence, the support of your tranquility at home, your peace abroad; of your safety; of your prosperity; of that very liberty which you so highly prize. But as it is easy to foresee that, from different causes and from different quarters, much pains will be taken, many artifices employed to weaken in your minds the conviction of this truth; as this is the point in your political fortress against which the batteries of internal and external enemies will be most constantly and actively (though often covertly and insidiously) directed, it is of infinite moment that you should properly estimate the immense value of your national union to your collective and individual happiness; that you should cherish a cordial, habitual, and immovable attachment to it; accustoming yourselves to think and speak of it as of the palladium of your political safety and prosperity; watching for its preservation with jealous anxiety; discountenancing whatever may suggest even a suspicion that it can in any event be abandoned; and indignantly frowning upon the first dawning of every attempt to alienate any portion of our country from the rest, or to enfeeble the sacred ties which now link together the various parts.

For this you have every inducement of sympathy and interest. Citizens, by birth or choice, of a common country, that country has a right to concentrate your affections. The name of American, which belongs to you in your national capacity, must always exalt the just pride of patriotism more than any appellation derived from local discriminations. With slight shades of difference, you have the same religion, manners, habits, and political principles. You have in a common cause fought and triumphed together; the independence and liberty you possess are the work of joint counsels, and joint efforts of common dangers, sufferings, and successes.

But these considerations, however powerfully they address themselves to your sensibility, are greatly outweighed by those which apply more immediately to your interest. Here every portion of our country finds the most commanding motives for carefully guarding and preserving the union of the whole.

The North, in an unrestrained intercourse with the South, protected by the equal laws of a common government, finds in the productions of the latter great additional resources of maritime and commercial enterprise and precious materials of manufacturing industry. The South, in the same intercourse, benefiting by the agency of the North, sees its agriculture grow and its commerce expand. Turning partly into its own channels the seamen of the North, it finds its particular navigation invigorated; and, while it contributes, in different ways, to nourish and increase the general mass of the national navigation, it looks forward to the protection of a maritime strength, to which itself is unequally adapted. The East, in a like intercourse with the West, already finds, and in the progressive improvement of interior communications by land and water, will more and more find a valuable vent for the commodities which it brings from abroad, or manufactures at home. The West derives from the East supplies requisite to its growth and comfort, and, what is perhaps of still greater consequence, it must of necessity owe the secure enjoyment of indispensable outlets for its own productions to the weight, influence, and the future maritime strength of the Atlantic side of the Union, directed by an indissoluble community of interest as one nation. Any other tenure by which the West can hold this essential advantage, whether derived from its own separate strength, or from an apostate and unnatural connection with any foreign power, must be intrinsically precarious.

While, then, every part of our country thus feels an immediate and particular interest in union, all the parts combined cannot fail to find in the united mass of means and efforts greater strength, greater resource, proportionably greater security from external danger, a less frequent interruption of their peace by foreign nations; and, what is of inestimable value, they must derive from union an exemption from those broils and wars between themselves, which so frequently afflict neighboring countries not tied together by the same governments, which their own rival ships alone would be sufficient to produce, but which opposite foreign alliances, attachments, and intrigues would stimulate and embitter. Hence, likewise, they will avoid the necessity of those overgrown military establishments which, under any form of government, are inauspicious to liberty, and which are to be regarded as particularly hostile to republican liberty. In this sense it is that your union ought to be considered as a main prop of your liberty, and that the love of the one ought to endear to you the preservation of the other.

These considerations speak a persuasive language to every reflecting and virtuous mind, and exhibit the continuance of the Union as a primary object of patriotic desire. Is there a doubt whether a common government can embrace so large a sphere? Let experience solve it. To listen to mere speculation in such a case were criminal. We are authorized to hope that a proper organization of the whole with the auxiliary agency of governments for the respective subdivisions, will afford a happy issue to the experiment. It is well worth a fair and full experiment. With such powerful and obvious motives to union, affecting all parts of our country, while experience shall not have demonstrated its impracticability, there will always be reason to distrust the patriotism of those who in any quarter may endeavor to weaken its bands.

In contemplating the causes which may disturb our Union, it occurs as matter of serious concern that any ground should have been furnished for characterizing parties by geographical discriminations, Northern and Southern, Atlantic and Western; whence designing men may endeavor to excite a belief that there is a real difference of local interests and views. One of the expedients of party to acquire influence within particular districts is to misrepresent the opinions and aims of other districts.

You cannot shield yourselves too much against the jealousies and heartburnings which spring from these misrepresentations; they tend to render alien to each other those who ought to be bound together by fraternal affection. The inhabitants of our Western country have lately had a useful lesson on this head; they have seen, in the negotiation by the Executive, and in the unanimous ratification by the Senate, of the treaty with Spain, and in the universal satisfaction at that event, throughout the United States, a decisive proof how unfounded were the suspicions propagated among them of a policy in the General Government and in the Atlantic States unfriendly to their interests in regard to the Mississippi; they have been witnesses to the formation of two treaties, that with Great Britain, and that with Spain, which secure to them everything they could desire, in respect to our foreign relations, towards confirming their prosperity. Will it not be their wisdom to rely for the preservation of these advantages on the Union by which they were procured? Will they not henceforth be deaf to those advisers, if such there are, who would sever them from their brethren and connect them with aliens?

To the efficacy and permanency of your Union, a government for the whole is indispensable. No alliance, however strict, between the parts can be an adequate substitute; they must inevitably experience the infractions and interruptions which all alliances in all times have experienced. Sensible of this momentous truth, you have improved upon your first essay, by the adoption of a constitution of government better calculated than your former for an intimate union, and for the efficacious management of your common concerns. This government, the offspring of our own choice, uninfluenced and unawed, adopted upon full investigation and mature deliberation, completely free in its principles, in the distribution of its powers, uniting security with energy, and containing within itself a provision for its own amendment, has a just claim to your confidence and your support. Respect for its authority, compliance with its laws, acquiescence in its measures, are duties enjoined by the fundamental maxims of true liberty. The basis of our political systems is the right of the people to make and to alter their constitutions of government. But the Constitution which at any time exists, till changed by an explicit and authentic act of the whole people, is sacredly obligatory upon all. The very idea of the power and the right of the people to establish government presupposes the duty of every individual to obey the established government.

All obstructions to the execution of the laws, all combinations and associations, under whatever plausible character, with the real design to direct, control, counteract, or awe the regular deliberation and action of the constituted authorities, are destructive of this fundamental principle, and of fatal tendency. They serve to organize faction, to give it an artificial and extraordinary force; to put, in the place of the delegated will of the nation the will of a party, often a small but artful and enterprising minority of the community; and, according to the alternate triumphs of different parties, to make the public administration the mirror of the ill-concerted and incongruous projects of faction, rather than the organ of consistent and wholesome plans digested by common counsels and modified by mutual interests.

However combinations or associations of the above description may now and then answer popular ends, they are likely, in the course of time and things, to become potent engines, by which cunning, ambitious, and unprincipled men will be enabled to subvert the power of the people and to usurp for themselves the reins of government, destroying afterwards the very engines which have lifted them to unjust dominion.

Towards the preservation of your government, and the permanency of your present happy state, it is requisite, not only that you steadily discountenance irregular oppositions to its acknowledged authority, but also that you resist with care the spirit of innovation upon its principles, however specious the pretexts. One method of assault may be to effect, in the forms of the Constitution, alterations which will impair the energy of the system, and thus to undermine what cannot be directly overthrown. In all the changes to which you may be invited, remember that time and habit are at least as necessary to fix the true character of governments as of other human institutions; that experience is the surest standard by which to test the real tendency of the existing constitution of a country; that facility in changes, upon the credit of mere hypothesis and opinion, exposes to perpetual change, from the endless variety of hypothesis and opinion; and remember, especially, that for the efficient management of your common interests, in a country so extensive as ours, a government of as much vigor as is consistent with the perfect security of liberty is indispensable. Liberty itself will find in such a government, with powers properly distributed and adjusted, its surest guardian. It is, indeed, little else than a name, where the government is too feeble to withstand the enterprises of faction, to confine each member of the society within the limits prescribed by the laws, and to maintain all in the secure and tranquil enjoyment of the rights of person and property.

I have already intimated to you the danger of parties in the State, with particular reference to the founding of them on geographical discriminations. Let me now take a more comprehensive view, and warn you in the most solemn manner against the baneful effects of the spirit of party generally.

This spirit, unfortunately, is inseparable from our nature, having its root in the strongest passions of the human mind. It exists under different shapes in all governments, more or less stifled, controlled, or repressed; but, in those of the popular form, it is seen in its greatest rankness, and is truly their worst enemy.

The alternate domination of one faction over another, sharpened by the spirit of revenge, natural to party dissension, which in different ages and countries has perpetrated the most horrid enormities, is itself a frightful despotism. But this leads at length to a more formal and permanent despotism. The disorders and miseries which result gradually incline the minds of men to seek security and repose in the absolute power of an individual; and sooner or later the chief of some prevailing faction, more able or more fortunate than his competitors, turns this disposition to the purposes of his own elevation, on the ruins of public liberty.

Without looking forward to an extremity of this kind (which nevertheless ought not to be entirely out of sight), the common and continual mischiefs of the spirit of party are sufficient to make it the interest and duty of a wise people to discourage and restrain it.

It serves always to distract the public councils and enfeeble the public administration. It agitates the community with ill-founded jealousies and false alarms, kindles the animosity of one part against another, foments occasionally riot and insurrection. It opens the door to foreign influence and corruption, which finds a facilitated access to the government itself through the channels of party passions. Thus the policy and the will of one country are subjected to the policy and will of another.

There is an opinion that parties in free countries are useful checks upon the administration of the government and serve to keep alive the spirit of liberty. This within certain limits is probably true; and in governments of a monarchical cast, patriotism may look with indulgence, if not with favor, upon the spirit of party. But in those of the popular character, in governments purely elective, it is a spirit not to be encouraged. From their natural tendency, it is certain there will always be enough of that spirit for every salutary purpose. And there being constant danger of excess, the effort ought to be by force of public opinion, to mitigate and assuage it. A fire not to be quenched, it demands a uniform vigilance to prevent its bursting into a flame, lest, instead of warming, it should consume.

*C*onsider the source and the audience.

- Although this address was never given by Washington in person, it was clearly intended to be. To whom is Washington addressing his words primarily? The American public? Fellow politicians? Political adversaries?

*L*ay out the argument, the values, and the assumptions.

- What are Washington's basic assumptions about human nature? What is the link between human nature and parties?
- What values does Washington believe government should protect above all else?
- In what ways does Washington think parties threaten those values?

*U*ncover the evidence.

- What evidence does Washington provide to support his contention that a unified country is a good thing?
- Is that evidence sufficient to convince people that parties are consequently bad, or should he have provided something more?

*E*valuate the conclusion.

- Washington makes a powerful logical and rhetorical case. Are passion, logic, and eloquence enough to convince you?
- What does Washington want Americans to do about the dangers of parties?

*S*ort out the political implications.

- In what ways do modern-day politics support or weaken Washington's contention? Would he think that his fears had been realized, or that they were unnecessary?

12

Interest Groups

French philosopher Alexis de Tocqueville, writing about American culture and government during his trip to the United States in the early 1830s, noted that "Americans of all ages, all conditions, and all dispositions, constantly form associations. They not only have commercial and manufacturing companies, in which all take part, but associations of a thousand other kinds—religious, moral, serious, futile, general, or restricted, enormous or diminutive."[1] Tocqueville's observation more than 175 years ago still applies today. In fact, while we often criticize Americans for their lack of political engagement, more than 80 percent of us belong to at least one interest group.[2] An interest group is simply an organization of individuals who share a common political goal and unite for the purpose of influencing government decisions.

Indeed, one theory of representative democracy notes the incredible importance of interest groups in our society. Believers in pluralist democracy argue that while individually we may not have much power to influence government, our voices are magnified through our membership in interest groups. Representatives may discount our single vote, or ignore our single letter, but they are likely to listen to the Sierra Club, the National Rifle Association (NRA), or AARP (formerly the American Association for Retired Persons) when their professional representatives, known as lobbyists, come to call.

We may be, as Tocqueville wrote, a country of "joiners," but that doesn't necessarily mean we hold interest groups in the highest regard. The founders were quite wary of factions (their term for interest groups) because they feared it would then be easy for a majority to suppress the minority. James Madison made this argument persuasively in *Federalist* No. 10, included in this chapter. Today, when there are more interest groups than at any other time in our history, citizens often view interest groups as defenders of "special interests"—interests that, as far as Madison was concerned, do not represent the general public good. Interest groups such as the NRA and the Association of Trial Lawyers of America seem to have immense influence with elected officials, but their views are not necessarily consistent with the majority of the public. We also are skeptical of the role of interest groups in elections, and we fear that interest

248

group money buys or unduly influences elected officials' votes. While political scientists haven't conclusively demonstrated this to be true, they have found evidence that money buys access, which could indirectly influence votes.

The articles in this chapter examine several aspects of interest groups and social movements. The first looks at the active role a college student has played in civil disobedience protests on campus and the price he has had to pay for his involvement. The next article, from the *Washington Monthly*, examines the role of one particular interest group, the American Council on Education, a group that lobbies government on behalf of higher education. Third, Gary Andres, in a piece in the *Weekly Standard*, argues that President Barack Obama's attempts to limit the role of lobbyists will fail because his policies encourage the development of more lobbying organizations. Finally, we close with Madison's famous *Federalist* No. 10, in which he warns against the negative effects of factions.

Notes

1. Alexis de Tocqueville, *Democracy in America*, Richard D. Heffner, ed. (New York: New American Library, 1956), 198.
2. *The Public Perspective*, April/May 1995.

 12.1 "My Life Is Shaped by the Border"

Student Activist Faces Fallout from Mideast Protest

Tanya Schevitz, San Francisco Chronicle

Why We Chose This Piece

Interest groups organize around a common interest to try to influence public policy. Usually they work through the system, directly or indirectly targeting government as the focus of their efforts. Sometimes groups, such as African Americans in the 1950s and 1960s, or women at the turn of the twentieth century, have difficulty getting into the system to work to bring about the change they value. When an interest group is unable to work within the political system, we usually call it a social movement. Such groups may use nonviolent civil disobedience or more active forms of demonstration. As we see here, the line between freedom of speech and assembly and breaking the law can be hard to draw. Those actors who want to keep a group outside the system have every incentive to define their efforts as law breaking; the social movement itself usually claims the protection of the First Amendment.

The sit-ins during the 1960s, for example, were a major success in forcing department stores to integrate their lunch counters. Throughout the South (and even in parts of the North), African Americans—in this case, mostly college students—ignored integration

---

Selection published: November 18, 2002

laws by refusing to give up their seats. In many instances, they were arrested. In the end, however, the protests forced many stores to change their policies. Civil disobedience also played a major role on college campuses as students protested the Vietnam War. While controversial, civil disobedience is a classic example of political participation.

The following article from the San Francisco Chronicle *documents the plight of a UC Berkeley student who faced severe punishment because of his involvement in campus protests aimed at altering university policy. It illustrates many of the same issues confronted by earlier social movements. Where should the line be drawn between free speech and criminal activity in these cases?*

Roberto Hernandez remembers looking out the window of his San Ysidro elementary classroom and seeing the Border Patrol chasing people "who look like me" across the playground.

When he got older, he was often stopped by the Border Patrol near his San Diego County home, even though he had a green card.

"The military checkpoints are much worse in Palestine," he says, "but for me there is a natural link there."

These days, Hernandez's strong feelings about the Israeli-Palestinian quagmire have gotten him in big trouble at his school, UC Berkeley.

Hernandez was one of 79 protesters arrested during an April 9 demonstration held by the Students for Justice in Palestine, as part of a campaign to force the university to divest from companies with business ties to Israel.

While the Alameda County District Attorney's office did not file criminal charges against those arrested, the university is pursuing campus disciplinary charges against Hernandez and 31 other students.

Hernandez will face a campus hearing Wednesday—a battle that students characterize as a free speech issue but one that the university considers a simple matter of protecting other students' rights to an education.

The university has put a hold on Hernandez's degree, which is preventing him from officially graduating and enrolling in his graduate program. That means he isn't a student and cannot collect the fellowship he was relying on to pay tuition and living expenses.

"Everything in my life, my politics, is shaped and changed by the border," said Hernandez, 23, who grew up as a Mexican citizen just seven blocks from the U.S.-Mexican border.

From one perspective, Roberto Hernandez personifies the traditional American success story. His parents are poor immigrants from Guadalajara and Chiapas who have little education.

But he made it to UC Berkeley and excelled throughout his undergraduate years, getting involved in the campus community, and earning a campus fellowship and a spot in Berkeley's doctoral program in ethnic studies.

University officials paint quite a different portrait: a rabble-rouser who attends virtually every campus protest and who jeopardized his future by participating in a takeover of Wheeler Hall last spring.

Hernandez, they say, not only defied the rules by occupying a campus building but also bit a campus police officer while he was being arrested.

And they say that Hernandez and the other students arrested were warned repeatedly against disrupting the "academic mission" of the campus and that they have a right to pursue disciplinary charges dealing with the campus code of conduct.

UC administrators are seeking up to a year's suspension for each of the students.

But Hernandez, who became a U.S. citizen two years ago, says he is just following the values his mother instilled in him. His mother was so proud of her Mexican heritage that when she went into labor with him, she traveled to a hospital across the border to retain the family's "Mexican nationality."

Although she had just an eighth-grade education, his mother was always active in his school, organizing other parents to improve things and encouraging Hernandez and his sister to get involved.

"My mom brought me up to be involved in the schools," he said, "but it became larger than that."

He became politicized at age 13, when he got swept up in his first "real demonstration," a 1992 protest of the celebration of the 500th anniversary of Christopher Columbus' "discovery" of America.

"It was so huge, and it was beautiful. Five thousand people coming together to say no, to take a stand," he said. "That was the beginning for me. It had never really clicked for me before. Until that point, I was confused and full of rage, but I didn't know how to channel it."

He began protesting police and Border Patrol brutality and providing support and security to the Pastors for Peace caravans headed with food and supplies to Cuba.

In ninth grade, he wrote a paper on what it means to be an American and received an F for writing of America as a continent, including Mexico. He then joined MEChA, a Chicano student group, for support.

He was involved in the campaign against Proposition 187, organizing student walkouts to protest the measure to deprive undocumented workers of education and health and welfare services. (The measure was approved but has since been halted by the courts.)

From then on, he was active on every state proposition affecting minorities, including Proposition 209, which eliminated the use of race in university admissions.

"I think back now not in terms of time, but in terms of propositions," he said.

He was admitted to UC Berkeley in the last year that affirmative action was in place and isn't ashamed to say he probably benefited from the use of racial preferences.

"Affirmative action only opens the door," he said. "We have to work our a—off and earn our degree."

His apartment is one of an intellectually and politically engaged student, with a bed crowded into the corner of a tiny room filled with eight towering book-shelves packed with books, mostly about minority issues. The walls are papered with Mexican flags, posters of Che Guevara and announcements of political demonstrations.

"People know of my place here as a mini-Chicano resource center," Hernandez said. "I don't have formal library cards, but people do come check out books here."

Even in his academic life at UC Berkeley, he focused on political issues that arose from his upbringing. He has researched the social, political and cultural aspects of the border and the functionality of borders internationally.

Hernandez admits he is involved in a lot of campus political actions but says it is because he has been frustrated every time he has tried to work within the system. He served as a student senator on campus but found his agenda thwarted by politics and partisanship, he said.

"I try these other formal means of enacting change, but a lot of times we come up against these roadblocks," he said.

Hernandez has been arrested before, during a September 2001 protest of a *Daily Californian* cartoon that many considered racist and anti-Muslim. The charges were dropped.

And he was involved in the highly publicized 1999 demonstrations, where students demanded increased support for the ethnic studies program by fasting and camping outside Chancellor Robert Berdahl's office.

But he says his participation is always peaceful. He says the university is targeting him because he is so politically active.

Hernandez's professors—and even a University of California regent who knows him—believe the university is overreacting to this latest incident because of political pressures that label any criticism of Israel as anti-Semitic.

The entire ethnic studies department signed a letter of support for Hernandez.

"To see this kid get trashed this way, I just can't see it," said UC Regent Alfredo Terrazas, who first met Hernandez in 1998 at a scholarship fund-raising event by the Chicano Latino Alumni Club. "For him, it is devastating for his career. For the university, it is a shame. And we lose an individual in the Latino community who I really believe is going to be a leader."

Campus spokeswoman Janet Gilmore says that the university's disciplinary charges have nothing to do with politics and that pro-Palestinian students who were merely protesting and marching around campus have not faced any charges.

"Clearly, there is not an effort to stop them from exercising their free speech," Gilmore said.

For Hernandez, political dissent could come at a price he was not prepared to pay.

"I wasn't expecting the university to come down on us as hard as they have," he said.

*C*onsider the source and the audience.

- The *San Francisco Chronicle* is the major newspaper in the Bay Area, located near the University of California at Berkeley. This was clearly a local story for the *Chronicle*—but does it also have a more general relevance?

*L*ay out the argument, the values, and the assumptions.

- How has Hernandez's background influenced his values? What changes does he want to bring about? Why does he feel that more "traditional" forms of participation have not been effective? How does he think the university should respond to his actions?

- How does the University of California view Hernandez's behavior? What does it consider its "academic mission" to be, and how does Hernandez damage this mission?
- One of Hernandez's supporters says that the loss of Hernandez is a shame for the university. What contribution might Hernandez be making to the university? What could be the costs of suspending him?

Uncover the evidence.

- Is there any kind of evidence that either side could provide to back its arguments, or is this just a case of opposing viewpoints? How do the conflicting interests here shape the way the two sides interpret events?

Evaluate the conclusion.

- Why would the university react so harshly to these students? What is at stake for them?
- What is at stake for Hernandez? Were other avenues open to him to achieve his ends?

Sort out the political implications.

- Can universities promote free speech and academic freedom without disrupting students' educations? What rights do students have to express their views? What can they do if they feel that their rights are being violated?
- How might this campus climate affect students who want to demonstrate in favor of or against military action around the world?

 12.2 Inside the Higher Ed Lobby

Welcome to One Dupont Circle, Where Good Education-Reform Ideas Go to Die

Ben Adler, Washington Monthly

Why We Chose This Piece

> *When you think about interest groups lobbying government—in other words, attempting to persuade policymakers to support their positions—organizations like the NRA, AARP, or the American Civil Liberties Union likely come to mind. Yet there are literally thousands of interests that must be protected, many by organizations not nearly as visible as some of the groups mentioned previously but quite powerful nonetheless. The higher education lobby is one such example. You may not be aware that your school likely has someone on staff who lobbies Congress or the state legislature on its behalf. Additionally, the American Council on Education (ACE) represents colleges and universities on a variety of issues related to higher education.*

Selection published: July 9, 2007

We chose this article because, unlike many lobbying organizations, the higher ed lobby should be quite relevant to most of you. As the article makes clear, though, on some issues ACE has students' interests in mind, but its job is to protect the interests of colleges and universities—not students. Sometimes, according to Ben Adler, ACE works against policies that could be good education reform (and beneficial to students) but that go against the interest of higher education. We also include this piece because it does a nice job illustrating the lobbying process—an essential subject when learning about interest groups.

In 2003, Ted Kennedy tried to nudge America's colleges and universities toward changing two of the least defensible practices in the modern admissions process. The first is legacy preferences, in which schools heavily favor applications from the children of alumni, often ahead of students with stronger academic resumes but less-well-connected parents. The second practice, early decision, where schools make it easier for prospective students to get admitted if they'll commit to attending at the time they apply, has a similar effect, since wealthier candidates don't need to compare financial aid packages and can therefore more easily commit to a school early. Taken together, the two practices fly in the face of the ideal of American meritocracy, and reduce the opportunities for young people of more modest backgrounds to go to selective colleges.

Under Kennedy's proposal, schools that used both tools and also graduated students of color at a disproportionately low rate—at the time, that meant eighty-seven schools, including five Ivies—would be required to try to boost that rate, and would receive federal money to do so. If they failed, the schools would be required to give up legacy preferences or early decision, or else forgo other forms of federal aid.

Kennedy was touching the third and fourth rails of higher education, a particularly courageous move for a senator who represents the state with perhaps the most powerful colleges in the country. Yet as a longtime leader on education issues, who two years earlier had worked with President Bush to pass the No Child Left Behind Act, Kennedy had sufficient clout to get his measure considered, even in a GOP Congress. Indeed, the proposal held out some appeal to certain of the Senate's Republican populists, who tend to be well disposed toward any effort to stick it to the East Coast elite.

But before Kennedy's proposal could even be formally introduced, One Dupont Circle weighed in. That's the address of the marble-and-glass office building that serves as the de facto headquarters for the array of groups representing the organized interests of America's colleges and universities. Prominently located in a fashionable D.C. neighborhood that's home to many of the better-funded nonprofits, One Dupont (or the "National Center for Higher Education," as its awning appropriately proclaims) is owned by the largest and most powerful of the higher ed associations, the American Council on Education. In order to facilitate coordination of policy and strategy, ACE leases the rest of the space, at below-market rates, exclusively to other higher ed groups (from the National Association of College and University Attorneys to the American College Personnel Association). That sense of cohesion tends to come through in the lobby's work: one higher ed expert I spoke to called One Dupont "a building that speaks, like the White House."

When the denizens of One Dupont learned of the Kennedy proposal, they pulled out all the stops to fight it. Legacy preferences are a key way for many colleges to maintain favor with deep-pocketed alumni, and early decision allows them to manage the admissions process with more predictability, and to lock in certain coveted applicants—often wealthy athletic recruits, who play sports like squash and lacrosse and whose parents can be expected to pay full price.

Higher ed lobbyists quickly mobilized their member colleges, encouraging them to go directly to senators on the key committee. Publicly, the lobby stressed the effect the measure would have on small religious institutions and historically black colleges, some of which, they claimed, depend for their existence on using the admissions process to maintain alumni loyalty. But in reality, say Hill staffers who worked on the issue, it was the elite New England private colleges and universities, appealing directly to their home-state senators Kennedy and Chris Dodd of Connecticut, who applied particularly effective behind-the-scenes pressure. When Dodd began to waver, Kennedy was forced to back off, and the two instead proposed a largely toothless alternative that merely required colleges to report on the number, socioeconomic status, and race of students who were relatives of alumni or were admitted through early decision. It involved no penalties of any kind. Yet ultimately, under pressure from One Dupont, even this measure was never brought up for a vote.

The fight to hold on to preferential admissions practices was only one example of what might be called the higher education lobby's misplaced priorities. For years, colleges and universities have hidden behind the argument that America's system of higher education is the best in the world to insulate themselves from scrutiny and accountability, and to operate with a remarkable degree of autonomy from Washington, given the funds lavished on them by the federal government. The claim that our higher ed system really is the best in the world, however, is becoming less and less true every year. In 1980, the United States led Canada by 10 percent in the percentage of its population with a college degree, and was ahead of the United Kingdom by 11 percent and France by 19 percent, according to a recent study by the Organization for Economic Cooperation and Development. By 2000, those leads had shrunk to 3, 6, and 10 percent respectively—and the evidence suggests that the gaps have continued to narrow since then. Meanwhile, colleges, especially elite private institutions, have been raising tuition far faster than the rate of inflation year after year after year, outpacing the meager growth in federal tuition subsidies. That's put a squeeze on middle-class families and forced students deeper and deeper into debt. Worst of all, the information that policy makers and the public need to begin turning these problems around—which schools are educating their students effectively, and how tuition dollars are really being spent—remains locked in the ivory tower.

That's not to say that higher ed doesn't champion righteous causes. In the 1990s, they stood up to attempts by the Republican Congress to cut student aid, and went on to team with the Clinton administration to expand the Pell Grant program. And when, after 9/11, the Bush administration, in its zeal to keep out terrorists, imposed overly harsh visa requirements that ended up keeping out large numbers of foreign professors and grad students—exactly the kind of people who keep our universities humming with fresh ideas—higher ed led the successful effort to pressure the government to adopt a more sensible policy.

But the same lobbying muscle they've often put in the service of worthy causes they've also used to thwart promising reforms. On a range of issues, higher ed has stood up for its own narrow strategic or pecuniary concerns, rather than the broader interests of students or the country at large. In short, though it represents institutions that loudly proclaim a mission of public service, the higher education lobby more often acts like any other Washington trade group. Today, one of the most significant roadblocks to fixing many of the pressing problems of our troubled system of higher education is the higher education lobby itself.

Though organized associations of colleges and universities have been lobbying the federal government on behalf of their interests since the nineteenth century, it wasn't until the 1950s that higher education began to exert influence in Washington in a systematic way. The GI Bill and the spreading prosperity of the postwar years helped create a society in which a college degree for the first time became a common middle-class aspiration. As higher education became increasingly central to American life, its Washington representatives began to work together to take advantage of this growing prominence, and to ensure that colleges and universities were getting their share of federal spending. In 1968, the American Council on Education—which represents both public and private universities as well as smaller regional and national associations, and bills itself as the "unifying voice" of higher ed—took over One Dupont and established it as the lobby's power center.

But there was trouble on the horizon. The political unrest on college campuses in the late 1960s provoked a conservative backlash. Concerned that the federal government would react by cracking down on colleges' historic autonomy, higher ed stepped up its Washington presence. Nonetheless, in 1972 it suffered a major legislative defeat: the Democratic Congress was considering ways to help expand access to higher education, and colleges advocated an approach by which they would receive aid as institutions, which would then allow them to offer tuition breaks to poorer students. But instead, Congress created federal grants that would be given directly to college students, to use at the school of their choice. (The program, conceived by Democratic Senator Claiborne Pell of Rhode Island, now bears his name.) Many in higher education circles blamed the defeat on a lack of lobbying sophistication. As a result, in 1976 a coalition of private schools founded the National Association of Independent Colleges and Universities (NAICU), with the explicit purpose of lobbying the federal government more effectively.

During this same period, the federal government's role in higher education began to increase, as Washington started subsidizing research more heavily, and regulating aspects of college life that had heretofore been seen as the exclusive purview of the institutions themselves—from the gender equity of their sports programs to the safety of their campuses. In response, higher education continued to beef up its lobbying presence. Then, in 1994, the Republican takeover of Congress brought to power a new wave of leaders with an essentially antagonistic attitude toward higher education as a whole, triggering a countermobilization by the lobby. With the Clinton White House as an ally, it successfully fought off Newt Gingrich's efforts to gut federal student financial aid, and helped block a bid by then Senate Majority Leader Bob Dole—who was looking to burnish his conservative credentials in advance of his presidential run—to eliminate affirmative action programs. Over the next few years, the lobby won steady or increased funding for almost every key program.

But it also learned how to use its growing Washington know-how to work not just against Republicans but with them, when doing so served its interests. For instance, in the early nineties, the Democratic Congress had created a system to allow the Education Department to audit the finances of colleges that triggered warning signs of mismanagement. Resenting this challenge to higher education's autonomy, NAICU skillfully framed the issue as a case of big government run wild, and in 1995 teamed with Gingrich and his conservative acolytes in Congress to eliminate the program.

The higher ed lobby is plenty aggressive, but in an understated way—money is not its main lever of power. In 2005, the last year for which figures are available, higher education associations officially spent just $6.2 million on lobbying, according to figures from Inside Higher Ed. (By contrast, General Electric alone spent $24.2 million, much of which went to the kind of high-priced outside law and PR firms that higher ed almost never employs.) Nor does it rely on mass grassroots campaigns to make its voice heard. Since most of the associations are organized under the tax code as 501(c)(3) organizations, they're legally allowed to spend only a limited amount of money on the kind of conventional mass political tactics—holding rallies and organizing letter- and e-mail-writing campaigns in order to affect legislation—that the teachers unions or environmental groups routinely use.

Instead, higher ed wields power in two effective if subtle ways. First, it plays an inside game, conducting quiet, sit-down meetings with policy makers in which it trades on its expertise on the often technical questions of education policy. Hill staffers looking to make sense of complicated legislative proposals, and to understand the impact on those most directly affected, have little alternative but to turn to higher ed lobbyists.

Second, higher ed makes skillful use of its hometown ties. Colleges typically occupy prominent positions in the economic, cultural, and civic life of their communities, and they're adept at using those positions to win influence. They can curry favor with legislators by conferring honorary degrees or inviting them to give commencement addresses, usually generating a round of positive PR back home. In some communities, college presidents are high-profile public figures, with ready access to the media and the power to help shape local opinion. Like large corporations, universities are often major employers in their districts, and their financial fortunes have a spillover effect on the local economy. More personal ties can also weigh heavily: according to some Hill staffers, legislators often have a soft spot for their alma mater, or for the state university whose football team they grew up rooting for.

Perhaps just as important, colleges are aware that they have control over a process—admissions—that looms large in the lives of powerful decision makers and their families. According to Daniel Golden, the author of *The Price of Admission: How America's Ruling Class Buys Its Way Into Elite Colleges—And Who Gets Left Outside the Gates*, they routinely admit the children of legislators who aren't the best candidates. (For example, Golden cites the case of then Senate Majority Leader Bill Frist's son, who in 2005, despite not being in the top 20 percent of his high school class, was admitted to Vanderbilt, an elite private school at which 80 percent of students finished in the top tenth of their class.) Barmak Nassirian, a lobbyist for the

American Association of Collegiate Registrars and Admissions Officers (AACRAO), admitted to me, "We live in a system in which people take care of each other. I'm not going to say that doesn't happen."

The aggressiveness with which higher ed has come to oppose even Washington's gentlest attempts to improve its performance was on display last year, when a high-level commission appointed by Education Secretary Margaret Spellings produced its first draft of a report on the state of higher education. The commission, led by Charles Miller, a no-nonsense accountability hawk who in the 1990s had a hand in efforts to reform Texas's public K–12 schools, pulled no punches. It noted that graduation rates remain unimpressive, and that too many qualified students don't go to college, or drop out for financial reasons. "Among the vast and varied institutions that make up U.S. higher education," the draft declared, "we have found equal parts meritocracy and mediocrity."

ACE President David Ward, who served on the commission, told me he found this first version "unnecessarily polemical and confrontational." Not wanting to alienate higher ed, whose cooperation would be needed to implement the proposed reforms, the other commissioners acquiesced to changes in the report's language, in response to higher ed's complaints. Nonetheless, some on the commission were shocked by the lobby's utter resistance to the inclusion of any forthright criticism. "It was the closest thing I've seen to censorship in my life," says Miller. In the final, public version, the reference to mediocrity was gone, replaced by this more diplomatic statement: "Among the vast and varied institutions that make up U.S. higher education, we have found much to applaud but also much that requires urgent reform." Still, Ward refused to sign the final report.

If higher ed's reaction to a nonbinding report that merely sought to identify strategies for improvement provoked charges of censorship, it isn't surprising that the lobby has been even less willing to compromise when Washington has actually tried to legislate reform. For decades, education experts have been concerned about declining teacher quality in K–12 schools, and in the late 1990s the Clinton administration tried to address the problem by improving colleges' notoriously lackluster teacher-training programs. The Education Department put together a proposal requiring states to report the percentage of teacher-training-program graduates from each school who pass the state licensure exam, and to report which of their education schools, many of which are affiliated with major universities, were underperforming. Schools that consistently failed to produce graduates capable of passing the exams would lose their eligibility to receive federal aid for teacher training.

For many colleges, teacher-training programs, which can count on a steady stream of applicants and have relatively low administrative costs, represent a crucial revenue source—and the higher ed lobby went into overdrive to protect it. "They didn't want publicly accessible info for the performance of their graduates," says Sara Mead, who worked on implementation at the Education Department. "They didn't want to be held accountable. They would come up with all sorts of technical objections, but that was the real issue." Sarah Flanagan of NAICU insists that the proposal would have discriminated against historically black colleges, or any colleges that let in low-income students, since standardized tests like state licensure exams are racially and socioeconomically biased. But Kati Haycock of Education Trust, a nonprofit education organization, calls that notion "preposterous...These are low-level exams. People who cannot pass the exam should not be teachers. There are plenty of African Americans who can pass these exams and then some."

This time, higher ed lost, and a version of the proposal passed Congress. But the lobby didn't give up. During the department's rule-making process on implementing the law in 1999, lobbyists showed up at every meeting with complaints and objections, watering down the effect of the legislation. In addition, higher ed mobilized at the state level, prevailing upon state governments to set absurdly lenient testing standards—in some cases, schools essentially avoided compliance by simply defining a "program completer" as someone who had passed the licensing exam, ensuring a 100 percent success rate. Nine years after its passage, most experts agree the law has done little to improve teacher quality.

Another area in which higher ed has hardly been a profile in courage is the issue of private lending. Currently, students can receive loans for college either directly from the government or through federally subsidized private lenders. Direct loans are cheaper for the taxpayer, both because they don't include the subsidy to the lender and because the federal government can borrow money at a better rate. Indeed, when President Clinton introduced direct lending, he sought to phase out the private-lender-based program altogether. But the private-sector bias of congressional Republicans (and their reliance on campaign contributions from the lending companies) thwarted that effort. Instead, schools are allowed to choose whether to participate in the direct-loan or the private-lender-based program.

This arrangement creates an obvious incentive toward corruption, and over the last decade evidence began to mount that lenders and financial aid officers at some schools were building improperly close relationships. When the Clinton administration tried to look into the issue in the late 1990s, the higher ed lobby showed little interest. Only in the last two years, when outright corruption became undeniable, did higher ed get behind anything that might hurt the lending industry. And even then, it hardly went out on a limb, backing legislation—the College Cost Reduction Act, which passed both houses of Congress in July—that merely cuts subsidies to lenders, and that already had massive bipartisan support.

What they didn't do was get behind a more far-reaching approach when they had the chance. Last February, legislators from both parties proposed the Student Aid Reward Act (STAR), which sought to encourage schools to choose direct lending over private lending, by allowing them to keep three-quarters of the savings that direct loans generate—to be spent on additional Pell Grants for their students—with the remaining one-quarter going to deficit reduction. Schools that continued to participate in the lender-based program would face no penalty. In other words, schools would receive free federal money for Pell Grants, or would get increased leverage in negotiating with private lenders for a better deal.

One might expect, then, that the proposal would have received the enthusiastic support of the higher education lobby. But none of the Big Six associations (see "The Higher Ed Lobby: A Glossary"), and very few of the smaller lobbies, came out for STAR, much less put their political muscle behind passing it. "The silence was deafening," says Michael Dannenberg, an education expert at the New America Foundation. Without higher ed pushing back against the deep-pocketed lenders' opposition to STAR, it went nowhere.

What explains the lobby's reticence? NAICU's Flanagan says her organization opposed STAR because it would have meant that some students ended up receiving more aid than others. But that stance makes little sense, since no student would have ended up with less aid because of STAR. Many higher education experts suggest a more plausible reason. The relationship between the higher ed lobby and the lenders is complex and multifaceted. The two groups are allies in the fight for increased federal student aid. Lending company officials make it their business to get to know college administrators personally, and many have worked in higher ed themselves. Lenders have often provided financial backing for charitable organizations like the Nellie Mae Foundation and Knowledge Works, which further the cause of higher education by supporting research on college access and student achievement. Barmak Nassirian, whose organization, AACRAO, was one of the only members of the lobby to support STAR, explains the thinking: "The largesse and generosity of lenders has created enough friendship that you don't want to trample on it so easily for the sake of one piece of legislation."

Perhaps higher ed was politically shrewd not to alienate their sometime allies in the lending industry on this one. But there's no doubt that their hands-off approach worked to benefit the lenders—who Dannenberg calls "some of the worst actors in the higher education system"—at the expense of the students who are denied extra Pell Grants, and the taxpayers who continue to foot the bill for corporate subsidies.

But perhaps the most damaging example of the lobby standing in the way of efforts to improve the system involves its opposition to efforts to make public more information on educational outcomes. Currently, colleges report schoolwide statistics on tuition and graduation rates to the federal government, but they've resisted providing Washington with more student-specific information.

The consequences of this lack of data are severe: Suppose you're a high school senior trying to pick a college. You might want to know how a given school's graduates go on to do in the job market. The information would not be hard to assemble, since states already collect workforce data, which could then be cross-referenced with student records. But for now, you'd be out of luck, because schools keep their side of the information under wraps. Just as important, policy makers wanting to create better incentives for schools to improve first need to know how well individual schools are serving their students, and at what cost. But again, they're currently in the dark. It's as if the Federal Reserve were trying to set monetary policy without access to information about how well the economy was performing. As last year's Spellings Commission report dryly but firmly put it: "Right now, policymakers, scholarly researchers, and members of the public lack basic information on institutional performance and labor market outcomes for postsecondary institutions."

Last year, the Education Department recommended to Congress that it address this problem by passing a law to create a single federal student-unit-record system. But though one major higher ed group—the American Association of State Colleges and Universities, which represents the less prestigious, more regional public schools—supported the idea, many of the associations went into overdrive to fight it. Their chief argument against the proposal was that such a system could violate student privacy. But that position doesn't withstand even gentle scrutiny. The federal government routinely gathers far more sensitive personal data on private citizens—every year at tax time, for instance—but uses standard privacy protections to ensure that the information remains confidential. And the database would have been managed by the National Center for Education Statistics, a quasi-independent division of the Department of Education that has an excellent track record of protecting personal information.

Again, many higher ed experts say there are more self-interested reasons for the lobby's opposition. A student-unit-record system would lay bare some of the tricks of the trade that higher ed would just as soon keep under wraps. First, it would make public just how much aid many institutions give to academically strong middle- and upper-class students, simply to encourage them to attend and thereby boost the school's academic ranking in college guides like U.S. News's. Perhaps more important, the system would undercut higher ed's longstanding efforts to keep the federal government out of the business of regulating college tuition in order to deal with the growing problem of college affordability. As average tuition has continued to rise since the early '90s, making college increasingly unaffordable for students from low-income families, the lobby's chief argument against federal regulation is that, thanks to financial aid and scholarship programs, many students—more than half, at some schools—don't pay the full "sticker price." And since no one knows exactly how much they do pay on average, the government shouldn't try to intervene based on incomplete information. The existence of a record system would fix this problem by giving the government that information, paving the way, higher ed fears, for the feds to regulate tuition rates. It would also reveal to students that many of their peers don't pay full price, making those who do pony up the full rate less willing to keep doing so as costs rise, according to some experts.

As a result, when the student-unit-record system came before Congress, it stood little chance. With senators pressured by higher ed—one-third of the members of the key committee were from the private-college-heavy Northeast—the writing was on the wall. In the end, not only did the proposal fail to make it out of committee, but the Senate went on to pass a measure flatly prohibiting the creation of such a system.

That the higher ed lobby acts in the narrow self-interest of the industry it represents is not, in a way, a big shocker; all lobbyists do this. Many Americans, however—liberals especially—expect a little more from the Washington representatives of colleges and universities. These are the institutions, after all, that are in loco parentis for their children. And they enjoy a nonprofit status that should oblige them to weigh larger societal interests more heavily in their calculations.

At the very least, it would be wise for higher ed to consider that acts that seem to be in their self-interest today may not be in the long run. The public's tolerance for the status quo is wearing a bit thin, and some in Washington are pushing radical action. A cautionary example helps prove the point: in 2003, California Republican Representative Buck McKeon offered a bill to withdraw federal student aid from colleges that raised tuition at a rate greater than inflation for three straight years. The measure played well with some angry parents, but it amounted to a form of government price control—a blunt and seldom effective instrument, and a curious one for a Republican to be proposing. That effort died in committee, but efforts like McKeon's could become commonplace unless colleges and universities begin to modify their knee-jerk opposition to reform.

Being responsive to the public doesn't have to mean being micromanaged by Washington. Instead of imposing price controls, the federal government should demand, and colleges should accept, the disclosure of key information—like what colleges are spending money on, and how well they're teaching—so that it can be made available to ordinary citizens, who can then decide what to do with their own tuition dollars. Doing so would create market pressures on universities to cut costs and increase the quality of their services. That won't necessarily be pleasant for the higher ed sector, but it may make voters more amenable to increasing subsidies on things the higher ed lobby cares about, like research and student financial aid. If America's system of higher education really is going to continue to be the best in the world, its Washington lobbyists will have to spend a little more time thinking about what's best for America.

*C*onsider the source and the audience.

- Ben Adler is affiliated with Campus Progress, an organization that, according to its web site, "acts to empower new progressive leaders nationwide as they develop fresh ideas, communicate in new ways, push policy outcomes in a progressive direction, and build a strong progressive movement." What does this tell you about the kinds of educational issues that are likely to be important to him?

*L*ay out the arguments, the values, and the assumptions.

- What are the "good education-reform" bills that Adler criticizes the higher ed lobby for defeating? Does Alder see any good in the higher ed lobby?
- According to Adler, why is the higher ed lobby so powerful? Are there any limits on its power?

*U*ncover the evidence.

- What evidence does Adler offer that the higher ed lobby has been responsible for the defeat of the education-reform bills he mentions? How do we know that something else was not the reason for the bills' failure?

*E*valuate the conclusion.

- Adler is critical of the higher ed lobby on many issues because he believes it protects bad policy. If you don't hold the same political views as Adler, can you support his conclusion?

*S*ort out the political implications.

- Let's assume that Adler is correct—that the higher ed lobby has prevented good education policy from passing, a debatable assumption. What, if anything, could be done to counter the education lobby?
- Is it problematic in a representative democracy that groups representing some interests may be more powerful and influential than groups representing other interests? Is it inevitable?

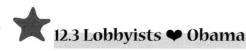

12.3 Lobbyists ❤ Obama

It's a Golden Age for the "Advocacy" Business
Gary Andres, Weekly Standard

Why We Chose This Piece

> *This article complements Reading 12.2, on the higher education lobby. The author, Gary Andres, does a nice job of explaining the complexities of defining who exactly is a lobbyist. Moreover, the article is timely given that it critiques President Obama's attempts to try to limit lobbying. If the United States is indeed a pluralist democracy in which groups are supposed to represent the interests of the public before legislative bodies, why are lobbyists viewed so negatively? Why do some people want to limit the influence of lobbyists?*

L ike most political reforms, the Obama administration's attempt to clean up lobbying is beset with unintended consequences. The president's policies are producing an explosion in interest-group activity, and much of the growth is taking place outside the scope of federal disclosure and other regulations.

The expansion of government always causes lobbying to grow, and Obama is enlarging Washington's reach. The bigger, more complicated, and more activist the federal government becomes, the more the affected interests mobilize. Columnist Robert Samuelson calls Obama's bigger government a "gift for K Street." The president's promise to banish special interests from the political arena, Samuelson writes, is "doomed to fail" because "the only way to eliminate lobbying and special interests is to eliminate government."

Samuelson is partly right. Lobbying growth in the last four decades closely tracks the expansion of the federal government. More complicated laws, a proliferation of congressional subcommittees, the expansion of legislative staff, and increased federal regulatory volume all induce affected parties to devote more resources to Washington. Since the 1970s, the number of associations moving to the District, the percentage of large corporations with a presence inside the Beltway, and the roster of issue-based advocacy groups have all spiked. Political scientist Beth Leech and her colleagues published a paper in 2005 concluding, "Groups do not automatically form and come to Washington; there must be a demand for them. Government creates that demand." Government is doing so now at an accelerating pace as the federal leviathan marches further into the auto, financial services, and health care sectors.

What's more, those affected by President Obama's promise to bring "change" to Washington play both defense and offense. Anytime a new policy challenges the status quo, interests respond by maneuvering to avoid risk and exploit opportunity. Labor unions, environmental groups, business organizations, and professional societies seek to reshape bad proposals to avoid costs (higher taxes, new rules) and secure advantages (new spending, the shifting of costs to competitors). At present, while many business interests are on their heels, liberal groups like trial lawyers, unions, and greens are making gains unthinkable during the last eight years.

Selection published: June 8, 2009

Yet perhaps the most important change is taking place in the world of advocacy itself. Here, the president's caricature of special interests perpetuates and masks another important shift. Obama's narrative is simplistic and ugly: Lobbying is all about some fat cat in an expensive suit handing out cash and cigars to lawmakers, while plying them with three-martini lunches in exchange for Bridges to Nowhere. This doesn't resemble the real world.

Today, lobbying, like government itself, is a large and complex enterprise. While the number of registered lobbyists in Washington doubled between 2000 and 2006 (from about 15,000 to 30,000), many believe that is just the tip of the iceberg. Political scientist James Thurber of American University believes the real number is three or four times larger.

In structure and tactics, the lobbying world looks a lot more like a well-organized political campaign than the classic individual "influence peddler." Its denizens are engaged in direct advocacy, but also in research, polling, message development, advertising, grassroots organizing, new media, and more.

Like many other aspects of politics—such as the proliferation of so-called 527 campaign finance organizations, following the "reforms" to ban soft money—lobbying has changed faster than the government's ability to regulate it.

Consider two lobbyists. The first arranges for 10 face-to-face visits with lawmakers to urge the defeat of a piece of legislation. He or she should register as a lobbyist. The second produces a media or grassroots campaign with exactly the same message, aimed at the same 10 lawmakers. He or she is not considered a lobbyist under the law. Only some modes of lobbying activity are regulated, and use of the new, unregulated lobbying tools is growing.

Many get around Obama's "Scarlet L" by giving their work another name. Former lawmakers and former senior administration officials offer high-priced advice, strategic information, and intelligence about how to affect public policy but call themselves "strategists" instead of using the "L" word—and don't register as lobbyists.

Consider "Business Forward," a group whose formation was announced last week. According to the *New York Times*, it will engage in "public advocacy" on behalf of President Obama's agenda, including health care and climate change, but will not "lobby" administration officials or members of Congress. It is, in effect, an organization of non-lobbyist lobbyists.

Finally, some government relations executives who previously registered as lobbyists are now "delisting"—causing a growing number of former interest group advocates to move out of the federal disclosure regime entirely. "Why should I take all the cheap shot criticism for being a 'lobbyist' when I spend most of my time doing other things, like managing my staff and giving advice to senior management about public policy?" an executive with a major corporation asked me.

Others see "deregistering" as a problematic trend. "One of the unintended effects of President Obama's anti-lobbyist reforms," Thurber told me, "is fewer advocates are registering and more are deregistering, thus creating less transparency in Washington."

So despite the president's political rhetoric and protestations, lobbying is entering a golden age, with much of the activity hidden from public view. Curtailing the size and reach of government—as Samuelson suggests—would be one way to curb it. The other would be to amend the Constitution to eliminate Americans' First Amendment right to petition the government for redress of grievances, for, given the Obama trajectory of government expansion, the list of grievances and of lobbyists out to remedy them will certainly grow.

*C*onsider the source and the audience.

- Andres is vice chairman of research at Dutko Worldwide, a lobbying firm. He also was a former legislative aide. What kind of perspective does this background give him on lobbying in general and the attempts to control lobbying specifically?

*L*ay out the arguments, the values, and the assumptions.

- What has led to the increase in lobbying since the 1970s?
- Why does Andres believe that lobbying will only increase during Obama's presidency?

*U*ncover the evidence.

- Andres cites statistics on the number of registered lobbyists but claims that the real number is actually much higher. How does he know?

*E*valuate the conclusion.

- Does Andres conclude that the increase in lobbying that he predicts will happen is a positive?
- Has Andres shown that the increase in lobbying is attributed to the Obama administration's policies, or could it simply be a result of a general increase in lobbying?

*S*ort out the political implications.

- What might be some consequences of the movement toward "'non-lobbyist' lobbyists"?

 ## 12.4 *Federalist* No. 10

James Madison, The Federalist Papers

Why We Chose This Piece

> *Of all the Federalist Papers, perhaps none has received as much scrutiny and discussion as Madison's* Federalist No. 10. *One simply cannot be a student of interest groups without understanding Madison's argument in this essay. Whereas supporters of pluralist democracy—a theory of representative democracy that holds that citizen membership in groups is the key to political power—argue that interest groups are an essential component of a republic, Madison claims that the formation of interest groups—or factions, as he calls them—can potentially threaten the very health of a society. In* Federalist No. 10, *Madison argues that the proposed new republic offers the perfect opportunity to control "the violence of faction" while, at the same time, not limiting individual freedoms. How does Madison's view of factions in 1787 compare with our view of interest groups today?*

Selection published: November 23, 1787

T

o the People of the State of New York:

Among the numerous advantages promised by a well constructed Union, none deserves to be more accurately developed than its tendency to break and control the violence of faction. The friend of popular governments never finds himself so much alarmed for their character and fate, as when he contemplates their propensity to this dangerous vice. He will not fail, therefore, to set a due value on any plan which, without violating the principles to which he is attached, provides a proper cure for it. The instability, injustice, and confusion introduced into the public councils, have, in truth, been the mortal diseases under which popular governments have everywhere perished; as they continue to be the favorite and fruitful topics from which the adversaries to liberty derive their most specious declamations. The valuable improvements made by the American constitutions on the popular models, both ancient and modern, cannot certainly be too much admired; but it would be an unwarrantable partiality, to contend that they have as effectually obviated the danger on this side, as was wished and expected. Complaints are everywhere heard from our most considerate and virtuous citizens, equally the friends of public and private faith, and of public and personal liberty, that our governments are too unstable, that the public good is disregarded in the conflicts of rival parties, and that measures are too often decided, not according to the rules of justice and the rights of the minor party, but by the superior force of an interested and overbearing majority. However anxiously we may wish that these complaints had no foundation, the evidence, of known facts will not permit us to deny that they are in some degree true. It will be found, indeed, on a candid review of our situation, that some of the distresses under which we labor have been erroneously charged on the operation of our governments; but it will be found, at the same time, that other causes will not alone account for many of our heaviest misfortunes; and, particularly, for that prevailing and increasing distrust of public engagements, and alarm for private rights, which are echoed from one end of the continent to the other. These must be chiefly, if not wholly, effects of the unsteadiness and injustice with which a factious spirit has tainted our public administrations.

By a faction, I understand a number of citizens, whether amounting to a majority or a minority of the whole, who are united and actuated by some common impulse of passion, or of interest, adversed to the rights of other citizens, or to the permanent and aggregate interests of the community.

There are two methods of curing the mischiefs of faction: the one, by removing its causes; the other, by controlling its effects.

There are again two methods of removing the causes of faction: the one, by destroying the liberty which is essential to its existence; the other, by giving to every citizen the same opinions, the same passions, and the same interests.

It could never be more truly said than of the first remedy, that it was worse than the disease. Liberty is to faction what air is to fire, an aliment without which it instantly expires. But it could not be less folly to abolish liberty, which is essential to political life, because it nourishes faction, than it would be to wish the annihilation of air, which is essential to animal life, because it imparts to fire its destructive agency.

The second expedient is as impracticable as the first would be unwise. As long as the reason of man continues fallible, and he is at liberty to exercise it, different opinions will be formed. As long as the connection subsists between his reason and his self-love, his opinions and his passions will have a reciprocal influence on each other; and the former will be objects to which the latter will attach themselves. The diversity in the faculties of men, from which the rights of property originate, is not less an insuperable obstacle to a uniformity of interests. The protection of these faculties is the first object of government. From the protection of different and unequal faculties of acquiring property, the possession of different degrees and kinds of property immediately results; and from the influence of these on the sentiments and views of the respective proprietors, ensues a division of the society into different interests and parties.

The latent causes of faction are thus sown in the nature of man; and we see them everywhere brought into different degrees of activity, according to the different circumstances of civil society. A zeal for different opinions concerning religion, concerning government, and many other points, as well of speculation as of practice; an attachment to different leaders ambitiously contending for preeminence and power; or to persons of other descriptions whose fortunes have been interesting to the human passions, have, in turn, divided mankind into parties, inflamed them with mutual animosity, and rendered them much more disposed to vex and oppress each other than to co-operate for their common good. So strong is this propensity of mankind to fall into mutual animosities, that where no substantial occasion presents itself, the most frivolous and fanciful distinctions have been sufficient to kindle their unfriendly passions and excite their most violent conflicts. But the most common and durable source of factions has been the various and unequal distribution of property. Those who hold and those who are without property have ever formed distinct interests in society. Those who are creditors, and those who are debtors, fall under a like discrimination. A landed interest, a manufacturing interest, a mercantile interest, a moneyed interest, with many lesser interests, grow up of necessity in civilized nations, and divide them into different classes, actuated by different sentiments and views. The regulation of these various and interfering interests forms the principal task of modern legislation, and involves the spirit of party and faction in the necessary and ordinary operations of the government.

No man is allowed to be a judge in his own cause, because his interest would certainly bias his judgment, and, not improbably, corrupt his integrity. With equal, nay with greater reason, a body of men are unfit to be both judges and parties at the same time; yet what are many of the most important acts of legislation, but so many judicial determinations, not indeed concerning the rights of single persons, but concerning the rights of large bodies of citizens? And what are the different classes of legislators but advocates and parties to the causes which they determine? Is a law proposed concerning private debts? It is a question to which the creditors are parties on one side and the debtors on the other. Justice ought to hold the balance between them. Yet the parties are, and must be, themselves the judges; and the most numerous party or, in other words, the most powerful faction must be expected to prevail. Shall domestic manufactures be encouraged, and in what degree, by restrictions on foreign manufactures? are questions which would be differently decided by the landed and the manufacturing classes, and probably by neither with a sole regard to justice and the public good. The apportionment of taxes on the various descriptions of property is an act which seems to require the most exact impartiality; yet there is, perhaps, no legislative act in which greater opportunity and temptation are given to a predominant party to trample on the rules of justice. Every shilling with which they overburden the inferior number, is a shilling saved to their own pockets.

It is in vain to say that enlightened statesmen will be able to adjust these clashing interests, and render them all subservient to the public good. Enlightened statesmen will not always be at the helm. Nor, in many cases, can such an adjustment be made at all without taking into view indirect and remote considerations, which will rarely prevail over the immediate interest which one party may find in disregarding the rights of another or the good of the whole.

The inference to which we are brought is, that the CAUSES of faction cannot be removed, and that relief is only to be sought in the means of controlling its EFFECTS.

If a faction consists of less than a majority, relief is supplied by the republican principle, which enables the majority to defeat its sinister views by regular vote. It may clog the administration, it may convulse the society; but it will be unable to execute and mask its violence under the forms of the Constitution. When a majority is included in a faction, the form of popular government, on the other hand, enables it to sacrifice to its ruling passion or interest both the public good and the rights of other citizens. To secure the public good and private rights against the danger of such a faction, and at the same time to preserve the spirit and the form of popular government, is then the great object to which our inquiries are directed. Let me add that it is the great desideratum by which this form of government can be rescued from the opprobrium under which it has so long labored, and be recommended to the esteem and adoption of mankind.

By what means is this object attainable? Evidently by one of two only. Either the existence of the same passion or interest in a majority at the same time must be prevented, or the majority, having such coexistent passion or interest, must be rendered, by their number and local situation, unable to concert and carry into effect schemes of oppression. If the impulse and the opportunity be suffered to coincide, we well know that neither moral nor religious motives can be relied on as an adequate control. They are not found to be such on the injustice and violence of individuals, and lose their efficacy in proportion to the number combined together, that is, in proportion as their efficacy becomes needful.

From this view of the subject it may be concluded that a pure democracy, by which I mean a society consisting of a small number of citizens, who assemble and administer the government in person, can admit of no cure for the mischiefs of faction. A common passion or interest will, in almost every case, be felt by a majority of the whole; a communication and concert result from the form of government itself; and there is nothing to check the inducements to sacrifice the weaker party or an obnoxious individual. Hence it is that such democracies have ever been spectacles of turbulence and contention; have ever been found incompatible with personal security or the rights of property; and have in general been as short in their lives as they have been violent in their deaths. Theoretic politicians, who have patronized this species of government, have erroneously supposed that by reducing mankind to a perfect equality in their political rights, they would, at the same time, be perfectly equalized and assimilated in their possessions, their opinions, and their passions.

A republic, by which I mean a government in which the scheme of representation takes place, opens a different prospect, and promises the cure for which we are seeking. Let us examine the points in which it varies from pure democracy, and we shall comprehend both the nature of the cure and the efficacy which it must derive from the Union.

The two great points of difference between a democracy and a republic are: first, the delegation of the government, in the latter, to a small number of citizens elected by the rest; secondly, the greater number of citizens, and greater sphere of country, over which the latter may be extended.

The effect of the first difference is, on the one hand, to refine and enlarge the public views, by passing them through the medium of a chosen body of citizens, whose wisdom may best discern the true interest of their country, and whose patriotism and love of justice will be least likely to sacrifice it to temporary or partial considerations. Under such a regulation, it may well happen that the public voice, pronounced by the representatives of the people, will be more consonant to the public good than if pronounced by the people themselves, convened for the purpose. On the other hand, the effect may be inverted. Men of factious tempers, of local prejudices, or of sinister designs, may, by intrigue, by corruption, or by other means, first obtain the suffrages, and then betray the interests, of the people. The question resulting is, whether small or extensive republics are more favorable to the election of proper guardians of the public weal; and it is clearly decided in favor of the latter by two obvious considerations:

In the first place, it is to be remarked that, however small the republic may be, the representatives must be raised to a certain number, in order to guard against the cabals of a few; and that, however large it may be, they must be limited to a certain number, in order to guard against the confusion of a multitude. Hence, the number of representatives in the two cases not being in proportion to that of the two constituents, and being proportionally greater in the small republic, it follows that, if the proportion of fit characters be not less in the large than in the small republic, the former will present a greater option, and consequently a greater probability of a fit choice.

In the next place, as each representative will be chosen by a greater number of citizens in the large than in the small republic, it will be more difficult for unworthy candidates to practice with success the vicious arts by which elections are too often carried; and the suffrages of the people being more free, will be more likely to centre in men who possess the most attractive merit and the most diffusive and established characters.

It must be confessed that in this, as in most other cases, there is a mean, on both sides of which inconveniences will be found to lie. By enlarging too much the number of electors, you render the representatives too little acquainted with all their local circumstances and lesser interests; as by reducing it too much, you render him unduly attached to these, and too little fit to comprehend and pursue great and national objects. The federal Constitution forms a happy combination in this respect; the great and aggregate interests being referred to the national, the local and particular to the State legislatures.

The other point of difference is, the greater number of citizens and extent of territory which may be brought within the compass of republican than of democratic government; and it is this circumstance principally which renders factious combinations less to be dreaded in the former than in the latter. The smaller the society, the fewer probably will be the distinct parties and interests composing it; the fewer the distinct parties and interests, the more frequently will a majority be found of the same party; and the smaller the number of individuals composing a majority, and the smaller the compass within which they are placed, the more easily will they concert and execute their plans of oppression. Extend the sphere, and you take in a greater variety of parties and interests; you make it less probable that a majority of the whole will have a common motive to invade the rights of other citizens; or if such a common motive exists, it will be more difficult for all who feel it to discover their own strength, and to act in unison with each other. Besides other impediments, it may be remarked that, where there is a consciousness of unjust or dishonorable purposes, communication is always checked by distrust in proportion to the number whose concurrence is necessary.

Hence, it clearly appears, that the same advantage which a republic has over a democracy, in controlling the effects of faction, is enjoyed by a large over a small republic,—is enjoyed by the Union over the States composing it. Does the advantage consist in the substitution of representatives whose enlightened views and virtuous sentiments render them superior to local prejudices and schemes of injustice? It will not be denied that the representation of the Union will be most likely to possess these requisite endowments. Does it consist in the greater security afforded by a greater variety of parties, against the event of any one party being able to outnumber and oppress the rest? In an equal degree does the increased variety of parties comprised within the Union, increase this security? Does it, in fine, consist in the greater obstacles opposed to the concert and accomplishment of the secret wishes of an unjust and interested majority? Here, again, the extent of the Union gives it the most palpable advantage.

The influence of factious leaders may kindle a flame within their particular States, but will be unable to spread a general conflagration through the other States. A religious sect may degenerate into a political faction in a part of the Confederacy; but the variety of sects dispersed over the entire face of it must secure the national councils against any danger from that source. A rage for paper money, for an abolition of debts, for an equal division of property, or for any other improper or wicked project, will be less apt to pervade the whole body of the Union than a particular member of it; in the same proportion as such a malady is more likely to taint a particular county or district, than an entire State.

In the extent and proper structure of the Union, therefore, we behold a republican remedy for the diseases most incident to republican government. And according to the degree of pleasure and pride we feel in being republicans, ought to be our zeal in cherishing the spirit and supporting the character of Federalists.

PUBLIUS.

*C*onsider the source and the audience.

- *Federalist* No. 10 was an editorial, written anonymously under the name "Publius," in an effort to get the citizens of New York to sign on to the Constitution. *Federalist* No. 10 was especially aimed at people who feared the possibilities for corruption in a large country. How does that fact affect how Madison couches his arguments about factions?

*L*ay out the argument, the values, and the assumptions.

- What does Madison believe are the root causes of factions?
- Why does he think factions are problematic?
- Does he want to control the causes of factions or the effects of them—and why? What's the difference? Why does he think the root causes of factions cannot be controlled, but the effects of factions can?
- How, in Madison's view, will the new republic contain the dangers of factions? What is the key role that its size will play?

*U*ncover the evidence.

- Does Madison provide any evidence to support his arguments, or are they all theory driven? Is there any type of evidence he could have added to make his argument more persuasive?

*E*valuate the conclusion.

- Hindsight is 20/20. Historical works allow us to go back and ask, "Was the author right?" Was he? Has the Constitution limited the power of factions?
- Even if Madison was right—specifically, in saying that the Constitution would control the effects of factions—was his premise correct? Are factions bad? What good, if any, can come from them?

*S*ort out the political implications.

- Conditions have changed since Madison's day. With phones, e-mails, and fax machines, we can now get in touch with someone on the other side of the country in seconds. The land-mass of the United States is significantly larger than when Madison was writing; yet, in a sense, the country is much smaller today. Does the shrinking of America negate the force of Madison's argument about the containment of the ill effects of factions?
- What would Madison say if he could come back today? Would he think his expectations in *Federalist* No. 10 had been borne out? Would he be pleased or displeased? Why?

13

Voting and Elections

Elections are at the very heart of a representative democracy, based on the principle that the public interest is best served by many individuals each choosing those leaders they feel will make decisions in their particular interests. Politics is about power, after all. It's about winners and losers, and nowhere is this more evident than in elections in the United States. Parties, interest groups, individuals, and candidates throw hundreds of millions of dollars into campaigns for one reason: so that their team (or at least their candidate) will win and their interests will be served.

Because winning is what really counts in electoral politics, campaigns have become more expensive, more negative, and more long-lived. Political consulting has become a lucrative business. Today's candidates have not only policy advisors but also campaign strategists, pollsters, opposition researchers, and speechwriters all working to put, and keep, them in office.

Even with the rise of candidate-centered elections, we still measure who wins and who loses based on how well the two major parties do. The importance of winning means that parties must have a strategy. There may be small policy differences among party members, but the party needs a message. It must make clear what it stands for and what it will do if it wins. The party that has the more effective, persuasive message typically will set the agenda for the next few years.

All campaign strategy is created with voters in mind. Who votes? Who doesn't? How will the candidate do among women voters? African Americans? The poor? The educated? The first major theory of voting developed in the 1940s argued that campaigns don't matter because we simply vote with the groups with which we identify. If we are wealthy, we vote Republican. If we come from a blue-collar family, we vote Democratic. If we are Protestant, we vote Republican. If we are Jewish, we vote Democratic. Although more recently many political scientists have criticized this theory of voting, campaigns still devise their strategies as if it were valid. During the next election, pay attention. You will surely hear pundits make such comments as "Candidate X must win at least 60 percent of the white vote to be successful" or "Candidate Y is really struggling with women. If he can't improve women's perceptions of him, he will lose." Candidates keep altering their strategies to make themselves more appealing to certain groups that are essential for them to win. They can't rest on their laurels; they must continually try to expand that winning electoral coalition.

Obviously campaign strategy depends on who the voters are. But just as important may be who the voters aren't, and unfortunately most of us aren't voters. The United States prides itself on being the model democracy, the one that others should look to as an example. But in this model democracy, only about half of all eligible voters will cast their ballots in a presidential election. This percentage is even worse when we look at midterm elections, where voter turnout hovers around 35 percent, or primaries and caucuses, where turnout is even lower. In 1996, 915 people came to Wyoming's Republican caucus meeting! And in contrast to the Olympic medal count, in which the United States prides itself on finishing toward the top, few people seem to care that we consistently rank near the very bottom of the list regarding voter turnout in industrialized countries.

In this chapter we look at some recent controversies and debates that have surrounded elections in the United States. First, Nate Silver presents what he considers to be the "real" reason why Barack Obama won the 2008 presidential election. Next, we examine an editorial, by Patrick McIlheran, criticizing the most recent attempt to reform the Electoral College. The third article, written by Norman Ornstein for *Roll Call*, argues in favor of voter identification laws, if certain provisions are included, to help reduce voter fraud. However, Ornstein contends that absentee voting is the real concern regarding voter fraud. We conclude with the concession speech by one of the most famous electoral losers of the past few years—former vice president Al Gore, who shows how elections promote stability when all agree on the rules of the game, even when they dislike the outcome.

 ## 13.1 How Obama Really Won the Election

Nate Silver, Esquire

Why We Chose This Piece

By now you have no doubt heard numerous explanations for Barack Obama's victory in the 2008 presidential election, whether it was chalked up to an unpopular sitting president from the other party, to a weakened economy, to Obama's money and organization advantages, to his appeal to young voters, or to some combination of these factors. Here, Nate Silver, a statistician who also coauthored Reading 6.4, on Congress, offers a different account for why Obama won. We chose this article in part because it presents a different spin on the reason behind Obama's victory, but also because Silver's argument is about more than just an electoral victory. He is documenting a trend that he believes will affect not just American politics in the future but also the American way of life in general.

Silver is an interesting person to meet because he is not necessarily the kind of author one typically encounters in a book such as this one. He is best known for inventing a system

Selection published: January 14, 2009

for predicting the career development of baseball players, which he then extended to elec-tion forecasting. His web site FiveThirtyEight.com was required reading for many election prognosticators during 2008. How might understanding baseball statistics be helpful in predicting presidential elections?

I f Bill Clinton was the first black president, then Barack Obama might be the first urban one. He is the only American president in recent history to seem unembar-rassed about claiming a personal residence in a major American city. Instead, presidents have tended to hail from homes called ranches or groves or manors or plan-tations, in places called Kennebunkport or Santa Barbara or Oyster Bay or Northamp-ton. There were times, certainly, during the course of the presidential campaign when Barack Obama seemed less than proud of his Chicago heritage. Indeed, Obama treated Chicago as little more than a bedroom community during parts of his presidential bid, choosing to launch his campaign downstate in Springfield instead, and not holding a major public rally in the city until his climactic event in Grant Park on November 4. As John McCain's commercials yapped about the "corrupt Chicago political machine," Obama seemed as though he was worried about bumping into Bill Ayers at Manny's Deli or Tony Rezko at the Frontera Grill. As Rudy Giuliani—the former mayor of the hamlet called New York City—tried to portray Obama as an out-of-touch elitist, Obama seemed to strain to avoid the caricature.

Like many incoming presidents, Barack Obama was elected partly in reaction to the failures of the previous one, a president who was dogmatic, insecure, white-bread, and—at least ostensibly—rural. By contrast, Obama is unmistakably urban: prag-matic, superior, hip, stubborn, multicultural. But Obama's election may also represent something more—if not a sign that America's psyche has changed then at least that its demographics are on the move. We may still romanticize some of the more familiar, rurally oriented narratives of presidents past: the Ronald Reagan frontiersman carica-ture (which both Sarah Palin and John McCain tried to co-opt at various times) or the Bill Clinton born-in-a-small-town shtick (see also: Edwards, John; Huckabee, Mike). Fewer and fewer of us, however, have actually lived those experiences. In 1992, when Bill Clinton won his first term, 35 percent of American voters were identified as rural according to that year's national exit polls, and 24 percent as urban. This year, how-ever, the percentage of rural voters has dropped to 21 percent, while that of urban voters has climbed to 30. The suburbs, meanwhile, have been booming: 41 percent of America's electorate in 1992, they represent 49 percent now. . . .

In other words, if you are going to pit big cities against small towns, it is probably a mistake to end up on the rural side of the ledger. Last year, Obama accumulated a margin of victory of approximately 10.5 million votes in urban areas. . . far bettering John Kerry's 3.6 million. Obama improved his performance not only among black and Latino voters but also among urban whites, with whom he performed 9 points better than Kerry. Obama also won each of the seventeen most densely populated states, a list that includes such nontraditional battlegrounds as Virginia, North Carolina, and Indiana. (One hidden advantage of urban areas: They're easier to canvass to get the vote out.) By contrast, for all their bluster about small towns, John McCain and Sarah Palin beat Obama by just 2.4 million votes in rural areas, actually a bit worse than the 4.3-million-vote margin that Bush racked up in 2004.

With the votes that he banked in the cities, Obama did not really need to prevail in the suburbs. But he did anyway—as every winning presidential candidate has done since 1980—bettering McCain by 2 points there. Indeed, among the many mistakes the McCain campaign made was targeting the rural vote rather than the suburban one, as Bush and Karl Rove did in 2000 and 2004.

It may also be that suburban voters are starting to look—and behave—more like their urban brethren. According to a poll by the National Center for Suburban Studies, 20 percent of suburban voters are nonwhite—not much behind the national average of 27 percent—and 44 percent live in a racially mixed neighborhood (versus a national average of 46 percent). Suburban voters are just as likely to be concerned about the economy as other voters are and just as likely to know someone who has lost a job. Moreover, many suburbanites who do not live in cities may nevertheless be thoroughly familiar with them; according to the Census Bureau, at least eight to nine million persons commute into urban areas each day. As a result, urban bashing isn't what it once was at the height of white flight and the Reagan revolution. Whereas in 1980, according to the biannual General Social Survey conducted by the University of Chicago, 24.4 percent of Americans thought that the government was spending too much money to solve the problems of big cities, nowadays that number is down to 12.8 percent. The suburbs are immune to neither urban America's problems nor its promise.

Barack Obama, the former community organizer, may be the first president in a generation to actively seed urban renewal. His proposals include creating an Office of Urban Policy, restoring the Bush cuts to the Community Development Block Grant program, financing so-called regional-innovation clusters to link smaller cities together, and establishing twenty "Promise Neighborhoods"—essentially, oases of social services—in inner cities. Closer to home, he has already started to pitch Chicago as the prospective home of the 2016 Olympic Games, a potentially climactic event that—if all goes well—could give a bounce in the polls to his Democratic successor in the midst of an election year.

We have, of course, started to get a little ahead of ourselves. But the future of America is an urban one—among the twenty largest metropolitan areas in 2000, nineteen had added population by 2007, a trend likely to sustain itself as rising gas prices place more pressure on exurban commuters. Republicans trail Democrats among essentially every fast-growing demographic except the elderly—the youth vote, the Latino vote; they never had the black vote. It is long past time that they hone their pitch to urban voters, and find their shining city upon a hill.

*C*onsider the source and the audience.

- *Esquire* is a magazine that historically has focused on men's fashion. Why would Silver's argument appeal to its readers?

*L*ay out the argument, the values, and the assumptions.

- According to Silver, why did Obama win the election? What had changed from previous presidential elections?
- Silver implies that the trend he is documenting is much bigger than simply the result of a presidential election. How so?

U*ncover the evidence.*

- Silver has spent his career analyzing various kinds of data. What data does Silver use here? Is it enough to make his case?
- Many factors can explain why a person won a presidential election. How can we be sure that other factors weren't at play as well?

E*valuate the conclusion.*

- The title of the article implies that there are other explanations for Obama's victory, some of which were mentioned in the introduction to this reading, but that they are incorrect. In other words, they are not the *real* reason Obama won. Are those explanations necessarily incompatible with Silver's argument?

S*ort out the political implications.*

- If Silver is correct, what might be the implications for the future of the Democratic and Republican Parties? How might this affect the 2012 presidential election?

13.2 Electoral College: Keep It or Dump It?

Patrick McIlheran, Milwaukee Journal Sentinel

Why We Chose This Piece

Perhaps no aspect of the U.S. Constitution is more controversial than the Electoral College. As a result, no analysis of American presidential elections is complete without a discussion of the pros and cons of such a system. This particular article critiques a proposal, by an organization named FairVote, that would fundamentally alter the Electoral College without abolishing it. To understand this article, you need to know how the Electoral College works. If you don't know already, you can find a description of the Electoral College in any introductory American Government textbook or online.

The Electoral College is difficult to do away with, because it would require an amendment to the Constitution. The FairVote proposal would essentially undo some unattractive features of the Electoral College without abolishing it. Because the state legislatures and not the federal government determine how each state's electors are selected, FairVote created a plan by which states would agree to cast their electoral votes for the national popular vote winner, not the popular vote winner in the states. So, for example, if Florida's state legislature had adopted FairVote's proposal, the state's twenty-five electoral votes would have gone to Al Gore in 2000, since he won the national popular vote, even though George W. Bush was declared to have won the state. Consequently, Gore would have then

---

Selection published: June 16, 2006

won the election. If enough heavily populated states agreed to enact FairVote's proposal, then the popular vote winner would always win the election.

Here, Patrick McIlheran criticizes FairVote's plan, calling it a "New Coke moment" (after the ill-fated effort to change a soft drink that most consumers thought was fine the way it was). When McIlheran wrote the article, FairVote's plan had just been introduced. Since that time, the plan has been signed in to law in five states. As you read the article, ask yourself whether you would be happy if your state adopted the proposal.

I f you ponder it long enough, you suspect the Electoral College got invented in a bar.

You see Madison and Hamilton already half in the bag and some Philadelphia inn-keeper wishing they'd call it a night.

"Really," says Madison, swaying. "It's state-by-state, and make sure to say legislatures will 'chuse' the electors."

Hamilton can't get the quill to work, so they rewrite from memory the next day. Still, it seems to have worked out.

Clanking and jerking, with rebuilt plumbing to keep the loser from getting to be veep, this social studies trick question nonetheless has given us functional presidents most of the time.

We ought to hesitate before blowing up the Electoral College, ungainly though it is.

There are people who want to do this. The latest is FairVote. It wants to nullify the system by getting electors to follow the national result rather than their state's. Say Hillary Clinton wins Wisconsin, but Condoleezza Rice scores down South and takes 51% nationally. Wisconsin's 11 electors would ignore Wisconsin's voters and go with Rice.

Whether this is destroying democracy in order to save it is worth a debate in itself. So is the end-run way it evades having to amend the Constitution. Advocates say the cause is so just it trumps such worries.

What so vexes them about the Electoral College? They have three main complaints.

First, they say, the winner-take-all nature of most states' electoral votes makes some states contestable prizes—battleground states, showered with attention. Most others, comfortably in one camp or the other, are ignored.

But critics never say how this is the fault of the Electoral College, other than to admit Democrats have written off any place without a Whole Foods while Republicans skip those without a Wal-Mart.

In fact, while this started with California feeling ignored, critics note most small states aren't battlegrounds, either. This suggests electoral votes themselves aren't the issue.

What unites the ignored states is that they're already convinced. States become battlegrounds by being fickle. The reason President Bush and John Kerry met every cow in Wisconsin in 2004 was because we toyed with their affections.

There are cures, aside from California going GOP once in a while. The Constitution doesn't specify a state's electors must move in a clump. Maine and Nebraska divvy theirs by congressional district.

If California wants some love, it can do as Nebraska. Bush won in 22 of California's 53 congressional districts; had he a shot at getting their electors, of course he'd have shown up.

Dumping the Electoral College will still leave people on the sidelines. It just won't be by state. Blacks still will be taken for granted by Democrats as long as they vote in a bloc. And Air Force One won't land in La Crosse or anywhere else within 10 miles of a hayfield. You can slug it out in small towns when only 10 states are in play. When it's national, coastal soccer moms eclipse the entire Midwest.

The critics also complain the system is undemocratic: It overrepresents small states. California, with 55 votes, is slighted because Wyoming, with three, really merits only two-thirds of a vote.

Yet 55 nonetheless outweighs three by a lot, while both states are equal in the Senate. Will we rip that up next? We're a union of states, not one big centralized country, after all.

Besides, democracy's great, but it's not first among our founding principles. Our Constitution's all about limiting government, not about saying, "The majority rules, so we get to abridge your freedom of speech." If the Electoral College hinders a majority's absolute sway, that was the founders' point.

The third claim is the supposed danger of the electoral vote contradicting the popular vote. This has happened four times, all but once more than a century ago. While 2000 was galling to lefties, there's no sign we're on a streak. If anything, the hazard is sloppy voting procedure.

There's danger in an election result that seems to break the rules. But the Electoral College doesn't do that, unless you never noticed those red and blue maps with numbers on each state. The system's arcane, but it is tested and the results follow known rules.

The bigger risk lies in tossing those out. We don't know what happens to our politics if we dump the odd system that nonetheless has produced an unusually free and enduring nation.

Maybe it'll work, though it's a disquieting sign when a scheme lists former congressman and failed kook candidate John Anderson and *The New York Times* Editorial Page among its leading advocates.

My main worry, however, is that this seems like curing a headache with a brain transplant. Before a New Coke moment leads us to toss out something that's strange but functional, we need evidence that it's the thing that's broken.

*C*onsider the source and the audience.

- Patrick McIlheran is an editorial writer for the *Milwaukee Journal Sentinel*, and this piece is his opinion. As an editorial writer, does he have any obligation to give a hearing to opinions other than his own?
- How might McIlheran's political views shape his perception of the Electoral College?
- The *Milwaukee Journal Sentinel* is Wisconsin's largest paper. Why might people in Wisconsin have different views about the pros and cons of the Electoral College than, say, people in California or Wyoming?

*L*ay out the argument, the values, and the assumptions.

- What reasons does McIlheran give for retaining the Electoral College as is?
- How does McIlheran think that the Electoral College might be tweaked to meet some of the objections of its critics?

*U*ncover the evidence.

- How does McIlheran refute the arguments made by people opposed to the Electoral College?
- One concern about changing institutions such as the Electoral College is that we can't be sure of the benefits or consequences of the change until after the fact. Is that the case here? Can either side provide conclusive evidence that its view is best?

*E*valuate the conclusion.

- Has McIlheran successfully made the claim that the Electoral College isn't "broken?" Do you need to accept his political views to accept his conclusion?

*S*ort out the political implications.

- If FairVote's proposal is passed in enough states (each state has to decide whether to pass the proposal), how will that change the way presidential candidates campaign? Which states will benefit the most? The least?
- If the proposal is enacted and it guarantees that the candidate who wins the national popular vote also wins the election, will that quell the controversy over the Electoral College or will it create new problems?

13.3 There's Value in Voter ID Requirement—If It's Done Properly

Norman Ornstein, Roll Call

Why We Chose This Piece

In any democracy, citizens should be concerned both that all eligible voters have equal access to the voting booth and that no one besides those eligible voters can gain access to the polls. However, not everyone is convinced that American elections meet those criteria. Some people, usually Republicans, worry that ineligible voters might be affecting election outcomes and have pushed states, including Georgia and Indiana, to pass laws requiring people to show some sort of identification, such as a driver's license, to vote. Such legislation infuriates many Democrats, who argue that photo identification simply leads to more suppression of minorities and those with less income, groups likely to vote Democratic. In

---

Selection published: May 7, 2008

short, the issue of voter ID has become one of the most contentious debates regarding election law in the past several years.

In this article, Norman Ornstein argues in favor of voter identification as long as certain provisions are included. We like this article because it provides a nice overview of the debate and highlights other aspects of the electoral system that may be more prone to fraud than in-person voting. Why would something that seemingly everyone would support—eliminating election fraud—be so controversial?

One of the most interesting and significant recent Supreme Court decisions concerned the Indiana voter identification law, in which the court by a 6–3 vote upheld the law despite zero evidence of in-person voting fraud in the state. In a major surprise, Justice John Paul Stevens led the opinion, saying the state's interest in preventing such fraud justifies the Legislature's action. Stevens did leave the door open to challenges to other states' laws if they create too much of a burden on many voters.

Indiana's law was better by far than the awful Georgia law that was overturned by the courts; in Indiana, the state would provide voters with the appropriate government-issue photo ID for free, while Georgia charged a significant fee, the equivalent of a poll tax. But Indiana's requirements are plenty burdensome.

Elections need to be fair, and fraud is a real concern, especially in an era where the stakes are very high and the parties are close enough that many elections will be decided by razor-thin margins.

If a person cannot present a passport, driver's license or other similar form of official identification, he or she must supply an official document, such as a birth certificate, to get the free ID, and getting a copy of a birth certificate is quite costly. The fact is that many elderly people and many poor people don't drive, don't fly and don't have copies of their birth certificates.

The voter ID issue has divided sharply on partisan lines. Republicans have pushed hard for photo requirements in many states, and Democrats have resisted. Republicans have been passionate about the cancer of voter fraud, and Democrats have brushed that issue aside while being equally passionate about expanding voter access. The decision is not going to open the floodgates to dozens of onerous statutes, but it does create running room for more controversy in this area, and it leaves an opening for Congress to think through and perhaps act in a way that will bring some balance and uniformity on this issue for voters in federal elections.

Is there voter fraud? Yes, there is—but it is not the kind done in person on Election Day. The real voter fraud for which we have evidence is in voting by mail. We know, for example, what happened in one of the incredibly rare cases where an election result was actually overturned—in the 1997 Miami mayoral race, when courts threw out 5,000 absentee ballots, removed presumed winner Xavier Suarez and replaced him with his opponent, Joe Carollo. Thirty-six people were charged with absentee ballot vote fraud (most working for the Suarez campaign, but a couple on the Carollo side as well).

A part of the problem was the peculiarity of Florida law that made it easy to forge absentee ballot results, but there were and are larger problems with voting by mail. There is no zone of privacy like the one that comes with going into a voting booth and closing a curtain to all, including one's spouse, boss or pastor. There is a great temptation to coerce or sweet-talk older or slower voters into letting campaign workers "help" them fill out their ballots. And when the ballots are filled out and mailed in, sometimes several weeks before the election itself, they can sit unguarded in a municipal building or voting official's office, with the potential for partisans inside or outside the office to jettison some or skew others.

As for in-person polling place voter fraud, it was widespread at the turn of the 20th century (which led to such path-breaking reforms as the Australian ballot and the norm of the secret ballot), and it certainly took place in sizable amounts a few decades ago. But there is no credible evidence that it is a serious problem now.

I do not have any Pollyannish notion that most people in politics are good and fair—lots of 'em on both sides would steal an election in a New York minute if they could. But frankly, engaging in systematic in-person voting fraud is way too much effort for way too little payoff. To be sure, there are occasional instances of either sloppiness or chicanery in voter registration drives, and individual instances of wrongdoing. But every allegation of big-time fraud ends up being shot down by the evidence.

Elections need to be fair, and fraud is a real concern, especially in an era where the stakes are very high and the parties are close enough that many elections will be decided by razor-thin margins. But I would have more confidence in the concerns that legislators in states like Indiana and Georgia raise if they were equally passionate about fraud in voting by mail. But for the most part—with exceptions such as the *Wall Street Journal*'s John Fund—the same people who scream from the rafters about rampant in-person fraud say nothing at all about the other kind (could it be that more of "their" voters vote absentee?).

In many states, the safeguard against forged absentee ballots is a signature match. It is done with considerable sophistication these days. If a simple signature match—one in which the initial signature does not have to be accompanied by any official government-sponsored photo ID—suffices for votes-by-mail, why is it not enough for votes at the polling place?

This is not just an issue of motive and fairness. The fact is that no-excuses absentee voting and voting by mail are expanding rapidly out there, and may be as much as 30 percent or more of all the votes cast in November. If the trends continue, they may soon be the norm. At that point, fraud will be a huge concern.

In the meantime, we will have to deal with the larger questions posed by voter ID laws. I do not think, in principle, that requiring a photo ID is evil or onerous. An official photo ID can protect voters against charges that they are ineligible to vote. I agree with civil rights activist Andrew Young that a photo ID would be a huge help to poor people who are often victimized by huge fees they are charged to cash paychecks because they lack any such identification.

But there are certain clear principles that need to be applied. Any such ID has to be offered for free—including no-cost access to whatever support documents are required. In a free society, no one should have to pay to vote, and there should not be any unequal burden on those citizens who want to vote. Not only should the ID be free, but it must be readily accessible—in multiple places convenient to the poor and elderly, and through mobile vans to reach those who can't get out easily to the fixed sites.

With these conditions, a voter ID is not an undue burden. But to get to that point requires two things: federal guidelines for the states, under Congress' constitutional power to regulate federal elections, and federal money to make the system work for all. This issue is significant and controversial enough that it ought to be on Congress' agenda this year. But Congress' track record on election reform this year suggests that the chance of that happening is zero.

*C*onsider the source and the audience.

- Ornstein is a resident scholar at the American Enterprise Institute, a think tank—an organization that conducts research on policy—that is generally considered to be right of center. Does this fact lead you to have any preconceived notions about what Ornstein's position might be? Was his actual position consistent with your expectations?
- *Roll Call* is a newspaper that covers the U.S. Congress almost exclusively. Why would its readers be interested in an op-ed on voter identification?

*L*ay out the argument, the values, and the assumptions.

- Why does Ornstein believe there is some value in voter identification? What conditions need to be applied to a voter identification law?
- According to Ornstein, what kind of voting is most responsible for voter fraud?
- How could Ornstein's position be seen as a middle ground between those of liberals and conservatives?

*U*ncover the evidence.

- What evidence does Ornstein provide that voter fraud—in person or otherwise—is a problem?

*E*valuate the conclusion.

- After reading this article, how convinced are you that voter fraud is a problem? If it is a problem, how convinced are you that photo identification is the solution?
- Are Ornstein's ideas likely to appease either liberals or conservatives? Why or why not?

*S*ort out the political implications.

- How, if at all, would requiring voter identification change elections? Why do Democrats generally oppose such reforms and Republicans support them? Is either side right?
- What nonpartisan reforms, if any, could safeguard the electoral process without advantaging or disadvantaging any particular group?

13.4 Concession Speech

Al Gore

Why We Chose This Piece

Elections serve lots of purposes in democratic society: They give people a voice in their government, they lend legitimacy to leadership change, they offer an alternative to fighting in the streets when people disagree. Another function of elections is to provide political stability. The 2000 presidential election was unusual on several counts. A state's election results were contested, amid accusations of fraud and misleading ballot design; that state's supreme court was overruled by the U.S. Supreme Court in the matter of recounts; and the results of that contested state election gave an Electoral College victory to a candidate who had lost the popular vote. To top it off, the governor of the state in question was the brother of the candidate who was eventually declared the winner. In many societies, such a series of events could have led to rioting, violence, or revolution. But in the United States, where there is commitment to the Constitution and to the idea of procedural justice (that is, if the rules are fair, then the results will be fair), the outcome, though distressing to many, was accepted by most.

Among the disappointed was Vice President Al Gore, who believed that he would have won the election in Florida if all the votes had been counted, and who knew that he had won the popular vote in any case. The night of the election, he had called George W. Bush to concede, only to be told afterward that the networks had erred in projecting Bush the winner in Florida, and that this state was still in play. He called Bush back and retracted his concession. Over a month later, he finally phoned Bush again.

We chose to include this speech because it highlights how elections, even as odd as this one, serve to legitimate government when people agree on the rules. How did the country manage to go on after this event—as if nothing, really, had happened—with a majority of voters, including some of those who had voted for Gore, giving Bush high approval ratings as he came into office?

Good evening.

Just moments ago, I spoke with George W. Bush and congratulated him on becoming the 43rd president of the United States, and I promised him that I wouldn't call him back this time.

I offered to meet with him as soon as possible so that we can start to heal the divisions of the campaign and the contest through which we just passed.

Selection delivered: December 13, 2000

Almost a century and a half ago, Senator Stephen Douglas told Abraham Lincoln, who had just defeated him for the presidency, "Partisan feeling must yield to patriotism. I'm with you, Mr. President, and God bless you."

Well, in that same spirit, I say to President-elect Bush that what remains of partisan rancor must now be put aside, and may God bless his stewardship of this country.

Neither he nor I anticipated this long and difficult road. Certainly neither of us wanted it to happen. Yet it came, and now it has ended, resolved, as it must be resolved, through the honored institutions of our democracy.

Over the library of one of our great law schools is inscribed the motto, "Not under man but under God and law." That's the ruling principle of American freedom, the source of our democratic liberties. I've tried to make it my guide throughout this contest as it has guided America's deliberations of all the complex issues of the past five weeks.

Now the U.S. Supreme Court has spoken. Let there be no doubt, while I strongly disagree with the court's decision, I accept it. I accept the finality of this outcome which will be ratified next Monday in the Electoral College. And tonight, for the sake of our unity of the people and the strength of our democracy, I offer my concession.

I also accept my responsibility, which I will discharge unconditionally, to honor the new president elect and do everything possible to help him bring Americans together in fulfillment of the great vision that our Declaration of Independence defines and that our Constitution affirms and defends.

Let me say how grateful I am to all those who supported me and supported the cause for which we have fought. Tipper and I feel a deep gratitude to Joe and Hadassah Lieberman who brought passion and high purpose to our partnership and opened new doors, not just for our campaign but for our country.

This has been an extraordinary election. But in one of God's unforeseen paths, this belatedly broken impasse can point us all to a new common ground, for its very closeness can serve to remind us that we are one people with a shared history and a shared destiny.

Indeed, that history gives us many examples of contests as hotly debated, as fiercely fought, with their own challenges to the popular will.

Other disputes have dragged on for weeks before reaching resolution. And each time, both the victor and the vanquished have accepted the result peacefully and in the spirit of reconciliation.

So let it be with us.

I know that many of my supporters are disappointed.

I am too. But our disappointment must be overcome by our love of country.

And I say to our fellow members of the world community, let no one see this contest as a sign of American weakness. The strength of American democracy is shown most clearly through the difficulties it can overcome.

Some have expressed concern that the unusual nature of this election might hamper the next president in the conduct of his office. I do not believe it need be so.

President-elect Bush inherits a nation whose citizens will be ready to assist him in the conduct of his large responsibilities.

I personally will be at his disposal, and I call on all Americans—I particularly urge all who stood with us to unite behind our next president. This is America. Just as we fight hard when the stakes are high, we close ranks and come together when the contest is done.

And while there will be time enough to debate our continuing differences, now is the time to recognize that that which unites us is greater than that which divides us.

While we yet hold and do not yield our opposing beliefs, there is a higher duty than the one we owe to political party. This is America and we put country before party. We will stand together behind our new president.

As for what I'll do next, I don't know the answer to that one yet. Like many of you, I'm looking forward to spending the holidays with family and old friends. I know I'll spend time in Tennessee and mend some fences, literally and figuratively.

Some have asked whether I have any regrets and I do have one regret: that I didn't get the chance to stay and fight for the American people over the next four years, especially for those who need burdens lifted and barriers removed, especially for those who feel their voices have not been heard. I heard you and I will not forget.

I've seen America in this campaign and I like what I see. It's worth fighting for and that's a fight I'll never stop.

As for the battle that ends tonight, I do believe as my father once said, that no matter how hard the loss, defeat might serve as well as victory to shape the soul and let the glory out.

So for me this campaign ends as it began: with the love of Tipper and our family; with faith in God and in the country I have been so proud to serve, from Vietnam to the vice presidency; and with gratitude to our truly tireless campaign staff and volunteers, including all those who worked so hard in Florida for the last 36 days.

Now the political struggle is over and we turn again to the unending struggle for the common good of all Americans and for those multitudes around the world who look to us for leadership in the cause of freedom.

In the words of our great hymn, "America, America": "Let us crown thy good with brotherhood, from sea to shining sea."

And now, my friends, in a phrase I once addressed to others, it's time for me to go.

Thank you and good night, and God bless America.

Consider the source and the audience.

- Gore is speaking to several audiences here. Who are they? Why does he address "our fellow members of the world community"?
- At the time, Gore was certainly considering a run for the presidency in the future. How might that have shaped his message?
- How could he have used this speech to rally supporters if he had wanted to?

Lay out the argument, the values, and the assumptions.

- What personal values of Gore's become apparent in this speech? How do they affect his political views?
- What is Gore's view of the common good here? How does that differ from partisan advantage, and when should the former take precedence over the latter?

- When should a political outcome be accepted even when one doesn't like it? How do the "honored institutions of our democracy" help to resolve contests like this? In what context does Gore refer to the Supreme Court and the Electoral College?

*U*ncover the evidence.

- What kinds of evidence does Gore use to support his argument that the result of the election process should be accepted even if one doesn't agree with it, and that George W. Bush is the legitimate president of the United States?

*E*valuate the conclusion.

- Did Gore's use of symbolism and references to history, law, and religion convince supporters to accept the election result?
- Did they convince the world that the United States was a stable and solid nation?
- Did they convince the nation to put the trauma of the partisan backbiting behind it and move on?

*S*ort out the political implications.

- Many electoral reforms were debated following the election, but few were enacted. Who would have resisted reform, and why?

★ 14 ★

The Media

Of all the things that have changed in the United States since the country's founding, it is perhaps the media that have changed the most. Where once we got our news, often months old, from weekly papers and in Sunday sermons, we can now access worldwide news in real time on devices we carry in our pockets. We have truly experienced a revolution in communication in the last one hundred years.

In a democratic society, access to accurate, timely news is essential so that we can make informed decisions at the voting booth but also so that we can keep tabs on what government does, and keep our representatives honest. Free speech and press freedom were some of the key values preserved by the framers, who knew that a stifled press could not work to protect any of our other liberties.

The threat to press freedom that the authors of the Constitution were concerned about was the government, and they had reason to be concerned. During colonial times, printers had to get government approval for the work they turned out. Even after independence, the newspaper business was often subsidized by politicians in exchange for favorable coverage. It was not until mass circulation papers acquired some measure of financial independence that journalistic objectivity and detachment from political patronage became economically feasible and in fact commercially savvy. The effort to appeal to a broad audience was enhanced if a paper did not risk alienating part of that audience by taking up controversial political positions.

The objectivity spawned by mass circulation news organizations is jealously guarded today by partisans on both sides of the ideological spectrum who eagerly scan the media's output for signs of liberal or conservative bias. We know that, on average, journalists tend to be slightly more liberal than the average American, media owners and editorial writers slightly more conservative (the conservatives at Fox News and the liberals at MSNBC notwithstanding, of course.) But in any case, most Americans are amply armed to deflect any political bias that sneaks into the media because we bring our own ideological filters to the business of reading the paper and watching the news.

We are less primed to watch for the effects of other kinds of pressures on the media that may have a more serious influence on the news that we get. Today the mainstream media (major city newspapers and the television networks) are part of corporate America, where the drive for profits helps define the news and how it is presented and packaged. In addition to the commercial pressures coming from the corporate owners, journalists have to contend with the efforts of politicians to control the way they are presented by the media. But today's mainstream media also find themselves challenged by a new threat to their existence. As news-seekers increasingly go online to get their information, as bloggers and tweeters and others set themselves up as free disseminators of the news, and as traditional sources of the news fail to find ways to charge people for accessing their work, the media landscape is being transformed in ways we don't yet quite appreciate. All these forces can make the journalist's public job—to provide accurate and timely news to citizens and to provide a check on government—increasingly difficult.

The articles in this chapter deal with some of the pressures faced by journalists today. The first piece is a Pulitzer Prize–winning article from *New York Times* writer David Barstow, who exposed a Pentagon program under the Bush administration to shape public perceptions of the war in Iraq by using retired members of the military as "independent" media analysts. The second piece, by *Slate*'s John Dickerson, looks at whether the Obama administration was similarly trying to control the news when it asked a blogger to present a question from an Iranian at a presidential press conference. In the third piece, Markos Moulitsas, of the liberal blog *Daily Kos*, looks at the political role played by bloggers and what he calls the "netroots," as the line between journalist and activist blurs in the new media. In the fourth piece, an Internet writer, Clay Shirky, speculates about the future of newspapers. Finally, we look backward in time to the arguments made by media giant William Randolph Hearst, about the evils of government-controlled newspapers.

 14.1 Message Machine

Behind TV Analysts, Pentagon's Hidden Hand
David Barstow, New York Times

Why We Chose This Piece

> *When the Bush administration came into office in 2001, it was particularly adept at managing the message it wanted the media to convey about its actions. Although it became more difficult as the insurgency in Iraq proved intractable, the administration's efforts to control the way the media covered the Iraq war seemed golden in its early years. In this*

Selection published: April 20, 2008

Pulitzer Prize–winning article for the New York Times, *David Barstow shows why that was. Immediately following the publication of Barstow's article, Democratic members of Congress called for an investigation into the Pentagon's military experts program. On January 16, 2009, with just four days left to go in the Bush administration, the Pentagon's own internal investigation reported that it had done nothing inappropriate. In May the Pentagon took the unusual step of retracting its report, saying it was flawed, but as the program had been terminated and the officials who had participated no longer worked for the Pentagon, it was not pursuing the investigation.*

Although this article is long and detailed, we want you to read it not only for what it reveals about how easily the news we get can be manipulated by a government determined to push its point of view, but also because it demonstrates by example the value of an independent press free to investigate and criticize what government does. Though the Pentagon tried to manipulate public opinion, Barstow was able to pull back the curtain to show us what was going on. Will investigative journalism such as Barstow's still be possible if the mainstream media are too weak to fund it?

In the summer of 2005, the Bush administration confronted a fresh wave of criticism over Guantánamo Bay. The detention center had just been branded "the gulag of our times" by Amnesty International, there were new allegations of abuse from United Nations human rights experts and calls were mounting for its closure.

The administration's communications experts responded swiftly. Early one Friday morning, they put a group of retired military officers on one of the jets normally used by Vice President Dick Cheney and flew them to Cuba for a carefully orchestrated tour of Guantánamo.

To the public, these men are members of a familiar fraternity, presented tens of thousands of times on television and radio as "military analysts" whose long service has equipped them to give authoritative and unfettered judgments about the most pressing issues of the post-Sept. 11 world.

Hidden behind that appearance of objectivity, though, is a Pentagon information apparatus that has used those analysts in a campaign to generate favorable news coverage of the administration's wartime performance, an examination by The New York Times has found.

The effort, which began with the buildup to the Iraq war and continues to this day, has sought to exploit ideological and military allegiances, and also a powerful financial dynamic: Most of the analysts have ties to military contractors vested in the very war policies they are asked to assess on air.

Those business relationships are hardly ever disclosed to the viewers, and sometimes not even to the networks themselves. But collectively, the men on the plane and several dozen other military analysts represent more than 150 military contractors either as lobbyists, senior executives, board members or consultants. The companies include defense heavyweights, but also scores of smaller companies, all part of a vast assemblage of contractors scrambling for hundreds of billions in military business generated by the administration's war on terror. It is a furious competition, one in which inside information and easy access to senior officials are highly prized.

Records and interviews show how the Bush administration has used its control over access and information in an effort to transform the analysts into a kind of media Trojan horse—an instrument intended to shape terrorism coverage from inside the major TV and radio networks.

Analysts have been wooed in hundreds of private briefings with senior military leaders, including officials with significant influence over contracting and budget matters, records show. They have been taken on tours of Iraq and given access to classified intelligence. They have been briefed by officials from the White House, State Department and Justice Department, including Mr. Cheney, Alberto R. Gonzales and Stephen J. Hadley.

In turn, members of this group have echoed administration talking points, sometimes even when they suspected the information was false or inflated. Some analysts acknowledge they suppressed doubts because they feared jeopardizing their access.

A few expressed regret for participating in what they regarded as an effort to dupe the American public with propaganda dressed as independent military analysis.

"It was them saying, 'We need to stick our hands up your back and move your mouth for you,'" Robert S. Bevelacqua, a retired Green Beret and former Fox News analyst, said.

Kenneth Allard, a former NBC military analyst who has taught information warfare at the National Defense University, said the campaign amounted to a sophisticated information operation. "This was a coherent, active policy," he said.

As conditions in Iraq deteriorated, Mr. Allard recalled, he saw a yawning gap between what analysts were told in private briefings and what subsequent inquiries and books later revealed.

"Night and day," Mr. Allard said, "I felt we'd been hosed."

The Pentagon defended its relationship with military analysts, saying they had been given only factual information about the war. "The intent and purpose of this is nothing other than an earnest attempt to inform the American people," Bryan Whitman, a Pentagon spokesman, said.

It was, Mr. Whitman added, "a bit incredible" to think retired military officers could be "wound up" and turned into "puppets of the Defense Department."

Many analysts strongly denied that they had either been co-opted or had allowed outside business interests to affect their on-air comments, and some have used their platforms to criticize the conduct of the war. Several, like Jeffrey D. McCausland, a CBS military analyst and defense industry lobbyist, said they kept their networks informed of their outside work and recused themselves from coverage that touched on business interests.

"I'm not here representing the administration," Dr. McCausland said.

Some network officials, meanwhile, acknowledged only a limited understanding of their analysts' interactions with the administration. They said that while they were sensitive to potential conflicts of interest, they did not hold their analysts to the same ethical standards as their news employees regarding outside financial interests. The onus is on their analysts to disclose conflicts, they said. And whatever the contributions of military analysts, they also noted the many network journalists who have covered the war for years in all its complexity.

Five years into the Iraq war, most details of the architecture and execution of the Pentagon's campaign have never been disclosed. But The Times successfully sued the Defense Department to gain access to 8,000 pages of e-mail messages, transcripts and records describing years of private briefings, trips to Iraq and Guantánamo and an extensive Pentagon talking points operation.

These records reveal a symbiotic relationship where the usual dividing lines between government and journalism have been obliterated.

Internal Pentagon documents repeatedly refer to the military analysts as "message force multipliers" or "surrogates" who could be counted on to deliver administration "themes and messages" to millions of Americans "in the form of their own opinions."

Though many analysts are paid network consultants, making $500 to $1,000 per appearance, in Pentagon meetings they sometimes spoke as if they were operating behind enemy lines, interviews and transcripts show. Some offered the Pentagon tips on how to outmaneuver the networks, or as one analyst put it to Donald H. Rumsfeld, then the defense secretary, "the Chris Matthewses and the Wolf Blitzers of the world." Some warned of planned stories or sent the Pentagon copies of their correspondence with network news executives. Many—although certainly not all—faithfully echoed talking points intended to counter critics.

"Good work," Thomas G. McInerney, a retired Air Force general, consultant and Fox News analyst, wrote to the Pentagon after receiving fresh talking points in late 2006. "We will use it."

Again and again, records show, the administration has enlisted analysts as a rapid reaction force to rebut what it viewed as critical news coverage, some of it by the networks' own Pentagon correspondents. For example, when news articles revealed that troops in Iraq were dying because of inadequate body armor, a senior Pentagon official wrote to his colleagues: "I think our analysts—properly armed—can push back in that arena."

The documents released by the Pentagon do not show any quid pro quo between commentary and contracts. But some analysts said they had used the special access as a marketing and networking opportunity or as a window into future business possibilities.

John C. Garrett is a retired Marine colonel and unpaid analyst for Fox News TV and radio. He is also a lobbyist at Patton Boggs who helps firms win Pentagon contracts, including in Iraq. In promotional materials, he states that as a military analyst he "is privy to weekly access and briefings with the secretary of defense, chairman of the Joint Chiefs of Staff and other high level policy makers in the administration." One client told investors that Mr. Garrett's special access and decades of experience helped him "to know in advance—and in detail—how best to meet the needs" of the Defense Department and other agencies.

In interviews Mr. Garrett said there was an inevitable overlap between his dual roles. He said he had gotten "information you just otherwise would not get," from the briefings and three Pentagon-sponsored trips to Iraq. He also acknowledged using this access and information to identify opportunities for clients. "You can't help but look for that," he said, adding, "If you know a capability that would fill a niche or need, you try to fill it. "That's good for everybody."

At the same time, in e-mail messages to the Pentagon, Mr. Garrett displayed an eagerness to be supportive with his television and radio commentary. "Please let me know if you have any specific points you want covered or that you would prefer to downplay," he wrote in January 2007, before President Bush went on TV to describe the surge strategy in Iraq.

Conversely, the administration has demonstrated that there is a price for sustained criticism, many analysts said. "You'll lose all access," Dr. McCausland said.

With a majority of Americans calling the war a mistake despite all administration attempts to sway public opinion, the Pentagon has focused in the last couple of years on cultivating in particular military analysts frequently seen and heard in conservative news outlets, records and interviews show.

Some of these analysts were on the mission to Cuba on June 24, 2005—the first of six such Guantánamo trips—which was designed to mobilize analysts against the growing perception of Guantánamo as an international symbol of inhumane treatment. On the flight to Cuba, for much of the day at Guantánamo and on the flight home that night, Pentagon officials briefed the 10 or so analysts on their key messages—how much had been spent improving the facility, the abuse endured by guards, the extensive rights afforded detainees.

The results came quickly. The analysts went on TV and radio, decrying Amnesty International, criticizing calls to close the facility and asserting that all detainees were treated humanely.

"The impressions that you're getting from the media and from the various pronouncements being made by people who have not been here in my opinion are totally false," Donald W. Shepperd, a retired Air Force general, reported live on CNN by phone from Guantánamo that same afternoon.

The next morning, Montgomery Meigs, a retired Army general and NBC analyst, appeared on "Today." "There's been over $100 million of new construction," he reported. "The place is very professionally run."

Within days, transcripts of the analysts' appearances were circulated to senior White House and Pentagon officials, cited as evidence of progress in the battle for hearts and minds at home.

Charting the Campaign

By early 2002, detailed planning for a possible Iraq invasion was under way, yet an obstacle loomed. Many Americans, polls showed, were uneasy about invading a country with no clear connection to the Sept. 11 attacks. Pentagon and White House officials believed the military analysts could play a crucial role in helping overcome this resistance.

Torie Clarke, the former public relations executive who oversaw the Pentagon's dealings with the analysts as assistant secretary of defense for public affairs, had come to her job with distinct ideas about achieving what she called "information dominance." In a spin-saturated news culture, she argued, opinion is swayed most by voices perceived as authoritative and utterly independent.

And so even before Sept. 11, she built a system within the Pentagon to recruit "key influentials"—movers and shakers from all walks who with the proper ministrations might be counted on to generate support for Mr. Rumsfeld's priorities.

In the months after Sept. 11, as every network rushed to retain its own all-star squad of retired military officers, Ms. Clarke and her staff sensed a new opportunity. To Ms. Clarke's team, the military analysts were the ultimate "key influential"—authoritative, most of them decorated war heroes, all reaching mass audiences.

The analysts, they noticed, often got more airtime than network reporters, and they were not merely explaining the capabilities of Apache helicopters. They were framing how viewers ought to interpret events. What is more, while the analysts were in the news media, they were not of the news media. They were military men, many of them ideologically in sync with the administration's neoconservative brain trust, many of them important players in a military industry anticipating large budget increases to pay for an Iraq war.

Even analysts with no defense industry ties, and no fondness for the administration, were reluctant to be critical of military leaders, many of whom were friends. "It is very hard for me to criticize the United States Army," said William L. Nash, a retired Army general and ABC analyst. "It is my life."

Other administrations had made sporadic, small-scale attempts to build relationships with the occasional military analyst. But these were trifling compared with what Ms. Clarke's team had in mind. Don Meyer, an aide to Ms. Clarke, said a strategic decision was made in 2002 to make the analysts the main focus of the public relations push to construct a case for war. Journalists were secondary. "We didn't want to rely on them to be our primary vehicle to get information out," Mr. Meyer said.

The Pentagon's regular press office would be kept separate from the military analysts. The analysts would instead be catered to by a small group of political appointees, with the point person being Brent T. Krueger, another senior aide to Ms. Clarke. The decision recalled other administration tactics that subverted traditional journalism. Federal agencies, for example, have paid columnists to write favorably about the administration. They have distributed to local TV stations hundreds of fake news segments with fawning accounts of administration accomplishments. The Pentagon itself has made covert payments to Iraqi newspapers to publish coalition propaganda.

Rather than complain about the "media filter," each of these techniques simply converted the filter into an amplifier. This time, Mr. Krueger said, the military analysts would in effect be "writing the op-ed" for the war.

[...]

The Selling of the War

From their earliest sessions with the military analysts, Mr. Rumsfeld and his aides spoke as if they were all part of the same team.

In interviews, participants described a powerfully seductive environment—the uniformed escorts to Mr. Rumsfeld's private conference room, the best government china laid out, the embossed name cards, the blizzard of PowerPoints, the solicitations of advice and counsel, the appeals to duty and country, the warm thank you notes from the secretary himself.

"Oh, you have no idea," Mr. Allard said, describing the effect. "You're back. They listen to you. They listen to what you say on TV." It was, he said, "psyops on steroids"—a nuanced exercise in influence through flattery and proximity. "It's not like it's, 'We'll pay you $500 to get our story out,'" he said. "It's more subtle."

The access came with a condition. Participants were instructed not to quote their briefers directly or otherwise describe their contacts with the Pentagon.

In the fall and winter leading up to the invasion, the Pentagon armed its analysts with talking points portraying Iraq as an urgent threat. The basic case became a familiar mantra: Iraq possessed chemical and biological weapons, was developing nuclear weapons, and might one day slip some to Al Qaeda; an invasion would be a relatively quick and inexpensive "war of liberation."

At the Pentagon, members of Ms. Clarke's staff marveled at the way the analysts seamlessly incorporated material from talking points and briefings as if it was their own.

"You could see that they were messaging," Mr. Krueger said. "You could see they were taking verbatim what the secretary was saying or what the technical specialists were saying. And they were saying it over and over and over." Some days, he added, "We were able to click on every single station and every one of our folks were up there delivering our message. You'd look at them and say, 'This is working.'"

On April 12, 2003, with major combat almost over, Mr. Rumsfeld drafted a memorandum to Ms. Clarke. "Let's think about having some of the folks who did such a good job as talking heads in after this thing is over," he wrote.

By summer, though, the first signs of the insurgency had emerged. Reports from journalists based in Baghdad were increasingly suffused with the imagery of mayhem.

The Pentagon did not have to search far for a counterweight.

It was time, an internal Pentagon strategy memorandum urged, to "re-energize surrogates and message-force multipliers," starting with the military analysts.

The memorandum led to a proposal to take analysts on a tour of Iraq in September 2003, timed to help overcome the sticker shock from Mr. Bush's request for $87 billion in emergency war financing.

The group included four analysts from Fox News, one each from CNN and ABC, and several research-group luminaries whose opinion articles appear regularly in the nation's op-ed pages.

The trip invitation promised a look at "the real situation on the ground in Iraq."

The situation, as described in scores of books, was deteriorating. L. Paul Bremer III, then the American viceroy in Iraq, wrote in his memoir, "My Year in Iraq," that he had privately warned the White House that the United States had "about half the number of soldiers we needed here."

"We're up against a growing and sophisticated threat," Mr. Bremer recalled telling the president during a private White House dinner.

That dinner took place on Sept. 24, while the analysts were touring Iraq.

Yet these harsh realities were elided, or flatly contradicted, during the official presentations for the analysts, records show. The itinerary, scripted to the minute, featured brief visits to a model school, a few refurbished government buildings, a center for women's rights, a mass grave and even the gardens of Babylon.

Mostly the analysts attended briefings. These sessions, records show, spooled out an alternative narrative, depicting an Iraq bursting with political and economic energy, its security forces blossoming. On the crucial question of troop levels, the briefings echoed the White House line: No reinforcements were needed. The "growing and sophisticated threat" described by Mr. Bremer was instead depicted as degraded, isolated and on the run.

"We're winning," a briefing document proclaimed.

One trip participant, General Nash of ABC, said some briefings were so clearly "artificial" that he joked to another group member that they were on "the George Romney memorial trip to Iraq," a reference to Mr. Romney's infamous claim that American officials had "brainwashed" him into supporting the Vietnam War during a tour there in 1965, while he was governor of Michigan.

But if the trip pounded the message of progress, it also represented a business opportunity: direct access to the most senior civilian and military leaders in Iraq and Kuwait, including many with a say in how the president's $87 billion would be spent. It also was a chance to gather inside information about the most pressing needs confronting the American mission: the acute shortages of "up-armored" Humvees; the billions to be spent building military bases; the urgent need for interpreters; and the ambitious plans to train Iraq's security forces.

[…]

The Pentagon, though, need not have worried.

"You can't believe the progress," General Vallely told Alan Colmes of Fox News upon his return. He predicted the insurgency would be "down to a few numbers" within months.

"We could not be more excited, more pleased," Mr. Cowan [a Fox analyst and retired Marine Colonel] told Greta Van Susteren of Fox News. There was barely a word about armor shortages or corrupt Iraqi security forces. And on the key strategic question of the moment—whether to send more troops—the analysts were unanimous.

"I am so much against adding more troops," General Shepperd said on CNN.

Access and Influence

Inside the Pentagon and at the White House, the trip was viewed as a masterpiece in the management of perceptions, not least because it gave fuel to complaints that "mainstream" journalists were ignoring the good news in Iraq.

"We're hitting a home run on this trip," a senior Pentagon official wrote in an e-mail message to Richard B. Myers and Peter Pace, then chairman and vice chairman of the Joint Chiefs of Staff.

Its success only intensified the Pentagon's campaign. The pace of briefings accelerated. More trips were organized. Eventually the effort involved officials from Washington to Baghdad to Kabul to Guantánamo and back to Tampa, Fla., the headquarters of United States Central Command.

The scale reflected strong support from the top. When officials in Iraq were slow to organize another trip for analysts, a Pentagon official fired off an e-mail message warning that the trips "have the highest levels of visibility" at the White House and urging them to get moving before Lawrence Di Rita, one of Mr. Rumsfeld's closest aides, "picks up the phone and starts calling the 4-stars."

Mr. Di Rita, no longer at the Defense Department, said in an interview that a "conscious decision" was made to rely on the military analysts to counteract "the increasingly negative view of the war" coming from journalists in Iraq. The analysts, he said, generally had "a more supportive view" of the administration and the war, and the combination of their TV platforms and military cachet made them ideal for rebutting critical coverage of issues like troop morale, treatment of detainees, inadequate equipment or poorly trained Iraqi security forces. "On those issues, they were more likely to be seen as credible spokesmen," he said.

For analysts with military industry ties, the attention brought access to a widening circle of influential officials beyond the contacts they had accumulated over the course of their careers.

Charles T. Nash, a Fox military analyst and retired Navy captain, is a consultant who helps small companies break into the military market. Suddenly, he had entree to a host of senior military leaders, many of whom he had never met. It was, he said, like being embedded with the Pentagon leadership. "You start to recognize what's most important to them," he said, adding, "There's nothing like seeing stuff firsthand."

Some Pentagon officials said they were well aware that some analysts viewed their special access as a business advantage. "Of course we realized that," Mr. Krueger said. "We weren't naïve about that."

They also understood the financial relationship between the networks and their analysts. Many analysts were being paid by the "hit," the number of times they appeared on TV. The more an analyst could boast of fresh inside information from high-level Pentagon "sources," the more hits he could expect. The more hits, the greater his potential influence in the military marketplace, where several analysts prominently advertised their network roles.

"They have taken lobbying and the search for contracts to a far higher level," Mr. Krueger said. "This has been highly honed."

Mr. Di Rita, though, said it never occurred to him that analysts might use their access to curry favor. Nor, he said, did the Pentagon try to exploit this dynamic. "That's not something that ever crossed my mind," he said. In any event, he argued, the analysts and the networks were the ones responsible for any ethical complications. "We assume they know where the lines are," he said.

The analysts met personally with Mr. Rumsfeld at least 18 times, records show, but that was just the beginning. They had dozens more sessions with the most senior members of his brain trust and access to officials responsible for managing the billions being spent in Iraq. Other groups of "key influentials" had meetings, but not nearly as often as the analysts.

[...]

"We knew we had extraordinary access," said Timur J. Eads, a retired Army lieutenant colonel and Fox analyst who is vice president of government relations for Blackbird Technologies, a fast-growing military contractor.

Like several other analysts, Mr. Eads said he had at times held his tongue on television for fear that "some four-star could call up and say, 'Kill that contract.'" For example, he believed Pentagon officials misled the analysts about the progress of Iraq's security forces. "I know a snow job when I see one," he said. He did not share this on TV.

"Human nature," he explained, though he noted other instances when he was critical.

Some analysts said that even before the war started, they privately had questions about the justification for the invasion, but were careful not to express them on air.

Mr. Bevelacqua, then a Fox analyst, was among those invited to a briefing in early 2003 about Iraq's purported stockpiles of illicit weapons. He recalled asking the briefer whether the United States had "smoking gun" proof.

"'We don't have any hard evidence,'" Mr. Bevelacqua recalled the briefer replying. He said he and other analysts were alarmed by this concession. "We are looking at ourselves saying, 'What are we doing?'"

Another analyst, Robert L. Maginnis, a retired Army lieutenant colonel who works in the Pentagon for a military contractor, attended the same briefing and recalled feeling "very disappointed" after being shown satellite photographs purporting to show bunkers associated with a hidden weapons program. Mr. Maginnis said he concluded that the analysts were being "manipulated" to convey a false sense of certainty about the evidence of the weapons. Yet he and Mr. Bevelacqua and the other analysts who attended the briefing did not share any misgivings with the American public.

Mr. Bevelacqua and another Fox analyst, Mr. Cowan, had formed the wvc3 Group, and hoped to win military and national security contracts.

"There's no way I was going to go down that road and get completely torn apart," Mr. Bevelacqua said. "You're talking about fighting a huge machine."

Some e-mail messages between the Pentagon and the analysts reveal an implicit trade of privileged access for favorable coverage. Robert H. Scales Jr., a retired Army general and analyst for Fox News and National Public Radio whose consulting company advises several military firms on weapons and tactics used in Iraq, wanted the Pentagon to approve high-level briefings for him inside Iraq in 2006.

"Recall the stuff I did after my last visit," he wrote. "I will do the same this time."

Pentagon Keeps Tabs

As it happened, the analysts' news media appearances were being closely monitored. The Pentagon paid a private contractor, Omnitec Solutions, hundreds of thousands of dollars to scour databases for any trace of the analysts, be it a segment on "The O'Reilly Factor" or an interview with The Daily Inter Lake in Montana, circulation 20,000.

Omnitec evaluated their appearances using the same tools as corporate branding experts. One report, assessing the impact of several trips to Iraq in 2005, offered example after example of analysts echoing Pentagon themes on all the networks.

"Commentary from all three Iraq trips was extremely positive over all," the report concluded.

In interviews, several analysts reacted with dismay when told they were described as reliable "surrogates" in Pentagon documents. And some asserted that their Pentagon sessions were, as David L. Grange, a retired Army general and CNN analyst put it, "just upfront information," while others pointed out, accurately, that they did not always agree with the administration or each other. "None of us drink the Kool-Aid," General Scales said.

Likewise, several also denied using their special access for business gain. "Not related at all," General Shepperd said, pointing out that many in the Pentagon held CNN "in the lowest esteem."

Still, even the mildest of criticism could draw a challenge. Several analysts told of fielding telephone calls from displeased defense officials only minutes after being on the air.

On Aug. 3, 2005, 14 marines died in Iraq. That day, Mr. Cowan, who said he had grown increasingly uncomfortable with the "twisted version of reality" being pushed on analysts in briefings, called the Pentagon to give "a heads-up" that some of his comments on Fox "may not all be friendly," Pentagon records show. Mr. Rumsfeld's senior aides quickly arranged a private briefing for him, yet when he told Bill O'Reilly that the United States was "not on a good glide path right now" in Iraq, the repercussions were swift.

Mr. Cowan said he was "precipitously fired from the analysts group" for this appearance. The Pentagon, he wrote in an e-mail message, "simply didn't like the fact that I wasn't carrying their water." The next day James T. Conway, then director of operations for the Joint Chiefs, presided over another conference call with analysts. He urged them, a transcript shows, not to let the marines' deaths further erode support for the war.

"The strategic target remains our population," General Conway said. "We can lose people day in and day out, but they're never going to beat our military. What they can and will do if they can is strip away our support. And you guys can help us not let that happen."

"General, I just made that point on the air," an analyst replied.

"Let's work it together, guys," General Conway urged.

The Generals' Revolt

The full dimensions of this mutual embrace were perhaps never clearer than in April 2006, after several of Mr. Rumsfeld's former generals—none of them network military analysts—went public with devastating critiques of his wartime performance. Some called for his resignation.

On Friday, April 14, with what came to be called the "Generals' Revolt" dominating headlines, Mr. Rumsfeld instructed aides to summon military analysts to a meeting with him early the next week, records show. When an aide urged a short delay to "give our big guys on the West Coast a little more time to buy a ticket and get here," Mr. Rumsfeld's office insisted that "the boss" wanted the meeting fast "for impact on the current story."

That same day, Pentagon officials helped two Fox analysts, General McInerney and General Vallely, write an opinion article for The Wall Street Journal defending Mr. Rumsfeld.

"Starting to write it now," General Vallely wrote to the Pentagon that afternoon. "Any input for the article," he added a little later, "will be much appreciated." Mr. Rumsfeld's office quickly forwarded talking points and statistics to rebut the notion of a spreading revolt.

"Vallely is going to use the numbers," a Pentagon official reported that afternoon.

The standard secrecy notwithstanding, plans for this session leaked, producing a front-page story in The Times that Sunday. In damage-control mode, Pentagon officials scrambled to present the meeting as routine and directed that communications with analysts be kept "very formal," records show. "This is very, very sensitive now," a Pentagon official warned subordinates.

On Tuesday, April 18, some 17 analysts assembled at the Pentagon with Mr. Rumsfeld and General Pace, then the chairman of the Joint Chiefs.

A transcript of that session, never before disclosed, shows a shared determination to marginalize war critics and revive public support for the war.

"I'm an old intel guy," said one analyst. (The transcript omits speakers' names.) "And I can sum all of this up, unfortunately, with one word. That is Psyops. Now most people may hear that and they think, 'Oh my God, they're trying to brainwash.'"

"What are you, some kind of a nut?" Mr. Rumsfeld cut in, drawing laughter. "You don't believe in the Constitution?"

There was little discussion about the actual criticism pouring forth from Mr. Rumsfeld's former generals. Analysts argued that opposition to the war was rooted in perceptions fed by the news media, not reality. The administration's overall war strategy, they counseled, was "brilliant" and "very successful."

"Frankly," one participant said, "from a military point of view, the penalty, 2,400 brave Americans whom we lost, 3,000 in an hour and 15 minutes, is relative."

An analyst said at another point: "This is a wider war. And whether we have democracy in Iraq or not, it doesn't mean a tinker's damn if we end up with the result we want, which is a regime over there that's not a threat to us."

"Yeah," Mr. Rumsfeld said, taking notes.

But winning or not, they bluntly warned, the administration was in grave political danger so long as most Americans viewed Iraq as a lost cause. "America hates a loser," one analyst said.

Much of the session was devoted to ways that Mr. Rumsfeld could reverse the "political tide." One analyst urged Mr. Rumsfeld to "just crush these people," and assured him that "most of the gentlemen at the table" would enthusiastically support him if he did.

"You are the leader," the analyst told Mr. Rumsfeld. "You are our guy."

At another point, an analyst made a suggestion: "In one of your speeches you ought to say, 'Everybody stop for a minute and imagine an Iraq ruled by Zarqawi.' And then you just go down the list and say, 'All right, we've got oil, money, sovereignty, access to the geographic center of gravity of the Middle East, blah, blah, blah.' If you can just paint a mental picture for Joe America to say, 'Oh my God, I can't imagine a world like that.'"

Even as they assured Mr. Rumsfeld that they stood ready to help in this public relations offensive, the analysts sought guidance on what they should cite as the next "milestone" that would, as one analyst put it, "keep the American people focused on the idea that we're moving forward to a positive end." They placed particular emphasis on the growing confrontation with Iran.

"When you said 'long war,' you changed the psyche of the American people to expect this to be a generational event," an analyst said. "And again, I'm not trying to tell you how to do your job..."

"Get in line," Mr. Rumsfeld interjected.

The meeting ended and Mr. Rumsfeld, appearing pleased and relaxed, took the entire group into a small study and showed off treasured keepsakes from his life, several analysts recalled.

Soon after, analysts hit the airwaves. The Omnitec monitoring reports, circulated to more than 80 officials, confirmed that analysts repeated many of the Pentagon's talking points: that Mr. Rumsfeld consulted "frequently and sufficiently" with his generals;

that he was not "overly concerned" with the criticisms; that the meeting focused "on more important topics at hand," including the next milestone in Iraq, the formation of a new government.

Days later, Mr. Rumsfeld wrote a memorandum distilling their collective guidance into bullet points. Two were underlined:"Focus on the Global War on Terror—not simply Iraq. The wider war—the long war."

"Link Iraq to Iran. Iran is the concern. If we fail in Iraq or Afghanistan, it will help Iran."

But if Mr. Rumsfeld found the session instructive, at least one participant, General Nash, the ABC analyst, was repulsed.

"I walked away from that session having total disrespect for my fellow commentators, with perhaps one or two exceptions," he said.

View From the Networks

[...]

"I don't think NBC was even aware we were participating," said Rick Francona, a longtime military analyst for the network.

Some networks publish biographies on their Web sites that describe their analysts' military backgrounds and, in some cases, give at least limited information about their business ties. But many analysts also said the networks asked few questions about their outside business interests, the nature of their work or the potential for that work to create conflicts of interest. "None of that ever happened," said Mr. Allard, an NBC analyst until 2006.

"The worst conflict of interest was no interest."

Mr. Allard and other analysts said their network handlers also raised no objections when the Defense Department began paying their commercial airfare for Pentagon-sponsored trips to Iraq—a clear ethical violation for most news organizations.

CBS News declined to comment on what it knew about its military analysts' business affiliations or what steps it took to guard against potential conflicts.

NBC News also declined to discuss its procedures for hiring and monitoring military analysts. The network issued a short statement: "We have clear policies in place to assure that the people who appear on our air have been appropriately vetted and that nothing in their profile would lead to even a perception of a conflict of interest."

Jeffrey W. Schneider, a spokesman for ABC, said that while the network's military consultants were not held to the same ethical rules as its full-time journalists, they were expected to keep the network informed about any outside business entanglements. "We make it clear to them we expect them to keep us closely apprised," he said.

A spokeswoman for Fox News said executives "refused to participate" in this article.

CNN requires its military analysts to disclose in writing all outside sources of income. But like the other networks, it does not provide its military analysts with the kind of written, specific ethical guidelines it gives its full-time employees for avoiding real or apparent conflicts of interest.

Yet even where controls exist, they have sometimes proven porous.

CNN, for example, said it was unaware for nearly three years that one of its main military analysts, General Marks, was deeply involved in the business of seeking government contracts, including contracts related to Iraq.

General Marks was hired by CNN in 2004, about the time he took a management position at McNeil Technologies, where his job was to pursue military and intelligence contracts. As required, General Marks disclosed that he received income from McNeil Technologies. But the disclosure form did not require him to describe what his job entailed, and CNN acknowledges it failed to do additional vetting.

"We did not ask Mr. Marks the follow-up questions we should have," CNN said in a written statement.

In an interview, General Marks said it was no secret at CNN that his job at McNeil Technologies was about winning contracts. "I mean, that's what McNeil does," he said.

CNN, however, said it did not know the nature of McNeil's military business or what General Marks did for the company. If he was bidding on Pentagon contracts, CNN said, that should have disqualified him from being a military analyst for the network. But in the summer and fall of 2006, even as he was regularly asked to comment on conditions in Iraq, General Marks was working intensively on bidding for a $4.6 billion contract to provide thousands of translators to United States forces in Iraq. In fact, General Marks was made president of the McNeil spin-off that won the huge contract in December 2006.

General Marks said his work on the contract did not affect his commentary on CNN. "I've got zero challenge separating myself from a business interest," he said.

But CNN said it had no idea about his role in the contract until July 2007, when it reviewed his most recent disclosure form, submitted months earlier, and finally made inquiries about his new job.

"We saw the extent of his dealings and determined at that time we should end our relationship with him," CNN said.

*C*onsider the source and the audience.

- Barstow is writing in the *New York Times*, probably the most prestigious daily newspaper in the United States. Does the fact that the editorial pages of the *Times* can have a liberal tilt make this investigation and report any less believable?
- Who is likely to be reading this story? How does that shape its political impact?

*L*ay out the argument, the values, and the assumptions.

- This is a straight news report, not an ideological argument, but there are clear underlying values that make what the Pentagon did newsworthy. What does Bartow assume is the role of the media in a democracy?
- What does he imply is the failure on the part of the cable stations who hired the military analysts? What is the failure on the part of the Bush administration? What is the failure on the part of the analysts themselves?

*U*ncover the evidence.

- This article is evidence-filled. What kinds of information did Barstow's investigation turn up? How does it strengthen his case? Is there any way for defenders of Bush's administration to argue against this evidence?

E*valuate the conclusion.*

- Barstow does not state his conclusions overtly, but they are clearly implied. Who is at fault here and why? Does he need to spell it out?

S*ort out the political implications.*

- Barstow's article had immediate political significance—members of Congress called loudly for an investigation into the Pentagon's actions even though that investigation proved to be a sham. What longer-term implications did the article have? Would it have had any effect on the 2009 election?
- Why do you think the Pentagon retracted its January report in May 2009?

 ## 14.2 Mr. President, Iran Has a Question

How Obama Is Using the Media to Destroy and Improve the Traditional Press Conference

John Dickerson, Slate

Why We Chose This Piece

In June 2009 Iran appeared to be on the brink of a revolution. President Obama was handling the situation with kid gloves, to avoid being seen as intervening in Iran's domestic affairs and to prevent the revolutionaries from being tagged as American puppets. He was careful not to answer questions about the events in Iran too directly. When he scheduled a press conference on other topics, however, his press office let Nico Pitney, a blogger on the liberal Huffington Post *who had been covering the Iranian unrest and communicating with Iranian citizens, know that if he could get a question from one of those citizens he would be called on to ask it. Pitney acquired such a question from his Iranian sources, and it proved to be one of the toughest that Obama received that day. Because the question had clearly been solicited in advance, the president was accused by some critics of manipulating the news, even though he had no idea what it would be about ahead of time (and in fact answered it badly).*

Slate's chief political correspondent John Dickerson has a long relationship with presidential press conferences. His mother, Nancy Dickerson, was a pioneer in broadcast journalism who turned her personal connection with various White House occupants into major scoops. Dickerson himself was a White House correspondent for Time *magazine before*

***

Selection published: June 26, 2009

moving to Slate. He has a reputation for asking killer questions. It was Dickerson's query to George W. Bush about his biggest post-9/11 mistake in office that reduced Bush to incoherence at a 2004 press conference. What underlying tension is Dickerson concerned about in this article?

There was a tiny tempest this week in the Washington press corps. The White House arranged to have Nico Pitney of the Huffington Post ask a question he received over the Web from an Iranian. This caused mild upset among some traditional news organizations, which, in turn, prompted harsh derision from many in the Web-only world. (On Sunday, the tempest became a fracas on CNN's media-affairs show *Reliable Sources* as Pitney traded accusations with the *Washington Post*'s Dana Milbank.)

This is an intramural fight that won't go away. We love to talk about ourselves. (If you think this is navel-gazing, move on or close your browser. If you do read on, don't say you weren't warned, and don't complain.) Beyond the media world, this small fracas is interesting because it's a predictable clash between various media outlets in a swiftly changing world. Pitney is a new kind of journalist not just because he works for a Web site but because on the Iran story, he's been a first-rate aggregator—sifting all different kinds of media for the narrative of an ongoing story. This is an entirely new kind of animal, available not just at the Huffington Post but at the *New York Times*.

What's new about this little press conference episode is not the arrangement but the context. The White House arranges things all the time with reporters. It just doesn't usually happen during a press conference. (The Jeff Gannon incident was the exception that proves the rule.)

In a better world, reporters would not rely on the White House for access to the president. But we do. The administration decides who gets called on and who gets sit-down interviews and who gets all-day access complete with a trip to a hamburger joint with the president. So there's nothing new about a reporter getting a choice piece of access because there's something in it for the White House.

In the Bush years, the mere notion that reporters would engage in any kind of arranging at all was a cause for criticism. The argument was that reporters were captive because they relied on the White House to allow them even in the door to do their jobs. I remember being on a panel with Arianna Huffington, who argued persuasively that because the White House press corps relied on access, the transaction between it and the White House was inherently tainted. (She wrote an account of that panel.)

There was, and is, merit to this charge. Reporters and news organizations have, at times, traded away toughness for access.

But access does not *guarantee* softness. Pitney got his shot and asked a good question, proof of which is that the president fled from it. (Further proof is that Obama started his answer with the word *well*—a little tic that tells you he's not so enthusiastic.)

Now Arianna Huffington and her defenders are on the other side of this intramural spat. They are arguing a version of what the mainstream media used to argue: It's not the access; it's what you do with it. That's a healthy evolution. It's true that some of the same writers now praising the Obama administration for its openness to a new kind of journalism would probably have howled in protest if Bush had done something similar at a press conference. How much this hypocrisy bothers you probably depends on how partisan you are.

But what's truly silly is pretending the arrangement doesn't exist. This is either a delusion or a strained rationale the mainstream media use to justify its choice access. Fear of losing that access, by the way, isn't necessarily selfish sour grapes: Mainstream media outlets pay a lot of money to cover the White House, and the information they provide (presumably) is a public good. For this expenditure of money and resources, they might argue, they should receive some preferential treatment. If they don't get at least pride of place in the Q&A pecking order at a press conference, they'll go away—and we'll all suffer. (The counterargument is that they get plenty of access.)

There are members of the traditional press who concede that there is a symbiotic relationship between the White House and its press corps—but they're still bothered by this episode because it took place *at a press conference*, which turned the other reporters into props.

Pitney's question helped create a tableau that benefited the White House on this specific story: A president who was being criticized for insufficient fellow-feeling with Iranian protesters got a chance to show that he was making a special effort to field a question from an Iranian. After all, the president could have answered Pitney's questions in private. But he wanted to show his empathy to the world, and to create this tableau, he needed the Huffington Post to agree to this arrangement. As an enabling of tableaux, however, this was puny compared with the tableau created by the recent ABC and NBC specials, which were longer and reached far more people than the press conference.

If the president had sat down with Pitney, the mainstream press wouldn't have minded so much. They cared, in part, because the episode made them participants. The White House used the press conference stage for the arrangement.

As a civilian, how upset you are about this depends on how much importance you give White House press conferences. There is a school of thought that nothing much useful comes out of presidential press conferences. I disagree. They may be staged events—the president picks the questioners, and they're held on his turf, usually—but they are among the least staged interactions between the president and the press.

While the Obama team has meddled in press conferences in a new way, it's also made them less planned. Obama calls on a wider range of reporters than the Bush team did—reporters from Web sites, reporters from smaller magazines, *Stars and Stripes*—and those questions are likely to be more unpredictable, which is good. On balance, then, this White House has actually made the press conference more likely to generate useful news.

Finally, a personal perspective on the members of the White House press corps: For a lot of them, the press conference is the only place where they get a crack at the president. The White House beat can make stars out of network TV correspondents and big-city newspaper reporters, but there are a lot of other members of the press corps you've never heard of and probably never will. There are fewer of these types now, because these are the people losing their jobs as the media contract.

Press conferences are often their one chance to ask a question of a president they've watched and studied for months. They prepare their questions, remind themselves of the last time someone from an obscure outlet got called on, and hope they get their shot. Then they watch as the traditional big-media outlets get their questions, and when it all ends yet again without them being able to ask anything, they're disappointed.

Now, as they are moved farther to the back of the room, they have one more reason to be disappointed. Even if you buy the White House's rationale, you can appreciate how they may find this new arrangement hard to take.

*C*onsider the source and the audience.

- *Slate* is part of the new media, a liberal leaning online journal owned by the old media (the *Washington Post*). Dickerson himself is a member of the new media with a pedigree straight from the old. How might that shape the way he saw the tension at the Obama press conference?
- To which audience is Dickerson directing this piece? Will the general public care about the issue as much as his fellow journalists?

*L*ay out the argument, the values, and the assumptions.

- Dickerson's mother lost her job at NBC in the early 1970s amid criticism that she had traded personal relationships for access in the Kennedy and Johnson administrations and could not be tough enough on them. Might that shape Dickerson's views here? What implicit values about the way journalism ought to be conducted does he reveal?
- On which relationships and tensions does Dickerson focus? Can one short article deal meaningfully with the tension between the White House and the press, the old and the new media, and journalists with access and those who have none?

*U*ncover the evidence.

- Dickerson's thoughts here range widely over the field of journalism, but his evidence comes mostly from a single incident at a single press conference, plus several other discussions by media insiders. Does he need some other kind of evidence, or is his own thinking enough for this analysis?

*E*valuate the conclusion.

- In what ways does Dickerson think Obama has damaged the press conference? In what ways has he improved it? Would other journalists agree?

*S*ort out the political implications.

- The Bush administration tried to manage the media in some definitive ways, for example, by giving press credentials to a friendly but marginal media figure and then calling on him at a press conference, by paying columnists to write favorable analyses of Bush policy, and by engaging in the Pentagon program we looked at in Reading 14.1. How is the Obama practice documented here similar to and different from those practices?

14.3 Why Brian Keeler Is a Netroots Hero

Markos Moulitsas, Daily Kos

Why We Chose This Piece

Blogging is a multifaceted media form. While The Huffington Post *is named for founder Arianna Huffington and her writings are prominent, it is really like a multiauthored online opinion journal to which people can post comments. Other blogs focus more on the personality of a single blogger and have much stronger activist intentions. One of the most widely read political blogs, receiving over 650,000 hits per day, is* Daily Kos *(dailykos. com), named for its founder and primary blogger, Markos Moulitsas Zuñiga.*

Moulitsas's goals for his blog are not objective journalism, and he does not see himself as competing with the mainstream media. Rather, he sees his blog as part of a movement, a "people-powered" effort to upend the traditional power elite in the Democratic Party and make it responsive to the netroots—the Internet community that he sees as the new version of grassroots in American democracy. In this short post applauding the candidacies of Ned Lamont, who defeated Sen. Joe Lieberman for the Democratic nomination for the U.S. Senate in the 2006 Connecticut primary, and Brian Keeler, a Daily Kos *poster who was running for the New York state senate, he describes the role he sees himself and other bloggers playing in American politics. How does that role differ from that of a mainstream journalist?*

We are all part of a movement that has, over the past two years, begun flexing its political muscle. We are a people-powered movement, using technology to aggregate the masses to bypass the entrenched media and political establishments. It's been exciting times, especially for those of us who believe in the wisdom of the masses over the wisdom of entrenched and monied interests.

My ultimate vision is to get away from the current politics, in which politicians tout their endorsements from various issue and constituency groups, toward a world in which politicians tout the sheer number of *people* engaging their campaigns. That's why I get excited when people contribute to Ned Lamont. Not because Ned is desperate for money (I mean, he's worth between $90–300 million). But because it sends a clear message that people are backing him, and are doing so by giving their time and hard-earned money. That's how people-power manifests itself—with volunteer hours and small dollar donations.

But this is a long-term vision. A Congress made up of people-powered candidates will have to wait. In the short term, we have to work with the lobbyist-powered candidates we're stuck with in DC. And while we may pick a few off here and there (I'm looking at you, Joementum), it'll be a while before we can get good people-powered candidates into Congress.

Selection published: May 26, 2006

So here's the long-term part of the strategy: When old Democrats and Republicans retire or otherwise leave office (handcuffs, stretcher, etc), there are now two kinds of candidates that can currently replace them—the self-funded gazillionaire, or the long-time party operative/hack. And while these candidates can be well meaning, good progressives at times, ultimately, I want a Congress that better reflects America.

So we need a farm system. We need to start identifying young progressives and encouraging them to run for local and state offices. And as they get elected and move up the ranks, they can build their fundraising and volunteer base while learning valuable lessons on how to govern and campaign.

And when one of those establishment politicians leaves office, we suddenly have the right kind of progressives ready to contest for those seats.

So to summarize, short-term, we generally deal with the hand we've been dealt, but long-term we build the farm team to engineer a people-powered takeover of Congress.

Which brings me to NYBri, or Brian Keeler. As a long-time, valued member of this community, Brian has shown the values that we'd all love to see in office. In Congress? Yes, but it's tough for a regular person to make that jump. So he's running for State Senate in New York. Susan G, who has worked with him, already gave Brian's race a plug. Let me try to give it a big push—

People squawk when I give my "I'm not a leader" spiel. I'm not. My job is to create an infrastructure to support the emergence of new progressive leaders, and then to support their efforts. Brian is Exhibit A. He has emerged, now let's support his efforts.

Visit his website Keeler2006.com. If you live in the area, join the effort and volunteer. Everyone can contribute to Keeler's campaign. A simple $10 sends the message that we all believe in people-powered politics. That we all believe in a world where good progressives can run and be supported by regular people, not corporate or special interests.

It's not enough to bitch and moan, banging furiously on a keyboard to show your outrage at a broken political system. We have the ability to change it dramatically. So stop complaining. Stop feeling powerless. And start lending a hand.

Whether it's Keeler (and he's a perfect choice), or some other local candidate in your town or county or city or state, it's time to start building the long-term bench for our new people-powered progressive movement.

So do it.

*C*onsider the source and the audience.

- Moulitsas is writing in his own blog, for his own readers, and in that sense he is writing for a sympathetic audience. But he is also addressing critics who accuse him of being fixated on his own power, on being a "king maker" in American politics. How does having his own forum allow him to respond to his critics? Are there any limits on what he can say?

*L*ay out the argument, the values, and the assumptions.

- Moulitsas is defining the "netroots" when he speaks of "people-powered politics." What does he mean by this phrase? What is its opposite?

- What is the strategy that Moulitsas outlines for changing the face of Congress? What does he mean by a "farm system?"
- Why does he consider Brian Keeler a netroots hero?

*U*ncover the evidence.

- This piece is about Moulitsas's own views and strategy—does he need to supply evidence? If so, what kind?

*E*valuate the conclusion.

- This blog post is more of a call to action than an argument (although Moulitsas makes an argument along the way). Is it effective? If you shared his views, would you act?

*S*ort out the political implications.

- As blogs become more popular, with their blurring of the line between providing information and inciting to activism, what might this mean for political participation in America? How might it alter our views of citizenship?

 ## 14.4 Newspapers and Thinking the Unthinkable

Clay Shirky, **www.shirky.com**

Why We Chose This Piece

One of the main reasons people worry about the shrinking audience of the mainstream media is that, until now, it has been the big papers and networks that have funded the investigation and reporting of the news (that is, journalism) through the advertising they sell. They maintain bureaus in faraway places around the world and find and disseminate information about those places, as well as about locales closer to home.

It is ironic and fitting that this article about the "unthinkable" end of newspapers is written by an expert on the Internet and is published on the Internet, at www.shirky.com (the author's Web site.) Shirky looks at the various attempts newspapers have made to stave off the challenge of the Internet, and he argues that the one possibility they don't consider is the unthinkable one, that we are in the midst of a revolution that spells their demise. Is he right that it is time to start thinking about the unthinkable?

Back in 1993, the Knight-Ridder newspaper chain began investigating piracy of Dave Barry's popular column, which was published by the Miami Herald and syndicated widely. In the course of tracking down the sources of unlicensed distribution, they found many things, including the copying of his column to alt.fan.

Selection published: March 13, 2009

dave_barry on usenet; a 2000-person strong mailing list also reading pirated versions; and a teenager in the Midwest who was doing some of the copying himself, because he loved Barry's work so much he wanted everybody to be able to read it.

One of the people I was hanging around with online back then was Gordy Thompson, who managed internet services at the New York Times. I remember Thompson saying something to the effect of "When a 14 year old kid can blow up your business in his spare time, not because he hates you but because he loves you, then you got a problem." I think about that conversation a lot these days.

The problem newspapers face isn't that they didn't see the internet coming. They not only saw it miles off, they figured out early on that they needed a plan to deal with it, and during the early 90s they came up with not just one plan but several. One was to partner with companies like America Online, a fast-growing subscription service that was less chaotic than the open internet. Another plan was to educate the public about the behaviors required of them by copyright law. New payment models such as micropayments were proposed. Alternatively, they could pursue the profit margins enjoyed by radio and TV, if they became purely ad-supported. Still another plan was to convince tech firms to make their hardware and software less capable of sharing, or to partner with the businesses running data networks to achieve the same goal. Then there was the nuclear option: sue copyright infringers directly, making an example of them.

As these ideas were articulated, there was intense debate about the merits of various scenarios. Would DRM or walled gardens work better? Shouldn't we try a carrot-and-stick approach, with education *and* prosecution? And so on. In all this conversation, there was one scenario that was widely regarded as unthinkable, a scenario that didn't get much discussion in the nation's newsrooms, for the obvious reason.

The unthinkable scenario unfolded something like this: The ability to share content wouldn't shrink, it would grow. Walled gardens would prove unpopular. Digital advertising would reduce inefficiencies, and therefore profits. Dislike of micropayments would prevent widespread use. People would resist being educated to act against their own desires. Old habits of advertisers and readers would not transfer online. Even ferocious litigation would be inadequate to constrain massive, sustained law-breaking. (Prohibition redux.) Hardware and software vendors would not regard copyright holders as allies, nor would they regard customers as enemies. DRM's requirement that the attacker be allowed to decode the content would be an insuperable flaw. And, per Thompson, suing people who love something so much they want to share it would piss them off.

Revolutions create a curious inversion of perception. In ordinary times, people who do no more than describe the world around them are seen as pragmatists, while those who imagine fabulous alternative futures are viewed as radicals. The last couple of decades haven't been ordinary, however. Inside the papers, the pragmatists were the ones simply looking out the window and noticing that the real world was increasingly resembling the unthinkable scenario. These people were treated as if they were barking mad. Meanwhile the people spinning visions of popular walled gardens and enthusiastic micropayment adoption, visions unsupported by reality, were regarded not as charlatans but saviors.

When reality is labeled unthinkable, it creates a kind of sickness in an industry. Leadership becomes faith-based, while employees who have the temerity to suggest that what seems to be happening is in fact happening are herded into Innovation

Departments, where they can be ignored *en masse*. This shunting aside of the realists in favor of the fabulists has different effects on different industries at different times. One of the effects on the newspapers is that many of their most passionate defenders are unable, even now, to plan for a world in which the industry they knew is visibly going away.

* * *

The curious thing about the various plans hatched in the '90s is that they were, at base, all the same plan: "Here's how we're going to preserve the old forms of organiza-tion in a world of cheap perfect copies!" The details differed, but the core assumption behind all imagined outcomes (save the unthinkable one) was that the organizational form of the newspaper, as a general-purpose vehicle for publishing a variety of news and opinion, was basically sound, and only needed a digital facelift. As a result, the conversation has degenerated into the enthusiastic grasping at straws, pursued by skeptical responses.

"The Wall Street Journal has a paywall, so we can too!" (Financial information is one of the few kinds of information whose recipients don't want to share.) "Micropayments work for iTunes, so they will work for us!" (Micropayments work only where the provider can avoid competitive business models.) "The New York Times should charge for con-tent!" (They've tried, with QPass and later TimesSelect.) "Cook's Illustrated and Con-sumer Reports are doing fine on subscriptions!" (Those publications forgo ad revenues; users are paying not just for content but for unimpeachability.) "We'll form a cartel!" (… and hand a competitive advantage to every ad-supported media firm in the world.)

Round and round this goes, with the people committed to saving newspapers demanding to know "If the old model is broken, what will work in its place?" To which the answer is: Nothing. Nothing will work. There is no general model for newspapers to replace the one the internet just broke.

With the old economics destroyed, organizational forms perfected for industrial production have to be replaced with structures optimized for digital data. It makes increasingly less sense even to talk about a publishing industry, because the core problem publishing solves—the incredible difficulty, complexity, and expense of mak-ing something available to the public—has stopped being a problem.

* * *

Elizabeth Eisenstein's magisterial treatment of Gutenberg's invention, *The Printing Press as an Agent of Change*, opens with a recounting of her research into the early his-tory of the printing press. She was able to find many descriptions of life in the early 1400s, the era before movable type. Literacy was limited, the Catholic Church was the pan-European political force, Mass was in Latin, and the average book was the Bible. She was also able to find endless descriptions of life in the late 1500s, after Guten-berg's invention had started to spread. Literacy was on the rise, as were books written in contemporary languages, Copernicus had published his epochal work on astron-omy, and Martin Luther's use of the press to reform the Church was upending both religious and political stability.

What Eisenstein focused on, though, was how many historians ignored the transition from one era to the other. To describe the world before or after the spread of print was child's play; those dates were safely distanced from upheaval. But what was happening in 1500? The hard question Eisenstein's book asks is "How did we get from the world before the printing press to the world after it? What was the revolution *itself* like?"

Chaotic, as it turns out. The Bible was translated into local languages; was this an educational boon or the work of the devil? Erotic novels appeared, prompting the same set of questions. Copies of Aristotle and Galen circulated widely, but direct encounter with the relevant texts revealed that the two sources clashed, tarnishing faith in the Ancients. As novelty spread, old institutions seemed exhausted while new ones seemed untrustworthy; as a result, people almost literally didn't know what to think. If you can't trust Aristotle, who can you trust?

During the wrenching transition to print, experiments were only revealed in retrospect to be turning points. Aldus Manutius, the Venetian printer and publisher, invented the smaller *octavo* volume along with italic type. What seemed like a minor change—take a book and shrink it—was in retrospect a key innovation in the democratization of the printed word. As books became cheaper, more portable, and therefore more desirable, they expanded the market for all publishers, heightening the value of literacy still further.

That is what real revolutions are like. The old stuff gets broken faster than the new stuff is put in its place. The importance of any given experiment isn't apparent at the moment it appears; big changes stall, small changes spread. Even the revolutionaries can't predict what will happen. Agreements on all sides that core institutions must be protected are rendered meaningless by the very people doing the agreeing. (Luther and the Church both insisted, for years, that whatever else happened, no one was talking about a schism.) Ancient social bargains, once disrupted, can neither be mended nor quickly replaced, since any such bargain takes decades to solidify.

And so it is today. When someone demands to know how we are going to replace newspapers, they are really demanding to be told that we are not living through a revolution. They are demanding to be told that old systems won't break before new systems are in place. They are demanding to be told that ancient social bargains aren't in peril, that core institutions will be spared, that new methods of spreading information will improve previous practice rather than upending it. They are demanding to be lied to.

There are fewer and fewer people who can convincingly tell such a lie.

* * *

If you want to know why newspapers are in such trouble, the most salient fact is this: Printing presses are terrifically expensive to set up and to run. This bit of economics, normal since Gutenberg, limits competition while creating positive returns to scale for the press owner, a happy pair of economic effects that feed on each other. In a notional town with two perfectly balanced newspapers, one paper would eventually generate some small advantage—a breaking story, a key interview—at which point both advertisers and readers would come to prefer it, however slightly. That paper would in turn find it easier to capture the next dollar of advertising, at lower expense, than the competition.

This would increase its dominance, which would further deepen those preferences, repeat chorus. The end result is either geographic or demographic segmentation among papers, or one paper holding a monopoly on the local mainstream audience.

For a long time, longer than anyone in the newspaper business has been alive in fact, print journalism has been intertwined with these economics. The expense of printing created an environment where Wal-Mart was willing to subsidize the Baghdad bureau. This wasn't because of any deep link between advertising and reporting, nor was it about any real desire on the part of Wal-Mart to have their marketing budget go to international correspondents. It was just an accident. Advertisers had little choice other than to have their money used that way, since they didn't really have any other vehicle for display ads.

The old difficulties and costs of printing forced everyone doing it into a similar set of organizational models; it was this similarity that made us regard *Daily Racing Form* and *L'Osservatore Romano* as being in the same business. That the relationship between advertisers, publishers, and journalists has been ratified by a century of cultural practice doesn't make it any less accidental.

The competition-deflecting effects of printing cost got destroyed by the internet, where everyone pays for the infrastructure, and then everyone gets to use it. And when Wal-Mart, and the local Maytag dealer, and the law firm hiring a secretary, and that kid down the block selling his bike, were all able to use that infrastructure to get out of their old relationship with the publisher, they did. They'd never really signed up to fund the Baghdad bureau anyway.

* * *

Print media does much of society's heavy journalistic lifting, from flooding the zone—covering every angle of a huge story—to the daily grind of attending the City Council meeting, just in case. This coverage creates benefits even for people who aren't newspaper readers, because the work of print journalists is used by everyone from politicians to district attorneys to talk radio hosts to bloggers. The newspaper people often note that newspapers benefit society as a whole. This is true, but irrelevant to the problem at hand; "You're gonna miss us when we're gone!" has never been much of a business model. So who covers all that news if some significant fraction of the currently employed newspaper people lose their jobs?

I don't know. Nobody knows. We're collectively living through 1500, when it's easier to see what's broken than what will replace it. The internet turns 40 this fall. Access by the general public is less than half that age. Web use, as a normal part of life for a majority of the developed world, is less than half *that* age. We just got here. Even the revolutionaries can't predict what will happen.

Imagine, in 1996, asking some net-savvy soul to expound on the potential of craigslist, then a year old and not yet incorporated. The answer you'd almost certainly have gotten would be extrapolation: "Mailing lists can be powerful tools," "Social effects are intertwining with digital networks," blah blah blah. What no one would have told you, could have told you, was what actually happened: craigslist became a critical piece of infrastructure. Not the idea of craigslist, or the business model, or even the software driving it. Craigslist itself spread to cover hundreds of cities and has become a part of public consciousness about what is now possible. Experiments are only revealed in retrospect to be turning points.

In craigslist's gradual shift from 'interesting if minor' to 'essential and transformative,' there is one possible answer to the question "If the old model is broken, what will work in its place?" The answer is: Nothing will work, but everything might. Now is the time for experiments, lots and lots of experiments, each of which will seem as minor at launch as craigslist did, as Wikipedia did, as *octavo* volumes did.

Journalism has always been subsidized. Sometimes it's been Wal-Mart and the kid with the bike. Sometimes it's been Richard Mellon Scaife. Increasingly, it's you and me, donating our time. The list of models that are obviously working today, like Consumer Reports and NPR, like ProPublica and WikiLeaks, can't be expanded to cover any general case, but then nothing is going to cover the general case.

Society doesn't need newspapers. What we need is journalism. For a century, the imperatives to strengthen journalism and to strengthen newspapers have been so tightly wound as to be indistinguishable. That's been a fine accident to have, but when that accident stops, as it is stopping before our eyes, we're going to need lots of other ways to strengthen journalism instead.

When we shift our attention from 'save newspapers' to 'save society,' the imperative changes from 'preserve the current institutions' to 'do whatever works.' And what works today isn't the same as what used to work.

We don't know who the Aldus Manutius of the current age is. It could be Craig Newmark, or Caterina Fake. It could be Martin Nisenholtz, or Emily Bell. It could be some 19 year old kid few of us have heard of, working on something we won't recognize as vital until a decade hence. Any experiment, though, designed to provide new models for journalism is going to be an improvement over hiding from the real, especially in a year when, for many papers, the unthinkable future is already in the past.

For the next few decades, journalism will be made up of overlapping special cases. Many of these models will rely on amateurs as researchers and writers. Many of these models will rely on sponsorship or grants or endowments instead of revenues. Many of these models will rely on excitable 14 year olds distributing the results. Many of these models will fail. No one experiment is going to replace what we are now losing with the demise of news on paper, but over time, the collection of new experiments that do work might give us the journalism we need.

*C*onsider the source and the audience.

- Shirky writes about the Internet for people who are interested in Internet issues. This article does not appear in a book or magazine; it is self-published on the Web, exactly the kind of threat to traditional methods of disseminating information that the mainstream media worry about. How can you learn more about who Shirky is and what he thinks?

*L*ay out the argument, the values, and the assumptions.

- Shirky is clearly comfortable with the Internet and sees the plight of the mainstream media without the fear that those who strive to save them feel. What does he think is worth saving in the traditional channels through which we get the news?

- What is the value of the comparison Shirky makes to the revolution brought on by the invention of the printing press?

*U*ncover the evidence.

- Shirky's argument here is based largely on his own insights about the modern media and on historical analogy. What evidence does he use? Could he bring in other evidence, or is this sufficient?

*E*valuate the conclusion.

- Shirky says it is not newspapers we need to worry about saving, but rather journalism. What does he mean by that?
- How does he think journalism can be saved?

*S*ort out the political implications.

- What would a world without newspapers look like? How might it change the practice of American politics?
- What will happen if we are not able to find a way to save journalism?

 ## 14.5 Mr. Hearst Answers High School Girl's Query

William Randolph Hearst, San Francisco Examiner

Why We Chose This Piece

In times of war and national insecurity there are many pressures on the media, both from within government and without, to control their coverage of national affairs. In the days immediately after the September 11 terrorist attacks, President Bush's press secretary told a questioner that people needed to be very careful about what they said. Although he later retracted the statement, he was clearly warning people to be cautious about their comments on the government's antiterror efforts. Journalists covering the war in Afghanistan said that there were tighter limits on the information available to them than in previous military actions they had covered. During wartime there are security concerns that obviously demand secrecy, but governments also have an incentive to use national security as an excuse to control the information and images that go out to the public. The Vietnam War is a lesson in what public opinion can do to a war effort of which people do not approve.

Media censorship is an issue that pertains not just to the war on terror, as demonstrated by this editorial letter by William Randolph Hearst, the great newspaper publisher and editor. Hearst was often blamed for contributing to the sensationalism of the news in the

Selection published: October 8, 1935

early decades of the twentieth century, but, in fact, that gossipy, exaggerated, human-interest form of journalism allowed newspapers to garner sufficiently large circulations that they could afford to free themselves from the government financial support (and control) they had required before the Civil War. In this letter, written in response to a high school girl's question, Hearst makes clear that he thinks the worst fate that can befall the news is to be government controlled. Are his arguments valid today?

T here is no such thing and can be no such thing as government control of NEWSPAPERS.

There may be and there is government control of publications, including daily papers.

But daily papers cease to be NEWSPAPERS as soon as they come under governmental control.

Please observe Germany and Russia and Italy, and all the nations where governments control the daily press.

Papers in such countries print only what the Government wants them to print.

The Government suppresses anything which it does not want printed; and if the editor prints anything which the Government does not approve, he goes to jail and the paper is compelled to suspend publication.

Consequently the public never get the full facts about anything.

They never get the actual NEWS.

They always get just one side of every question,—and that is the government side.

When I was last in England, I met an old friend who was London correspondent for what had once been a great German newspaper. He said: "I have been relieved of my post and am going back to Germany."

"Good heavens," I said, "what have you done?"

"Oh," he said, "I have not done anything, but I cannot send any news from London. My editor says that he is not allowed to print any more news from or about England excepting what the German Government gives him to print.

"He cannot print the real news. He must print what the Government desires to have the people believe. Consequently he says he has no need for a news correspondent. The foreign office of the Government hands him his so-called foreign news."

Again, when I was in Germany, a paper was closed up and its editor deprived of the privilege of ever again editing a paper because he had printed in his paper some absolutely true account of occurrences that the Government did not want printed.

In Russia the same conditions prevail in more aggravated form, and more drastic degree. Editors who do not print what the Government wants or who print what the Government does not want are sent to Siberia or shot.

Under such circumstances, there cannot be any real news or any real newspapers.

Consequently the people never know the TRUTH.

In a despotism perhaps this does not matter much.

It would not do the people any good if they did know the truth. They could not do anything about it. The iron heel of a military dictator is on their necks.

But in a democracy the people MUST know the facts, and must know all sides of all questions.

Good government in a democracy depends upon the enlightenment of the electorate. They cannot vote right unless they are completely informed.

They must have the right to read not merely one newspaper but many newspapers, and get all the facts and shades of opinion.

Free speech and free publication are the cornerstones of democracy—the keystones of liberty.

The first step towards tyranny is the suppression of free speech, and the government control of the press.

When the Government controls the press the people no longer get true accounts of what their Government is doing; and the successive steps to tyranny come quickly and surely.

Therefore, those who advocate government control of the press advocate the downfall of democracy and the end of liberty.

Consider the source and the audience.

- This letter appeared on the front page of Hearst's *San Francisco Examiner*. What does the front-page placement of a letter better suited for the editorial pages tell us about how Hearst regarded his message?

Lay out the argument, the values, and the assumptions.

- What is the relationship between Hearst's key values of truth and democracy? Can we have one without the other?
- What does he see as the citizen's role in democratic government? What happens if citizens are unable to perform that role?
- Would Hearst think that it is ever allowable to have government control of the press? What would happen if we did?

Uncover the evidence.

- Is Hearst's use of comparative examples persuasive? Is what happens in Germany or Russia relevant to what happens in the United States? Why or why not?

Evaluate the conclusion.

- Hearst is uncompromising in his conclusions on this subject. Is he unnecessarily harsh, or is government censorship an all-or-nothing proposition? What would he think would happen once the door to government control was opened?

Sort out the political implications.

- Is censorship permissible under any conditions? When? How do we avoid setting a precedent?

15 ★ ★ ★

Domestic Policy

So far we have spent a good deal of time looking at governmental actors and processes—the *who* and the *how* of politics. In this chapter we turn our attention to the *what*. What does government do with all the personnel, resources, and rules at its disposal? What is at stake in the nitty-gritty political struggles we have examined in this book?

When all is said and done, what government does (or does not do) is called policy. What the U.S. government does here in the United States is domestic policy; what it does in other countries is foreign policy (the subject of Chapter 16). Domestic policies can concern anything government decides is its business—transportation, drugs, security, defense, welfare, education, economic regulation, or environmental protection. The list is endless.

Some of the biggest political battles in the United States involve decisions regarding what is government's business and, if something is an appropriate target for government action, which level of government should act. Historically the U.S. federal government had only a limited policymaking role. The Great Depression of the 1930s changed that dramatically, however, as people demanded that government do something to regulate the ailing economy, get them back to work, and provide them with some security. President Franklin Roosevelt's New Deal offered a way out of many of the social ills that plagued the country after the Depression, and it ushered in a new era of American policymaking.

Since the New Deal, in general (though in politics there are always exceptions), Democrats have tended to approve a larger role for the federal government in solving social problems, and they have tended to hold an expansive idea of what a social problem is. They are often reluctant to leave problems in the hands of the states, fearing uneven or inadequate responses. Republicans, on the other hand, have generally believed that problems should be solved first at the individual level, and then at the state level, with federal action a last resort except for such policy areas as national defense and domestic security.

Members of the two parties also differ in their constituencies, so they are often at odds about whom they think government action should assist. To give just a few examples, Democrats tend to respond to issues affecting workers, minorities, and the environment, while Republicans are more responsive to issues affecting business, religious conservatives, and the military. Another way to think about this is to consider three kinds of policies: *distributive policies*, those that benefit targeted portions of the population (homeowners, for instance, or students, or veterans) and are paid for by all taxpayers; *redistributive policies*, which shift resources from the wealthier part of the population to the less well off; and *regulatory policies*, which seek to restrict or change the actions of a business or an individual. While both parties frequently support distributive policies (though they do not always agree on the groups who should be assisted), Democrats tend to favor redistributive polices, which Republicans are more likely to oppose. Democrats also favor regulation of business, whereas Republicans are more likely to favor regulation of personal and religious life.

Policymaking is tricky for lawmakers. Not only do they have to agree on the problem to be solved and on how to solve it, but also they need to monitor the policy once it is made to see if the solution works and to be sure that it does not cause new, unexpected problems. All kinds of political actors are joined in the enterprise of policymaking—members of Congress, but also the president, the bureaucracy, the courts, and groups of interested citizens along with their professional organizations and lobbyists. Policymaking is the main job of American government, and all the available political resources come to be involved in it.

The selections in this chapter look at a variety of different policies. The first article, from the *Los Angeles Times*, discusses the plight of an honor student who unknowingly violated his school's zero-tolerance policy regarding weapons on campus. This story raises important questions about balancing the regulation of individual behavior with the protection of civil liberties, and about the unintended consequences of a well-intentioned law. The second article, from the *Wall Street Journal* and written by Karl Rove, former deputy chief of staff and senior adviser to President George W. Bush, criticizes President Barack Obama's health care proposal. Third, *Washington Post* and *Newsweek* columnist Robert Samuelson argues that the country's rising debt brings with it dangerous risks for the future. Finally, we provide a transcript of a radio address by President Franklin Roosevelt detailing his actions and plans for combating high unemployment during the Great Depression. In this speech we can see FDR redefining the role of government, setting the stage for many of the policy debates we have today.

15.1 Zero Tolerance Lets a Student's Future Hang on a Knife's Edge

A Utensil Fell into Taylor Hess' Pickup, Dropping Him into a Storm over School Policy

Barry Siegel, Los Angeles Times

Why We Chose This Piece:

In the aftermath of a wave of school violence that hit a horrible climax with the 1999 Columbine High School shootings, several states and localities decided to clean up their schools by enacting zero-tolerance laws designed to keep weapons off campus. These laws meant that any transgression of the rules, no matter how seemingly insignificant or unintentional, would result in a student's expulsion.

We chose the following article from the Los Angeles Times *because it shows that the best intentions can result in unexpected consequences that can return to haunt policymakers. This story profiles an honor student who was expelled for unknowingly bringing a bread knife to school. Although he was eventually readmitted to school, the case raised many questions. Why are zero-tolerance policies attractive to policymakers? What are their limitations? How can lawmakers control the unforeseen consequences of the policies they make?*

No big deal. That's what 16-year-old Taylor Hess thought, watching the assistant principal walk into his fourth-period class.

For Taylor, life was good, couldn't be better. He was an honors student. He was a star on the varsity swim team. That morning, he'd risen at 5:30 for practice. It was agonizing, diving into the school pool before sunrise, but Taylor liked getting something done early. He also liked the individuality of his sport, how in swimming you can only blame yourself.

The assistant principal, he now realized, was looking at him. In fact, Nathaniel Hearne was pointing at him. "Get your car keys," Hearne said. "Come with me."

Taylor still thought, no big deal. Maybe he'd left his headlights on. Maybe he'd parked where he shouldn't.

"A knife has been spotted in your pickup," Hearne said.

He'd gone camping with friends on Saturday, Taylor told him. Maybe someone left a machete in the truck.

"OK," Hearne said. "We'll find out."

In the parking lot, beside the 1993 cranberry red Ford Ranger he'd worked all summer to buy, Taylor saw Alan Goss, the Hurst city policeman assigned full time to

---

Selection published: August 11, 2002

L. D. Bell High. He also saw two private security officers holding a pair of dogs trained to find drugs and weapons.

Taylor looked at the bed of his pickup. It wasn't a machete after all, but an unserrated bread knife with a round point. A long bread knife, a good 10 inches long, lying right out in the open.

Now it clicked. That's my grandma's kitchen knife, Taylor explained. She had a stroke, we had to move her to assisted living, put her stuff in our garage. Last night we took it all to Goodwill. This must have fallen out of a box. I'll lock it up in the cab. Or you can keep it. Or you can call my parents to come get it.

The others just kept staring at the knife. Taylor thought they looked confused, like they didn't know what to do.

"Is it sharp?" Hearne finally asked.

Officer Goss ran his finger along the blade. "It's fairly sharp in a couple of spots."

Hearne slipped the knife inside his sport coat. Taylor walked with him back to class, wondering what his punishment might be. Saturday detention hall, maybe. He'd never pulled D hall before, never been in any trouble.

"Get your stuff and come to my office," Hearne said. "I've got to warn you, Taylor, this is a pretty serious thing."

Beginnings at Columbine

The Hurst-Euless-Bedford Independent School District, about 12 miles west of Dallas, resembles so many others that have fashioned zero-tolerance policies to combat mounting fears of campus violence. For most districts, it began in 1994 with the federal Gun-Free Schools Act, which required all schools receiving federal aid to expel students who bring firearms to campus. Many states and school boards, appalled by the shootings that culminated in the 1999 Columbine High School massacre in Colorado, adopted policies even wider and tougher than the federal law. Everything from paper guns to nail files became weapons, everything from second-grade kisses to Tylenol tablets cause for expulsion. In countless rule books, "shall" and "must" replaced administrative discretion.

There'd been crazy situations ever since: Eighth-graders arrested for bringing "purple cocaine"—grape Kool-Aid—in lunch boxes; a sixth-grader suspended for bringing a toy ax as part of his Halloween fireman costume; a boy expelled for having a "hit list" that turned out to be his birthday party guests. Pundits clucked and civil rights lawyers protested, but for the most part, parents liked the changes, in fact campaigned for them. They wanted more rules, stricter rules. They also wanted consistency. They wanted students treated equally.

Jim Short, the principal of L. D. Bell High, understood all this as he sat at his desk on Monday afternoon, Feb. 25. Just minutes before, they'd found Taylor Hess' knife. Short's heart told him to ignore the matter. He knew Taylor well, thought him a great kid, a terrific young man. He believed the boy's story, he understood what had happened. He didn't believe Taylor had done anything wrong. Yet as principal, Short didn't think he could turn a blind eye.

Before him he had the Texas Education Code's Chapter 37 and his own school district's student code of conduct. They both told him the same thing: He had no latitude. There it was in the state code: A student shall be expelled … if the student on school property ... possesses an illegal knife. There it was in the district code: Student will be expelled for a full calendar year....

Nothing got people's attention more quickly than weapons on campus. Short appreciated this. He was 50 years old. For 26 years, he'd worked in the Abilene, Texas, schools, the last 15 as a principal, before coming to L. D. Bell this year. He knew schools could be dangerous places. An Abilene teacher had been shot on campus. Kids were good generally, but some just didn't care. If Short ignored an infraction, it could blow up in his face. If he ignored Taylor Hess' knife, people would hear about it. Then he'd be assailed for paying no heed to a big carving knife. He had to follow the rules.

Still—Short had a sick feeling. He kept asking himself, what did he expect Taylor to have done differently?

At 2 P.M. that day, Short met with five assistant principals and the Hurst police officer, Alan Goss. They traded opinions without reaching a consensus. Most, even while hoping Taylor might win a later appeal, thought the state and district codes mandated expulsion.

We don't make the laws, the way Officer Goss saw it. Their hands were tied. If he were working as a street cop, if he had pulled Taylor over and seen an illegal knife in his pickup, Goss had discretion on whether even to write a report. He'd probably let him go with a warning. But he couldn't do that on school grounds. Not under the district's zero-tolerance policy.

Short found himself sounding the most liberal. Yet he saw his colleagues' viewpoints. It seemed to him they were honorable people with different opinions. Honorable people who all left the meeting with long faces.

More voices soon chimed in. The Texas Education Agency advised that the district had to proceed against Taylor. A county prosecuting attorney said yes, this was a case he'd accept, this was a violation of the penal code.

That made a difference. Officer Goss had been expecting the prosecuting attorney to say no, don't bring it to me. Expecting—and hoping.

At 2:40 P.M., Taylor Hess, summoned from his 11th-grade advanced-placement chemistry class, stepped into the principal's office. This will all blow over, he'd been telling himself. If no one else knows, they can let it pass. He didn't feel guilty or anxious, the way you did when you knew you'd messed up. Besides, he had a history with this principal. Jim Short had been supportive of the swim team. He'd sat around with them, talking to Taylor, congratulating him for being regional backstroke champ. Short knew him, knew what kind of kid he was.

A non-event. That's what all this was, Taylor figured. A non-event.

He explained again, telling Short about his grandma's stroke, packing up her stuff, driving to Goodwill. Short appeared to believe him but still looked mighty serious. When Taylor stopped talking, Short said, "Taylor, are you aware this calls for mandatory expulsion?"

Parents' Disbelief

Robert and Gay Hess, Taylor's parents, have an unspoken rule. She doesn't call him at work unless it's urgent. She's a physical therapist's assistant at North Hills Hospital; he's a customer service manager for American Eagle airline at the Dallas–Fort Worth airport. At 3 P.M. that Monday, his pager beeped while he sat in a staff meeting. He bolted from the room to call his wife.

"You're not going to believe this," she began, sounding distraught. Taylor's principal had just phoned her. She'd realized right off what this was about. She'd explained everything to Jim Short. He'd appreciated her account, Gay thought. After all, she'd corroborated Taylor's story without knowing what Taylor had told them. Yet Gay didn't think she'd swayed the principal. This is very serious, he'd kept telling her. This is very serious.

Robert Hess tried to calm his wife. He was good at solving problems and easing tension. That's what he did all day with aggravated airline travelers. He could fix this. It was a bread knife, after all. Taylor obviously never even saw it. They were all grownups, weren't they?

"The school district has competent leaders," Robert told Gay. "Surely they will be fair and logical."

Late that day, he called Jim Short's office and arranged to meet with him the next afternoon. During dinner, the Hess family—Taylor has one older brother, Jordan, 17, then an L. D. Bell senior—talked things over. Gay thought it ironic that their family had always wanted to make schools safer; she'd never expected it would backfire on them. Taylor thought, this just shows that no good deed goes unpunished.

Robert Hess' mind drifted to Sunday, to their hours in the garage packing up his mother Rose's stuff. Going through everything had sparked such memories. The glassware, for instance. He was 46 now, yet there were glasses he remembered drinking from as a child, glasses his mom had used to serve Kool-Aid at Cub Scout meetings. She must have kept them, he imagined, because they took her back to a time when she was a young, beautiful woman with small children. Now 80, she sat in assisted living, unaware of Taylor's plight, for they'd chosen not to upset her.

It was funny. Robert and Gay had debated about the cutlery set. Gay had decided not to keep it, so it went into a box. Dusk fell before they finished. In the dark, Robert and Taylor drove a mile to the Goodwill center, bouncing along on the Ranger's old springs. The night drop-off area was poorly lighted, so they could barely see as they unloaded. They worked fast, eager to get home.

Don't worry, Robert Hess told his family now. Maybe Taylor will have to write an essay. Something like that. Something that fits the event.

A Word Study

Again and again, Principal Jim Short flipped through the penal code, the state code, the school code. He asked himself, how do you define "possession"? He studied the words: "knowingly.".."willingly.".."recklessly." The first two didn't apply, but "recklessly"—there were those in the district, both below and above him, who thought Taylor's conduct reckless.

Another word drew Short's attention: "shall." Shall be expelled, not "may" be expelled....

Ten years ago, he would have handled the Taylor Hess situation by himself. No longer. Now Short had to talk to his district supervisors, who talked to the district superintendent, Gene Buinger. People in Buinger's office had to talk to the Texas

Education Agency and local police authorities. The rules and codes kept evolving. Although the federal Gun-Free Schools Act had allowed them "case by case" flexibility, the state refined and the districts refined even further. It was Texas that required expulsion of a student with an "illegal knife," but it was Short's own district that insisted the expulsion be for a full year.

Some school administrators found it insulting or preposterous to lose personal discretion. Zero-tolerance panels at school board conferences often drew overflow crowds. There was always talk of the foolish cases. In recent years in Short's district, there'd been half a dozen as perplexing as Taylor Hess,' half a dozen where district Supt. Buinger believed the punishment had been excessive. "Feel-good legislation" is what Buinger called the state laws; legislation that is "supposed to solve, but deep down, everyone knows it just addresses issues superficially."

Still, Buinger had to admit—zero-tolerance rules made life easier. They eased the burden. By applying consistency instead of subjective judgment, you had support for your actions rather than claims of discrimination. If Jim Short disregarded the Taylor Hess case and six months later a different principal responded another way with, say, a Latino student, you would surely hear cries about prejudice.

That, above all, was why Short's supervisors wanted firm formulas. Their school district was in transition, undergoing "a change in demographics." It was one-third minority now, mostly Latino. There was a distinct and growing gap between poorer and more affluent students. For people to have faith in the school system, they had to believe everyone was being treated equally.

Deep down, despite his unease, Jim Short agreed. He had to admit: He derived a certain comfort in not having discretion. He could lean on that. He could then say he followed the formula.

As arranged, Robert Hess appeared in his office at 2:15 P.M. on Tuesday. Assistant Principal Nathaniel Hearne joined them. So did the Hurst police officer, Alan Goss. Hess sat down, ready to settle this as he did most problems. Right off, though, Short handed him a letter and asked him to sign a receipt for it.

For the first time, Hess began to feel a little nervous. "Wait a minute," he said. "Let me read it."

"This letter is to notify you that your son, Ryan Taylor Hess, is being considered for expulsion from L. D. Bell High School.... We have scheduled a Due Process Hearing for Friday, March 1 at 9:00 A.M...."

Hess' nervousness grew. This looked more significant than he'd expected. He asked, "Would I be overreacting if I brought an attorney?"

"I can't say," Short told him. "But if you do, you need to notify us so we have ours too."

The principal felt he owed it to Hess to be truthful. Short himself would preside at the due process hearing, he explained. He'd be following the code of conduct. It would be unlikely that he'd be able to recommend anything but expulsion.

Hess, normally easy with conversation, sat speechless. OK, he thought, OK. This has gone a step or two further than he'd expected. But surely they'd resolve this at the hearing. They just needed to prepare; they just needed to get ready.

They needed to do one other thing, Robert Hess decided. They needed to call a lawyer.

Quizzing the Educators

A door at the rear of the principal's office leads into a private conference room. There everyone gathered at 9 A.M Friday, settling around a rectangular table. On the table, a tape recorder turned silently. Facing the Hess family now, along with Short, Hearne and Goss, was Dianne Byrnes, who directs the district's "alternative education programs" for problem kids.

This wouldn't be adversarial, Short had advised. Yet it seemed that way to the Hesses. Taylor felt numb, in shock, ready for anything, He talked little, trying instead to grasp what was going on. Same with his mother, who couldn't believe this was even happening. Mainly, Robert Hess spoke for the family.

He'd been preparing for two days, studying the codes, scouring the Internet, consulting an attorney, drafting specific questions for each person present. Whoever loses his temper, he reminded himself, is at a disadvantage. So he spoke politely, without a hint of antagonism, something that Short noted and appreciated. Yet as they walked through the facts of the case, Hess poured on the questions, unrelenting.

You don't have the knife or a photo of the knife at this hearing? You don't have a copy of the police report? You're sitting here today without any of the evidence? Do you really think these proceedings are fair? Do you really feel you're following the spirit of the law? Do any of you in the least doubt the truth of Taylor's explanation? What are your feelings about the school district's zero-tolerance policies? How do you feel about what you're doing to Taylor?

Dianne Byrnes, who wrote the district's code of conduct and spends most of her time on matters of discipline, took the hardest line. Her stance made the Hess family feel uncomfortable. "Taylor did have a knife visible in his truck...," she said. "Taylor did put students at risk.... The spirit of the law is to ensure the safety of students.... I think there was a risk factor."

Jim Short sounded much more ambivalent. Where Byrnes resisted questions about personal feelings, he responded. He thought zero-tolerance policies "a two-edged sword." They made it possible for him to "look myself in the mirror and know that I treated the students as equally as I possibly could." On the other hand, the policies "make you feel like you lose some judgment." So it was for him "a love-hate thing."

Short turned to Hess. "I don't know if that answers your question."

Hess said, "Yes, you answered it eloquently. I can appreciate how frustrating it must be to have your hands tied."

Short sighed. "I'd be lying if I said any aspect of this is pleasant. This is a sorrowful experience."

As they talked, Hess kept looking for signs. No one else had files or questions or evidence. They've already made their decision, he concluded. Reading their body language, he believed he saw people eager to go. To him, Dianne Byrnes seemed particularly antsy, glancing often at her watch. She had another appointment, she declared finally. They would have to postpone this hearing.

"No," Robert Hess said. "We're not through."

Short eventually sided with Hess. At 11 A.M., two hours into the hearing, Dianne Byrnes left. Hess seized the opportunity. Again he asked Short how he felt.

"Miserable," the principal said, with a rueful laugh. "How's that?" He paused. "There's not a good feeling in my body about this."

Half an hour later, they all rose. Short usually ruled right away in these situations, but not today. "I want to think about this over the weekend," he told the Hess family.

Doing the "Right Thing"

Late on Monday afternoon, Robert Hess called the L. D. Bell office. "I need another day," Jim Short told him. "I want to make sure we do the right thing for Taylor and for the student population of Bell High."

Hess' heart sank. Right thing for the student population. Oh my God, he thought. They're going to expel Taylor.

That night he warned his family. Taylor reeled. He'd been in turmoil for a week. Like his principal, he'd been wondering why he hadn't just denied any knowledge of the knife. It hadn't occurred to him, though. There'd been no reason to lie. Besides, he'd always been taught to tell the truth.

Taylor had career plans. He wanted to get a private pilot's license; he wanted to study aeronautical engineering. Now what would happen? Taylor couldn't help but think this whole thing made the school administrators look cowardly. Nobody was asking, what should we do? Instead, everyone was asking, what do we have to do?

The call from Short finally came at 3:15 P.M. Tuesday. "I've decided to expel Taylor," the principal told Robert Hess. "You can appeal. I encourage you to appeal. If you do, I'll be one of Taylor's biggest advocates." Short also asked, "Do you want me to tell Taylor, or should you?"

"We'll both tell him," Hess said. "I'm on my way there." ...

In Short's office. Hess and the principal swapped letters.

Legalese filled Short's: "This is to inform you of my decision to recommend expulsion of Ryan Taylor Hess from L. D. Bell High School."

Hess' cited a federal appellate court ruling in another zero-tolerance case: A school administrator that executed such an action could be held personally liable and would not have the luxury of his qualified immunity.

Hess vainly implored Short to reconsider. Hess said, "Mr. Short, the only thing that can happen from this point on is, this could get bigger and uglier."

Short replied, "I'll try not to take that as a threat." Yet to himself, he thought: This man is just being an advocate for his child. I would do exactly the same.

They called Taylor in. He'd been waiting in the anteroom, summoned once again from his advanced-placement chemistry class. Short explained his decision. Taylor felt gut-punched, stung with pain. All my hard work shot to hell, he thought. Honors classes, the swim team, all a waste of time. He held his tongue, though. Jim Short thought him amazingly courteous.

The principal let Taylor stay at L. D. Bell for two more days, Wednesday and Thursday. Taylor told all his friends now, after keeping things mostly to himself. A couple of teachers had him get up, explain to the class. He asked his English teacher to spread the word wider, to tell other students. Taylor preferred that everyone hear the true story rather than think he'd gone and stabbed someone....

Debate Goes Public

On the Thursday afternoon of spring break, district Supt. Gene Buinger arrived home to find a note on his front door. It was from Monica Mendoza, a reporter for the *Fort Worth Star-Telegram*. Robert Hess had contacted her, she advised, and had provided her a tape recording of Taylor's due process hearing. She'd be writing a story for the Sunday paper. Did Buinger want to respond?

Buinger had heard about the Taylor Hess case. There were 20,000 students in his district, though, 30 schools in all, so he didn't have a complete grasp of the matter. His first response to the reporter's note was surprise—surprise that the Hess family had gone to a newspaper. In his 20 years as a superintendent, that had never happened. Most parents didn't want the notoriety. The Hesses were waiving lots of confidentiality rights.

That didn't mean Buinger believed he could waive confidentiality. He declined to comment to the reporter, explaining that federal law prevented him from responding. Then he braced himself for the article.

Jim Short's phone rang at 4:30 that Sunday morning. You going to call off school? an anonymous voice inquired. Short didn't know what the man was talking about. He was still in bed and hadn't seen the newspaper. The caller explained: They're going to have lots of sharp pencils out.

By 10 that morning, the onslaught had begun, mostly directed at Short. Phone calls, e-mails, radio talk shows, TV cameras, CNN, NBC—from all quarters, pundits and outraged citizens were lambasting him. He'd never imagined being the subject of radio talk shows; he'd never grasped the full might of the Internet.

Zero tolerance is a cop-out. Here my tax dollars are paying a principal to not use his judgment.... Ludicrous.... I am so disgusted.... Not only insane, but cruel and unnecessary.... Any administrator who supports this should resign immediately....

Other messages scared Short even more. The loudest voices came not from civil libertarians but from the antigovernment, right-to-bear-arms crowd. Free men are armed, slaves are disarmed. The Constitution guarantees the right of the people to bear arms.... You're just a bunch of left-wing nazi indoctrinators.... Take away the arms and you break a nation.

Most damaging of all were the Hess family's comments. They were doing back-to-back interviews now, filling TV screens by the hour. It had been their attorney's idea to contact the news media. They agreed, seeing no other alternative, but called only the one Fort Worth reporter. They'd not expected the enormous response. They'd not realized that people would sense this could happen to their own kids, to anyone. The feedback felt good to the Hess family, but also scary. "We're just regular working folks," Robert Hess kept saying. "We're not used to TV trucks and reporters outside our door. This feels so alien."

All the same, they handled it with aplomb. Hess observed that "an act of being a good Samaritan now has this fine young man expelled from school.... Having zero tolerance doesn't mean having zero judgment or zero rights." Taylor, amid bashful shrugs, said, "Somehow a knife had to fall out. A fork couldn't fall out, a spoon couldn't fall out.... It's criminal trespass if I go on campus, which means I can't see my brother graduate."

Gene Buinger and Jim Short realized there was no way to look good. Truth was, they didn't feel good. Buinger thought of his old Marine adage: There's a time when you have to stand at attention and take it.

By Tuesday, though, he'd decided to respond. The school district called a news conference for 2 P.M., timed to make the evening news. Buinger still wouldn't discuss the details of the Hess case, but he wanted to explain the state laws and district codes that mandated their zero-tolerance policy. With printed handouts and a big-screen PowerPoint presentation, he emphasized the "musts" and "shalls."

"We're very limited in what we can do," he said. "I understand the public's frustration. I'm frustrated too.... Individuals opposed to such policies should take their concerns to their respective state legislators."

Watching from the back of the hall, Robert Hess thought Buinger handled himself well. The superintendent had said something about possibly being able to shorten the expulsion because the offense involved a knife, not a gun. Hess sensed that Buinger was trying to find a way out.

The outcry wouldn't stop, though. Hess couldn't believe the momentum. The national newspapers were calling him now, alerted by a story distributed by Associated Press. The school district was getting crucified. The Hurst Police Department had backed away, deciding not to file a complaint with the county prosecutor. So had the Texas Education Agency, telling AP that local districts did have discretion, that "every case has to be looked at individually."

Enough, the Hess family resolved. For Taylor, the first couple of times on TV had been neat, but the back-to-back interviews lost their sparkle real quick. For his father, it began to feel like piling on. When would it just become cruel? It wasn't his intent to ruin the school system, to hurt these people's careers. He just wanted Taylor back in school.

He would turn down further interviews, Hess decided. He'd take all the reporters' phone numbers, stick them in his hip pocket. If his family lost their appeal, scheduled for Thursday at 11 A.M., he could always pull them out again.

By Wednesday night, that didn't seem likely. Early in the evening, the phone rang at the Hess home. It was an assistant superintendent in Gene Buinger's office. Would the Hesses be agreeable to a 9 A.M. meeting, he wondered, before the scheduled appeal? The district had some ideas. The district thought matters maybe could be resolved.

Finding a Way to Bend

In the end, it all came down to what had been lacking, to what everyone said the law didn't allow: personal judgment.

The federal Gun-Free Schools Act had always included a clause specifying that state laws "shall" allow school superintendents to modify expulsion requirements. The Texas Education Agency, in a letter to district administrators, had made clear that the term of expulsions "may be reduced from the statutory one year." Yet it was the Hurst-Euless-Bedford district's own code that governed in the Hess case—and like many others across the country, the HEB district had handcuffed itself by mandating inflexible one-year expulsions.

Now, one day before the Hesses' appeal, Gene Buinger decided to remove the self-imposed handcuffs. He'd simply waive district policy; he'd rescind the expulsion.

Following a conversation with the Texas Education Agency's school safety division, he thought he could do that, especially since the police had never filed a complaint. And if he could do that, why even hold an appeal hearing?

When the Hesses arrived at his office on Friday morning, Buinger began to explain his plan. Just then, however, an assistant came in carrying a newly arrived fax from the state agency's legal department. No, the fax advised, Buinger couldn't rescind the expulsion. He could only reduce the expulsion to time served.

Buinger wasn't sure whether the Hesses would buy this. He shared with them the conflicting advice he'd received. This does call for expulsion, he said, but we can adjust the amount of time. Is that OK with you?

Robert Hess had a typed list of conditions. "Yes," he said. "If we can agree on these."

The Hesses wanted Taylor readmitted immediately to L. D. Bell, his record expunged of any reference to the expulsion, tutorials to help him catch up on missed classes and a public announcement of the resolution. Buinger's staff readily agreed, but since it was already Thursday, they thought Taylor should come back to Bell on Monday.

No, Robert Hess said. Tomorrow.

Applause greeted the announcement, at an 11 A.M. joint news conference, that Taylor Hess would be returning to L. D. Bell the next morning. Taylor said it hadn't been "a pleasant experience, but I hold no personal grudges." Robert Hess said, "What I was hoping for is exactly what I got." Gene Buinger said, "Zero-tolerance policies have become excessive.... The school board is now undertaking a complete review of district policy. We want to give as much discretion as possible to local administrators so we don't have to repeat this situation."

In time, the district would revise its policy, among other things ending the mandatory one-year term for expulsions. All that remained unresolved were the fundamental reasons for zero-tolerance policies in the first place. Gene Buinger knew as much; he knew that if another student had lifted the knife from Taylor's pickup and used it in an altercation, they would have endured an even more impassioned response. He knew also what he would hear in the next knife-on-campus case: I want the same as Taylor Hess. If I don't get the same, it's discrimination.

There were no simple answers. Still, returning to L. D. Bell after the final news conference, Jim Short saw one thing clearly. This day happened to be the occasion for another random security sweep of the campus, complete with drug-sniffing dogs. There they were, out on the parking lot, just as they were the morning they spotted Taylor's knife. This crew had never found drugs, hardly ever weapons. Littering and tardiness had been the biggest problems at Bell all year.

"No thank you," Short told the dog handlers. "You're not going to do this today. Stay out of the parking lot. Stay out of our classes."

---

*C*onsider the source and the audience.

- Why would a national newspaper like the *Los Angeles Times* run a story about a small town in Texas?
- This is a human-interest story with lots of personal detail. How does that fact affect your feelings about it? Can you tell where Siegel's sympathies lie?

*L*ay out the argument, the values, and the assumptions.

- Both the people advocating zero-tolerance laws and those opposing them are concerned about "fairness," but they define it differently. What two definitions of "fairness" are at work here?
- How do values like safety, flexibility, due process, and equality figure into the arguments made by each side? What trade-offs among these values is each side willing to make?

*U*ncover the evidence.

- How does Siegel know what happened, who thought what, and who said what to whom? What motives might his sources have had in talking to him?
- What evidence do the two sides bring to bear in making their cases for and against the policy?

*E*valuate the conclusion.

- The advocates of zero tolerance believe that schools can be safe, and students treated fairly, only if all transgressions of the no-weapons rule are swiftly and evenly met with expulsion. Opponents also want safety and fairness, but they want administrators to be able to use discretion in applying sanctions. Can either side get what it wants?
- What are the implications of this article for zero-tolerance policies? Are such implications stated clearly?

*S*ort out the political implications.

- Ultimately, even with a zero-tolerance policy in place, Taylor Hess was treated differently due to the individual circumstances of his case, his own personal merits, and the advantages his family could bring to his defense. What is the lesson here for the makers of zero-tolerance policies?

15.2 How to Stop Socialized Health Care

Five Arguments Republicans Must Make

Karl Rove, Wall Street Journal

Why We Chose This Piece

Health care reform was a central part of President Obama's platform on the campaign trail. Yet few issues are more complex and controversial. Democrats often argue that reform is needed to lower costs and provide health care to more citizens. Republicans, such as the author of this op-ed, generally claim that the reforms usually championed by Democrats would lower the quality of health care services and amount to socialized medicine. We include this article because health care reform is a seemingly perennial policy debate.

Selection published: June 11, 2009

I t was a sobering breakfast with one of the smartest Republicans on Capitol Hill. We can fix a lot of bad stuff President Barack Obama might do, he told me. But if Mr. Obama signs into law a "public option," government-run insurance program as part of health-care reform we won't be able to undo the damage.

I'd go the Republican member of Congress one further: If Democrats enact a public-option health-insurance program, America is on the way to becoming a European-style welfare state. To prevent this from happening, there are five arguments Republicans must make.

The first is it's unnecessary. Advocates say a government-run insurance program is needed to provide competition for private health insurance. But 1,300 companies sell health insurance plans. That's competition enough. The results of robust private competition to provide the Medicare drug benefit underscore this. When it was approved, the Congressional Budget Office estimated it would cost $74 billion a year by 2008. Nearly 100 providers deliver the drug benefit, competing on better benefits, more choices, and lower prices. So the actual cost was $44 billion in 2008—nearly 41% less than predicted. No government plan was needed to guarantee competition's benefits.

Second, a public option will undercut private insurers and pass the tab to taxpayers and health providers just as it does in existing government-run programs. For example, Medicare pays hospitals 71% and doctors 81% of what private insurers pay.

Who covers the rest? Government passes the bill for the outstanding balance to providers and families not covered by government programs. This cost-shifting amounts to a forced subsidy. Families pay about $1,800 more a year for someone else's health care as a result, according to a recent study by Milliman Inc. It's also why many doctors limit how many Medicare patients they take: They can afford only so much charity care.

Fixing prices at less than market rates will continue under any public option. Sen. Edward Kennedy's proposal, for example, has Washington paying providers what Medicare does plus 10%. That will lead to health providers offering less care.

Third, government-run health insurance would crater the private insurance market, forcing most Americans onto the government plan. The Lewin Group estimates 70% of people with private insurance—120 million Americans—will quickly lose what they now get from private companies and be forced onto the government-run rolls as businesses decide it is more cost-effective for them to drop coverage. They'd be happy to shift some of the expense—and all of the administration headaches—to Washington. And once the private insurance market has been dismantled it will be gone.

Fourth, the public option is far too expensive. The cost of Medicare—the purest form of a government-run "public choice" for seniors—will start exceeding its payroll-tax "trust fund" in 2017. The Obama administration estimates its health reforms will cost as much as $1.5 trillion over the next 10 years. It is no coincidence the Obama budget nearly triples the national debt over that same period.

Medicare and Medicaid cost much more than estimated when they were adopted. One reason is there's no competition for these government-run insurance programs. In the same way, Americans can expect a public option to cost far more than the Obama administration's rosy estimates.

Fifth, the public option puts government firmly in the middle of the relationship between patients and their doctors. If you think insurance companies are bad, imagine what happens when government is the insurance carrier, with little or no competition and no concern you'll change to another company.

In other words, the public option is just phony. It's a bait-and-switch tactic meant to reassure people that the president's goals are less radical than they are. Mr. Obama's real aim, as some candid Democrats admit, is a single-payer, government-run health-care system.

Health care desperately needs far-reaching reforms that put patients and their doctors in charge, bring the benefits of competition and market forces to bear, and ensure access to affordable and portable health care for every American. Republicans have plans to achieve this, and they must make their case for reform in every available forum.

Defeating the public option should be a top priority for the GOP this year. Otherwise, our nation will be changed in damaging ways almost impossible to reverse.

*C*onsider the source and the audience.

- As noted, Rove is a well-known political strategist. Is his argument here intended to detail the cons of Obama's health care plan, or is his argument political? In other words, is it focused on the drawbacks of the plan, or on the ways in which the plan can be defeated? Is there a difference between the two?

*L*ay out the argument, the values, and the assumptions.

- Rove clearly lays out five arguments he believes Republicans must make against the Obama health care proposal. What are they?
- How does Rove's view of government compare to Obama's? What does Rove believe is Obama's ultimate goal?

*U*ncover the evidence.

- Rove provides several statistics to support his claim. Do you have enough information regarding the background of these statistics to assess their persuasiveness? What other statistics, if any, would you like to see?

*E*valuate the conclusion.

- Rove concludes that if Obama's plan is passed, "our nation will be changed in damaging ways almost impossible to reverse." Does he articulate what those damaging ways are? Are you persuaded?

*S*ort out the political implications.

- Like Bill Clinton, Barack Obama ran on a platform that included expanding health care coverage. Clinton failed to enact meaningful health care reform, and, at the time of this writing at least, Obama is finding it exceedingly difficult to get his proposal passed. What do you think it is about the issue of health care that makes change to the system so difficult?
- If Obama fails on health care reform, how might that affect his ability to pass other aspects of his agenda? Would failure on this issue affect his prospects for 2012?

15.3 Obama's Risky Debt

Robert J. Samuelson, Washington Post

Why We Chose This Piece

With few exceptions, in recent American history the national government has racked up substantial deficits—shortfalls in the budget due to government spending more in a year than it takes in. These deficits have led to a ballooning national debt—the accumulation of deficits. Much has been written on the rising debt, not so much because of the problems it creates today, but because of the problems analysts believe it will create in the future. Here, Robert Samuelson, a columnist who writes regularly on economic issues, contributes to that argument. Samuelson's piece is interesting because, if he is correct, the current generation of college students will be left to deal with the issues he documents.

Just how much government debt does a president have to endorse before he's labeled "irresponsible"? Well, apparently much more than the massive amounts envisioned by President Obama. The final version of his 2010 budget, released last week, is a case study in political expediency and economic gambling.

Let's see. From 2010 to 2019, Obama projects annual deficits totaling $7.1 trillion; that's atop the $1.8 trillion deficit for 2009. By 2019, the ratio of publicly held federal debt to gross domestic product (GDP, or the economy) would reach 70 percent, up from 41 percent in 2008. That would be the highest since 1950 (80 percent). The Congressional Budget Office, using less optimistic economic forecasts, raises these estimates. The 2010-19 deficits would total $9.3 trillion; the debt-to-GDP ratio in 2019 would be 82 percent.

But wait: Even these totals may be understated. By various estimates, Obama's health plan might cost $1.2 trillion over a decade; Obama has budgeted only $635 billion. Next, the huge deficits occur despite a pronounced squeeze of defense spending. From 2008 to 2019, total federal spending would rise 75 percent, but defense spending would increase only 17 percent. Unless foreign threats recede, military spending and deficits might both grow.

Except from crabby Republicans, these astonishing numbers have received little attention—a tribute to Obama's Zen-like capacity to discourage serious criticism. Everyone's fixated on the present economic crisis, which explains and justifies big deficits (lost revenue, anti-recession spending) for a few years. Hardly anyone notes that huge deficits continue indefinitely.

One reason Obama is so popular is that he has promised almost everyone lower taxes and higher spending. Beyond the undeserving who make more than $250,000, 95 percent of "working families" receive a tax cut. Obama would double federal spending for basic research in "key agencies." He wants to build high-speed-rail

---

Selection published: May 18, 2009

networks that would require continuous subsidy. Obama can do all this and more by borrowing.

Consider the extra debt as a proxy for political evasion. The president doesn't want to confront Americans with choices between lower spending and higher taxes—or, given the existing deficits, perhaps both *less spending and more taxes*. Except for talk, Obama hasn't done anything to reduce the expense of retiring baby boomers. He claims to be containing overall health costs, but he's actually proposing more government spending (see above).

Closing future deficits with either tax increases or spending cuts would require gigantic changes. Discounting the recession's effect on the deficit, Marc Goldwein of the Committee for a Responsible Federal Budget puts the underlying "structural deficit"— the basic gap between the government's spending commitments and its tax base—at 3 to 4 percent of GDP. In today's dollars, that's roughly $400 billion to $600 billion.

It's true that since 1961 the federal budget has run deficits in all but five years. But the resulting government debt has consistently remained below 50 percent of GDP; that's the equivalent of a household with $100,000 of income having a $50,000 debt. (Note: Deficits are the annual gap between government's spending and its tax revenue. The debt is the total borrowing caused by past deficits.) Adverse economic effects, if any, were modest. But Obama's massive, future deficits would break this pattern and become more threatening.

At best, the rising cost of the debt would intensify pressures to increase taxes, cut spending—or create bigger, unsustainable deficits. By the CBO's estimates, interest on the debt as a share of federal spending will double between 2008 and 2019, to 16 percent. Huge budget deficits could also weaken economic growth by "crowding out" private investment.

At worst, the burgeoning debt could trigger a future financial crisis. The danger is that "we won't be able to sell [Treasury debt] at reasonable interest rates," says economist Rudy Penner, head of the CBO from 1983 to 1987. In today's anxious climate, this hasn't happened. American and foreign investors have favored "safe" U.S. Treasurys. But a glut of bonds, fears of inflation—or something else—might one day shatter confidence. Bond prices might fall sharply; interest rates would rise. The consequences could be worldwide because foreigners own half of U.S. Treasury debt.

The Obama budgets flirt with deferred distress, though we can't know what form it might take or when it might occur. Present gain comes with the risk of future pain. As the present economic crisis shows, imprudent policies ultimately backfire, even if the reversal's timing and nature are unpredictable.

The wonder is that these issues have been so ignored. Imagine hypothetically that a President McCain had submitted a budget plan identical to Obama's. There would almost certainly have been a loud outcry: "McCain's Mortgaging Our Future." Obama should be held to no less exacting a standard.

*C*onsider the source and the audience.

- Samuelson is a columnist for the *Washington Post* and *Newsweek*. This column appeared in both news outlets. Who is Samuelson appealing to here? A general audience? A specific group?

*L*ay out the argument, the values, and the assumptions.

- Why is Samuelson so concerned with the Obama budget? Why does he argue that deficits have increased?
- What effects does Samuelson believe increasing deficits (hence, an increasing debt) will have?

*U*ncover the evidence.

- Samuelson provides numerous statistics documenting the increasing deficits. Does he provide any evidence that the increasing deficits will have the negative effects he predicts?
- What empirical data could Samuelson provide to support his argument, or is his argument more theoretical?

*E*valuate the conclusion.

- What solution does Samuelson give to halt the increasing deficits? How politically feasible is that solution?
- Has Samuelson convinced you that growing deficits are a problem? Why or why not?

*S*ort out the political implications.

- If the national debt continues to grow, how might that affect government services in the future? The economy? The United States' standing as a superpower?
- A common refrain is that budgets should be balanced. However, can some debt be good? What issues might arise if the national government always balanced its budget?

 15.4 Fireside Chat

The Work Relief Program

Franklin Delano Roosevelt

Why We Chose This Piece

When President Franklin Roosevelt was inaugurated in the winter of 1933, roughly a third of Americans were unemployed. When he told the nation, in his inaugural address, that the only thing we have to fear is fear itself, he was referring in part to the devastating effects that economic panic had had on the system. Many Americans were fearful that good times had come to an end permanently.

By the spring of 1935, FDR was halfway through his first term. He had already set in motion new legislation, including reforms designed to help heal the American banking

---

Selection aired: April 28, 1935

system, but he had much more planned in his New Deal for America. In this "fireside chat" he outlined his ideas for a works relief policy—a temporary program to get people back to work at the public's expense—as well as for Social Security, the program for worker compensation and old-age pensions that is still with us, albeit in somewhat rocky financial shape today. We include this speech because it was one of many examples during Roosevelt's presidency that changed the scope of domestic policymaking. In what ways does this speech show how FDR was redefining the way Americans thought about the purpose of government and the role of the presidency? Also, the speech allows for an interesting comparison to the challenges facing President Obama as he entered office.

Since my annual message to the Congress on January fourth, last, I have not addressed the general public over the air. In the many weeks since that time the Congress has devoted itself to the arduous task of formulating legislation necessary to the country's welfare. It has made and is making distinct progress.

Before I come to any of the specific measures, however, I want to leave in your minds one clear fact. The Administration and the Congress are not proceeding in any haphazard fashion in this task of government. Each of our steps has a definite relationship to every other step. The job of creating a program for the Nation's welfare is, in some respects, like the building of a ship. At different points on the coast where I often visit they build great seagoing ships. When one of these ships is under construction and the steel frames have been set in the keel, it is difficult for a person who does not know ships to tell how it will finally look when it is sailing the high seas.

It may seem confused to some, but out of the multitude of detailed parts that go into the making of the structure the creation of a useful instrument for man ultimately comes. It is that way with the making of a national policy. The objective of the Nation has greatly changed in three years. Before that time individual self-interest and group selfishness were paramount in public thinking. The general good was at a discount.

Three years of hard thinking have changed the picture. More and more people, because of clearer thinking and a better understanding, are considering the whole rather than a mere part relating to one section or to one crop, or to one industry, or to an individual private occupation. That is a tremendous gain for the principles of democracy. The overwhelming majority of people in this country know how to sift the wheat from the chaff in what they hear and what they read. They know that the process of the constructive rebuilding of America cannot be done in a day or a year, but that it is being done in spite of the few who seek to confuse them and to profit by their confusion. Americans as a whole are feeling a lot better—a lot more cheerful than for many, many years.

The most difficult place in the world to get a clear open perspective of the country as a whole is Washington. I am reminded sometimes of what President Wilson once said: "So many people come to Washington who know things that are not so, and so few people who know anything about what the people of the United States are thinking about." That is why I occasionally leave this scene of action for a few days to go fishing or back home to Hyde Park, so that I can have a chance to think quietly about the country as a whole. "To get away from the trees," as they say, "and to look at the whole forest." This duty of seeing the country in a long-range perspective is one which, in a very special manner, attaches to this office to which you have chosen me. Did you ever stop to think that there are, after all, only two positions in the Nation that are filled by the vote of all of the voters—the President and the Vice-President? That makes it particularly necessary for the Vice-President and for me to conceive of our duty toward the entire country. I speak, therefore, tonight, to and of the American people as a whole.

My most immediate concern is in carrying out the purposes of the great work program just enacted by the Congress. Its first objective is to put men and women now on the relief rolls to work and, incidentally, to assist materially in our already unmistakable march toward recovery. I shall not confuse my discussion by a multitude of figures. So many figures are quoted to prove so many things. Sometimes it depends upon what paper you read and what broadcast you hear. Therefore, let us keep our minds on two or three simple, essential facts in connection with this problem of unemployment. It is true that while business and industry are definitely better our relief rolls are still too large. However, for the first time in five years the relief rolls have declined instead of increased during the winter months. They are still declining. The simple fact is that many million more people have private work today than two years ago today or one year ago today, and every day that passes offers more chances to work for those who want to work. In spite of the fact that unemployment remains a serious problem here as in every other nation, we have come to recognize the possibility and the necessity of certain helpful remedial measures. These measures are of two kinds. The first is to make provisions intended to relieve, to minimize, and to prevent future unemployment; the second is to establish the practical means to help those who are unemployed in this present emergency. Our social security legislation is an attempt to answer the first of these questions. Our work relief program the second. The program for social security now pending before the Congress is a necessary part of the future unemployment policy of the government. While our present and projected expenditures for work relief are wholly within the reasonable limits of our national credit resources, it is obvious that we cannot continue to create governmental deficits for that purpose year after year. We must begin now to make provision for the future. That is why our social security program is an important part of the complete picture. It proposes, by means of old age pensions, to help those who have reached the age of retirement to give up their jobs and thus give to the younger generation greater opportunities for work and to give to all a feeling of security as they look toward old age.

The unemployment insurance part of the legislation will not only help to guard the individual in future periods of lay-off against dependence upon relief, but it will, by sustaining purchasing power, cushion the shock of economic distress. Another helpful feature of unemployment insurance is the incentive it will give to employers to plan more carefully in order that unemployment may be prevented by the stabilizing of employment itself.

Provisions for social security, however, are protections for the future. Our responsibility for the immediate necessities of the unemployed has been met by the Congress through the most comprehensive work plan in the history of the Nation. Our problem is to put to work three and one-half million employable persons now on the relief rolls. It is a problem quite as much for private industry as for the government.

We are losing no time getting the government's vast work relief program underway, and we have every reason to believe that it should be in full swing by autumn. In directing it, I shall recognize six fundamental principles:

(1) The projects should be useful.

(2) Projects shall be of a nature that a considerable proportion of the money spent will go into wages for labor.

(3) Projects which promise ultimate return to the Federal Treasury of a considerable proportion of the costs will be sought.

(4) Funds allotted for each project should be actually and promptly spent and not held over until later years.

(5) In all cases projects must be of a character to give employment to those on the relief rolls.

(6) Projects will be allocated to localities or relief areas in relation to the number of workers on relief rolls in those areas.

... For many months preparations have been under way. The allotment of funds for desirable projects has already begun. The key men for the major responsibilities of this great task already have been selected. I well realize that the country is expecting before this year is out to see the "dirt fly," as they say, in carrying on the work, and I assure my fellow citizens that no energy will be spared in using these funds effectively to make a major attack upon the problem of unemployment.

Our responsibility is to all of the people in this country. This is a great national crusade to destroy enforced idleness which is an enemy of the human spirit generated by this depression. Our attack upon these enemies must be without stint and without discrimination. No sectorial, no political distinctions can be permitted. It must, however, be recognized that when an enterprise of this character is extended over more than three thousand counties throughout the Nation, there may be occasional instances of inefficiency, bad management, or misuse of funds. When cases of this kind occur, there will be those, of course, who will try to tell you that the exceptional failure is characteristic of the entire endeavor. It should be remembered that in every big job there are some imperfections. There are chiselers in every walk of life; there are those in every industry who are guilty of unfair practices, every profession has its black sheep, but long experience in government has taught me that the exceptional instances of wrong-doing in government are probably less numerous than in almost every other line of endeavor. The most effective means of preventing such evils in this work relief program will be the eternal vigilance of the American people themselves. I call upon my fellow citizens everywhere to cooperate with me in making this the most efficient and the cleanest example of public enterprise the world has ever seen. It is time to provide a smashing answer for those cynical men who say that a democracy cannot be honest and efficient. If you will help, this can be done. I, therefore, hope you will watch the work in every corner of this Nation. Feel free to criticize. Tell me of instances where work can be done better, or where improper practices prevail. Neither you nor I want criticism conceived in a purely fault-finding or partisan spirit, but I am jealous of the right of every citizen to call to the attention of his or her government examples of how the public money can be more effectively spent for the benefit of the American people.

I now come, my friends, to a part of the remaining business before the Congress. It has under consideration many measures which provide for the rounding out of the program of economic and social reconstruction with which we have been concerned for two years. I can mention only a few of them tonight, but I do not want my mention of specific measures to be interpreted as lack of interest in or disapproval of many other important proposals that are pending. The National Industrial Recovery Act expires on the sixteenth of June. After careful consideration, I have asked the Congress to extend the life of this useful agency of government. As we have proceeded with the administration of this Act, we have found from time to time more and more useful ways of promoting its purposes. No reasonable person wants to abandon our present gains—we must continue to protect children, to enforce minimum wages, to prevent excessive hours, to safeguard, define and enforce collective bargaining, and, while retaining fair competition, to eliminate, so far as humanly possible, the kinds of unfair practices by selfish minorities which unfortunately did more than anything else to bring about the recent collapse of industries. There is likewise pending before the Congress legislation to provide for the elimination of unnecessary holding companies in the public utility field. . . .

Not only business recovery, but the general economic recovery of the Nation will be greatly stimulated by the enactment of legislation designed to improve the status of our transportation agencies. There is need for legislation providing for the regulation of interstate transportation by buses and trucks, to regulate transportation by water, new provisions for strengthening our Merchant Marine and air transport, measures for the strengthening of the Interstate Commerce Commission to enable it to carry out a rounded conception of the national transportation system in which the benefits of private ownership are retained, while the public stake in these important services is protected by the public's government.

Finally, the reestablishment of public confidence in the banks of the Nation is one of the most hopeful results of our efforts as a Nation to reestablish public confidence in private banking. We all know that private banking actually exists by virtue of the permission of and regulation by the people as a whole, speaking through their government. Wise public policy, however, requires not only that banking be safe but that its resources be most fully utilized, in the economic life of the country. To this end it was decided more than twenty years ago that the government should assume the responsibility of providing a means by which the credit of the Nation might be controlled, not by a few private banking institutions, but by a body with public prestige and authority. The answer to this demand was the Federal Reserve System. Twenty years of experience with this system have justified the efforts made to create it, but these twenty years have shown by experience definite possibilities for improvement. Certain proposals made to amend the Federal Reserve Act deserve prompt and favorable action by the Congress. They are a minimum of wise readjustment of our Federal Reserve system in the light of past experience and present needs.

These measures I have mentioned are, in large part, the program which under my constitutional duty I have recommended to the Congress. They are essential factors in a rounded program for national recovery. They contemplate the enrichment of our national life by a sound and rational ordering of its various elements and wise provisions for the protection of the weak against the strong. Never since my inauguration in

March, 1933, have I felt so unmistakably the atmosphere of recovery. But it is more than the recovery of the material basis of our individual lives. It is the recovery of confidence in our democratic processes and institutions. We have survived all of the arduous burdens and the threatening dangers of a great economic calamity. We have in the darkest moments of our national trials retained our faith in our own ability to master our destiny. Fear is vanishing and confidence is growing on every side, renewed faith in the vast possibilities of human beings to improve their material and spiritual status through the instrumentality of the democratic form of government. That faith is receiving its just reward. For that we can be thankful to the God who watches over America.

Consider the source and the audience.

- Roosevelt gave this speech to the American public over the radio. He was the first president to regularly sidestep the critical voice of the media to speak directly with his constituency en masse. Why did FDR choose to "go public?"

Lay out the argument, the values, and the assumptions.

- What does FDR see as the basic purpose of government in a time of crisis? How does this differ from the view of government as basically an administrative apparatus?
- What does FDR see as the fundamental difference between his social security proposals and the work relief program?
- Even though FDR's audience wants him to fix its broken system, the solutions he proposes are unorthodox and even threatening to many Americans. How does he try to diffuse the public's fear?

Uncover the evidence.

- To make the point that the public should support his policies, FDR needs to argue that what he has done so far has been effective, but that more needs to be done. What evidence does he offer to support this claim? Is it enough?

Evaluate the conclusion.

- Is FDR right in saying that it is government's job to restore economic security, the enrichment of national life, confidence in democracy, and faith in human beings?

Sort out the political implications.

- Although obvious exceptions exist, some analysts have drawn parallels between the problems facing Roosevelt and Obama when they entered office. Based on your reading of this speech, what similarities exist? What issues and obstacles did Roosevelt face that Obama has not? Has Obama had any challenges that Roosevelt did not encounter?
- It is now close to seventy years since FDR's New Deal changed our expectations of government and altered the way we perceive the office of the presidency. What would life today be like if we still believed that government should have a narrowly prescribed role and that the president's job is just to be chief among the bureaucrats running the administrative apparatus of government?

16

Foreign Policy

It is clear from Chapter 15 that Americans are split over the role of the national government on domestic issues. Liberals generally want more government involvement, conservatives less. Americans are often just as divided over foreign policy. In fact, some of the most heated political debates deal with issues of foreign policy. In what world affairs should we involve ourselves? Who are our allies? When do we use diplomacy as a tool, and when do international affairs require the use of force?

How do the parties divide on foreign policy issues? Keeping in mind that there are always exceptions, we can say that liberals are more likely to support aid to other countries and efforts to build democratic regimes abroad (although, as illustrated by Reading 16.2, this goal was a central part of President George W. Bush's foreign policy). Liberals are more willing to support the United Nations (UN) and to engage in multilateral foreign policy—building support among several nations. In matters of war they tend to be doves; that is, they hesitate to use force.

Conservatives, on the other hand, are generally nationalistic. They are more likely to be hawks (they tend to support military action) and are skeptical of the UN. As a consequence, they are more likely to endorse unilateral action, in which the United States goes it alone without the support of our allies or international organizations. They question aid to foreign governments or for building up regimes because of the cost, and they believe that money is better spent on programs at home—or not spent at all.

The United States is the only remaining superpower; no other country in the world has as complex a foreign policy or plays as large a global role. Yet that hasn't always been the case. Not until our belated, reluctant involvement in World War II did the United States emerge as a major player on the world stage. After World War II the fascist governments of Germany and Italy were defeated, but a new enemy emerged, the totalitarian and communist Soviet Union. The development of hydrogen and nuclear weapons changed diplomacy as well, adding a weapon of mass destruction that the world had never seen before.

In the 1960s and 1970s controversy surrounding U.S. involvement in Vietnam forced many observers to question the goals of American foreign policy. During the 1980s the arms race heated up as President Ronald Reagan convinced Congress to put millions of dollars into military buildup and the development of missile defense technology. The collapse of the Soviet Union in the late 1980s brought the Cold War to an end but raised a number of new questions regarding U.S. foreign policy. The United States was now the world's only superpower, but that did not mean it was without enemies.

As a result of the terrorist attacks of September 11, 2001, foreign policy issues have emerged once again at the top of a president's issue agenda. The Soviet Union is no longer the enemy—now it is a group of rogue nations and terrorist organizations, such as al Qaeda, that many people believe present the biggest threat to the United States. The enemy may have changed, but the questions posed earlier have not. In fact, they remain as important and controversial as ever.

In this chapter we tackle some of those foreign policy questions. We begin with an article written by then–presidential candidate Barack Obama outlining his positions on several foreign policy issues. Next, Peter Baker of the *New York Times* analyzes two different approaches—one by the George W. Bush administration, the other by the Obama administration—to promoting democracy abroad. Then we examine an article from the conservative *New American*, in which Steve Bonta argues that the events of September 11 have forced us to focus on a new threat—terrorism—and have made us forget about what he still considers the real threat to the country, a nuclear attack. Finally, for this chapter's classic piece, we turn to President Reagan's address to the National Association of Evangelicals, in which he warned that we need to maintain national strength and defense capabilities against "evil empires" like the former Soviet Union.

 ## 16.1 Renewing American Leadership

Barack Obama, Foreign Affairs

Why We Chose This Piece

Throughout this reader, you have heard from scholars, op-ed writers, reporters, and political consultants who have either criticized or supported aspects of the Obama administration. Here, you hear directly from the president—who at the time of this writing was a candidate.

We include this article for several reasons. First, it covers numerous important topics that cannot be addressed individually in such a short chapter. Your instructor will have the opportunity to broadly cover all of the topics or speak to some in greater detail. Second, what better way to study foreign policy than to analyze the writing of the person with the most control over U.S. foreign policy—the president?

Selection published: July/August 2007

This leads us to a third reason for including the article. This piece was written before Barack Obama was elected president. He was not even the Democratic nominee at the time of the writing, but rather one of several hopefuls to represent his party in the 2008 presidential election. People have long argued that campaigning and governing are two different things. On the campaign trail, candidates can make promises that, once they become president, either are difficult to implement or are no longer prudent. As you read the article, ask yourself whether Obama has followed through on what he said he would do. In other words, would Barack Obama the president write the same article today as Barack Obama the candidate did a year before he was elected?

Common Security for Our Common Humanity

At moments of great peril in the last century, American leaders such as Franklin Roosevelt, Harry Truman, and John F. Kennedy managed both to protect the American people and to expand opportunity for the next generation. What is more, they ensured that America, by deed and example, led and lifted the world—that we stood for and fought for the freedoms sought by billions of people beyond our borders.

As Roosevelt built the most formidable military the world had ever seen, his Four Freedoms gave purpose to our struggle against fascism. Truman championed a bold new architecture to respond to the Soviet threat—one that paired military strength with the Marshall Plan and helped secure the peace and well-being of nations around the world. As colonialism crumbled and the Soviet Union achieved effective nuclear parity, Kennedy modernized our military doctrine, strengthened our conventional forces, and created the Peace Corps and the Alliance for Progress. They used our strengths to show people everywhere America at its best.

Today, we are again called to provide visionary leadership. This century's threats are at least as dangerous as and in some ways more complex than those we have confronted in the past. They come from weapons that can kill on a mass scale and from global terrorists who respond to alienation or perceived injustice with murderous nihilism. They come from rogue states allied to terrorists and from rising powers that could challenge both America and the international foundation of liberal democracy. They come from weak states that cannot control their territory or provide for their people. And they come from a warming planet that will spur new diseases, spawn more devastating natural disasters, and catalyze deadly conflicts.

To recognize the number and complexity of these threats is not to give way to pessimism. Rather, it is a call to action. These threats demand a new vision of leadership in the twenty-first century—a vision that draws from the past but is not bound by outdated thinking. The Bush administration responded to the unconventional attacks of 9/11 with conventional thinking of the past, largely viewing problems as state-based and principally amenable to military solutions. It was this tragically misguided view that led us into a war in Iraq that never should have been authorized and never should have been waged. In the wake of Iraq and Abu Ghraib, the world has lost trust in our purposes and our principles.

After thousands of lives lost and billions of dollars spent, many Americans may be tempted to turn inward and cede our leadership in world affairs. But this is a mistake we must not make. America cannot meet the threats of this century alone, and the world cannot meet them without America. We can neither retreat from the world nor try to bully it into submission. We must lead the world, by deed and by example.

Such leadership demands that we retrieve a fundamental insight of Roosevelt, Truman, and Kennedy—one that is truer now than ever before: the security and well-being of each and every American depend on the security and well-being of those who live beyond our borders. The mission of the United States is to provide global leadership grounded in the understanding that the world shares a common security and a common humanity.

The American moment is not over, but it must be seized anew. To see American power in terminal decline is to ignore America's great promise and historic purpose in the world. If elected president, I will start renewing that promise and purpose the day I take office.

Moving Beyond Iraq

To renew American leadership in the world, we must first bring the Iraq war to a responsible end and refocus our attention on the broader Middle East. Iraq was a diversion from the fight against the terrorists who struck us on 9/11, and incompetent prosecution of the war by America's civilian leaders compounded the strategic blunder of choosing to wage it in the first place. We have now lost over 3,300 American lives, and thousands more suffer wounds both seen and unseen.

Our servicemen and servicewomen have performed admirably while sacrificing immeasurably. But it is time for our civilian leaders to acknowledge a painful truth: we cannot impose a military solution on a civil war between Sunni and Shiite factions. The best chance we have to leave Iraq a better place is to pressure these warring parties to find a lasting political solution. And the only effective way to apply this pressure is to begin a phased withdrawal of U.S. forces, with the goal of removing all combat brigades from Iraq by March 31, 2008—a date consistent with the goal set by the bipartisan Iraq Study Group. This redeployment could be temporarily suspended if the Iraqi government meets the security, political, and economic benchmarks to which it has committed. But we must recognize that, in the end, only Iraqi leaders can bring real peace and stability to their country.

At the same time, we must launch a comprehensive regional and international diplomatic initiative to help broker an end to the civil war in Iraq, prevent its spread, and limit the suffering of the Iraqi people. To gain credibility in this effort, we must make clear that we seek no permanent bases in Iraq. We should leave behind only a minimal over-the-horizon military force in the region to protect American personnel and facilities, continue training Iraqi security forces, and root out al Qaeda.

The morass in Iraq has made it immeasurably harder to confront and work through the many other problems in the region—and it has made many of those problems considerably more dangerous. Changing the dynamic in Iraq will allow us to focus our attention and influence on resolving the festering conflict between the Israelis and the Palestinians—a task that the Bush administration neglected for years.

For more than three decades, Israelis, Palestinians, Arab leaders, and the rest of the world have looked to America to lead the effort to build the road to a lasting peace. In recent years, they have all too often looked in vain. Our starting point must always be a clear and strong commitment to the security of Israel, our strongest ally in the region and its only established democracy. That commitment is all the more important as we contend with growing threats in the region—a strengthened Iran, a chaotic Iraq, the resurgence of al Qaeda, the reinvigoration of Hamas and Hezbollah. Now more than ever, we must strive to secure a lasting settlement of the conflict with two states living side by side in peace and security. To do so, we must help the Israelis identify and strengthen those partners who are truly committed to peace, while isolating those who seek conflict and instability. Sustained American leadership for peace and security will require patient effort and the personal commitment of the president of the United States. That is a commitment I will make.

Throughout the Middle East, we must harness American power to reinvigorate American diplomacy. Tough-minded diplomacy, backed by the whole range of instruments of American power—political, economic, and military—could bring success even when dealing with long-standing adversaries such as Iran and Syria. Our policy of issuing threats and relying on intermediaries to curb Iran's nuclear program, sponsorship of terrorism, and regional aggression is failing. Although we must not rule out using military force, we should not hesitate to talk directly to Iran. Our diplomacy should aim to raise the cost for Iran of continuing its nuclear program by applying tougher sanctions and increasing pressure from its key trading partners. The world must work to stop Iran's uranium-enrichment program and prevent Iran from acquiring nuclear weapons. It is far too dangerous to have nuclear weapons in the hands of a radical theocracy. At the same time, we must show Iran—and especially the Iranian people—what could be gained from fundamental change: economic engagement, security assurances, and diplomatic relations. Diplomacy combined with pressure could also reorient Syria away from its radical agenda to a more moderate stance—which could, in turn, help stabilize Iraq, isolate Iran, free Lebanon from Damascus' grip, and better secure Israel.

Revitalizing the Military

To renew American leadership in the world, we must immediately begin working to revitalize our military. A strong military is, more than anything, necessary to sustain peace. Unfortunately, the U.S. Army and the Marine Corps, according to our military leaders, are facing a crisis. The Pentagon cannot certify a single army unit within the United States as fully ready to respond in the event of a new crisis or emergency beyond Iraq; 88 percent of the National Guard is not ready to deploy overseas.

We must use this moment both to rebuild our military and to prepare it for the missions of the future. We must retain the capacity to swiftly defeat any conventional threat to our country and our vital interests. But we must also become better prepared to put boots on the ground in order to take on foes that fight asymmetrical and highly adaptive campaigns on a global scale.

We should expand our ground forces by adding 65,000 soldiers to the army and 27,000 marines. Bolstering these forces is about more than meeting quotas. We must recruit the very best and invest in their capacity to succeed. That means providing our servicemen and servicewomen with first-rate equipment, armor, incentives, and training—including in foreign languages and other critical skills. Each major defense program should be reevaluated in light of current needs, gaps in the field, and likely future threat scenarios. Our military will have to rebuild some capabilities and transform others. At the same time, we need to commit sufficient funding to enable the National Guard to regain a state of readiness.

Enhancing our military will not be enough. As commander in chief, I would also use our armed forces wisely. When we send our men and women into harm's way, I will clearly define the mission, seek out the advice of our military commanders, objectively evaluate intelligence, and ensure that our troops have the resources and the support they need. I will not hesitate to use force, unilaterally if necessary, to protect the American people or our vital interests whenever we are attacked or imminently threatened.

We must also consider using military force in circumstances beyond self-defense in order to provide for the common security that underpins global stability—to support friends, participate in stability and reconstruction operations, or confront mass atrocities. But when we do use force in situations other than self-defense, we should make every effort to garner the clear support and participation of others—as President George H. W. Bush did when we led the effort to oust Saddam Hussein from Kuwait in 1991. The consequences of forgetting that lesson in the context of the current conflict in Iraq have been grave.

Halting the Spread of Nuclear Weapons

To renew American leadership in the world, we must confront the most urgent threat to the security of America and the world—the spread of nuclear weapons, material, and technology and the risk that a nuclear device will fall into the hands of terrorists. The explosion of one such device would bring catastrophe, dwarfing the devastation of 9/11 and shaking every corner of the globe.

As George Shultz, William Perry, Henry Kissinger, and Sam Nunn have warned, our current measures are not sufficient to meet the nuclear threat. The nonproliferation regime is being challenged, and new civilian nuclear programs could spread the means to make nuclear weapons. Al Qaeda has made it a goal to bring a "Hiroshima" to the United States. Terrorists need not build a nuclear weapon from scratch; they need only steal or buy a weapon or the material to assemble one. There is now highly enriched uranium—some of it poorly secured—sitting in civilian nuclear facilities in over 40 countries around the world. In the former Soviet Union, there are approximately 15,000-16,000 nuclear weapons and stockpiles of uranium and plutonium capable of making another 40,000 weapons—all scattered across 11 time zones. People have already been caught trying to smuggle nuclear material to sell on the black market.

As president, I will work with other nations to secure, destroy, and stop the spread of these weapons in order to dramatically reduce the nuclear dangers for our nation and the world. America must lead a global effort to secure all nuclear weapons and material at vulnerable sites within four years—the most effective way to prevent terrorists from acquiring a bomb.

This will require the active cooperation of Russia. Although we must not shy away from pushing for more democracy and accountability in Russia, we must work with the country in areas of common interest—above all, in making sure that nuclear weapons and material are secure. We must also work with Russia to update and scale back our dangerously outdated Cold War nuclear postures and de-emphasize the role of nuclear weapons. America must not rush to produce a new generation of nuclear warheads. And we should take advantage of recent technological advances to build bipartisan consensus behind ratification of the Comprehensive Test Ban Treaty. All of this can be done while maintaining a strong nuclear deterrent. These steps will ultimately strengthen, not weaken, our security.

As we lock down existing nuclear stockpiles, I will work to negotiate a verifiable global ban on the production of new nuclear weapons material. We must also stop the spread of nuclear weapons technology and ensure that countries cannot build—or come to the brink of building—a weapons program under the auspices of developing peaceful nuclear power. That is why my administration will immediately provide $50 million to jump-start the creation of an International Atomic Energy Agency-controlled nuclear fuel bank and work to update the Nuclear Nonproliferation Treaty. We must also fully implement the law Senator Richard Lugar and I passed to help the United States and our allies detect and stop the smuggling of weapons of mass destruction throughout the world.

Finally, we must develop a strong international coalition to prevent Iran from acquiring nuclear weapons and eliminate North Korea's nuclear weapons program. Iran and North Korea could trigger regional arms races, creating dangerous nuclear flashpoints in the Middle East and East Asia. In confronting these threats, I will not take the military option off the table. But our first measure must be sustained, direct, and aggressive diplomacy—the kind that the Bush administration has been unable and unwilling to use.

Combating Global Terrorism

To renew American leadership in the world, we must forge a more effective global response to the terrorism that came to our shores on an unprecedented scale on 9/11. From Bali to London, Baghdad to Algiers, Mumbai to Mombasa to Madrid, terrorists who reject modernity, oppose America, and distort Islam have killed and mutilated tens of thousands of people just this decade. Because this enemy operates globally, it must be confronted globally.

We must refocus our efforts on Afghanistan and Pakistan—the central front in our war against al Qaeda—so that we are confronting terrorists where their roots run deepest. Success in Afghanistan is still possible, but only if we act quickly, judiciously, and decisively. We should pursue an integrated strategy that reinforces our troops in Afghanistan and works to remove the limitations placed by some NATO allies on their forces. Our strategy must also include sustained diplomacy to isolate the Taliban and more effective development programs that target aid to areas where the Taliban are making inroads.

I will join with our allies in insisting—not simply requesting—that Pakistan crack down on the Taliban, pursue Osama bin Laden and his lieutenants, and end its relationship with all terrorist groups. At the same time, I will encourage dialogue between Pakistan and India to work toward resolving their dispute over Kashmir and between Afghanistan and Pakistan to resolve their historic differences and develop the Pashtun border region. If Pakistan can look toward the east with greater confidence, it will be less likely to believe that its interests are best advanced through cooperation with the Taliban.

Although vigorous action in South Asia and Central Asia should be a starting point, our efforts must be broader. There must be no safe haven for those who plot to kill Americans. To defeat al Qaeda, I will build a twenty-first-century military and twenty-first-century partnerships as strong as the anticommunist alliance that won the Cold War to stay on the offense everywhere from Djibouti to Kandahar.

Here at home, we must strengthen our homeland security and protect the critical infrastructure on which the entire world depends. We can start by spending homeland security dollars on the basis of risk. This means investing more resources to defend mass transit, closing the gaps in our aviation security by screening all cargo on passenger airliners and checking all passengers against a comprehensive watch list, and upgrading port security by ensuring that cargo is screened for radiation.

To succeed, our homeland security and counterterrorism actions must be linked to an intelligence community that deals effectively with the threats we face. Today, we rely largely on the same institutions and practices that were in place before 9/11. We need to revisit intelligence reform, going beyond rearranging boxes on an organizational chart. To keep pace with highly adaptable enemies, we need technologies and practices that enable us to efficiently collect and share information within and across our intelligence agencies. We must invest still more in human intelligence and deploy additional trained operatives and diplomats with specialized knowledge of local cultures and languages. And we should institutionalize the practice of developing competitive assessments of critical threats and strengthen our methodologies of analysis.

Finally, we need a comprehensive strategy to defeat global terrorists—one that draws on the full range of American power, not just our military might. As a senior U.S. military commander put it, when people have dignity and opportunity, "the chance of extremism being welcomed greatly, if not completely, diminishes." It is for this reason that we need to invest with our allies in strengthening weak states and helping to rebuild failed ones.

In the Islamic world and beyond, combating the terrorists' prophets of fear will require more than lectures on democracy. We need to deepen our knowledge of the circumstances and beliefs that underpin extremism. A crucial debate is occurring within Islam. Some believe in a future of peace, tolerance, development, and democratization. Others embrace a rigid and violent intolerance of personal liberty and the world at large. To empower forces of moderation, America must make every effort to export opportunity—access to education and health care, trade and investment—and provide the kind of steady support for political reformers and civil society that enabled our victory in the Cold War. Our beliefs rest on hope; the extremists' rest on fear. That is why we can—and will—win this struggle.

Rebuilding Our Partnerships

To renew American leadership in the world, I intend to rebuild the alliances, partnerships, and institutions necessary to confront common threats and enhance common security. Needed reform of these alliances and institutions will not come by bullying other countries to ratify changes we hatch in isolation. It will come when we convince other governments and peoples that they, too, have a stake in effective partnerships.

Too often we have sent the opposite signal to our international partners. In the case of Europe, we dismissed European reservations about the wisdom and necessity of the

Iraq war. In Asia, we belittled South Korean efforts to improve relations with the North. In Latin America, from Mexico to Argentina, we failed to adequately address concerns about immigration and equity and economic growth. In Africa, we have allowed genocide to persist for over four years in Darfur and have not done nearly enough to answer the African Union's call for more support to stop the killing. I will rebuild our ties to our allies in Europe and Asia and strengthen our partnerships throughout the Americas and Africa.

Our alliances require constant cooperation and revision if they are to remain effective and relevant. NATO has made tremendous strides over the last 15 years, transforming itself from a Cold War security structure into a partnership for peace. But today, NATO's challenge in Afghanistan has exposed, as Senator Lugar has put it, "the growing discrepancy between NATO's expanding missions and its lagging capabilities." To close this gap, I will rally our NATO allies to contribute more troops to collective security operations and to invest more in reconstruction and stabilization capabilities.

And as we strengthen NATO, we must build new alliances and partnerships in other vital regions. As China rises and Japan and South Korea assert themselves, I will work to forge a more effective framework in Asia that goes beyond bilateral agreements, occasional summits, and ad hoc arrangements, such as the six-party talks on North Korea. We need an inclusive infrastructure with the countries in East Asia that can promote stability and prosperity and help confront transnational threats, from terrorist cells in the Philippines to avian flu in Indonesia. I will also encourage China to play a responsible role as a growing power—to help lead in addressing the common problems of the twenty-first century. We will compete with China in some areas and cooperate in others. Our essential challenge is to build a relationship that broadens cooperation while strengthening our ability to compete.

In addition, we need effective collaboration on pressing global issues among all the major powers—including such newly emerging ones as Brazil, India, Nigeria, and South Africa. We need to give all of them a stake in upholding the international order. To that end, the United Nations requires far-reaching reform. The UN Secretariat's management practices remain weak. Peacekeeping operations are overextended. The new UN Human Rights Council has passed eight resolutions condemning Israel—but not a single resolution condemning the genocide in Darfur or human rights abuses in Zimbabwe. Yet none of these problems will be solved unless America rededicates itself to the organization and its mission.

Strengthened institutions and invigorated alliances and partnerships are especially crucial if we are to defeat the epochal, man-made threat to the planet: climate change. Without dramatic changes, rising sea levels will flood coastal regions around the world, including much of the eastern seaboard. Warmer temperatures and declining rainfall will reduce crop yields, increasing conflict, famine, disease, and poverty. By 2050, famine could displace more than 250 million people worldwide. That means increased instability in some of the most volatile parts of the world.

As the world's largest producer of greenhouse gases, America has the responsibility to lead. While many of our industrial partners are working hard to reduce their emissions, we are increasing ours at a steady clip—by more than ten percent per decade. As president, I intend to enact a cap-and-trade system that will dramatically reduce our carbon emissions. And I will work to finally free America of its dependence on foreign oil—by using energy more efficiently in our cars, factories, and homes, relying more on renewable sources of electricity, and harnessing the potential of biofuels.

Getting our own house in order is only a first step. China will soon replace America as the world's largest emitter of greenhouse gases. Clean energy development must be a central focus in our relationships with major countries in Europe and Asia. I will invest in efficient and clean technologies at home while using our assistance policies and export promotions to help developing countries leapfrog the carbon-energy-intensive stage of development. We need a global response to climate change that includes binding and enforceable commitments to reducing emissions, especially for those that pollute the most: the United States, China, India, the European Union, and Russia. This challenge is massive, but rising to it will also bring new benefits to America. By 2050, global demand for low-carbon energy could create an annual market worth $500 billion. Meeting that demand would open new frontiers for American entrepreneurs and workers.

Building Just, Secure, Democratic Societies

Finally, to renew American leadership in the world, I will strengthen our common security by investing in our common humanity. Our global engagement cannot be defined by what we are against; it must be guided by a clear sense of what we stand for. We have a significant stake in ensuring that those who live in fear and want today can live with dignity and opportunity tomorrow.

People around the world have heard a great deal of late about freedom on the march. Tragically, many have come to associate this with war, torture, and forcibly imposed regime change. To build a better, freer world, we must first behave in ways that reflect the decency and aspirations of the American people. This means ending the practices of shipping away prisoners in the dead of night to be tortured in far-off countries, of detaining thousands without charge or trial, of maintaining a network of secret prisons to jail people beyond the reach of the law.

Citizens everywhere should be able to choose their leaders in climates free of fear. America must commit to strengthening the pillars of a just society. We can help build accountable institutions that deliver services and opportunity: strong legislatures, independent judiciaries, honest police forces, free presses, vibrant civil societies. In countries wracked by poverty and conflict, citizens long to enjoy freedom from want. And since extremely poor societies and weak states provide optimal breeding grounds for disease, terrorism, and conflict, the United States has a direct national security interest in dramatically reducing global poverty and joining with our allies in sharing more of our riches to help those most in need. We need to invest in building capable, democratic states that can establish healthy and educated communities, develop markets, and generate wealth. Such states would also have greater institutional capacities to fight terrorism, halt the spread of deadly weapons, and build health-care infrastructures to prevent, detect, and treat deadly diseases such as HIV/AIDS, malaria, and avian flu.

As president, I will double our annual investment in meeting these challenges to $50 billion by 2012 and ensure that those new resources are directed toward worthwhile goals. For the last 20 years, U.S. foreign assistance funding has done little more than keep pace with inflation. It is in our national security interest to do better. But if America is going to help others build more just and secure societies, our trade deals, debt relief, and foreign aid must not come as blank checks. I will couple our support with an insistent call for reform, to combat the corruption that rots societies and governments from within. I will do so not in the spirit of a patron but in the spirit of a partner—a partner mindful of his own imperfections.

Our rapidly growing international AIDS programs have demonstrated that increased foreign assistance can make a real difference. As part of this new funding, I will capitalize a $2 billion Global Education Fund that will bring the world together in eliminating the global education deficit, much as the 9/11 Commission proposed. We cannot hope to shape a world where opportunity outweighs danger unless we ensure that every child everywhere is taught to build and not to destroy.

There are compelling moral reasons and compelling security reasons for renewed American leadership that recognizes the inherent equality and worth of all people. As President Kennedy said in his 1961 inaugural address, "To those people in the huts and villages of half the globe struggling to break the bonds of mass misery, we pledge our best efforts to help them help themselves, for whatever period is required—not because the communists may be doing it, not because we seek their votes, but because it is right. If a free society cannot help the many who are poor, it cannot save the few who are rich." I will show the world that America remains true to its founding values. We lead not only for ourselves but also for the common good.

Restoring America's Trust

Confronted by Hitler, Roosevelt said that our power would be "directed toward ultimate good as well as against immediate evil. We Americans are not destroyers; we are builders." It is time for a president who can build consensus here at home for an equally ambitious course.

Ultimately, no foreign policy can succeed unless the American people understand it and feel they have a stake in its success—unless they trust that their government hears their concerns as well. We will not be able to increase foreign aid if we fail to invest in security and opportunity for our own people. We cannot negotiate trade agreements to help spur development in poor countries so long as we provide no meaningful help to working Americans burdened by the dislocations of a global economy. We cannot reduce our dependence on foreign oil or defeat global warming unless Americans are willing to innovate and conserve. We cannot expect Americans to support placing our men and women in harm's way if we cannot show that we will use force wisely and judiciously. But if the next president can restore the American people's trust—if they know that he or she is acting with their best interests at heart, with prudence and wisdom and some measure of humility—then I believe the American people will be eager to see America lead again.

I believe they will also agree that it is time for a new generation to tell the next great American story. If we act with boldness and foresight, we will be able to tell our grandchildren that this was the time when we helped forge peace in the Middle East. This was the time we confronted climate change and secured the weapons that could destroy the human race. This was the time we defeated global terrorists and brought opportunity to forgotten corners of the world. And this was the time when we renewed the America that has led generations of weary travelers from all over the world to find opportunity and liberty and hope on our doorstep.

It was not all that long ago that farmers in Venezuela and Indonesia welcomed American doctors to their villages and hung pictures of JFK on their living room walls, when millions, like my father, waited every day for a letter in the mail that would grant them the privilege to come to America to study, work, live, or just be free.

We can be this America again. This is our moment to renew the trust and faith of our people—and all people—in an America that battles immediate evils, promotes an ultimate good, and leads the world once more.

*C*onsider the source and the audience.

- What does the fact that Barack Obama is a Democrat tell you about what his worldview is likely to be? Had John McCain written this article, how might the message have differed?
- *Foreign Affairs* is a journal that is read regularly by foreign policy scholars and practitioners. Is Obama's pitch here made directly to them, or does he seem to have a broader audience in mind?

*L*ay out the argument, the values, and the assumptions.

- Why is Obama critical of George W. Bush's foreign policy? How does he believe Bush's foreign policy differed from that of Franklin Roosevelt, Harry Truman, and John Kennedy?
- Obama argues that we must renew American leadership in the world. What does he mean?
- According to Obama, how can the United States renew its leadership in world affairs?

*U*ncover the evidence.

- Obama is providing a list of actions that he will take as president. How does he know that these actions will have the intended effects? Does he rely on logic? History? Data?

*E*valuate the conclusion.

- It should come as no surprise that Democrats are likely to agree with much of what Obama wrote and Republicans are likely to disagree, but that support or opposition isn't universal. Where might some Democrats disagree with Obama? What ideas might some Republicans support?
- Based on what you know about the Obama administration's foreign policy, has it been successful or is it too early to tell? If you believe that it has been successful (or has not), what evidence do *you* have to make such a claim?

*S*ort out the political implications.

- Obama lists "Rebuilding Our Partnerships" and "Restoring America's Trust" as two of his goals. Is it important that other nations like and respect us? If we don't rebuild our partnerships and restore America's trust, then what price might we pay?

16.2 Following a Different Map to a Similar Destination

Peter Baker, New York Times

Why We Chose This Piece

Promoting democracy in countries with authoritarian governments—those in which the state holds all power over the social order—became the centerpiece of the Bush adminis-tration's foreign policy. This focus was particularly interesting because, as we note in the introduction to this chapter, democracy-building has traditionally been an issue that Democrats have championed and on which Republicans have been cautious. Indeed, candidate Bush ran against the idea in 2000.

Like George W. Bush, Barack Obama believes in promoting democracy around the world. However, many observers—mostly on the left—argue that the actions of Obama's prede-cessor have made this goal more difficult.

We include this article because it highlights the different approaches that two presidents have taken to achieve the same goal. Why would the idea of promoting democracy— something that is so cherished in the United States—be such a complex and controversial issue?

More than four years after his predecessor declared it America's mission to end tyranny around the world, President Obama is trying to reformulate a lofty goal that has become tarnished in many circles.

Mr. Obama used his address in Cairo last week to revive but recast the democracy agenda that was central to President George W. Bush's foreign policy. Yet even as he embraced the aspiration rhetorically, Mr. Obama left it uncertain how aggressively he planned to push repressive regimes that did not agree.

The president's focus on democracy—one of seven tenets of the speech—was his most expansive discussion of the issue since taking office. The decision to address it directly culminated a four-month struggle within the administration between those who want nothing to do with what they consider Mr. Bush's discredited ideological crusade and those who argue America should still promote freedom, just in a humbler manner.

"I think that sends a signal to people in his administration who have been moving in a steady neorealist direction that he doesn't want to abandon this," said Jennifer Windsor, executive director of Freedom House, an advocacy organization. "I know the battles were quite intense inside to even get it in there."

But the debate is probably not over. "I don't think this yet settles the question of how they are going to distance themselves from Bush, but still reclaim the tradition of

---

Selection published: June 9, 2009

American democracy promotion," said Tom Malinowski, Washington advocacy director for Human Rights Watch.

Mr. Bush put democracy at the center of American foreign policy in his second inaugural address, in 2005, vowing to challenge "every ruler and every nation" to guarantee freedom. But his fervor, his inconsistent application and the war in Iraq left many soured or suspicious. After Mr. Obama took office, 163 democracy advocates wrote a letter urging him to pick up the mantle while avoiding his predecessor's mistakes.

In the Cairo speech, Mr. Obama implicitly contrasted his vision of democracy promotion with Mr. Bush's by saying it cannot "be imposed by one nation," and by making clear that elections are not enough. He said America "would not presume to pick the outcome of a peaceful election," and would respect winners it disagreed with as long as they were peaceful and governed with respect for all of their people.

"I do have an unyielding belief that all people yearn for certain things—the ability to speak your mind and have a say in how you are governed, confidence in the rule of law and the equal administration of justice, government that is transparent and doesn't steal from the people, the freedom to live as you choose," the president said. "These are not just American ideas. They are human rights. And that is why we will support them everywhere."

Mr. Obama got applause the moment he used the word "democracy" and three more times during this section of his speech. When he finished this passage, someone in the crowd shouted, "Barack Obama, we love you!"

Yet Mr. Obama kept his words general and did nothing to challenge his Egyptian host, President Hosni Mubarak, whose government has jailed opponents, censored the news media and broken up protests. Indeed, the Obama administration, while increasing financing for democracy programs elsewhere, recently cut it for Egypt, and in an interview before leaving Washington, the president said he did not consider Mr. Mubarak an authoritarian.

"No, I tend not to use labels for folks," he told the BBC. Instead he called Mr. Mubarak "a force for stability and good" in the Middle East. While Mr. Obama acknowledged "there have been criticisms of the manner in which politics operates in Egypt," he said his job "is not to lecture but to encourage, to lift up what we consider to be the values" of all peoples.

For advocates like Larry Diamond, the gentle treatment of Mr. Mubarak undermined a strong speech. "I would have wished that he would have at some point in his visit to Egypt been a bit more explicit in raising concerns about what is a very hard authoritarian regime," said Mr. Diamond, a senior fellow at the Hoover Institution and director of Stanford University's Center on Democracy, Development and Rule of Law.

Robert Kagan, a scholar at the Carnegie Endowment for International Peace, said, "I thought he did the bare minimum." Mr. Kagan said: "Obviously he and his advisers knew that if he didn't mention democracy at all, that would be a news item. But he said very little that would cause Mubarak, or any other autocrat around the world, much if any heartburn."

Elliott Abrams, Mr. Bush's deputy national security adviser for global democracy strategy, was more supportive, noting that Mr. Obama backed the expansion of freedom and made the case that free governments were more secure and successful. But he questioned whether Mr. Obama would back up the words with actions.

"The problem is that the democracy and human rights offices in his government have fallen into disrepair, especially in the N.S.C.," said Mr. Abrams, referring to the National Security Council. "To carry out his stated policy, he needs to be sure he has the people in place and that they have the power to influence policy. So far this is simply not the case."

The uncertainty about how Mr. Obama will proceed was highlighted by the response of Human Rights Watch to his speech. At first, it issued a statement condemning the speech under the headline, "Obama Dodged Rights Issue." Then less than an hour later it retracted the statement. Finally, it issued a new one titled, "Obama Mid-East Speech Supports Rights, Democracy."

Mr. Malinowski said he did not see the first version before it went out, and when he did, found it "unfair." So he said he decided to swallow the embarrassment of retracting it and issued a new one to reflect "important and positive things" in the speech.

*C*onsider the source and the audience.

- In the speech referenced by Baker, Obama was addressing the Muslim world specifically. How might that have shaped his message?

*L*ay out the argument, the values, and the assumptions.

- Bush and Obama both want to spread democracy around the world. According to the article, how are their strategies different? Is it clear exactly what Obama's strategy will be?
- Why was there so much disagreement in the Obama administration regarding the inclusion in Obama's speech of a discussion of expanding democracy, an issue that Democrats have traditionally championed?

*U*ncover the evidence.

- This is a traditional news reporting piece. In other words, the author is not making the argument. Instead he is reporting on the arguments made by others. Does Baker provide any evidence that one side's "map" might be more effective than the other's?

*E*valuate the conclusion.

- The article states that Bush's attempts to promote democracy around the world left "many soured or suspicious." Is that a fair conclusion?
- How might Obama's approach improve U.S. relationships with other countries (a goal he highlights in Reading 16.1)? How might his approach be ineffective?

*S*ort out the political implications.

- What unintended consequences might result from trying to promote democracy in countries with authoritarian governments?

16.3 The Case for Missile Defense

The Fact That America Faces Novel Terrorist Threats Such as Hijacked Planes and Anthrax Spores Does Not Negate the Need for an Effective, Comprehensive Missile Defense

Steve Bonta, New American

Why We Chose This Piece

September 11, 2001, brought a new fear to the American public: terrorist attacks on our homeland. Until that point, while terrorism at home may have concerned some, most people believed that the biggest threat to the United States would come from a foreign missile attack. In the days of the Cold War, the United States and its chief superpower rival, the Soviet Union, had contained the threat posed by each nation with a policy of mutually assured destruction (MAD), based on the idea that if each had the ability to destroy the other, each had an incentive not to guarantee its own destruction by launching the first attack. As part of the principle of MAD, the nations signed the Anti-Ballistic Missile (ABM) Treaty in 1972, promising not to build a missile defense system. Such a system, by protecting one side from nuclear attack, would render the policy of MAD ineffective, and the threat of nuclear war would no longer be contained.

The ABM Treaty did not end discussion of missile defense. In the 1980s Ronald Reagan pushed Congress to authorize billions of dollars to create a missile defense system, nick-named Star Wars, designed to protect the country from a nuclear strike by the Soviet Union. Although the United States has worked on developing missile defense technology since the early 1980s, it has yet to build a system that works in test situations. Then, in 2001, George W. Bush announced his intention to withdraw the United States from the ABM Treaty arguing that it prevented the United States from defending itself against pos-sible terrorist or "rogue-state" missile attacks.

We no longer live in a world defined by two nuclear superpowers. The Cold War is over, the Soviet Union is gone, and its nuclear weapons are divided among its former republics, including Russia, now on more or less friendly terms with the United States. Today many other nations—some friends to the United States, some foes—have nuclear weapons or are attempting to build them, and there is no guarantee that these nations can be "contained" in the same way the United States and the Soviet Union once were.

Since September 11, some Americans have been divided between those who believe we should concentrate our resources on preventing threats like the terrorist attacks on the

---

Selection published: December 3, 2001

World Trade Center and the Pentagon and those, like the author of this piece, who think the reasons for pursuing missile defense are stronger than ever. Although this article was written shortly after 9/11, the issues raised in the article are as relevant today, as Congress regularly debates missile defense funding and some observers have questioned President Obama's commitment to missile defense systems. Moreover, concerns about nuclear proliferation in places like North Korea have made the debate all the more pertinent.

I n an October 28th op-ed piece for the *New York Times*, ex-Soviet dictator Mikhail Gorbachev wrote that, in light of the shocking breaches of American security on September 11th, the United States might begin making a priority out of unilateral national defense. "It would be a cause of great concern," he fretted, "if major nuclear powers abandoned or neglected multilateral forums, or took steps that would endanger the entire structure of arms control treaties, many of which, such as the 1972 ABM Treaty, are of as much value today as they were during the decades of nuclear confrontation."

Gorbachev isn't a lone voice, either. In the aftermath of September 11th, with the Bush administration's intention to scrap the ABM Treaty attracting a lot of political support, a chorus of Establishment voices have been clamoring to keep the 1972 agreement and to nix any national missile defense. "Even in the wake of Sept. 11, Bush clings to the wasteful, improbable Son of *Star Wars*," complained the *Houston Chronicle* on October 23rd. On the same day, the *San Francisco Chronicle* warned, "[N]ow, more than ever, an anti-missile defense system mocks the actual dangers that threaten Americans—as well as the rest of the world. It won't defend against terrorist weapons that, so far, have included boxcutters, planes and anthrax spores. Nor will it protect us from plastic explosives, cyberterrorism, or chemical warfare."

Arguments like these are nothing new. For several decades, since the United States embarked on the suicidal policy of Mutually Assured Destruction (MAD) and underscored it with an ABM Treaty forbidding any substantive missile defense measures, foreign policy experts with more Ivy-League credentials than common sense have been promoting abstract goals like "containment," "stabilization," and "deterrence" rather than national defense per se. In the process, they have successfully convinced a large number of gullible Americans, including congressional leaders, that defense against a missile attack is technologically impossible, politically unwise, and strategically unnecessary—and they have kept the United States pitifully vulnerable to nuclear attack. Exploiting our supposed nuclear Achilles' heel, the fanatical adherents of appeasement and arms control have extracted dangerous concessions in national sovereignty—like the ABM and SALT treaties—that unilaterally limit our ability to defend ourselves.

Changing Climate

With recent terrorist attacks, though, the political climate has changed. Suddenly national defense is a pressing urgency, and momentum is growing to scrap the ABM Treaty and other treasonous agreements with the former Soviet Union. But anti-American globalists, still eager to keep America weakened and vulnerable, have begun a campaign of withering propaganda to prevent this from happening.

The most common argument for continuing to neglect missile defense is that September 11th has shown us that, in the words of the *New York Times*, "the most immediate threat to the nation comes from terrorists, not nations with intercontinental ballistic missiles." Therefore, the critics argue, we should focus our resources on going after the men with the box cutters and the anthrax spores, rather than spend billions developing a system to shoot down Russian missiles.

That is, we should be *selective* in which threats to defend against. This is tantamount to choosing between a burglar alarm and a fire alarm, on the specious premise that we can't defend against both break-ins and fire hazards.

More importantly, a "threat" by its very nature is virtual, not actual. While no modern-day power has yet attempted a full-scale military assault, nuclear or otherwise, against the United States mainland, no one could credibly argue that any terrorist cell, however ingenious or well-equipped, could wreak as much havoc and loss of life as a Russian or Chinese nuclear missile attack. The most effective defense anticipates what might happen, rather than reacting too late to damage already done.

But, reply the critics, no country would dare launch a direct nuclear attack against the United States. As the *Houston Chronicle* put it, "such governments, even at their edge-of-reality looniest, would think twice about such an act because . . . U.S. retaliation would bring annihilation." This argument assumes that the only suicidal enemies of the United States are "non-state actors" like the terrorists who blew up the World Trade Center and the USS *Cole*.

But governments, even those of open societies, frequently act irrationally and against their best interests. The United States itself has done so consistently, under the influence of subversives hostile to American freedoms. And the verdict of history suggests that tyrannical regimes are even less rational. It is now well-known, for example, that some of imperial Japan's military and political leaders warned of the consequences of attacking Pearl Harbor. Saddam Hussein was deluded into believing that the West would not defend Kuwaiti oil fields. During the Gulf War, he even launched a barrage of SCUD missiles at Israel, undeterred by Israel's nuclear capability. The People's Republic of China has gone on record threatening to nuke Los Angeles if the United States comes to the defense of Taiwan in the event of a Chinese invasion. And a hypothetical nuclear regime like North Korea, facing military defeat in a future Korean conflict, might launch a desperation nuclear assault as a last-minute gesture of vengeful defiance. It is dangerously naive to assume that states and their leadership will behave rationally, especially in wartime.

Technological Capabilities

The next line of argument usually leveled against missile defense is the supposed technological limitations. "There is no indication that such a scheme would work and every sign it would cost billions even to find out," opined the *Los Angeles Times*. Wrong on both counts. Not only is a credible missile defense well within our technological capabilities, there is little question that such a system—if deployed—would work very effectively. As Sam Cohen, the inventor of the neutron bomb, wrote in these pages in

October 1998, nuclear-tipped missile interceptors would be an extremely effective and easily achievable missile-defense system:

> *Real strategic defense requires nuclear interceptors to overcome the huge economic and technical disadvantages of the non-nuclear defense systems that inherently favor attackers. . . . Nuclear explosives of the kind developed for Safeguard [a short-lived ABM system deployed in the '70s] included the six-kiloton Sprint, which could effectively take out attacking missiles within a radius of tens of yards, and the megaton Spartan, which could reach out to a radius of several miles to destroy missiles. These or similar systems could be launched from the ground, sea, air, or space, and a genuine ABM program would utilize a combination of these launch options to provide in-depth defense.*

Even leaving aside nuclear ABM defenses, conventional anti-missile missiles like the Patriot have proven effective—especially against obsolescent models like the Iraqi SCUDs, the type of missile most likely to be used by a third-world rogue regime.

For those who insist on some kind of defense against enemy missiles, Establishment liberals have a pat concession: Limited ABM defenses are okay, as long as they don't pose a serious threat to a major nuclear-armed adversary like the Russians. This is, in fact, the position of Bush administration "conservatives" who insist, even as they loudly promote a limited missile defense against rogue regimes, that America will not consider building any significant countermeasures against an all-out nuclear assault by a superpower adversary like Russia or China. The Bush administration's tough-talking Donald Rumsfeld implied as much by announcing on October 25th that the Pentagon had postponed antimissile tracking tests to avoid the appearance of violating the ABM Treaty or provoking the Russians.

But there is evidence that, despite the propaganda smokescreen, many Americans are awakening to America's dangerous vulnerability not only to terrorism but to old-fashioned military assaults. A new poll on internationalist views conducted by the Pew Research Center in conjunction with the Council on Foreign Relations found "growing public support for a missile defense system" since September 11th. The study admitted uneasily that "nearly two thirds [surveyed] favor the development of a missile shield and a growing number say we need such a system now."

Americans must not be deluded by the false alternatives offered by the Establishment on missile defense. They must insist that the excuses and prevarications stop, and that our elected leaders take all steps to defend our country, as completely as possible, from nuclear attack. No government that has frittered away billions of dollars on risky Mars missions, many of which have failed abysmally, can cite lack of technology, risk of failure, or budget shortfalls as excuses for not developing missile defense. And since September 11th, no one with a shred of human decency can justify any but a comprehensive approach to national defense. National defense, after all, is the first responsibility of any moral government. It's time to stop holding Americans hostage by playing games with America's enemies.

*C*onsider the source and the audience.

- The *New American* is a conservative magazine with the avowed purpose of protecting our freedom. What (or whom) does Bonta see as the threat to our freedom? Would a liberal publication define freedom in the same way?

*L*ay out the argument, the values, and the assumptions.

- What is Bonta's view of national power and sovereignty? What is the primary purpose of government, in his view? Bonta is worried about our leaders playing games with America's enemies. When it comes to protecting America, would he argue that we have any friends?
- According to Bonta, what was wrong with MAD, and why did it work against national defense? What arguments are frequently used by opponents of missile defense, and why, according to Bonta, are they wrong?

*U*ncover the evidence.

- Bonta cites many newspaper editorials and claims that they lack evidence to back up their arguments. Does he offer evidence to back up his own? What evidence does Bonta provide to counter the objection that the technology does not yet exist to create a successful missile defense system?

*E*valuate the conclusion.

- Does Bonta successfully make the case that we should expand our missile defense spending? Why or why not?
- Does Bonta successfully refute the claims of opponents of a missile defense system? Does he deal with any of the positive aspects of treaty making? Would he agree that any exist?

*S*ort out the political implications.

- If the U.S. government followed Bonta's suggestion, what trade-offs, if any, would it have to make? Can we deal effectively with all threats facing the United States at the same time?
- How might the rest of the world view our increased spending on missile defense? Should the United States be concerned with the reaction of other countries?

 ## 16.4 Speech Before the National Association of Evangelicals

Ronald Reagan

Why We Chose This Piece

Along with tax cuts, less intrusive government, and increased defense spending, Ronald Reagan made winning the Cold War a central part of his presidency. He believed that America needed to defend itself against a communist threat, promote free governments, and limit Soviet power and aggression. In this speech before the National Association of Evangelicals, Reagan made an impassioned plea to keep the "evil empire" in check and

Selection delivered: March 8, 1983

promote democracy throughout the world. Specifically, he argued that it would be fool-hardy for the West to freeze its development of nuclear forces because it is only by being strong and armed that the United States can bring about peace.

Although the United States' adversaries have changed, the issues raised in Reagan's speech remain pertinent today. Indeed, Reagan's views presented in this speech guided much of George W. Bush's philosophy on foreign policy. Moreover, the issues raised here are issues that President Obama must grapple with as well. Reading 16.1 laid out Obama's vision on foreign policy. What differences do you see between that reading and this one? What similarities?

[The beginning of this speech focused on President Reagan's views on the place of faith in public life. Toward the end of his talk he turned his attention to the role of faith in foreign affairs. We pick up the speech at that point.]

And this brings me to my final point today. During my first press conference as president, in answer to a direct question, I pointed out that, as good Marxist-Leninists, the Soviet leaders have openly and publicly declared that the only morality they recognize is that which will further their cause, which is world revolution. I think I should point out I was only quoting Lenin, their guiding spirit, who said in 1920 that they repudiate all morality that proceeds from supernatural ideas—that's their name for religion—or ideas that are outside class conceptions. Morality is entirely subordinate to the interests of class war. And everything is moral that is necessary for the annihilation of the old, exploiting social order and for uniting the proletariat.

Well, I think the refusal of many influential people to accept this elementary fact of Soviet doctrine illustrates a historical reluctance to see totalitarian powers for what they are. We saw this phenomenon in the 1930s. We see it too often today.

This doesn't mean we should isolate ourselves and refuse to seek an understanding with them. I intend to do everything I can to persuade them of our peaceful intent, to remind them that it was the West that refused to use its nuclear monopoly in the forties and fifties for territorial gain and which now proposes a 50-percent cut in strategic ballistic missiles and the elimination of an entire class of land-based, intermediate-range nuclear missiles.

At the same time, however, they must be made to understand we will never compromise our principles and standards. We will never give away our freedom. We will never abandon our belief in God. And we will never stop searching for a genuine peace. But we can assure none of these things America stands for through the so-called nuclear freeze solutions proposed by some.

The truth is that a freeze now would be a very dangerous fraud, for that is merely the illusion of peace. The reality is that we must find peace through strength.

I would agree to a freeze if only we could freeze the Soviets' global desires. A freeze at current levels of weapons would remove any incentive for the Soviets to negotiate seriously in Geneva and virtually end our chances to achieve the major arms reductions which we have proposed. Instead, they would achieve their objectives through the freeze.

A freeze would reward the Soviet Union for its enormous and unparalleled military buildup. It would prevent the essential and long overdue modernization of United States and allied defenses and would leave our aging forces increasingly vulnerable. And an honest freeze would require extensive prior negotiations on the systems and numbers to be limited and on the measures to ensure effective verification and compliance. And the kind of a freeze that has been suggested would be virtually impossible to verify. Such a major effort would divert us completely from our current negotiations on achieving substantial reductions.

A number of years ago, I heard a young father, a very prominent young man in the entertainment world, addressing a tremendous gathering in California. It was during the time of the cold war, and communism and our own way of life were very much on people's minds. And he was speaking to that subject. And suddenly, though, I heard him saying, "I love my little girls more than anything." And I said to myself, "Oh, no, don't. You can't-don't say that." But I had underestimated him. He went on: "I would rather see my little girls die now, still believing in God, than have them grow up under communism and one day die no longer believing in God."

There were thousands of young people in that audience. They came to their feet with shouts of joy. They had instantly recognized the profound truth in what he had said, with regard to the physical and the soul and what was truly important.

Yes, let us pray for the salvation of all of those who live in that totalitarian darkness—pray they will discover the joy of knowing God. But until they do, let us be aware that while they preach the supremacy of the state, declare its omnipotence over individual man, and predict its eventual domination of all peoples on the earth, they are the focus of evil in the modern world.

It was C. S. Lewis who, in his unforgettable *Screwtape Letters*, wrote: "The greatest evil is not done now in those sordid 'dens of rime' that Dickens loved to paint. It is not even done in concentration camps and labor camps. In those we see its final result. But it is conceived and ordered (moved, seconded, carried and minuted) in clean, carpeted, warmed, and well-lighted offices, by quiet men with white collars and cut fingernails and smooth-shaven cheeks who do not need to raise their voice."

Well, because these "quiet men" do not "raise their voices," because they sometimes speak in soothing tones of brotherhood and peace, because, like other dictators before them, they're always making "their final territorial demand," some would have us accept them at their word and accommodate ourselves to their aggressive impulses. But if history teaches anything, it teaches that simpleminded appeasement or wishful thinking about our adversaries is folly. It means the betrayal of our past, the squandering of our freedom.

So, I urge you to speak out against those who would place the United States in a position of military and moral inferiority. You know, I've always believed that old Screwtape reserved his best efforts for those of you in the church. So, in your discussions of the nuclear freeze proposals, I urge you to beware the temptation of pride—the temptation of blithely declaring yourselves above it all and label both sides equally at fault, to ignore the facts of history and the aggressive impulses of an evil empire, to simply call the arms race a giant misunderstanding and thereby remove yourself from the struggle between right and wrong and good and evil.

I ask you to resist the attempts of those who would have you withhold your support for our efforts, this administration's efforts, to keep America strong and free, while we negotiate real and verifiable reductions in the world's nuclear arsenals and one day, with God's help, their total elimination.

While America's military strength is important, let me add here that I've always maintained that the struggle now going on for the world will never be decided by bombs or rockets, by armies or military might. The real crisis we face today is a spiritual one; at root, it is a test of moral will and faith.

Whittaker Chambers, the man whose own religious conversion made him a witness to one of the terrible traumas of our time, the Hiss-Chambers case, wrote that the crisis of the Western world exists to the degree in which the West is indifferent to God, the degree to which it collaborates in communism's attempt to make man stand alone without God. And then he said, for Marxism-Leninism is actually the second-oldest faith, first proclaimed in the Garden of Eden with the words of temptation, "Ye shall be as gods."

The Western world can answer this challenge, he wrote, "but only provided that its faith in God and the freedom He enjoins is as great as communism's faith in Man."

I believe we shall rise to the challenge. I believe that communism is another sad, bizarre chapter in human history whose last pages even now are being written. I believe this because the source of our strength in the quest for human freedom is not material, but spiritual. And because it knows no limitation, it must terrify and ultimately triumph over those who would enslave their fellow man. For in the words of Isaiah: "He giveth power to the faint; and to them that have no might He increased strength. . . . But they that wait upon the Lord shall renew their strength; they shall mount up with wings as eagles; they shall run, and not be weary. . . ."

Yes, change your world. One of our Founding Fathers, Thomas Paine, said, "We have it within our power to begin the world over again." We can do it, doing together what no one church could do by itself.

God bless you, and thank you very much.

*C*onsider the source and the audience.

- President Reagan gave this speech to the National Association of Evangelicals. Would he have emphasized the same factors in a speech to a political group?

*L*ay out the argument, the values, and the assumptions.

- What, for Reagan, is the relationship among freedom, democracy, peace, and a belief in God? What defines the differences between "good" and "evil?" Why is the Soviet Union the "evil empire?"
- What does Reagan think is the route to peace? What is the role of arms and national strength? What is the role of faith in God?
- Who is Reagan arguing against here? What do his opponents want the United States to do? How do they think our problems with the Soviets can best be handled?

*U*ncover the evidence.

- Reagan claims that the best way to bring about world peace is by increasing America's strength and refusing to take part in a nuclear freeze. What evidence or logic does he offer for this claim?
- Does Reagan offer any evidence for the link between freedom and faith in God? Is it a link that can be verified? What kind of evidence would support it?

*E*valuate the conclusion.

- Can you accept Reagan's conclusions about the relationship of belief in God with freedom and democracy if you don't share his faith? What conclusions can nonbelievers take from his speech?

*S*ort out the political implications.

- President George W. Bush also used the word *evil* to refer to the United States' enemies. Did it have the same meaning for him as it did for Reagan?
- What are the advantages of framing one's political struggles in terms of good and evil? What are the disadvantages?

Credits

Chapter 1: Introduction to American Politics

p. 3: Reprinted by permission of the author. **p. 7:** © 2008, NPR®, News report by NPR's Scott Horsley was originally broadcast on NPR's All Things Considered® on July 2, 2008, and is used with the permission of NPR. Any unauthorized duplication is strictly prohibited.

Chapter 2: Political Culture

p. 14: From the New York Times, © 2009 The New York Times. All rights reserved. Used by permission and protected by the Copyright Laws of the United States. The printing, copying, redistribution, or retransmission of the Material without express written consent is prohibited. www.nytimes.com. **p. 17:** © 2009 Zadie Smith. Permission granted by AP Watt Ltd on behalf of Zadie Smith. **p. 25:** Reprinted by permission of the author. **p. 29:** Reprinted with author's permission. Michael Skube, winner of the Pulitzer Prize for Criticism, teaches journalism at Elon University. **p. 32:** Reprinted by arrangement with the Estate of Martin Luther King Jr., c/o Writers House as agent for the proprietor New York, NY. Copyright 1963 Martin Luther King Jr., copyright renewed 1991 Coretta Scott King.

Chapter 3: Federalism and the Constitution

p. 37: MSNBC.COM [ONLINE] by Keith Olbermann. Copyright 2009 by MSNBC INTERACTIVE NEWS, LLC. Reproduced with permission of MSNBC INTERACTIVE NEWS, LLC in the format Other book via Copyright Clearance Center. **p. 41:** CHICAGO TRIBUNE by Steve Chapman. Copyright 2009 by CHICAGO TRIBUNE COMPANY. Reproduced with permission of CHICAGO TRIBUNE COMPANY in the format Other book via Copyright Clearance Center. **p. 44:** Reprinted by permission of Sanford Levinson. **p. 47:** BOSTON GLOBE by Charlie Savage. Copyright 2006 by GLOBE NEWSPAPER COMPANY - MA. Reproduced with permission of GLOBE NEWSPAPER COMPANY - MA in the format Other book via Copyright Clearance Center.

Chapter 4: Civil Liberties

p. 61: From the Washington Post July 16, 2006 © 2006 The Washington Post. All rights reserved. Used by permission and protected by the Copyright Laws of the United States. The printing, copying, redistribution, or retransmission of the Material without express written permission is prohibited. **p. 67:** By Jane Lampman. Reproduced with permission from the June 1, 2006 issue of The Christian Science Monitor (www.CSMonitor.com). © 2006 The Christian Science Monitor. **p. 71:** Copyright TIME INC. Reprinted by permission. TIME is a registered trademark of Time Inc. All rights reserved. **p. 75:** © The Economist Newspaper Limited, London September 22, 2007.

Chapter 5: Civil Rights

p. 84: Reprinted by permission of International Creative Management, Inc. Copyright © 2009 by Sara Corbett for THE NEW YORK TIMES MAGAZINE **p. 87:** © 2006 by National Review Online, www.nationalreview.com. Reprinted by permission. **p. 90:** Reprinted by permission of the author.

Chapter 6: Congress

p. 105: Reprinted by permission of the author. **p. 107:** From the New York Times, © 2009 The New York Times. All rights reserved. Used by permission and protected by the Copyright Laws of the United States. The printing, copying, redistribution, or retransmission of the Material without express written consent is prohibited. www.nytimes.com. **p. 110:** WASHINGTON TIMES by S. A. Miller. Copyright 2009 by WASHINGTON TIMES CORPORATION. Reproduced with permission of WASHINGTON TIMES CORPORATION in the format Other book via Copyright Clearance Center. **p. 112:** From the New York Times, © 2009 The New York Times. All rights reserved. Used by permission and protected by the Copyright Laws of the United States. The printing, copying, redistribution, or retransmission of the Material without express written consent is prohibited. www.nytimes.com.

Chapter 7: The Presidency

p. 121: From the New York Times, © 2006 The New York Times. All rights reserved. Used by permission and protected by the Copyright Laws of the United States. The printing, copying, redistribution, or retransmission of the Material without express written consent is prohibited. www.nytimes.com. **p. 125:** Los Angeles Times, Copyright © 2003. Reprinted with Permission. **p. 129:** "The Presider" from The Daily Dish by Andrew Sullivan, published by *The Atlantic*. Copyright © 2009 by Andrew Sullivan, reprinted with permission of The Wylie Agency LLC. **p. 131:** CQ WEEKLY by David Nather. Copyright 2009 by CONGRESSIONAL QUARTERLY INC. Reproduced with permission of CONGRESSIONAL QUARTERLY INC in the format Other book via Copyright Clearance Center.

Chapter 8: Bureaucracy

p. 139: Los Angeles Times, Copyright © 2002. Reprinted with Permission. **p. 142:** From the New York Times, © 2008 The New York Times. All rights reserved. Used by permission and protected by the Copyright Laws of the United States. The printing, copying, redistribution, or retransmission of the Material without express written consent is prohibited. www.nytimes.com. **p. 144:** Reprinted by permission of the author.

Chapter 9: The Courts

p. 160: © Copyright 2009, Washingtonpost.Newsweek Interactive Company, LLC. All Rights Reserved. **p. 164:** Reprinted by permission of the author. **p. 178:** From the Washington Post July 14, 2009 © 2009 The Washington Post. All rights reserved. Used by permission and protected by the Copyright Laws of the United States. The printing, copying, redistribution, or retransmission of the Material without express written permission is prohibited. **p. 181:** This article originally appeared in The New York Times Magazine and is reprinted by permission. © Jeffrey Rosen.

Chapter 10: Public Opinion

p. 196: "Party on Dudes!" by Matthew Robinson © The American Spectator, March/April 2002. **p. 204:** © The Economist Newspaper Limited, London October 17, 2008. **p. 207:** Reprinted by permission of the author. **p. 209:** Reprinted with permission from The Washington Monthly. Copyright by Washington Monthly Publishing, LLC, www.washingtonmonthly.com. **p. 217:** Reprinted with the permission of Simon & Schuster, Inc., from The Pulse of Democracy by George Horace Gallup and Saul Forbes Raw. Copyright © 1940 by George H. Gallup and Saul F. Race. Copyright renewed © 1986 by George H. Gallup. All rights reserved.

Chapter 11: Political Parties

p. 227: Reprinted by permission of Robert J. Elisberg. **p. 230:** Copyright © 2009 by Ronald Brownstein, reprinted with permission of the author. **p. 233:** WEEKLY STANDARD (NEW YORK, NY) by Fred Barnes. Copyright 2009 by WEEKLY STANDARD. Reproduced with permission of WEEKLY STANDARD in the format Other book via Copyright Clearance Center. **p. 236:** Copyright © 2006 by Kurt Andersen. Reprinted by permission of William Morris Endeavor Entertainment, LLC on behalf of the Author.

Chapter 12: Interest Groups

p. 249: SAN FRANCISCO CHRONICLE (1865-) by Tanya Schevitz. Copyright 2002 by SAN FRANCISCO CHRONICLE. Reproduced with permission of SAN FRANCISCO CHRONICLE in the format Other book via Copyright Clearance Center. **p. 253:** Reprinted by permission of author. **p. 263:** WEEKLY STANDARD (NEW YORK, NY) by Gary Andres. Copyright 2009 by WEEKLY STANDARD. Reproduced with permission of WEEKLY STANDARD in the format Other book via Copyright Clearance Center.

Chapter 13: Voting and Elections

p. 273: Reprinted by permission of author. **p. 276:** MILWAUKEE JOURNAL SENTINEL [ONLY STAFF-PRODUCED MATERIALS MAY BE USED] by Patrick McIlheran. Copyright 2006 by JOURNAL/SENTINEL, INC. Reproduced with permission of JOURNAL/SENTINEL, INC. in the format Other book via Copyright Clearance Center. **p. 279:** © 2008. Reprinted by permission of Roll Call.

Chapter 14: The Media

p. 288: From the New York Times, © 2009 The New York Times. All rights reserved. Used by permission and protected by the Copyright Laws of the United States. The printing, copying, redistribution, or retransmission of the Material without express written consent is prohibited. www.nytimes.com. **p. 302:** © Copyright 2009, Washingtonpost.Newsweek Interactive Company, LLC. All Rights Reserved. **p. 306:** Reprinted with permission from Markos Moulitsas Zuniga.

Chapter 15: Domestic Policy

Chapter 16: Foreign Policy